RAW

Yatish Yadav is an investigative journalist with an experience of over two decades. He has spent more than fifteen years covering intelligence and investigative agencies, and extensively reported on conflicts in Kashmir, Northeast and the red corridor. He entered the field of journalism during the early days of digital media, an opportunity that turned him into a professional photographer. Subsequently, he moved to television and learnt filmmaking. In 2005, he was bestowed with the Best Director Award at the New York International Film Festival for Ropes in their Hands, a documentary exposing an international human trafficking ring operating from Nepal. In his journalistic career, he has worked with prominent newspapers and TV networks of India and the United States. He has had a chance to break some big-ticket stories that defined the news coverage of the time. He also served as Bureau Chief of *The New Indian Express* in Delhi, handling a team of reporters to generate content for 22 editions and *The Sunday Standard*, and as Associate Editor at Network18. As a hobby, he occasionally paints his thoughts. He is currently Media Advisor to the Lieutenant Governor of Jammu & Kashmir.

AF517634

A HISTORY OF INDIA'S COVERT OPERATIONS

RAW

YATISH YADAV

WESTLAND
NON-FICTION

WESTLAND
NON·FICTION

First published by Westland Publications Private Limited in 2020

Published by Westland Non-Fiction, an imprint of Westland Books, a division of Nasadiya Technologies Private Limited, in 2022

No. 269/2B, First Floor, 'Irai Arul', Vimalraj Street, Nethaji Nagar, Alapakkam Main Road, Maduravoyal, Chennai 600095

Westland, the Westland logo, Westland Non-Fiction and the Westland Non-Fiction logo are the trademarks of Nasadiya Technologies Private Limited, or its affiliates.

Copyright © Yatish Yadav, 2020

Yatish Yadav asserts the moral right to be identified as the author of this work.

ISBN: 9789395073264

10 9 8 7

The views and opinions expressed in this work are the author's own and the facts are as reported by him, and the publisher is in no way liable for the same.

All rights reserved

Typeset by SÜRYA, New Delhi

Printed at Parksons Graphics Pvt. Ltd

No part of this book may be reproduced, or stored in a retrieval system, or transmitted in any form or by any means, electronic, mechanical, photocopying, recording, or otherwise, without express written permission of the publisher.

CONTENTS

Author's Note vii

Prologue 1

1. Bloodbath in Bangladesh 9
2. Three Musketeers and a Bloody War in Fiji 66
3. A Warrior and the Warlords 104
4. Sri Lankan Affairs 152
5. Shadowy War in Washington 185
6. Hunting the R&AW Traitor 223
7. R&AW in Shackles 247
8. The Global Footprints of R&AW 260
9. Spies in Nepal 306
10. Operation Hornet 334
11. A Spy among the Dervish 353

Epilogue 364

Notes 367

Acknowledgements 378

Index 380

AUTHOR'S NOTE

Unlike the American CIA, British MI6 and Israel's espionage unit Mossad, the Indian intelligence community guards its critical operations, achievements and failures vigilantly. This book is an attempt to clear away the cobwebs. It is based on numerous conversations with intelligence operatives and spymasters. Declassified documents—exclusively accessed—have also helped in putting together lives of agents, assets and the history of India's external spy organisation, Research & Analysis Wing (R&AW). Many quotations and perspectives mentioned in this book are attributed to the source notes. If any attribution is missing, it is primarily to ensure anonymity. I have offered cover names to assets, agents and locations in certain missions for the sake of national security and to talk about the unsung heroes albeit, in the iron mask. However, the story remains close to the truth. Upholding the country's security and effectively countering the shadowy war of numerous forces is hardwired into R&AW's DNA. The narratives in this compilation are, in some sense, milestones of India's espionage history that needed to be told so that information-rich, global community comes to understand the 'mission impossible' attempted at different times and in difficult situations by Indian spies. The author is grateful to the men and women of the Indian intelligence community for letting him peek into the working of India's designated covert society that made this book possible.

March 2020

PROLOGUE

The parting of colleagues can incite emotional outbursts. That's what happened when India's only intelligence agency was split into two in September 1968. The two hundred officers who left the Intelligence Bureau (IB), India's primary intelligence agency, to join the newly created Research and Analysis Wing (R&AW) which focused on espionage operations abroad, were called 'traitors'.

For these two hundred former IB officers, the R&AW offered glamour and anonymity in uncharted territory. Those who remained in the domestic intelligence organisation continued to taunt them for the next few years.

Rameshwar Nath Kao, the founder of R&AW, knew that he and his team couldn't afford to fail. They didn't. The success of the Bangladesh Liberation War in 1971 caused a churn within the R&AW. Eventually, it began to look for specialised intelligence operatives with skills beyond the IB legacy. The first batch of the Research & Analysis Service (RAS) officers came into being in 1971. The officers were raw talent, recruited on the basis of rigorous scrutiny involving written exams and expertise in spy tradecraft. Unlike the IB network, which was manned by Indian Police Service (IPS) officers with direct recruits for the lower ranks, the R&AW finally had its own cadre. Even IPS officers who had joined the R&AW from the IB were encouraged to join the RAS permanently. This conversion of cadre was considered to be the best cure for the 'police hangover' in preparation for serious intelligence business. To this day, however, the debate over which cadre has the edge, the IPS or the RAS, continues. A senior R&AW operative, originally from the IPS, explained one side of the debate: 'IPS officers will always remain a step ahead of RAS officers because intense public interaction provides the perfect opportunity to understand and penetrate the minds of people. RAS officers are confined to a cocoon.'

The IPS officers who joined the R&AW from the IB were posted abroad with cover names to protect their identities since their real names appeared in civil lists which could easily be accessed by foreign missions in India. So, Vikram Singh had to go Moscow as Vishal Pandit and members of his family changed their names too. If his child was born while the family was abroad, the surname stuck for the child's entire life. Though this personal problem was limited to only a few IPS officers, it generated heat within the agency for quite some time, especially among the RAS's fresh recruits.

While coping with the social aspects of cover names, the new R&AW recruits were signed for four years' rigorous training that included specialisation in at least one strategically important language such as Chinese, Russian, Arabic, Sinhalese, German, Polish and Urdu. Communism was the target. New recruits were trained to identify, locate and neutralise communist influence. They were trained to better understand the functioning of the communist governments in China, the Soviet Union, Afghanistan, East Germany and other Eastern Bloc countries. Apart from this, commando and explosives trainings were mandatory.

To train recruits in spycraft, the R&AW opened offices in border states such as Rajasthan, Uttar Pradesh, West Bengal, Assam and Jammu and Kashmir. The nondescript R&AW office at Lucknow was to target Nepal and China while the Jammu and Kashmir station had to generate intelligence on Pakistan. The new spies spent their days learning codes and recruiting informers and their nights assembling and dismantling powerful explosives. In the meantime, Kao hunted across all the services for people with a knack for espionage, including the civil services and the paramilitary forces.

By the time Morarji Desai became the fourth prime minister of India in March 1977, the R&AW had a staff of more than five thousand on its payroll. The first thing Desai did after driving to Raisina Hill was tying the agents to their offices to reduce their political influence. The socialist prime minister suspected the R&AW of supporting his predecessor, Indira Gandhi, during the Emergency in India. In his meetings with R&AW officers, the prime minister blamed the agency for engineering atrocities against opposition leaders. The hapless intelligence officers argued that they had no mandate to operate inside the country and if any agency was to be blamed, it had to be the R&AW's bête noire, the IB. But Desai was unrelenting.

Kao, the founder of the agency, and his best officer, K. Sankaran Nair, had to leave the organisation under pressure from Desai's government. A major clean up followed in R&AW's operations abroad and recruitment came to a virtual halt. Covert actions were suspended and many recruits were left in the cold after their handlers failed to pull them back in time. Fortunately, Desai put N.F. Suntook in charge of the agency and somehow, he saved R&AW from being plundered by its own customer—the government. And following the return of Indira Gandhi as prime minister in January 1980, R&AW's mandate was restored. But it took almost four years for the agency to recuperate from the deep wounds inflicted by Morarji Desai and, subsequently, by his former comrade Chaudhary Charan Singh. By the time Rajiv Gandhi became prime minister in October 1984, the R&AW had begun supplying unhindered and actionable intelligence inputs from across the world. Rajiv Gandhi was happy but he was still in awe of the Chinese. A R&AW officer, who worked at the China desk at the time, was of the opinion that Rajiv suffered from a mental block created by the defeat inflicted on India by China in 1962 when his maternal grandfather Pandit Jawaharlal Nehru was the prime minister. 'Although he was briefed that there was nothing to fear from the Chinese, Rajiv stood like a school boy meeting the principal when he paid a visit to Deng Xiaoping, chairman of China's Central Military Commission in December 1988.'

Rajiv also kept the agency on its toes thanks to his ill-conceived decision to send peacekeeping troops to Sri Lanka, said R&AW insiders who still believe that this decision destroyed several R&AW operations in the neighbouring country. Rajiv Gandhi's successors V.P. Singh and Chandra Shekhar were not interested in India's foreign policy and paid little attention to the R&AW operations abroad. R&AW officers believe these two decision makers' primary aim was to establish a political legacy rather than look into the effectiveness and value of India's spy agency and the intelligence inputs and strategic analyses on various countries and events it provided. However, an officer code-named Prince had a different view. He said that the R&AW didn't care about political masters and between Rajiv's and Chandra Shekhar's regimes, the agency launched some spectacular spy operations.

This book explores the hits and misses of the espionage operations through the eyes of spymasters who are rarely in T20 masala-match mode. Courting a spy can be tougher than digging out a yorker. It requires endless wet evenings in bars, hours in dimly lit listening posts and miles-long walks to understand the nitty-gritties of espionage operations. But the results can be thrilling.

The R&AW has become synonymous with the liberation of Bangladesh. Though generations of spies grew up with various versions of how their agency severed East Pakistan from Pakistan and created Bangladesh, nothing was ever confirmed or denied because of the secrecy involved.

But many other exploits and setbacks are cardinal to the lives of Indian spies, some of which even their spouses are not aware of. Many of the stories in this book were scripted when R&AW had just turned adult as an organisation. In 1980s, Indian spies suddenly found themselves in the raging battlefields of Afghanistan. Mikhail Gorbachev had not yet arrived on the scene in the erstwhile USSR but the introduction of Stinger missiles by the USA had changed the Soviet game plan. India feared that the state of the art weapons meant for Afghan mujahideen—the resistance force against the Soviets—were being diverted by Pakistan's intelligence organisation, Inter Service Intelligence (ISI). On another front, in the island nation of Fiji, Sitiveni Rabuka, a Fijian army general and sworn enemy of ethnic Indians, had seized power from the elected Prime Minister Timoci Bavadra. Both the Afghanistan and Fiji fronts were treacherous for the Indian spies. The US did nothing in both the cases. It neither prevented the ISI from siphoning arms and money to raise proxy terror outfits against India, nor mounted pressure on Rabuka to stop the persecution of the Fiji Indians. Far from the diplomatic niceties initiated by the Rajiv Gandhi government, Indian spies tackled overpowering threats in Fiji in ways that do them credit.

For India, these operations anchored the challenges of future complex geopolitical structures in three words: secrecy, speed and success. Indian hunters had begun exerting their influence abroad. Eager agents on the ground effectively engineered situations from coups to the neutralisation of precarious affairs inimical to Indian interests. The intelligence community fought adversaries with blood and guts, fuelled by strategies of the mind.

These unprecedented operations were not just limited to regional troublemakers like Pakistan. The R&AW recruited, trained and deployed informers and covert action teams in the USA, Iran and several European countries as well as India's immediate neighbours. All this was carried out with incredible confidentiality.

While most of the tales of spycraft in this book centre on male operatives, the R&AW has had female officers in plenty since the agency was born in 1968. Female secret operatives are recruited as analysts, cartographers, polygraph examiners, instructors, linguists, economists and targeting officers. Today, they are also cyber security experts, counterintelligence operatives, human resources specialists and so on. Working behind the scenes, they have shaped major operations, big events and the destiny of the nation.

For instance, a female friend of mine works as an analyst at the R&AW and has made immense contributions in tracking down terror financing in Pakistan. Analysts piece together raw intelligence from field agents and prepare finished products for the agency's customers. The R&AW's first customer is India's prime minister, which means, reports must include every relevant detail to enable better decision-making. There is no substitute for an analyst in the espionage profession. Armed with raw intel from the field, my friend led an operation that dragged Pakistan onto the grey list of the Financial Action Task Force, the intergovernmental organisation that keeps an eye on money laundering. She may not operate in the wild, but her contributions to the global war on terror cannot be ignored.

Spies who work at the desk as analysts, linguists, cyber exploitation officers, country experts and so on are as important as those in covert ops, but their roles hold none of the glamour that James Bond films have imparted to agents in the field. Nevertheless, their methodical and tireless work at headquarters as well as abroad is always part of the most celebrated operations. A woman officer who started her career as an analyst went on to head a R&AW mission abroad. She is that rare spy: a trove of valuable intelligence on North Korea, Russia, Pakistan and Sri Lanka.

A legendary spy chief once observed that many women IPS officers who could have joined the R&AW but preferred to serve in domestic agencies, such as the paramilitary, the state police or the IB, due to family obligations. Right now, women officers are in charge of very important and sensitive operations within the IB and at least five SIBs (State Intelligence Bureaus, part of the IB) have senior women officers. But whether at the desk or on the field, all go through the same rigorous routine: physical training based on the template of the paramilitary, geopolitics and tradecraft. They also learn how to make friends, merge into the background, conduct surveillance, detect surveillance, run assets, brief and debrief sources, write reports, communicate clandestinely, observe warning signs and conduct covert operations. Human psychology and human weaknesses, topography to assess distances and heights, and ciphering and deciphering techniques are part of their training as well, as are mountaineering, swimming and practical sessions with units in different urban and rural locations.

Operatives live dangerously and on the edge. Their heroic exploits are locked away. There are no medals pinned on the chests of intelligence operatives. For spooks, emotions are killed before inception. For instance, the first successful strike against Pakistan during the 1999 Kargil war was mounted by eighty battle-trained covert action operatives of the R&AW. The team captured key locations and largely returned victorious. But some fell to the enemy's guns. Their names did not figure in the lists of martyrs. When TV channels began telecasting public ceremonies to honour the defence forces' fallen heroes, the agency's top brass were emotionally overwhelmed. Operatives who had lost friends and colleagues in the Kargil war watched the spectacle helplessly. An officer code-named Rehman requested the top boss to acknowledge the sacrifice of the operatives who never returned. A message was sent to Brajesh Mishra, then national security advisor and principal secretary to Prime Minister Atal Bihari Vajpayee. Mishra opposed the proposal. Nevertheless, the message was conveyed to Vajpayee. In a closed conference room at 7 Race Course Road, the prime minister's official residence, the names of eighteen R&AW officers were read aloud, along with details of their gallant performances on the Kargil battlefields. For the first time in the history of the R&AW, special medals were presented to these warriors in the shadows. Vajpayee shook hands with top R&AW officers and expressed his deep gratitude for the supreme sacrifice made by these unsung heroes. No records of this meeting were kept. No government press release was issued for the next day's newspapers. No photographs were published on the prime minister's website. After the ceremony, the officers quietly retreated to their invisible world to work, taking their secrets to bed.

1

BLOODBATH IN BANGLADESH

After dividing Pakistan in 1971 and establishing a democratically elected Bangladesh government under Sheikh Mujibur Rahman, the R&AW began to strengthen and spread its influence in other areas of conflict. India decided to withdraw its army and other officials from Bangladesh in 1972 and the R&AW's task was to bring back the Indians to Delhi, leaving only diplomats in Dhaka for backroom negotiations to help the newborn country in dealing with the ever-changing security dynamics of South Asia. Unfortunately, India's decision to pull out left Bangladesh open to a security nightmare in 1975 that forced the R&AW to fight a covert war for decades.

On 15 August 1975, while India celebrated Independence Day, a group of Bangladesh Army officers reportedly led by one Major Dalim successfully staged a coup d'état in Dhaka by storming Sheikh Mujib's house. They killed Mujib and his immediate family, as well as his two nephews—the influential Sheikh Moni of *Bangladesh Times* and Sahidul Islam, secretary of the Jatiya Chhatra League and Mujib's brother-in-law Abdur Rab Serniabat, who was the country's minister for water development. Sheikh Hasina, Mujib's daughter and the prime minister of Bangladesh today, was fortunately in Germany on that day and she was brought safely to Delhi by R&AW agents. Spies stationed far away in Poland were shocked. Sheikh Mujib had been expected to visit Warsaw between 15 and 18 September that year. Polish foreign officials could not understand why the Indian spies had not been able to foresee or influence the coup that slaughtered sixty-five of Mujib's relatives and followers.

The R&AW believed that Major Dalim, a freedom fighter of 1971, had personal vendetta against Sheikh Mujib, blaming the prime minister for his dismissal and that of twenty-seven other army officers. This happened after they had complained to Sheikh Mujib about a misdemeanour by the notoriously corrupt Ghulam Mustapha, chairman of the Bangladesh Red Cross and one of one of the Sheikh's protégés. Mujib did not act against Mustapha and Dalim wanted revenge.

The R&AW founder and chief R.N. Kao was just as shocked as the Polish officials. He didn't know how the situation had changed in just four years. The reports from Dhaka arriving via telegrams and notes suggested that altogether two hundred people had died in the fighting on the first day despite stiff resistance from Mujib's personal guards. An internal confidential note suggested that a group of pro-Mujib youth had come out on the streets of Dhaka but subsided when they saw the army firing at the troublemakers. The border with India was sealed and all communications were cut except for limited telephone and telegraph services.

The internal confidential note said: 'Forsaking the path of constitutional government and peaceful change, a new government has emerged in Bangladesh with its hands stained with the blood of Sheikh Mujib, the father figure and the moving spirit and hero of the liberation struggle of Bangladesh.'

Sheikh Mujib had been friendly towards India and stood for secular principles. But close scrutiny of the events leading to the coup suggested he had been losing his charm because of widespread corruption, nepotism, violence and lawlessness in the country.

The R&AW spies stationed at Dhaka said that there was no evidence of direct foreign complicity in the coup. One fact, though, was significant. Pakistan was the first country to recognise the new regime and lost no time in offering substantial aid of fifty thousand tonnes of rice and fifteen million metres of cloth. Even Saudi Arabia granted Bangladesh recognition immediately after the coup, which it had not done in the four years of Mujib's rule. The Indian government initially feared the involvement of pro-Maoist elements which had long been anti-Mujib. It is not known whether China had had a hand in the coup but the country welcomed the change, which was interpreted as a development favourable to its policy of promoting strife and tension in the subcontinent. Unlike other missions in Dhaka, the Indian embassy was cut off from the rest of the world for almost forty-eight hours. The telephone connections of the Indian High Commission, other offices and the official residence were neutralised just around the time of the coup.

An Indian government note said: 'The Bangladesh Ambassador in Kuwait General Wasiuddin appears to be involved in the coup. He was the senior most Bengali officer in the Pakistan army and was known to be bitter about having been denied his dues. We may also hear more of Brigadier Rauf formerly the Director of Forces Intelligence, who returned from London on 13 August 1975, when the Army finally revealed its hands. Bangladesh appears to be in for a period of unrest and instability with frequent changes of men and policies.'

What shocked the Indian government even more was President Khondaker Mostaq Ahmad's radio broadcast of 16 August. Ahmad did not name India in the broadcast but hinted that a 'particular power' allowed corruption, nepotism and political manipulations during Mujib's regime. Mostaq, who had appointed Major General Ziaur Rahman as army chief, went on to announce the keenness of his government to cultivate close and friendly ties with the Islamic countries, the big powers of the USA and the USSR, China and Pakistan. Just two days before the coup in Bangladesh, Prime Minister Indira Gandhi had imposed the Emergency in India. With political turmoil becoming the order of the day, India was virtually ruled with an iron hand.

J.N. Dixit, who had earlier served as India's deputy high commissioner in Bangladesh and was known to be an expert on the country, believed that Dhaka's policies would be communal, pan-Islamic and pro-Western. He foresaw a period of civil strife in Bangladesh which led to continuous political instability and economic chaos. He noted that there were many pro-India Bangladeshi politicians and recommended similar contacts in Bangladesh's defence forces as well.

'We should have similar extensive contacts in the army and paramilitary forces whom we should continue to cultivate to the extent possible. Our overall objective should be to encourage the re-emergence of a government which would be friendly to India and which is dedicated to the ideals of policies which motivated the liberation struggle of Bangladesh,' Dixit advocated in writing to Prime Minister Indira Gandhi.

Coup and the Murder of Sheikh Mujib

With limited snooping capability in Bangladesh, the R&AW was not certain about the CIA's role in the military coup. But a top-secret October 1975 note from the Ministry of External Affairs (MEA) provided another side to the story. S. Chattopadhyay, deputy secretary in the ministry, had a long meeting with Bangladesh's law minister Manoranjan Dhar in Calcutta on 9 October 1975. Chattopadhyay said in his note:

> Mostaq Ahmad was deeply involved in the coup from the very beginning. Although, there were a handful of young army officers who were directly involved in chalking out the whole

> plan with clock-like precision, the real brain behind [it] was Pakistan and the CIA. Due to the complacency of the three heads of the defence forces and also other senior and trusted officers of the army [the] coup could be staged. Mostaq Ahmad, according to Dhar, was [a] cunning and scheming fellow but he lacked the personality of Sheikh Mujib. Dhar said it was a fact that pro-Pak elements were jubilant at the turn of events and had started stirring up communal and anti-India propaganda. In the first cabinet meeting, Dhar made some plain speaking. He had told the President Mostaq Ahmad that all the Ministers were also close colleagues of Sheikh Mujib and as such, they couldn't deny their responsibilities in whatever had happened in Bangladesh under Sheikh Mujib. It is necessary, however, to take action against corrupt people but there should be no witch hunting as a matter of state principle. It is not that easy to obliterate the name of Sheikh Mujib and the slogan 'Jai Bangla' from the minds of people.

As far as suspicions of Chinese involvement were concerned, officials were worried. There was a telegram from the USA where the Chinese representative had made a statement about the Bangladesh situation. China had raised the issue of sharing the waters of the river Ganges while justifying the coup. The Chinese statement read:

> We sympathise with the situation of Bangladesh and support its just position. As Ganges is an international river, the upper and lower riparian should conduct consultations on an equal footing for an equitable distribution and utilisation of the water resources. A unilateral action by the upper riparian state (India) which impairs the lower riparian state does not conform with international norms.

In the days to come, several such telegrams were received by New Delhi indicating the increasing involvement of the USA and China in the bilateral affairs of India and Bangladesh.

The Shockwaves

A.K. Verma, a deputy director of the R&AW who became the head of the spy agency in 1987, said that the coup was the handiwork of the major rank officers. Other senior officers of the armed forces were not taken into confidence though some key anonymous officers of the army command at Dhaka were in the picture. Verma's investigation revealed the major instrument of the coup was the Bengal Lancers and its commanding officer, Major Farooq Rahman, but no troops or equipment from outside were utilised. Interestingly, spymaster Verma discovered that there had been no plans to take over the centres of power in other big cities and towns. The top military officers at Dhaka, who were taken by surprise by the coup, agreed to transfer their allegiance to the new government when presented with a fait accompli.

A month after the coup, Verma drafted a nine-page secret note for the various Indian government agencies responsible for national security. In Verma's analysis, Mostaq, who took over as the president after Mujib was killed, was privy to the planning of the coup. He also said that Major Farooq Rahman, one of the key plotters, was Mostaq's nephew and the manner in which they were able to establish quick control over the administration in the country and the ease with which Mostaq settled down as president strongly indicated prior knowledge and planning on his part and ready acceptance of his leadership by the conspirators. Verma noted that the USA could have played a major role. This is what he wrote:

> The possibility that it was another agency which made available its expertise for the effective planning of the coup and smooth transition of power that took place after the operation was over, cannot be still ruled out completely. There were certain developments, which seem somewhat significant in this regard. Firstly, the fact that no major problems have arisen among

> the conspirators, military or civilian, following the coup itself points to the existence of a mastermind. Secondly, a military advisory council, with the President as the Chairman and two officers of Major ranks instrumental in the coup, was formed without any loss of time. Thirdly, one of the Major rank officers involved in the coup had taken refuge at the American embassy at Dhaka on 20 August 1975, when he apprehended some danger to himself and the American embassy at Dhaka successfully interceded on his behalf with the army authorities and got certain assurances relating to his safety. The Americans have [had] nothing at all to do with Bangladesh armed forces in the past. This sudden linkage between the American embassy in Dhaka and those in authority on the military side and the ease with which the Americans were able to sort out the problems on behalf of one of the conspirators certainly creates suspicions as to whether the role of the American embassy was more than that of an honest broker.

Within four years of independence, a bias against India had taken deep root in Bangladesh. Mostaq's selection of army and civilian officials reflected that. General Osmani was given the new post of advisor to the defence ministry and Major General Khalilur Rahman, the senior most serving army officer, was designated as the chief of defence staff. Major General Shafifullah, the previous chief of the army staff who had been pro-Mujib, was replaced by Major General Ziaur Rahman. Brigadier Dastgir, commanding the 65 Brigade at Chittagong, was promoted to major general and made the commanding officer of the Bangladesh Rifles. All these officers had shown an anti-India bias in the past. Clearly, President Mostaq was placing people with anti-India sentiments in key positions. Mostaq followed the same policy with regard to key appointments on the civilian side. Mahbub Alam Chashi, who was appointed as the principal secretary to the president and Shafiul Azam, appointed as the new cabinet secretary, were similarly reputed to be not well disposed towards India for one reason or another. All the members of Mujib's cabinet were sidelined, indicating a policy to keep out those who might favour India and bring in others who were unlikely to tilt towards India. Protests against the new government were feeble. Some posters appeared in Dhaka and other cities accusing the USA's Central Intelligence Agency (CIA) of being responsible for the coup and a few underground activities by pro-Mujib activists were subdued within no time.

The officials knew Pakistan and China would exploit the changed situation in Bangladesh to the detriment of India. Pakistan was quick to grab the opportunity and recognised the new government though it had denied the same right to Mujib's government after the 1971 liberation war. Mostaq was a shrewd operator and he decided not to go overboard in accepting Pakistan's recognition and aid, fearing that it might offend India. The Pakistani authorities under Prime Minister Zulfikar Ali Bhutto sensed this reluctance on Bangladesh's part and, for the time being, they gave up any flamboyant approaches to bring the two countries together. Indian intelligence officers also picked up information that Bhutto had subtly refused Mostaq's offer immediately after the coup to send a Bangladeshi team to Pakistan to assist with rescue operations in flood-ravaged regions. However, there was no denying the fact that the Pakistanis were watching developments in Bangladesh carefully and were prepared to do all they could to get a foothold in the country as soon as possible.

Meanwhile, the R&AW felt that in the future, Indian and Soviet Union interests in Bangladesh would be effectively eroded and this might suit the USA. The Americans were already anxious about the growing Russian presence in Bangladesh and the USSR's attempts to penetrate all levels of Bangladesh society and centres of power. Verma said in his secret note:

> A more pro-west, pro-Pakistani and pro-Chinese outlook in Bangladesh will create problems which will have ramifications outside the borders of this subcontinent. If Bangladesh becomes a pawn in the clash of superpower interests in the region, this area will tend to develop into one of instability with obvious repercussions on us. In such an environment, the Chinese and the Pakistanis could feel encouraged to enlarge their conspiracies against us. Bhutto had always thought that the presence of East Pakistan close to the areas of instability in India was a matter of great luck to Pakistan, which should be fully exploited. It is possible that he may think on the same lines when Bangladesh and Pakistan become close to each other once again. The Chinese have also a similar interest. They would not allow themselves to fall behind once they arrive in Bangladesh.

But there was little that India could do at this stage beyond handling the situation diplomatically.

A secret note from the MEA dated 21 August 1975 sent to the PMO and R&AW headquarters said:

> As far as India is concerned, we have serious reservations about the brutal manner in which power was seized by the Bangladesh Army but it is not for us to comment on the internal affairs. Our relations with that country, as with others, are based strictly on the principle of equality, respect for mutual sovereignty and non-interference. We have never sought any exclusive relationship with Bangladesh. Bangladesh has as much a right as anyone else to have as many friends as possible. So long as Bangladesh's friendship with Pakistan, China or any other country is in the interest of Bangladesh and not aimed against India, we would not worry. If on the other hand, Bangladesh becomes a prey to foreign influence detrimental to India's interests, and if it presses its new pro-Islamic posture to a point where the minorities panic and begin to flee to India in large numbers, then that would be cause for

> grave concern for us. Ministry of Foreign Affairs of Bangladesh has sent us a note that gives a gist of new President Khondaker Mostaq Ahmad's address to the nation where he affirmed his government's resolve to promote Bangladesh's relations, goodwill, understanding and cooperation with all countries.

But India was worried. Not just about the influence of foreign powers in Bangladesh but also about the penetration of non-state actors in a country that had been liberated by Indian spies. In a secret note, government officials analysed what went wrong considering both internal and external factors.

Internal Factors Included:

(a) Economic collapse leading to the declaration of emergency in January 1975, followed by appointment of governors and other drastic steps.
(b) Failure of these steps to immediately produce results. Sheikh Mujib's idea of shifting the centre of gravity from the district headquarters to the Taluk headquarters was based upon the hope that there will be a shift from town to the villages. This pious hope has remained unfulfilled while the urban middle classes and intellectuals, indeed the whole Bangla elite, were alienated.
(c) Post-emergency measures were thus as yet ineffectual and Mujib government did nothing to remove the existing burden on ordinary Bangla citizens. There was also deep scepticism about Mujib's capacity to improve matters.
(d) This rather moderate reaction turned into fierce resentment in many cases when bullying tactics of strong troopers annoyed ordinary uncommitted people. High handedness of Mujib's troops against politically neutral masses triggered discontent.
(e) Chronic anti-India feeling was in no way discouraged by Mujib. The Pakistan Prime Minister Zulfikar Ali Bhutto's

visit provided the pro-Muslim groups to demonstrate their power. Mujib did not take the hint. (Here is one saving grace, Bhutto and Pakistan might be merely pegs on which anti-Mujib groups wanted to hang their coat. Pakistan could very well be exaggerating its influence or responsibility.)

(f) Specific groups, who would be interested in a change of government are:

  (i) The professional Bangladesh army consisting mainly of prisoners of war who came back from Pakistan with a positive view about Bhutto and the present Pakistan government because of the good treatment they had received.
  (ii) The malcontents from the Mukti Bahini and other volunteer forces, who were disillusioned by corruption.
  (iii) Sheer idealism and impatience might have enabled these two naturally disparate groups to form a temporary alliance.
  (iv) Simple pro-Islamic political leaders deeply worried about Hindu India's and West Bengal's cultural influence because of Mujib's secularism. This sentiment received some economic strengthening from the Abu Dhabi loan. Virtue, in other words, became profitable.

External Factors Suggested:

While these developments within Bangladesh dictated the need for an early coup, there is no doubt that there must have been encouragement and instigation from abroad, particularly from Pakistan. It is suggested that this could have been done only through the mixed Bangladesh-Pakistani population in the UK. In fact, the existence of highly organised pro-Pakistan anti-Mujib movement in the Bangladesh population in the UK has been known for a long time. Pakistani agents were active in London and as far as Bangladesh itself is concerned, the necessary details of the actual coup, the courier arrangements etc. must have been the work of conspiracy between anti-Mujib Bangladesh bureaucrats and army officers in the UK with the Pakistan government. The few reports we have indicate the actual coup was conducted by the younger army officers. Senior officers, particularly General Wasiuddin, the Bangladesh Ambassador in Kuwait, may be involved but it is extremely unlikely that they were the brains behind the plot. At best, the General could play the role of a spinola. It doesn't seem likely that US interests were necessarily involved in these developments. In the absence of hard evidence, it would be unwise to distribute responsibility over too wide an area. At the same time, we should take full notice of the fact that the Nepalese charge d'affaires in Dhaka is pro-Pakistani. He could have played a crucial role from the communication angle. Since neither Pakistan nor China was physically present in Dhaka, we should also avoid jumping to conclusions about actual physical interference by their agencies in Bangladesh. There is all the difference in the world between sympathy and actual conspiracy.

What perplexed the spies though, was the timing: 15 August was chosen primarily to coincide with India's Independence when the establishment could be caught off guard because of the celebration. Some argued that the day had been chosen because it was a Friday and Muslim sentiments could be exploited. The return to Dhaka from London of a crucial but anonymous figure on 12 August was also a matter of speculation: was the coup plot decided abroad with Pakistan at least being privy to it?

The MEA believed that India should not panic and the government must return to 'business as usual.' It said in a note:

> We should assume that anyone not overtly anti-Indian is for us and not the other way round. We have to be extremely subtle and delicate to the point of hypocrisy in attributing to Bangladeshi bureaucrats and politicians a virtue they may

> not possess. This is what Pakistanis are now doing. We should assume that the Bangla population continues to be grateful to us and would be with us if only their major economic ills are overcome.

While the Indians were discussing the country's future relationship with Bangladesh and the MEA was debating the kind of aid to be supplied to the Khondaker Mostaq Ahmad regime, on 3 November 1975, Mostaq was removed in yet another coup. This time, it was organised by the powerful Brigadier Khaled Mosharraf. There are various stories about Khaled's action but the one that had the most currency was that he had been pained by Mujib's death. Khaled put Ziaur Rahman under house arrest, but this coup resulted in another coup on the night of 6-7 November 1975. An army unit led by Abu Taher overthrew Khaled and freed Ziaur Rahman. An interim government was formed and Chief Abu Sadat Mohammad Sayem became the chief martial law administrator while Zia was appointed his deputy.

N.F. Suntook, a joint secretary level intelligence officer who went on to become the R&AW chief in 1977, provided a ringside view of Bangladesh's situation. Suntook believed that there was a general emphasis on Islamic identity by the majority community fanned by the 'Islampasand' (Islam lovers) group of Muslim parties like the Muslim League and Council Muslim League. Suntook said that in the minds of the Bangladesh's populace, India had been linked with the regime of Sheikh Mujib and the unpopularity of that regime and its failures resulted in India becoming unpopular with the masses as well. He drafted a note on 23 December 1975 to provide a proper perspective on the current situation in Bangladesh and its future scenario.

> The economy of Bangladesh is stagnant and the prospects of its revival in the next five years or so are remote, making Bangladesh very dependent on outside economic assistance which she can best hope to get from the oil-rich Muslim

countries or the US. All these factors would result in a certain undercurrent of anti-Indian feelings linked with the perception in the minds of many that Pakistan could play a useful role in advocating their case both in the Muslim world and in America. On the domestic scene, the allied problems of maintenance of law and order, and curbing of indiscipline in the armed forces will have the first priority with the new administration. Here again, the bogey of an outside threat would be a handy tool for the administration in rallying the troops and arousing a spirit of nationalism. This would again work to India's disadvantage, as the most plausible source of outside intervention would be in their minds because of its proximity. As far as the future power structure in Bangladesh is concerned, the armed forces are probably the most cohesive and effective organisation in existence in Bangladesh today and they would try to run the affairs of the country either with a façade of a civil administration or even without it. Within the armed forces, a struggle for power between the pro-Pakistani repatriates and the fundamentally nationalist freedom fighters led by Ziaur Rahman has surfaced. Zia has up to now effectively played the trump card of his popularity with the other ranks and has begun the process of weeding out likely opposition from important positions with access to the levers of power. The elimination of a large number of senior officers from amongst the freedom fighters as a result of first and third coups has left him, however, with very few senior colleagues to back him up.

The Resistance Force

The Indian spies knew that only a handful of major forces were in control in Bangladesh. The first was the Mujib Bahini founded by Sheikh Mujib but it was slowly losing mass support. The philosophy and aims of Mujib—secularism, socialism, non-alignment and a close relationship with India—had lost their appeal. The R&AW, which had started operating in Dhaka on a very small level, said that there was some support for the Mujib Bahini in the student community, particularly in Dhaka and Chittagong, but their militant activities failed to reach a level that could cause any serious difficulties for the administration.

Kader Bahini, which had participated in the liberation of Bangladesh under Abdul Kader Siddique, was the most active militant group opposed to the interim government that was virtually led by Ziaur Rahman. The R&AW examined its strength in case its future operations in Bangladesh needed local support. However, this group's effective sphere of operations was confined to the Mymensingh region with some sporadic activity in Pabna and Bogra districts. The strength of the Kader Bahini was also limited; it had just one thousand to three thousand armed guerrillas. A R&AW report said:

> A general study of their operations gives the impression that as organised at present, they are not equipped or trained to effectively face the regular troops of the Bangladesh army but have a continuing nuisance value. Kader Siddique utility as a focus for any national uprising, would therefore, be very limited unless a political opposition at the national level is created to which the militant group gets linked. Major Zia's was another group, which emerged after the third coup, but it was mainly active in the Sunderbans area. This group was primarily a body of about seventy deserters who had probably committed themselves too obviously in support of Khaled Mosharraf's abortive coup and deserted the army to avoid reprisals. During the brief period of their hey-day, their activities could mainly be described as those of freebooters and they did not show any particular political ideology or commitment. They were involved in stray attacks on isolated forest establishment and river craft in the Sundarbans region. In a concerted operation by Bangladesh army—Operation Python—about fifty-odd have either been captured or have surrendered. It is possible that the residue of this group may try to make their way to

> the stronghold of an established group like Kader Bahini as otherwise they would be completely destroyed and the leaders, at least, could not hope for mercy at the hands of present administration. As an effective fighting force, the group has, however, been eradicated by the operations that were mounted and the police forces are now being used for mopping up the stragglers. Another militant group in active conflict with the administration is the Shanti Bahini, the militant wing of the Chakma movement for autonomy, the Jana Sanghati Samiti. This group was also opposed to the Sheikh Mujib government, demanding for autonomy and protection of their customary rights. The level of their activities has not in any way increased since the coup of 15 August, though there are reports from time to time of intensified recruitment and training and of concentration of insurgents. The movement, while espousing the cause of secession, would probably fizzle out if a fair degree of autonomy is provided and certain safeguards against exploitation by non-tribals are assured. In any case, the Shanti Bahini's activities have a limited tribal appeal and would be of little importance on the national scene. The scope of their activities and their capabilities also are limited and can be contained by the troops available in the region, where 65 Brigade, based in Chittagong, has always been committed for dealing with the Chakma insurgents.

The Indians knew that Sheikh Mujib's Awami League had gone defunct as a political force immediately after the coup as many surviving leaders jumped ship in their need to be seen as supporters of the new regime. The Awami League had also been considerably discredited in the later years of Sheikh Mujib's regime because most of its prominent leaders had a reputation for corruption and nepotism. The euphoria of liberation had lasted just about a year; over the next three years there had been growing disenchantment with the party among the almost 85 per cent Muslim majority. Only Sheikh Mujib's personality and charisma as the father of the nation had prevented this disenchantment from growing to unimaginable proportions in his lifetime. While the intelligentsia probably missed the feeling of stability that Sheikh Mujib's regime provided, it had also been disenchanted with his government's activities. This was equally true for the bureaucracy. The best among the bureaucrats had been frustrated and humiliated by continuous interference from the political supporters of the Sheikh and what they considered the prime minister's lack of confidence in them. The economic degeneration during the Sheikh's regime with spiralling inflation, corruption, inefficiency in the distribution of relief materials and lack of any real effort by the regime to mitigate the hardships of the masses, had also left the country's labour and peasantry disillusioned by Mujib, the Awami League and what they stood for.

R&AW chief R.N. Kao was deeply disturbed by the events unfolding in Bangladesh and dissatisfied with the MEA's explanations about the clumsy handling of Bangladesh affairs. The birth of this nation, largely attributed to the R&AW, had been followed by the near annihilation of Indian influence there and Kao was looking for an honest and realistic assessment of what went wrong. His career as an Indian intelligence stalwart was still intact and his team had worked wonders in 1971. So what happened after the warriors in the shadow left Bangladeshi soil was a wake-up call for Indian diplomats.

Kao's query resulted in a twelve-page assessment report which came close to the truth and even admitted the failures of Indian diplomats in Delhi and Dhaka. It ended with a recommendation for serious thought into the main purposes and functioning of Indian diplomacy.

The Bungling Diplomats

After the liberation of Bangladesh in 1971, India needed to choose the perfect diplomatic personnel to station in Dhaka and strengthen the delicate Indo-Bangladeshi relationship. The coup showed that the MEA had chosen wrong. Though the Indian establishment knew that following its birth as a nation, Bangladesh would be a storm-centre of high-pressure international politics and intrigue, it sent Subimal Dutta, an older gentleman, to Dhaka as India's high commissioner when a younger and more dynamic person would probably have faced the challenging situation there more effectively while ostensibly maintaining a low profile. The report that looked into the diplomats' failures said:

> There were two personnel in the Indian diplomatic mission holding the third and fourth positions in the High Commission, who had a well-known pro-CPI background. They naturally befriended the NAP and CPB more than the ruling party, the Awami League, and thus, created a lot of misunderstanding in the high circles of the government and the ruling party in Bangladesh. This caused fresh suspicion about the motives of India. Soon after the liberation in 1971, the Joint Secretary in-charge of Bangladesh in the Ministry of External Affairs had a most fatalistic attitude towards Indo-Bangladesh relations. He was convinced that the relationship between the two countries would go from bad to worse and there was nothing that could be done about it. If the man in charge in Delhi was devoid of any imagination and drive, then one could not expect brilliant results in Dhaka. The general attitude of Indian diplomats in Delhi and Dhaka was: 'We have done enough for Bangladesh. It is now their turn to be grateful and to "behave nicely" towards us. Moreover, in any case, we have great advantage derived from geo-political and military-strategic considerations. If they choose to misbehave, we will put them in their right proper place at the right moment. In the meantime there was nothing much to do in Bangladesh.' What a mistaken and complacent attitude it was to take so many things for granted, while other foreign powers, not belonging to the same area, were working there in a feverish manner. Although there was exaggerated

> propaganda in Bangladesh about the Indian army dismantling factories and taking them away to India, it is known that this was actually done with the encouragement and active connivance of Marwari businessmen. Soon after liberation, there was massive smuggling of goods to and from Bangladesh. Indian businessmen in collaboration with unprincipled businessmen of Bangladesh and with the active support of security forces on the Indian side were carrying on smuggling. There was much hue and cry in Bangladesh and perhaps, some sporadic efforts were made on the Indian side to stop it but with very little effect. The press releases from the Indian High Commission denying the existence of smuggling had less and less credibility with the Bangladesh people. It lowered the prestige of Indian High Commissioner and his colleagues. It is true that it is not possible to stop smuggling effectively on such a long border as India has with Bangladesh. But the smugglers in league with the administration and politicians on both sides of the border played havoc with the Bangladesh economy. This not only had an adverse economic effect but also politically had a very unhealthy impact in Bangladesh. The lure of easy money corrupted an important section of the leadership of the Awami League and blackened its image in the popular mind. When the State Trading Corporation of India (STCI) took over the responsibility of sending dhotis and sarees to Bangladesh that created even greater scandal because they sent a large quantity of utterly rejected material. This came as a shock to the common man in Bangladesh.

The most important failure of Indian diplomacy in Bangladesh, however, was its indifference to and neglect of the country's pro-Indian elements. This, the Indian diplomats argued, was because there was no such pro-Indian core in Bangladesh. But the report which at times was brutally honest, said:

> This would be a wrong statement. We can say from our own experience that for diverse reasons—political, economic,

cultural and also sentimental—there are large sections of the people in Bangladesh who would like to develop the closest and friendliest of relations between the two countries. The Indian diplomacy allowed this hardcore to disintegrate from sheer indifference. Soon, a feeling spread that India was not interested in them. This proved utterly ruinous because when the anti-India feeling began to grow and spread rapidly, it became dangerous and risky to be identified as a pro-Indian element, then they did not feel any stake in trying to assert that they were pro-India. Why should they do so, if India was not interested in them? The disastrous result is that now, when Bangladesh is passing through a stage of utter confusion and intense conflict, with different foreign powers trying to take the fullest advantage of the situation, India is at the disadvantage of not having any genuine friends who have the necessary power to influence events there in any effective manner. It is true that primarily for their own interest some of the Bangladeshis might approach India but that should not be taken as a measure of the goodwill which prevails in Bangladesh towards India. Now, there is hardly any visible and effective influence of India in Bangladesh. This is absolutely disastrous for preservation of India's vital interests in the region.

Plot to Regain the Lost Country

There was intense debate in diplomatic circles and in the intelligence community about how to regain the lost ground in Bangladesh. India's relations with Bangladesh had to be thoroughly reappraised and the government had to formulate a long-term foreign relations strategy for Bangladesh with effective and efficient machinery to implement it. The top officials who analysed the psychological factors in Bangladesh before drafting a blueprint for future relations noted that Bangladeshis had been subjected to intense anti-India and anti-Hindu propaganda for nearly two decades before liberation when the country had been a part of Pakistan. The officials argued that this must have left some residue in the subconscious of most Muslim minds in Bangladesh, since for long years before its emergence as a nation, there had been very little connection on a the popular level between East Pakistan and India. As a new nation, Bangladeshis were very conscious of their new identity. At the same time, they were sensitive and apprehensive regarding India which had given its freedom fighters large-scale assistance. There was a natural sense of inferiority which every nation requiring aid resents and which finds expression in different ways. This phenomenon was nothing new. The Americans, for instance, were never as unpopular in Western Europe as they were during the Second World War when they sent their men to battle and, a few years later, when they poured billions of dollars into war-devastated Europe.

It was suggested to the Indira Gandhi government that India must adopt a mature approach which needed to be manifested in the behaviour of Indian personnel in Bangladesh. The general attitude of the Indian officials after Mujib had been killed was that they had been betrayed and this naturally evoked a feeling of resentment and created obstacles in formulating a well-balanced policy for the post-Mujib era in Bangladesh. A government note said:

> The attitude should be that what we did in Bangladesh was in our interest and that happened to coincide with the interests of the Bangladesh people as well. The attitude of mutuality and equality is absolutely essential for the success of Indian diplomacy in Bangladesh. That is why the selection of personnel who would be implementing the policies both at the official and non-official level is so very important.

Officials believed the problems in Bangladesh needed all the strength, machinery and contacts that the Indian diplomats had. They also discussed certain pre-conditions for the new Bangladesh policy. A conscious decision was taken to give Bangladesh the highest priority in India's foreign policy because there was every possibility that it might become a big base of joint China-Pak operations, aided and abetted by the USA, which could cause chaos in the whole of eastern India within a few years. Giving Bangladesh higher priority meant the involvement of a greater number of people and also greater financial expenditure. Moreover, the Indian officials decided to take a hard look at the personnel handling the Bangladesh situation to learn whether they were capable of facing the new situation. Just experience and competence would not be enough, the officials believed. Diplomats in Bangladesh would also need proper motivation and understanding to be effective. If necessary, suitable non-government people could also be involved.

India had four major objectives for Bangladesh, the achievement of which would be aided by aggressive bureaucracy.

1) To prevent anti-Indian foreign powers using Bangladesh as a base of operations for anti-Indian activities in the political, economic and military spheres.
2) To prevent the development of a situation in Bangladesh which might compel the Hindu minority to migrate to India.
3) To have a friendly government in Dhaka.
4) To forge as many mutually advantageous links as possible and get Bangladesh more and more involved with India.

While thinking about the Chinese, Pakistani and the USA penetration in the post-Mujib era, India was also deliberating its ties with the Soviet Union as far as Bangladesh was concerned. There was a unanimous feeling within the establishment that the Soviet capacity to do anything in Bangladesh on a major scale was limited. Yet, at the same time, any sizeable Soviet presence in Bangladesh could evoke extraordinarily sharp reactions in

Washington and Beijing. A note drafted by intelligence officers and diplomats said:

> Our interest should lie in keeping Bangladesh as much as possible as a sub-continental or South Asian affair. This cannot be achieved if India is too much identified with the Soviet Union in Bangladesh. In those circumstances, India's capacity to divide US, China and Pakistan will be completely nullified. The Soviet Union has to be persuaded to play second fiddle in Bangladesh and whatever understanding is arrived at with them should not be manifested publicly. It should be kept in mind except for a small number of people who are ideologically committed to Pakistan, China, US and Soviet Union, the overwhelming majority of the people of Bangladesh would not like to see their country transformed into a battleground of big powers and to be devastated once again. This fear should be fully exploited by India and this cannot be done effectively if India is too much identified with the Soviet Union in Bangladesh. At the same time, it must be stressed that this policy would not succeed if there were slightest indications of 'hegemonistic tendencies' on the part of India. One of the major efforts of Indian diplomacy in Dhaka should be to overcome the suspicion and fear that the Bangladesh policy-makers feel about the motives of India. A scientific and systematic strategy should be evolved to overcome this suspicion. Moreover, it has to be kept in mind that the Indian diplomacy in Dhaka has to function in a highly politicised atmosphere. Therefore, it is not a job which the ordinary run of diplomats can do effectively. Either diplomats with intense political awareness or politicians with necessary diplomatic skill can do justice to the challenging task.

There were also suggestions from the spy agency to increase people-to-people contact and invite influential leaders from the political, religious and educational spheres of Bangladeshi small towns to India to witness a secular society where Muslims enjoy religious freedom, so that, upon their return, they might be able to counter false anti-India propaganda. The espionage community felt that there were already sufficient grounds for a 'cultural conquest' of Bangladesh using media such as cinema, theatre, music and journals.

To avoid possible harm to the Hindu minorities of Bangladesh, the R&AW suggested that the Indira government warn the Bangladesh regime that any large exodus of Hindu minorities into India would be considered an unfriendly and hostile act. The agency believed that such a warning would have sufficient impact on any government in Dhaka, thanks to the indelible memory of India's active military action in 1971 that helped create Bangladesh.

The Heartbroken Spies

From the serpentine alleys of downtown Calcutta (now Kolkata), Baldev Krishna had watched the birth of Bangladesh. As a young R&AW operative, Krishna remembered the celebrations on the streets of Calcutta when Bangladesh achieved its independence. Although the move by India was a sort of political adventurism on the part of the Indira Gandhi government, the R&AW did not disappoint the prime minister. India's external spy agency announced its arrival in the world of shadows by liberating a new country with the help of the army.

Krishna had started his operations from a safe house in Calcutta in April 1970 under the protective cover of a bogus export-import company. 'I thought we were invincible but the bungling by diplomats in the following years made us vulnerable. And there was the possibility that our neighbours could unite against us,' he told me.

Alarmed, Krishna flew to Delhi in December 1975 to meet his boss R.N. Kao at his residence. The R&AW chief was worried about what he saw as Pakistan and China moving quietly to penetrate the Bangladeshi government and neutralise whatever little influence India still enjoyed in a certain section of the administration.

'There had to be coordinated action before Pakistan's Inter Service intelligence (ISI) led by Lt General Ghulam Jilani Khan created new uncertainties in Bangladesh. Above all, there was fear that Pakistan may soon enter every sphere of Bangladeshi life and India would pay a heavy political price. Kao agreed there was a serious threat that no one in the spy agency could ignore,' Krishna recalled.

Within days, the R&AW had drafted a note analysing the threat from Pakistan and a plan to confront it effectively. 'A decision was taken to recruit more informers in the areas covering the entire Bangladeshi coast and land boundaries. To pick up solid intelligence, we also decided to ensure close coordination of the activities of various Indian government organisations operating in Bangladesh so their offices could be used as listening posts,' Krishna revealed.

The initial information from Bangladesh had suggested that Pakistan was planning to open an embassy in Dhaka and was likely to operate in Bangladesh in a big way. The strength of the Pakistani mission was expected to be between one hundred and one hundred and fifty personnel, aside from a small consulate in Chittagong. The draft said:

> Once the Pakistani embassy starts functioning, they are likely to exercise a pervasive influence in various ministries and the departments of government of Bangladesh, especially in the foreign office. The officials in the Pakistani embassy will know everyone who matters in the official hierarchy of Bangladesh. The old bureaucrats' ties, which were snapped in 1971, would be restored and Pakistan would be able to operate on the old boys' network. As such, Pakistan will get to know practically everything that happens in the Bangladesh foreign office. As

> they would focus their energies primarily on India, Pakistan would know our problems with Bangladesh from A to Z and in any negotiations that we undertake with Bangladesh, Pakistan would be the invisible third party exercising influence on Bangladesh from behind the scenes. Pakistan's effort would be to widen the differences between India and Bangladesh and create all possible hindrances in the way of a smooth relationship between the two countries. Pakistan will seek to infiltrate every walk of life in Bangladesh and Pak-Bangladesh friendship societies may be set up at various levels. Pakistan would concentrate particularly on the mass media, the universities, the educational institutions and the religious organisations. The main purpose of their policy would be to foment pro-Islamic, pro-Pakistani feelings and encourage anti-Indian and anti-Hindu feelings. In due course, if the events in Bangladesh move in a direction favourable to them, Pakistan may promote the idea of a confederation between the two countries.

According to Krishna, the R&AW officers were more worried about Pakistan's plan to destabilise India's east and north-eastern regions working from Bangladesh, which is geographically close to India's West Bengal, the troubled tribal areas of the northeast, and also Nepal, Bhutan and Sikkim. The draft said:

> Zulfikar Ali Bhutto went so far as to say that this region has the potential of developing into another Vietnam. It is, therefore, likely that Pakistan will provide support and encouragement to the Nagas and Mizos as also to the Naxalites. Pakistan may also seek to foment disaffection against India among the Nepalese and try to create complications in our relationship with Nepal and Bhutan. Pakistan has—in the past—claimed to be the protector of the Muslims in India. Indeed, this claim is implicit in the two-nation theory. As such, once Pakistan re-establishes its presence in Bangladesh, they would extend

the network of their operations to the minority community in Bengal, Bihar, Tripura and Assam.

Internal Insecurity

India feared that Bangladesh was likely to become extremely vulnerable to foreign manipulations and pressures mainly from the USA and reactionary oil rich Arab states, compromising the idea of secularism espoused by Mujib. In consequence, the position of the minorities may be weakened, resulting in an exodus to India. When the country was portioned in 1947, a sizeable strength of Hindus remained in the then East Pakistan in great contrast to the position in West Pakistan from where most of the Hindus moved to India at the time of Partition. Due to linguistic and ethnic affinities as also to better their economic prospects, Hindus in Bangladesh felt a pull towards India. Therefore, whenever conditions were propitious, they tried to emigrate to India. Some unauthorised movement from Bangladesh into India had always existed on the border; sometimes, even members of the majority community emigrated to Assam and Meghalaya in search of land. According to information available in the Ministry of Home Affairs (MHA) in 1975, about forty-seven lakh people moved to India between 1947 and February 1971 from the then East Pakistan. Due to the worsening economic situation in Bangladesh, the influx had increased since September 1974 and the Border Security Force (BSF) had intercepted about fifty thousand Bangladeshis from August 1974 to July 1975. After the coup, the number of illegal immigrants from Bangladesh declined due to tight security at the border. But intelligence sources revealed that the worst was yet to come. Attempts were being made by some elements in Bangladesh to terrorise the minority communities, which would lead to an even greater exodus of those communities. Even Bihari Muslims who were well settled in Bangladesh were attempting to return to India. An MHA note said:

> After the assassination of Sheikh Mujib, a psychological warfare seems to have been started against the Hindus. There have been posters of communal nature and slogans against presence of Hindus in Bangladesh. Instances of harassment have been common. Fanatic Islamic organisations like Muslim League, Jamaat-e-Islami are at work in creating ill will against minorities in Bangladesh. All this may culminate in a large-scale exodus of minority groups from Bangladesh. Since there are about nine million Hindus in Bangladesh, India has to live with the problem of dealing with influx from Bangladesh.

The external spy agency believed that the implications of an influx of Bangladeshi minorities needed to be analysed. Apart from adding to India's economic burden, such a migration would create Hindu–Muslim tensions in India, particularly in the north-eastern regions of Bengal and Assam, creating a serious law and order problem even to the extent of jeopardising the tenets of secularism. The R&AW said:

> Should an exodus begin, any policy of stopping the refugees at the border by the use of force would be impracticable and we would inevitably be faced with the necessity of accepting these refugees not only on humanitarian grounds, but also due to the pressure of public sentiment particularly in West Bengal where the kith and kin of many of these people reside.

C.G. Somiah, joint secretary in the MHA, warned the states sharing borders with Bangladesh that India could not take upon itself the burden of maintaining Bangladesh nationals coming to India unauthorised and it would be necessary for state governments to take every possible step to locate and push back all illegal immigrants from Bangladesh. Somiah knew that the state governments might not have accurate information about unauthorised Bangladesh nationals in their territories and it was therefore necessary to review the existing intelligence set up in the states so an adequate information base could be created to locate and evict illegal immigrants. Therefore, he suggested a census operation in the border areas with special police powers provided to retired police and revenue officials to sign the eviction papers of illegal immigrants. Somiah's direction made the gravity of the situation clear. He said:

> State governments should evolve a system of supporting posts to the Border Security Forces to work as a second line of interception. These posts could be located in the rear areas at suitable checkpoints like railway stations and sensitive roads leading to the border. It is necessary to intensify riverine patrolling in Sunderbans area to block the influx of illegal immigrants as well as illicit movement of arms from Bangladesh. It is necessary to have timely exchange of information between the BSF and other central agencies and the state agencies regarding the happenings on the border. Events in Bangladesh and the influx of minority groups from there may create communal tension in India. There may be some agents behind the influx of Bangladesh nationals to India. It may be useful to collect intelligence about such agents with a view to keep watch over their activities. The police communication network in the border areas needs to be improved on a priority basis. All the border police stations should be provided with wireless network immediately. For push back operations, the infiltrators will have to be collected from areas of their illegal stay and taken to the border in batches. It may be necessary to keep them in transit camps for some time as pushing back operations can only be carried out in small groups.

The MHA was also worried about the BSF's strength at the border: was the force large enough to deal with a massive influx of illegal immigrants? In 1975, the border vigil force had deployed eighteen battalions with three placed in reserve. Though the ministry had decided to deploy the reserve battalions on the border as well, it understood that these resources were still inadequate. In those days, the BSF had four patrolling boats to monitor activities over fifty-eight miles of the riverine border in the Sunderbans area. The government decided to shop for more boats and equipment as well as raise four battalions of border wing home guards for effective liaison with the BSF. The MHA said:

> It would be necessary for the state level coordination committees presided over by the chief secretaries to periodically review the incidence of influx and steps taken to deal with the problem. Such meetings should be held at least once a month. The state level meetings should be attended by sector inspector general of the BSF and representatives of Intelligence Bureau and R&AW. At the district level, commandant of the BSF battalion deployed in the area and the local representatives of the Intelligence Bureau and R&AW would be associated with these meetings. It would be necessary for the central agencies and the state police to have quick and regular exchange of intelligence regarding influx from Bangladesh. The existing arrangements for collection and collation of intelligence will have to be reviewed and wherever necessary, strengthened. The influx of refugees may by itself create tensions in the border areas due to various socio-economic reasons. It would be necessary for the state governments and the district authorities to exercise necessary vigilance so that trouble, if any, can be nipped in the bud.

Meanwhile the MEA, which works to establish good diplomatic relationships with the other countries, worried that Indian actions might give the Bangladeshi regime the impression that New Delhi was not happy with it. K.R. Narayanan, additional secretary in the ministry, argued that even though the new government had declared itself an Islamic Republic, there was no reason for India to show coolness towards the regime or to write off Bangladesh in a mood of despondency. There were also strong views within the MEA that the Indian officials posted at the Dhaka mission who had returned after the coup should go back to Dhaka as a long stay in New Delhi could give the impression that India was still displeased with the new government. Besides, it was clear that India needed first-hand information as well as political analysis of the new forces and new personalities that had come up in Bangladesh after the coup. Narayanan said:

> My feeling is that immediately the new regime in Bangladesh would try to reassure India that no changes in relationship with India have taken place as a result of change in the government. Even if there will be greater friendliness towards Pakistan, Bangladesh is likely to remain an entity independent of Pakistan and also, of India. This would be a complicated situation, which would try our nerves very much in the future. However, on the diplomatic plane, the wisest course for us now would be to treat Bangladesh on a normal basis, recognising the new government and continuing our diplomatic representation.

The external spy agency still had a small network in Bangladesh, that supplied sketchy information. The sub-sources or paid agents had either dried up after the coup or gone underground fearing persecution if exposed. Nevertheless, the Indian spy agency continued to hunt for key figures in Bangladesh who might change the course of the country's political future.

Did the spy agency believe there was even the slightest possibility of a Bangladesh government in exile? Perhaps even operating out of India? Senior R&AW officer N.F. Suntook was disappointed with the leaders who had fled Bangladesh; he believed they had no stature to form a government in exile. He was right. The majority of those who decided to quietly leave Bangladesh after the coup belonged to the pro-Awami League Bangladesh Chhatra League (college students). Some MPs had also crossed the border, but none had enough prominence to provide a focus for a national government in exile. Suntook wrote:

> The two prominent leaders who are outside Bangladesh, namely Justice Abu Sayeed Chaudhury and Kamal Hossain, whilst personally not in favour of the developments in Bangladesh, have shown no stomach for a conflict with the regime in Bangladesh.

In the treacherous game of politics, friends and foes change their skins overnight. Chaudhury was appointed the new foreign minister of Bangladesh and he pledged allegiance to the new regime. In a meeting with a R&AW officer codenamed Shiva in New York, Chaudhury said that Kamal Hossain, who India believed was a friend, was in fact the opposite. Though Hossain outwardly expressed sentiments in favour of India, he strove to promote Pakistan's interests at the cost of India's. Chaudhury tried to sell himself as the true friend of India. 'He said he may have to say favourable things about Pakistan, but at heart he would always work to strengthen Indo-Bangladesh relations,' Shiva told me.

Chaudhury also told Shiva that he had been advised by the president of Bangladesh to not criticise China and Pakistan in international forums; in fact, he had been told to make favourable references to these two countries whenever opportunities arose.

The then foreign secretary Kewal Singh met Chaudhury at Lima, where Chaudhury told him that Sheikh Mujib had lost much of his charisma over the previous three years and that the drastic and arbitrary changes which Sheikh Mujib had made in the constitution were a great mistake since by putting himself above parliament, he had lost the basis for legitimacy. Kewal Singh said in a note:

> While agreeing that Sheikh Mujib was a great leader who had worked for Indo-Bangladesh friendship, Chaudhury was of the view that his advisors were not as sincere in their feelings towards India and, in this connection, he particularly referred to Kamal Hossain. Chaudhury said that he personally would like to maintain very friendly relations with India, but added that he would have to act very tactfully. Chaudhury also said that he had sometimes advised Sheikh Mujib that there was mounting discontentment in many circles and he should pay due regard to it but Sheikh, however, replied that he knew how to handle the situation and deal with the trouble makers. Chaudhury felt that Sheikh Mujib had become overconfident and didn't realise, even till the end, that there was grave danger to himself and his government. There had also been talk among the younger elements in the army that on the advice of India, Sheikh Mujib was keeping the Bangladeshi army small and weak. Sheikh Mujib even used to mention to his colleagues that in case of difficulty, he would call on the Indian army and this gave currency to rumours that his wrong actions were on the advice of India.

The R&AW worried that anti-Ziaur Rahman elements in Bangladesh had lost their lustre, even though hero-worship had immortalised Sheikh Mujib. The new government in Dhaka used anti-corruption and arms recovery drives to keep the few remaining followers of Sheikh Mujib on the run and Suntook believed that pro-Mujib elements would not support a national government in exile. However, he also felt that the Jatiya Samajtantrik Dal (JSD) headed by Major Jalil which had infiltrated the armed forces to a certain extent could become a potent force against Ziaur Rahman and his allies. The JSD, the R&AW knew, was in open conflict with Zia, and was probably the best-organised and most cohesive political force in Bangladesh. The JSD had a sizeable following in the armed forces and the R&AW was aware that it was solely responsible for encouraging widespread indiscipline. A R&AW report said:

> This indiscipline has—to some extent—been subdued by Ziaur Rehman's promises to take necessary steps for alleviating the grievances of the other ranks but demands are so far reaching that it is unlikely that the present administration would be able to actually meet them. The seeds of further discontent in the armed forces are, therefore, ever present. After the arrest of the JSD leaders, the administration has stepped up its drive to round up prominent JSD personalities even at the district and sub-divisional level. Quite a few have been rounded up, but it is unlikely that the regime has been able to break the back of the movement. The crackdown has, however, compelled the JSD to go underground in order to reorganise and reactivate its cadres. Whilst the philosophy of its leadership is incompatible with that of the pro-Mujib Awami League activists, we have been receiving reports of the JSD making efforts at establishing an alliance of convenience with straw leaders to form a combined opposition against the present regime. The Marxist-Leninist parties like the Purbo Banglar Communist Party, the Purba Banglar Samyabadi Dal, the East Pakistan Communist Party and the Purba Sarbahara Party has not yet indicated any active support for the present regime. They have fairly well-organised underground cadres who are guerrilla-oriented and could, if in opposition to the government, be expected to activate widespread minor attacks on isolated police stations, rural banks, etc. Their inspiration, however, is Maoist and they are unlikely to create any difficulty for the present regime for the time being till the attitude of China becomes clear.

The R&AW, which was keeping an eye on influential players after the Sheikh Mujib era, had identified A.V.M. Towab, chief of air staff, as a gradually emerging challenger to Zia's pre-eminence in Bangladesh. As a repatriated officer with avowed pro-West and pro-Pakistani leanings, his thinking was also in line with leaders embedded in the government yet unhappy over the recent developments in the country. There were intelligence reports to indicate that he had, behind the scenes, been trying to undermine Zia's position and move the government towards a more pro-Pakistani stance. R&AW had learnt that Towab was trying to get back some officers from Libya where they had fled after the coup, with an eye on creating a counterweight to the growing dominance of Ziaur Rahman.

Though he hoped for an internal uprising against Ziaur Rahman, Suntook believed that the armed forces were not in favour of supporting any particular party which was why no military leader had publicly expressed the view that elections should be delayed beyond the declared deadline of February 1977. The R&AW felt that the armed forces in power could be expected to resist a change if they felt that elections would bring in a government hostile to them. Suntook said:

> Zia is apprehensive of parties like JSD cashing in on the prevalent discontent in the armed forces or of the politicians creating dissatisfaction within particular armed forces units like Bangladesh Lancers to further their own political aims. His efforts would, therefore, most probably be directed towards consolidating his position to a point where he can influence the type of government that comes into power and which would enable him to effectively remain in control behind this façade. The instability and indiscipline, if it continues, may provide him with a handy pretext for continuing the present authoritarian regime and martial law and postponing the elections to a time which he considers more favourable to his aims. With the present divisions within the armed forces themselves, it is unlikely that either Zia's group or his opponents would be in a position to organise a party on the lines of BSPP, but if Zia is able to eliminate the opposition, a development on those lines and Zia finally emerging as the civilian head of state cannot also be ruled out. The most likely structure that will emerge will be a political front party with the effective power in the hands of the armed forces. The emphasis and policy of the governments

> would be dependent on whether the freedom fighters or the repatriates finally predominate in the armed forces.

Suntook's assessment was crystal clear. The uncertainties in Bangladesh and the anti-India feelings were not easy to erase. Although there was a clear rift within Bangladesh, no potent force existed to challenge martial law and Zia's power. The Bangladeshi armed forces were divided into two camps—freedom fighters who had participated in the 1971 liberation war and repatriates who were by and large pro-Pakistani. The division, to some extent, was further crystallised by the fact that the freedom fighters had obtained certain advantages and the repatriates some disadvantages by the creation of Bangladesh. However, the individual views and ambitions of senior officers blurred the line to some extent. The personal loyalties of units and formations also confused the situation. The influence of political parties like the JSD and Islamabad factions like the ex-Muslim Leaguers and their territorial and regional loyalties added another factor to the equation.

The R&AW felt, however, that the influence of a re-emphasised Islamic identity would be as strong in the Bangladeshi armed forces as it was in the rest of the country. The spies believed that in the wake of a tussle between senior officers, the loyalties of the armed forces could be influenced by some political parties. It was very much clear that of all the contenders for power amongst the senior armed forces officers, Ziaur Rahman wielded the greatest influence with the largest number of followers and had become effective enough to dampen the indiscipline instigated by political parties.

Indian spies who worked tirelessly to restore normalcy in Bangladeshi recalled the torments of waiting out a dark and cold night for a warm dawn. Since it was impossible to form a government in exile, given Bangladesh's political situation, the R&AW officers began recruiting people close to Ziaur Rahman.

The operation was purely political. The Indian interest was limited to restoring democratic rule in its neighbouring country. Zia was making several amendments to the Bangladeshi constitution to allow the army to rule with an iron hand and Indian spies were convinced that such arrangements couldn't last forever. Abu Sadat Mohammad Sayem, the former chief justice of Bangladesh who had become the president with Zia's blessings after the November 1975 coup, had discussions with a spy codenamed Raja Man Singh and acknowledged that participation of the people was vital for the development of Bangladesh. Sayem's advisor Abdus Sattar also played a key role during the deliberations to allow a multi-party system.

Raja Man Singh said that Zia's intention was to neutralise all opponents before allowing any democratic and political movement in the country. After elevating Sayem as president, Zia had become chief martial law administrator and his first target was the JSD and its leaders.

'In the next four months, between December 1976 and March 1977, Zia played his game perfectly. The crackdown against dissidents was planned, calculated and executed with precision. Zia was also inspired by Sanjay Gandhi's family planning initiatives and tried to replicate the sterilisation model in Bangladesh. This did create some noise, but he subdued the protests against it. At around the same time, India held its first elections after the Emergency and the Indira Gandhi regime ended. The ripple effect was felt in the agency. The top echelon was removed by the new prime minister, Morarji Desai, and Suntook, who was closely involved with developments in Bangladesh, was appointed the new chief of R&AW,' recalled Raja Man Singh.

Abdus Sattar was appointed vice president of Bangladesh after the referendum in May 1977 and his main task was to float a political front for the military government. The Jatiyatabadi Gantantrik Dal that emerged in February 1978 was the culmination of Sattar's effort to bring prominent figures of Bangladesh under a single political umbrella. The outfit was later merged with the Jatiyatabadi Front in May 1978 with Ziaur Rahman as its leader. In September, the same year, all the fledgling political fronts close to Zia were dissolved and the Bangladesh Nationalist Party (BNP) was born. The BNP swept the February 1979 election, winning two hundred and seven out of three hundred seats. The CIA, in a report, said that Zia had moved further away from India and the Soviet Union while deepening ties with the USA and China. The only solace for India was that Mohammed Ershad was head of the Bangladeshi army.

Raja Man Singh said that as a politician who tried to transform himself into a mass leader in the mould of Sheikh Mujib, Ziaur Rahman was a complete failure. When Indira Gandhi returned to power in early 1980, India tried to help Zia establish the rule of law and true democracy in Bangladesh, but he was suspicious of India's friendly overtures.

'His military approach in dealing with public issues and his ruthlessness towards army colleagues weakened his position. There was simmering anger in the army and we knew it was just a matter of time before another quake struck Bangladesh. We patiently waited for it,' Raja Man Singh told me.

On 30 May 1981, Ziaur Rahman was assassinated by a group of army officers in Chittagong. The development shocked China, the USA and close Islamic allies of Bangladesh, but according to Singh, India was not surprised.

'The BNP and its supporters had turned corrupt and were radicalised in a very short span of time. There was no space for secularism in Bangladesh under Zia and a group within the army that had fought for liberation was disenchanted with his rule,' Raja Man Singh said.

Hussain Mohammed Ershad as chief of army staff helped Vice President Abdus Sattar take over as acting president of Bangladesh after Zia's assassination. Sattar promised to hold elections soon. In November 1981, Sattar scored a landslide victory for the BNP. But within a few months, in March 1982, Mohammed Ershad executed a bloodless coup, ending Ziaur Rahman's legacy. A R&AW report said that such a move had been in the offing since the assassination of Ziaur Rahman in 1981. The report said:

> The development leading to army take over can be traced ultimately to President Zia's assassination. That episode removed most important leaders of the liberation wing in the Bangladesh army, one or two remaining senior Generals were eased out within two or three weeks, leaving the leadership entirely in the hands of repatriate group. The period between May and November 1981, when Sattar was acting President, was used to project Zia's party BNP as the only force which could run the country. Most of the officers involved in the assassination were tried and executed. During this period, the BNP appeared to present a united front under Sattar. Army Chief Ershad also appeared to be co-operative. The November Presidential election brought out the dangers in the situation. Since Sheikh Hasina was too young to contest, Kamal Hossain was the Awami League candidate. Both the sides made charges of rigging. The election campaign was violent. There were also strikes in many sectors of industry and government—altogether a very unconvincing election. However, Sattar's majority appears to have been genuine. The process of legitimisation does not seem to have helped Sattar. His first cabinet was a weak compromise in which balance between the right and the left in the BNP was upset. The Prime Minister, Shah Azizur Rehman, belongs to right wing, originally Muslim League. It was a large cabinet of forty-two. Many ministers were known to be corrupt. There was, however, no place for the pro-Chinese Awami League group, which has seventy-six seats in the Parliament. While the cabinet formation was a fiasco, there was another even more

> significant development—complete disagreement between Sattar and BNP men about the Vice President position. Against the views of many of his followers, Sattar decided to appoint a political non-entity, Mirza Nurul Huda, as Vice President. The next three months—November 1981 to January 1982—in fact, saw continuous fighting in the BNP between the left wing anti-corruption group and the Prime Minister's faction. This was compounded by an unseemly controversy about Zia's widow Begum Khaleda Zia in connection with the election to the post of president of the party. She was offered the post by Sattar, who, however, backed out of the commitment in mid-January, obviously under the Prime Minister's pressure. Begum Zia came out into the open, asking for a more balanced cabinet. Parallel to these developments in the ruling party, there was a controversy between the army and the President. Ershad put forward a formal claim for participation in the government and also criticised the corrupt elements in the cabinet. He demanded a presidential advisory group. Sattar responded by having a National Security Council in which the service chiefs would be in minority of three in a group of ten. This was publicly rejected by the army which resulted in a stalemate. Unable to govern with the corrupt cabinet, Sattar went back to the dissident leaders, promising reform on 13 February. The cabinet was dismissed and a much smaller Cabinet of eighteen people was sworn in. The immediate reason was to prevent a boycott of the president's speech in Parliament on 15 February. He also gave in to the army by dismissing the old Security Council and appointing a new one of six members, consisting of three service chiefs, himself, vice president and the prime minister. One factor in Sattar's capitulation was the food shortage. Many countries, including India, offered, at this time, to rush rice to the country, where prices were skyrocketing.

Indian intelligence officials believed that the emergence of Ershad in Bangladesh was mainly due to three parallel problems—

dissension within the ruling party, dissension within the Awami League after the return of Sheikh Hasina from abroad and the return of Khondaker Mostaq Ahmad to the political arena. They also believed that the developments leading to the coup against Sattar's regime had been complicated. They argued that three aspects were relevant—Bangladesh Prime Minister Rahman's close links with the army, a group of army officers visiting Indonesia just weeks before the coup to study the use of an army in national reconstruction and the army takeover preceded by the resignation of Vice President Huda who was unhappy about his position. The R&AW's analysis shed light on Ershad, who had effectively orchestrated the coup:

> Ershad's behaviour during the period leading to the coup has been fairly straightforward. His great political achievement has been to shed the image of a pure expatriate. He has made it a deliberate policy during the recent months to champion the cause of the freedom fighters within the army. This will widen his base, while at the same time, he would retain the loyalty of the large part of the army, which has a continuous professional record from 1971 within the Pakistan army. It is not clear whether the target of this action is the Awami League, Sheikh Hasina and Kamal Hossain, personally. If Ershad and his colleagues have a certain coherent philosophy of participation in or guidance of political activity of the army, we might see a brief period when all political activity is banned as in Pakistan, followed by the re-emergence of the parties. It is unlikely that the army would completely side with the reactionary groups in the country, even though they have links with the right wing Muslim League group in BNP.

The R&AW also believed that Ershad had no special anti-India record.

> He seems to have been a fairly happy officer in the National Defence College, Delhi, during the 1975 transition when

> Sheikh Mujib was assassinated, even though he did not conceal his differences from his Indian colleagues on many questions. He seems to be a professional soldier anxious to develop an efficient professional army. His statements during the last six months have been reasonably coherent and put forward the view that in the special circumstances of Bangladesh's recent history and the problems which the country is facing today, the army has to play a constitutionally legitimate role in spheres outside the purely professional field.

However, Ershad and his army were cautious of India's influence in Bangladesh. An incident in February 1982 showed that the Bangladeshis were almost paranoid about the presence of Indian officials in Dhaka. Surveillance on Indian diplomatic staff posted at the high commission was intense. On 25 February 1982, Bangladeshi security personnel tailed the car of Indian High Commissioner Muchkund Dubey on the Dhaka streets. External Affairs Minister P.V. Narasimha Rao was forced by the opposition to make a statement. On 4 March 1982, Rao said in Parliament:

> It is a matter of regret that the concerned Bangladesh authorities should have arranged surveillance of our High Commissioner in an objectionable manner while he was driving around Dhaka in pursuance of his normal and legitimate functions. The High Commissioner (Dubey) stopped his car, and asked his security guard to request the occupants of the car following him not to do so. This resulted in an altercation, which has since been exaggerated in the Bangladesh press. Unfounded allegations were also made that the High Commissioner was interfering in the domestic affairs of Bangladesh.

The issue of intense surveillance was taken up at the highest level in the Bangladesh government and Ershad was warned that any other similar incident may jeopardise the relationship between the two countries. A R&AW officer said the active tailing of Indian officers stopped for some time but resumed after a few months.

On 25 March 1982, Ershad announced the suspension of the constitution and the dissolution of the civil administration and parliament while declaring martial law. He became de facto chief martial law administrator, arguing that the action was necessary due to the critical state of the country and economy. In his address on Bangladesh radio, Ershad promised to hold elections after the situation improved.

Exploiting Weakness

'Winds are a significant element of weather in Bangladesh,' a CIA report once stated. The American analysts were right. A thunderstorm had brought misfortune to the once all-powerful BNP and the rainfall had helped Ershad harvest riches. By this time, the R&AW had increased the recruitment and deployment of human sources in Bangladesh. The operation was more about collecting intelligence inside the opaque military administration than about covert actions. The CIA too was interested in Bangladesh and its spies wrote several reports on the country. One such report said that to solidify his position, Ershad promoted an ambitious campaign to eradicate corruption in politics and business and many ministers were arrested for taking bribes and siphoning public funds. The Americans believed that Ershad's coup was a necessary evil although his hold on power was fragile and his survivability a big question.

American intelligence was always wary of an overwhelming penetration of Indian espionage apparatus in Bangladesh and this reflects in most intelligence analyses drafted by the CIA during those tumultuous days. A CIA report prepared after Ershad's coup said:

> Most Bangladeshis are innately suspicious of Indian intentions and tend to view any problems in relations with New Delhi as a sign that India is attempting to undermine

> their government. Acknowledging that it would prefer to deal with an elected administration, the Indian government has little alternative but to work with the military leadership. Although, New Delhi would favour the emergence of a more accommodating government in Dhaka, it recognises that blatant Indian interference in Bangladesh's internal affairs could be counterproductive for India. India's tough position on bilateral disputes with Bangladesh reflects Prime Minister Indira Gandhi's long-standing attitude that India is the predominant power in the subcontinent and that its neighbours must accommodate themselves to Indian interests. Ershad's administration has talked of not sacrificing national interests in dealing with outstanding bilateral problems between the two countries. Such a stance is only rhetorical, however, as Bangladesh lacks the leverage to give its remarks substance. Solutions will depend on the kind of relationship India decides it wants with its smaller and weaker neighbour and on the diplomatic skill [that] Bangladesh can muster in negotiating from a position of weakness. While Bangladesh's delicate political condition reduces its ability to resist external pressures, any sign of subservience to India on important issues would imperil the survival of any government in Dhaka.

On the diplomatic level, India acted as a large-hearted neighbour and tried to salvage the situation by opening communication lines with Dhaka. Ershad had invited External Affairs Minister P.V. Narasimha Rao to Dhaka months after declaring the martial law. Rao landed at Dhaka airport on 22 May 1982 and formal discussions were held on regional and international issues.

In October 1982, Ershad arrived in New Delhi. His visit was seen as a serious attempt to solidify the relationship between the two countries in the political, economic and cultural spheres. Indira Gandhi and Ershad agreed to set up a joint economic commission to increase commercial exchange with Dhaka. India signed an agreement on sharing the waters of the River Teesta with Bangladesh, but other critical issues like the augmentation of the Ganga waters at Farakka and large-scale infiltration from Bangladesh remained major worries.

According to documents in the MEA, Ershad told Indira, 'We must be friends—I mean, good friends. Our relations should be based on goodwill and neighbourliness, on large-heartedness and understanding, free from pre-independence and inherited inhibitions, and firmly established on the principles of sovereignty.'

Indira reminded Ershad that before Bangladesh could be free, the blood of Indian martyrs had cemented the country's foundation. Seldom in history have people had to pay so heavy a sacrifice for a goal.

Indira further said: 'We in India wish for our close friends what we want for ourselves—political strength and economic ability to fulfil the expectations of the people. It is our policy to see you stable and strong. We try constantly and earnestly to cooperate with you.'

These statements gave voice to the apprehensions of both Indira and Ershad. They needed an aggressive diplomatic exercise to soothe nerves in both countries. In 1983, External Affairs Minister P.V. Narsimha Rao flew to Dhaka to attend a bilateral meeting.

A R&AW agent codenamed Yasin Mohammed told me that the agency was particularly worried over the increasing influence of the Jamaat-e-Islami after Ershad came to power. The Jamaat cadre was swelling and anti-India propaganda was gaining traction among fundamentalists.

Yasin said, 'The fear among us was that Jamaat could transform itself into a mainstream force and play a crucial role whenever elections were held in Bangladesh. Although Ershad was quick to foresee the hazard an outfit like Jamaat posed for the country, he maintained a measured silence on certain activities fearing that he would be branded as pro-India.'

Sometime in October 1983, the US embassy in Dhaka reported that Ershad had been forced in his official role to recognise the reality of Indian dominance and tried to approach bilateral problems with moderation, to the point that some Bangladeshis considered him 'soft on India'. Probably in an attempt to counter this perception, Ershad publicly criticised New Delhi. The report further said:

> In our view, India would no doubt favour a return to power of the Awami League, which with Indian assistance, led Bangladesh to independence. However, India recognises that this is not likely to occur. We doubt, however, that India want[s] the political situation in Bangladesh to deteriorate to a point that would lead to control by radical parties of either extreme.
>
> 'We believe several areas of dispute between Bangladesh and India could strain relations and lead to instability in Bangladesh and regional turmoil on the sub-continent. The most pressing is the water-sharing problem. Seasonal water shortages and floods are chronic in Bangladesh, and the overpopulated, largely agrarian society depends heavily on the Ganges and Brahmaputra rivers, which flow through the country. Because both rivers enter Bangladesh from India, their technical management and control continue to be a sensitive political issue. We believe New Delhi recognises that instability in Bangladesh could affect the stability of the entire region.

A spy codenamed Vibhas who had served in Bangladesh told me that the USA was more worried about the Soviet Union's influence in Dhaka and that the CIA had deployed its covert machinery to neutralise Russian penetration. This was the period of intense cold war and the USSR was adamantly spreading communist propaganda far and wide. A CIA analysis said:

> The Soviets are trying to exploit the fluid internal situation in Bangladesh by encouraging the leftist political parties to increase agitation against the military regime of Ershad. In our

> view, Moscow's reasons for dabbling in Bangladesh internal politics stem from its perception that, because Ershad has not consolidated his control, the Soviets have an opportunity to check Bangladesh's drift to the West and the Islamic countries and to strengthen Leftist position. The Soviets probably recognise, however, that local pro-Soviets leftists are weak, factionalised and have little chance of bringing down Ershad's government without some major contributing issue and the support of other political groups. Instability in Bangladesh could provide an opportunity for further Soviet meddling in the subcontinent.

Vibhas told me: 'US spies were scared that the Soviet foothold in Bangladesh would provide an edge over American interests in South Asia. As an international ally, Bangladesh was a very minor interest but strategically, to counter the Soviets, it was crucial for US decision makers to keep a strong grip over the Bangladesh regime.'

Ershad may have publicly criticised New Delhi on certain foreign policy issues but by 1983, India had managed to rebuild its influence and a formidable network with the help of R&AW assets. The Indian intelligence agency's objective was very simple, 'Whoever is going to rule Dhaka must have a favourable approach towards India.'

'Since the liberation of Bangladesh, the R&AW had practiced this policy,' Vibhas told me. 'The setback of 1975 was enough to trigger a major policy shift. The event taught a basic lesson to the political decision makers that the neighbour's complex problems couldn't be resolved with fledgling diplomats at the helm of affairs. In December 1983, Ershad declared himself president and Indian intelligence officers knew the battle was going to be long and treacherous.'

In July 1984, just months before her assassination in October 1984, Prime Minister Indira Gandhi decided—during the South

Asian Regional Co-operation (SARC) meeting in the Maldives—to intensify operational activities with India's immediate neighbours including Bangladesh. India also convinced the leaders of other countries to convene the next meeting in Dhaka towards the end of 1985. After Rajiv Gandhi took over as prime minister of India, he made it clear in his first public statement in January 1985 that friendlier relations with the neighbouring countries would be the government's top priority. Gandhi visited Dhaka on 2 June 1985 after it was ravaged by a massive cyclone. The trip helped cement certain visible rifts between the two nations and Gandhi assured Ershad of India's help in rebuilding the cyclone-hit regions. Rajiv Gandhi and Ershad had two more meetings in 1985. In October, they met in the Bahamas and the talks were primarily focused on the long-standing problem of Ganga water shortages. They agreed to set up a ministerial level task force to discuss the issue and in November 1985 and a meeting was duly held in New Delhi. Gandhi and Ershad met again in December 1985 in Dhaka to discuss the bilateral relationship. A statement issued by the MEA at the time said:

> Some problems, however, persist. Among them is the continuing flow of illegal immigrants from Bangladesh into India. This has been discussed between the two governments on a number of occasions, including at a meeting between the Directors General of the Border Security Force and the Bangladesh Rifles. We have conveyed to Bangladesh our intention to stem this flow by whatever means possible.

Vibhas told me that the R&AW knew the Ershad was getting cosy with the West, particularly with the American intelligence agency which treated the dictator as their best bet against Soviet influence. The CIA was jubilant when the Ershad-led Jatiyo Party won the election in May 1986. The result of the completely rigged polls was already known to the world; however, the CIA insisted that it would provide some legitimacy for Ershad. A CIA report said:

> Ershad plans to use pro-government forces in [the] Parliament to pass an amendment ratifying his actions during four years of Martial Law. We expect the amendment to be approved; the leftist Awami League failed to gain the necessary seats to block it. The major opposition party BNP boycotted the polls and plans to pursue a disobedience campaign. The army is unhappy that the pro-government party did not win more seats but will continue its grudging support for Ershad. He was able to pull off the elections after months of wrangling with the Awami League and the BNP. According to the US embassy, Ershad secured Sheikh Hasina's agreement to participate in elections in return for relaxing Martial Law and promising to remain neutral during the elections.

Ershad won one hundred and eighty-three of three hundred seats and despite the noise about the rigged polls, swiftly took control of the administration. Ershad also planned to convene a presidential election in November 1986. In his meetings with CIA officials, Ershad had claimed that martial law in Bangladesh couldn't be completely lifted until his position as president had been secured either through popular elections or a martial law decree. The Indian government was perturbed by the development and when Ershad visited Delhi again, President Zail Singh reminded him about India's sacrifice in carving out Bangladesh. According to documents from the MEA, Singh told Ershad that there are perhaps few countries in the world with as much in common as India and Bangladesh. 'Not only have we shed our blood together in the cause of liberation and national independence, but we are bound together by common strands of history and culture,' President Singh told Ershad.

The Bangladeshi dictator turned leader, however, was unmoved. His focus was unresolved issues between the two countries rather than warmth. 'We are often asked, at home and abroad, about our unresolved issues with India. People have wondered how we can achieve a meaningful and enduring relationship when some important issues are still outstanding.' The MEA documents stated:

> The pivotal question in any bilateral relationship is, of course, how best such problems or differences can be tackled and resolved. Does the answer lie in confrontation, acrimony or pressure? Or will it not be far more effectual to approach them in a spirit of amity and accommodation? Surely, there cannot be any two opinions about the second option.

Ershad's comments rattled the Indian government officials. The external spy agency was shocked. Their response in various dispatches was clear: 'If Ershad's confrontational attitude persists, he needs to go.'

Return of the Shadow Operators

Within days of arriving in Dhaka in the first week of November 1988, the R&AW station head codenamed Krishna Patwardhan, held a meeting with junior agents. The first thing Patwardhan asked was whether agents operating under the overwhelming surveillance mounted by the Bangladesh dictatorship had been successful in maintaining their covers. The answer was no. The local staff employed at the mission were informers for Ershad and not a single Indian spy in Dhaka had been able to keep the iron mask intact.

Ershad had been under tremendous pressure from political movements of all shades to hold fresh elections. However, he dissolved parliament in December 1987 and declared an emergency before his government announced the dates for a fresh mandate. The dictator declared that the elections would be held in February 1988 and then, postponed them to March. The BNP, Awami League and Jamaat-e-Islami boycotted the polls, allowing Ershad's political front, the Jatiyo Party, to capture two hundred and fifty-one seats out of three hundred in parliament.

The Bangladesh army exercised absolute power and Indian officials operating in Dhaka were put under intense surveillance.

Patwardhan discovered other vulnerabilities of operations in Dhaka and decided to set up a standard procedure to facilitate targeting Ershad's opponents in. But he was more worried about the deep divisions between the political parties of Bangladesh. The primary concern was the much-publicised rift between the BNP's Begum Khaleda Zia and the Awami League's Sheikh Hasina. Patwardhan's coded message to both the leaders was clear. Ershad was their common enemy and the moment was ripe to renounce their bitter rivalry and join hands. Begum Zia and Sheikh Hasina both agreed that the removal of Ershad was their main objective and other issues could be ignored for a while. This understanding between political leaders who Patwardhan believed were potent forces against the dictator put more pressure on the Ershad regime which had successfully converted an illegitimate rule to legitimate governance.

Meanwhile, on the diplomatic level, every effort was being made to keep the ties between Ershad and the Indian government intact. According to Patwardhan, the Indian establishment aimed to show the world that India was not a troublemaker and its sole intention in Bangladesh was to help set up a people's government.

'I asked the staff to stop the practice of writing memoranda on meetings with sources and paid informers since the typist and the person who filed such memos could leak the information. Any documentation can be compromised. Instead, I encouraged the use of handwritten ciphers depending on the value of the information. Most of our plans were stored in our heads. There was a regime change in India in late 1989 but our operation continued without a glitch. We had recruited most of the leaders of student unions, managed to bring Begum Zia and Sheikh Hasina on the same platform and also ensured that Ershad and his spies knew nothing about our operation,' Patwardhan recalled.

For Patwardhan, January 1990 could not have had a better start. The R&AW spymaster was able to establish a powerful network of informers within the Bangladeshi government machinery which he tactfully used to counter anti-India elements embedded in the system. A month later, External Affairs Minister Inder Kumar Gujaral, serving under the new Indian prime minister, V.P. Singh, landed in Dhaka. The Indian delegation met Ershad to discuss all the vexing bilateral issues including the sharing of Ganga waters. In the background, Patwardhan and his team intensified their activities to bring down Ershad, who was turning bitter and hostile to India. An Indian intelligence review in early 1990 viewed him as a long-term threat to South Asia, a man who was acting on the directions of Western spy agencies that were now deeply entrenched in the Dhaka administration. A prized catch within Ershad's government codenamed Ismail was welcomed into the Indian informers' network. He was asked to help recruit political leaders to spearhead a campaign to restore democracy in Bangladesh.

Ismail and Patwardhan devised a unique method to communicate with each other. Whenever Ismail had information to share, the opinion page of the day's newspaper delivered to his controller, Rakesh Dixit, Patwardhan's junior colleague, was torn in half. It indicated the need for a meeting at an old jute warehouse on the banks of the Buriganga on the outskirts of Dhaka. In March 1990, Patwardhan and his team achieved another breakthrough when a top army commander serving under Ershad gave the R&AW the names of ISI and CIA officers who exercised considerable influence on the regime. The CIA used slush funds to ensure that Ershad's pro-West policy continued for decades to come. The then ISI chief Shamsur Rahman Kallue, loyal to Benazir Bhutto, was able to expand the Pakistani network with the help of the Americans and the nexus posed a formidable threat to R&AW operations. Sometime in May 1990, Ismail introduced a powerful politician to Rakesh Dixit. The politician was willing to work with the Indian agency to end the political oppression in Bangladesh and Ershad's rule.

'This powerful politician codenamed Amir told us that the only way to neutralise Ershad and counter the challenge of the ISI and CIA in the same breath was to confront them with a mass public movement. I agreed with his assessment. We always wanted a better relationship with our neighbouring country and tolerated Ershad as long as he remained neutral. But I believed he had been nurturing seeds of hatred against India since the coup and our conscious decision was to stop him by any means,' said Patwardhan, recalling the frantic debates between the R&AW spies on splitting Ershad's support base.

The R&AW analysts in Dhaka prepared an exhaustive handwritten assessment for Operation Farewell. In July 1990, four intelligence officers were given all the necessary resources including funds to execute the operation. The diplomats were kept far away from the espionage team. Ismail's and Amir's networks were tasked to act as listening posts for the R&AW and they too were given unparalleled access to funds and other resources. Although the CIA supported the Ershad government, its intelligence assessments were realistic about the dictator's future. An American intelligence memo candidly admitted that Ershad had no political legitimacy and even his so-called political front lacked popular public support. The CIA worried that the Bangladesh military might not follow Ershad's dictates in dealing with lawlessness due to a possible public uprising.

In late August that year, an expected scenario unfolded in Dhaka and other major cities. Political parties, student unions and various other social organisations indirectly supported by the R&AW launched the first stage of Operation Farewell. The streets were filled with protesters demanding the resignation of Ershad and fresh elections in the country under the supervision of the United Nations. By the beginning of September 1990, highly trained and motivated R&AW officers including Patwardhan and Rakesh Dixit exhibited remarkable strategic depths by mounting pressure on Ershad's administration. By the beginning of October, the tirades against Ershad had amplified and engulfed the hinterland.

'Not only Ershad but even the ISI and CIA were petrified by the sudden change in the atmosphere,' recalled Patwardhan. 'We used our networks in the domestic and international media to fan the fire. Public outbursts on the pages of newspapers highlighted Ershad's sustained assault on democratic values. Although Ershad reacted sharply by raiding the residences of some over ground leaders to offset the pressure, it didn't work. The spark we ignited to restore democracy in the country had fired the people's consciences. For us, it was just another day at work, though some of our junior colleagues doubted that things would go as planned.'

To ensure that the iron masks of the R&AW spies remained impregnable, telephonic communications and public meetings were prohibited for all intelligence officers involved in Operation Farewell. Patwardhan said he didn't want to give Ershad and the Western intelligence agencies the joy of surveillance and eavesdropping. On 1 October 1990, Operation Farewell gained further momentum when the powerful student body Chhatra Dal cobbled together various unions under the Sarbadaliya Chhatra Oikya Parishad (All-party Students Council) and mounted unprecedented protests against Ershad's government. The Awami League and the BNP successfully exploited the sentiments against the military dictatorship to rally the masses. For the next one week, Patwardhan and his team of seasoned spies focused on the second stage of the operation by gathering intelligence on Ershad's moves against the agitation. Foreknowledge of the government's military actions helped them further calibrate the plan. For their parts, Ismail and Amir developed tried and tested contacts in various organisations to garner support for a public movement. The major effort, Patwardhan recalled, was to ensure that Indian footprints on any such agitation were not visible.

'It was made clear to us by the top bosses that we could not afford to leave footprints of Indian intervention in Bangladesh's domestic affairs. We were on our own. Very few at the top were aware of the work [that] a small team of Indian spies were doing in hostile territory,' Patwardhan said.

Nevertheless, Patwardhan urged his colleagues to reassure the leaders of the movement and the informers that unflinching support from India would continue till Ershad was thrown out. The team handling Operation Farewell now needed to engineer a sustained and high-pressure movement for the final stage of the plan. By the first week of November 1990, the team had destroyed every single page of handwritten notes to ensure that India could never be tied to a people's uprising in case the plan went wrong. By this time, Ershad was helpless. He knew that absolute support from the military was impossible and that pinning any hopes on the USA and Pakistan could only be futile. Rakesh Dixit briefed Ismail and Amir that the battle had now moved from the street to the mind and Ershad could not keep his hold on the government for much longer. The only questions left were when he would go and how.

Clashes between protesters and a section of the security forces intensified towards late November and Ershad's administration brutally censored the media. Ismail informed Dixit that besides the Awami League and the BNP, over a dozen political parties had launched agitations against Ershad's corrupt and illegal rule.

On 25 November 1990, Patwardhan and his team retreated into the shadows. Two days later, Ershad declared a state of emergency in the country and curfew was imposed across major cities. The next day, the carefully crafted espionage operation produced the much-awaited result. Students and political parties defied the curfew and though, many lives were lost in the coming days, the movement against Ershad continued. The dictator tried to divert the attention of the international community and on 2 December 1990 announced that parliamentary and presidential elections would be held early next year. When the news of Ershad's latest move reached the team, the spies' immediate reaction was bouts of laughter. They knew Ershad would react again within twenty-four hours. And he did. On 4 December, about one lakh people marched through Dhaka in an unprecedented protest against Ershad, demanding that he step down with immediate effect. A few hours later, Ershad went on national television and announced his resignation. He also announced that parliament would decide on a caretaker government to run the country till the elections were held. Patwardhan and the rest of the team were jubilant though they could not set off firecrackers like the people on the streets.

A few days later, the Indian government came out with carefully drafted statement:

> Following two months of a sustained opposition agitation launched by the students and joined in by a wide cross section of Bangladesh society, President Ershad resigned on 6 December and handed over power to Mr Shahabuddin Ahmed, the chief justice of the Bangladesh Supreme Court, who assumed office as the acting president of Bangladesh.

Later, after the elections were held, the Indian government stated:

> Elections for Parliament were held on 27 February 1991. The restoration of the democratic rights of the people of Bangladesh was a welcome development and India is looking forward to working closely with a democratically elected government in Bangladesh.

Patwardhan said Ershad did not know about Operation Farewell until 11 December 1990 when he was placed under house arrest.

This surprise move by the interim government launched a further crackdown against Ershad's close aides. Former Vice President Moudud Ahmed, Prime Minister Kazi Zafar Ahmed and Foreign Minister Anisul Islam Mahmud were all picked up by the security forces.

'I think Nasiruddin Ahmed, commander of army intelligence, informed Ershad about the R&AW operation. I learnt a little later that Ershad was shocked. He wanted to know how the operation was executed and whether the counterespionage unit under his presidency was totally defunct. It was actually difficult for him to believe that we had played the game so brilliantly and with so much secrecy. We learnt later that Ershad even enquired about the Indian intelligence officers operating in Bangladesh. His trusted lieutenants had no names or faces to share,' Patwardhan told me.

'Did he ever learn about your identity?' I asked Patwardhan.

'I don't think so. But when the election was held and Begum Khaleda Zia came to power, I received several feelers about a meeting with General Ershad. I refused, but there were certain doubts in my mind that he knew or suspected that I had carried out Operation Farewell,' Patwardhan chuckled.

2

THREE MUSKETEERS AND A BLOODY WAR IN FIJI

Narayan Datt Tiwari, an old Congress party loyalist and India's external affairs minister, was sweating when he walked into Prime Minister Rajiv Gandhi's inner chamber on the sweltering evening of 14 May 1987. Not because of the summer heat, but because of the bundle of cables and intelligence analysis reports he was carrying that spoke of imminent Chinese aggression on the border.

Rajiv Gandhi carefully went through each page of the files, discussing various factors with Tiwari that might influence dealings on this external risk. When Tiwari left, the tension in the room left no space for an affable goodbye.

Rajiv Gandhi had settled well into the pace of his new life since the assassination of his charismatic mother, Indira Gandhi, in 1984. But since 1986, events in Bangladesh, Sri Lanka and Pakistan, which carried shadows of long term consequences in the neighbourhood, had threatened the relative peace of his days at the South Block. Before he could pack up for the day, the secure red phone on the right corner of his table crackled to life. The island nation of Fiji, seven thousand and two hundred miles from New Delhi, with 49 per cent of its population consisting of ethnic Indians, had had a bloodless coup just a few hours earlier, toppling the Indian-dominated Fijian government.

Gandhi was stunned. India was not only facing increasing threats from Pakistan and Sri Lanka, but the administration in 1987 was also dealing with both a terrible drought in some states and terrible floods in other states, threatening the livelihoods of 70 per cent of the labour forces employed in agriculture. Now, Fiji had been added to the prime minister's list of priorities. Within minutes, Tiwari was back in Gandhi's office.

The coup had taken place at about ten a.m. Fijian time (six hours ahead of Indian standard time), when ten soldiers entered the Fiji parliament and forcibly took over the barely one-month-old, multiracial government headed by Timoci Bavadra who had eight ethnic Indians in his cabinet.

Rajiv's mother, the late former Prime Minister Indira Gandhi, had been at the forefront in the fight for Fiji's independence from the British in the 1970s. Tiwari reminded Rajiv that in 1970, even before the birth of independent Fiji, an Indian diplomat, Surendra Singh, had warned that the island nation's ethnic Indians would be badly treated. For India, Fiji is not just another country, Tiwari told Gandhi. It is a little bit of India in the far-off South Pacific region and strategically important to India.

Indians first entered Fiji in 1879 as indentured labourers mostly shipped out of Uttar Pradesh and Bihar to work on sugarcane plantations owned by the British colonists. In 1916, when British plantation owners stopped sending demands for labourers, sponsored immigration virtually ceased, but about 40,000 to 50,000 Indians entered the Fiji colony in phases, thereafter. After indentured labour was abolished, most of these Indians chose to remain in Fiji and were settled by the British on two islands. In 1959, when the first census was conducted, the total population of Fiji was 3,87,646, out of whom 1,91,328 were

Indians. The Indian birth rate in 1959 was 46.46 per 1,000, the Fijian 36.36, the European 30.30 and the Chinese 37.01.

Gandhi and Tiwari were discussing Fiji's demography when R&AW Chief A.K. Verma walked in with a red file. The coup had been led by Colonel Sitiveni Rabuka, an ethnic Fijian military officer who wanted Indians to be thrown out of Fiji. The ethnic Indians called Rabuka a snake—a betrayer of trust and faith. Verma informed Gandhi that this was going to be a long and bloody war.

The R&AW had turned eighteen that year, the age of adulthood. The men and women of the agency had had hits and misses since its birth and were able to foresee and thwart devastating tragedies, beginning with the Bangladesh liberation. Gandhi believed in the highly resourceful R&AW and asked for an intelligence analysis on Fiji within twenty-four hours. In the meantime, Tiwari's ministry was asked to release a statement for the global media. The two-paragraph statement said:

> The government of India are distressed to hear reports of the military seizing power in Fiji and taking the Prime Minister and members of his cabinet into custody. The overthrow of a government elected through popular mandate only recently and the abrogation of the constitution are disquieting developments. The government of India views these developments with deep concern. We hope that racial harmony in Fiji will be maintained and that all parties will whole-heartedly work for the speedy return of Parliamentary democracy in Fiji.

Gandhi cleared the statement for release. He was determined to generate international sympathy for the deposed government in Fiji.

Road to Perdition

A nation of three hundred and thirty islands, Fiji was ruled by the British from 1874 to October 1970. According to R&AW reports, the erstwhile colony located two thousand miles east of Australia housed a US Air Force station in Viti Levu Island that primarily functioned as a refuelling base for aircraft between the US west coast and Australia–New Zealand. At the time of Fiji's independence in 1970, it had become a major transit hub, hosting more than forty transnational flights every day.

A report by the US's Central Intelligence Agency (CIA) provides a brief background on Fiji:

> When the Islands were first discovered by the British in 1643, they were populated by tribal peoples of essentially Melanesian descent, who now constitute the Fijian racial group. European colonisation was never appreciated. But after the British took control, large numbers of Indian labourers were imported from South Asia to work in the Island's sugar fields. Their descendants, most of whom are Hindus, presently outnumber the indigenous population. A few Chinese merchants and traders have also migrated to the Islands since the late 1800s.

In the 1970s, tension between the two major ethnic groups—Fijians and Indians—was the most serious threat to the island nation's stability. As the indigenous population, the Fijians had enjoyed protected status under colonial rules and the British had discriminated against the Indians. When the British granted Fiji independence, they ensured the inhabitants would repeat the bloody politics that the colonists had successfully engineered during the liberation of India. Before the final ship bearing the Union Jack sailed off the coast of Suva, the British had installed a pro-Western political front in Fiji—the Alliance Party headed by the elite Ratu Sir Kamisese Mara. He enjoyed the support of approximately two and a quarter lakh Fijians, while the two lakh and seventy thousand Indians who supported the Federation Party were side-lined. According to intelligence reports drafted immediately after Fiji's independence, distrust between the two major ethnic groups was deeply rooted in cultural differences. An uneven distribution of wealth and power had aggravated the situation. Fijians had moved into the modern economy very slowly and many felt their progress had been blocked by the better-educated and generally, more prosperous Indians who controlled much of the country's trade and finance. CIA analysts believed that the British would almost certainly oppose any electoral reforms that would provide power to the Indian majority. This is what the USA intelligence analysts observed in 1970:

> The question of land ownership also threatens to disrupt racial harmony. Under British rule, more than four over five of Fiji's land area was reserved for tribal ownership, with the balance mainly owned by Europeans and the government. Indians, although constituting about 50 per cent of the population, own less than 2 per cent of the land area. While Indians produced most of the country's cash crops, most of their output comes from land leased mainly from Fijians. The problem is that while Indians want access to additional land, many Fijians feel the Indians already farm the best areas and want to maintain present restrictions on land ownership. Indeed, some Fijians are refusing to renew leases, and a 1967 law designed to protect tenants (Indians) has recently been under review with an eye towards limiting their rights.

The first Fijian Prime Minister, Ratu Mara, essentially a tribal chief in the Lau Island group of the South Pacific island nation, was an opportunist. Intelligence reports suggest that Mara joined the British colonial service in Fiji in 1950 and rose to acquire membership in the legislative council and later, in the executive council. In 1984, a CIA report said growing political polarisation in Fiji was Mara's main hurdle and that Indian membership in his Alliance Party had dwindled since 1970, with ethnic Indians drifting to the National Federation Party of Fiji which was the main opposition political front. The CIA observed that constitutional safeguards enacted during the British colonial period to protect the Fijians from being overwhelmed by the more aggressive Indians contributed to Indian resentment and had created an unbridgeable gap between the two races. Despite the discrimination, Indians dominated business and the professional sphere in Fiji. They prevailed in institutions of higher learning in spite of government decreed advantages for Fijians, such as scholarships and lower entrance requirements. CIA reports observed:

> The Indians seem resigned to second class political status as long as they can prosper economically. Indians, for example, make up the majority of graduates of the University of the South Pacific in Fiji and almost the entire faculty and student body of its medical school.

Some agents of the R&AW suspected that Ratu Mara had been recruited by the USA administration to check Soviet influence in the South Pacific. He had barred the entry of Soviet ships in Fiji and even turned down Moscow's request to open an embassy in Suva.

'Mara was not an easy man to deal with. He warmly supported the US activities in Fiji's waters and had strong contempt for India and the Soviets. He never openly spoke about India but intelligence inputs during 1984–85 made it clear that the intention of his government was to curtail the rights of Indians,' a R&AW officer codenamed Prem Shekhawat told me.

A CIA report bolsters Shekhawat's observation. It said that sometime in 1982, Mara asserted that the opposition party dominated by ethnic Indians was being financed by the Soviets through the Indian embassy with the ultimate aim to oust his government. Mara had secretly appointed an internal probe which rubbished his views, but the findings of the investigation did not change his mind. Mara was quoted in an MEA cable as saying, 'Russia wants me out because it has been my influence that has successfully blocked Russian incursions into the Pacific. With me gone, they think they can gain a permanent foothold in the South Pacific.' His loyalty towards the Americans was evident from a declassified CIA report:

> In 1982, overreacting in the Parliamentary election year to what he perceived to be the Fijian populace's anti-nuclear mood, Ratu Mara announced implementation of a previously unenforced ban on port calls by nuclear ships. The ban could have hindered movements of the US Pacific fleet, now over 40 per cent nuclear-powered. Mara later became convinced of the safety of nuclear propulsion as a result of briefings at Honolulu, and in mid-1983, prevailed upon the Fijian cabinet to lift the ban. Since then, Fiji has not questioned whether visiting US Naval vessels are nuclear-armed. Mara's attitude is that such a query would be inappropriate in view of Fiji's dependence on US protection.

The R&AW chief and his team, recognising the depth of Indian roots in Fiji and India's larger interest in the region, went through several classified reports to understand the journey that had led to the coup. A fourteen-page secret note prepared in 1966, four years before Fiji's independence, said it all. The British had engineered the implementation of the new 'London' constitution before decolonising Fiji and sponsored the Fijian-led Alliance Party to fight the predominantly 'Indian' Federation Party. The Alliance Party claimed to be 'promoting orderly progress towards internal self-government while maintaining and strengthening Fiji's link with the crown. The Alliance will work to preserve basic human rights and to safeguard the interests of all the Fijian community with special regard to minority groups.'

A report from the Indian embassy in Suva, dated 5 April 1967, said that the Alliance was an attempt to bring together representatives from all the communities of Fiji, including the Fijians, Indians, Europeans, Chinese and so on to show the world that they represented all of Fiji, in contrast to the Federation Party which was led by an ethnic Indian named A.D. Patel. The report said:

> It was, in fact, a scheme obviously agreed upon by the Europeans and the Fijians to keep down the Federation which has been fighting for the cause of the people of Indian origin. The Alliance naturally sought for and took into their fold some Indians who joined them in the hope of getting rewards by way of appointment in the future government. As it proved later, when the election results came out, the Alliance was able to get their three Indians nominees elected in the cross voting constituencies and they accommodated two of them in the government which they formed: Vijay R. Singh as member for social services and K.S. Reddy as Parliamentary secretary in the same department. The net result is that the European and the Fijian group—the Fijians have implicit faith in the European leadership—have formed their own government with a couple of ineffective Indians to show to the world that they have representatives of the Indian community in the government.

R&AW Chief Verma and his spies were troubled by the last paragraph of this two decade-old note. This paragraph said:

> Fijians insist, obviously inspired and supported by the European community, that they have a special position in these Islands as compared with the Indian community and this position should be respected by the others, particularly by the majority Indian community. In other words, the European and Fijian obviously feel justified in whatever they do on

> the implicit basis that they are the owners and proprietors of Fiji and the Indian community which was here originally as indentured labour force, should be content to go on working for the proprietors on most favourable terms that could be secured.

Shekhawat told me he had been surprised by the reports. Whatever little he had read about Fiji in the mid-1980s had spoken of a multiracial society living in harmony. He went through another report which indicated that the trouble had started brewing just before the independence of Fiji in October 1970. Drafted in July 1970, the report said that some Muslim organisations had criticised the framework of the future constitution that was being deliberated between Fiji's Ratu Mara and the British government in London. The report sent to India's then foreign secretary T.N. Kaul as well as K. Natwar Singh, who was a director in the Prime Minister's Office (PMO), highlighted the Fiji Muslim Political Organisation's demand for separate representation for Muslims in the new parliament.

The comments on the margins of the intelligence note said:

> The Fiji Muslim Political Organisation is not as yet an influential body, consisting as it does of only 25 active members. There is no serious danger of a separatist Muslim movement receiving any encouragement or support in Fiji, particularly as Ratu Mara is also aware of the adverse implications of communal/ religious movement of this type. However, the initiative of Fiji Muslim Political Organisation and its sister organisation, the Fiji Muslim League, will bear watching.

On 15 May 1987, N.D. Tiwari made it clear in his briefing to Prime Minister Rajiv Gandhi that the Fiji coup had been in the making since 1970. He recalled how jubilant the then Prime Minister Indira Gandhi and officials of the MEA had been on 10 October 1970 when Fiji was finally decolonised. The independence celebration was marked by great cordiality amongst the different races and particularly between the two main racial groups, Fijians and Indians. India's main gift to Fiji on its independence was the speaker's chair for the new parliament as symbol of democracy and a personal gift from Indira Gandhi to Ratu Mara. However, Verma now told Prime Minister Rajiv Gandhi that the ethnic Fijians had been against the representation of Indians in Fiji's parliament at the time of independence and the situation had become worse since then. Mara had made false promises, said Verma. He showed Gandhi a secret report from Fiji that exposed the duality.

Ratu Mara had told a confidant:

> In one great united gathering, we had representatives of all the Christian churches, the various branches of the Hindu faith and of the Mohammedans. We believe that this service was not just a thing of the hour but also an enduring symbol of our unity and faith for the future, and we are determined, as far as it lies within our power to translate our promises into lasting reality. We don't think it is the best system for electing representatives in Parliament for a multiracial country. We believe that, for a multiracial country, there should be a guaranteed representation of those who compose the multiracial society. If there had been guaranteed representation for the Negros of the United States, the USA would perhaps not be in the trouble they are today. Our relations with India have been quite cordial even before independence and I think they will go on improving after independence. India has had a fairly wide experience of the problems which face us today and, when I visited India, I found our little problems there magnified to cinemascope size which made them more easy to understand.

According to a R&AW officer who had attended the meeting, after Gandhi read the note, he said, 'Ratu Mara was sowing the seed of enmity between Indians and Fijians. The coup did not take place now. In fact, Ratu Mara prepared the ground for a person like Rabuka to strike whenever Indians gained leverage in Fiji politics.'

Shekhawat told me that Mara was completely sold on the Americans and the British and hated the Indians. On the other hand, the Indian government had a very strong emotional connect with the Fiji Indians and they did not want it to be overpowered by diplomatic complexities engendered by the enhanced cultural and trade cooperation between Fiji and its neighbours, Australia and New Zealand.

'We wanted Indianness to survive in Fiji,' said Shekhawat. 'So, while Australia and New Zealand investors rushed to Fiji to invest in different sectors of the economy, the Indian government decided to install strong and permanent business enterprises.'

The intention of the Australian and New Zealand investors in the 1970s was to maintain control over the domestic Fiji market which they had ruled for the past many decades. As far as the India–Australia relationship was concerned, the two countries had a number of things in common—both were members of the British Commonwealth of Nations, enjoyed a parliamentary system of government and spoke English. But due to different historical backgrounds, the two countries did not have a common approach to various international issues. While India adopted the policy of non-alignment after Independence, Australia entered into a military alliance with the USA and New Zealand as early as in 1951. These differences, however, did not come in the way of the two countries improving their bilateral relations through mutual contacts and exchanges in economic and cultural fields.

Nevertheless, the Indian government felt that Indian entrepreneurs could provide invaluable assistance in Fiji through collaboration projects. An Indian techno-economic team was sent to Fiji to explore the possibilities of setting up small scale industries and also identify the different areas where investment could be best applied. This was followed by the first ever wholly Indian exhibition in Suva from 15–28 November 1970. Although, at that time, India was exporting goods to Fiji worth 3–4 million USD annually, no large scale efforts had been made to promote exports to Fiji. About a hundred and fifty firms from the public and private sectors participated in the exhibition. Nine of these firms decided to establish agencies in Suva. A number of other agencies made similar plans. No direct transport between India and Fiji existed at the time, so goods consigned to the island nation had to be transhipped at Singapore, Hong Kong or Sydney. The Indira Gandhi government therefore moved a proposal to open a direct line between Fiji and Bombay.

Despite India's efforts to strengthen ties with Fiji, it was clear to Rajiv Gandhi and the R&AW that systemic discrimination against the Indians of the island nation would have dire consequences. Shekhawat's deputy, a R&AW agent codenamed Kailash Singh, had been stationed in Suva in April 1987 when the ethnic Indian-backed National Federation Party (NFP) and the multiracial Fiji Labour Party (FLP) headed by Timoci Bavadra ended Ratu Mara's seventeen-year rule. The coalition had won twenty-eight out of fifty-two seats and the Indo-Fijian community was jubilant.

'Drawing up the layout of his future government from his Vatuwaqa residence, Bavadra had decided to give prominence to the NFP in his cabinet. They did not know that the government was about to head straight into a bloody war,' Shekhawat said, recalling some of the intelligence cables that the R&AW had received from Suva. He explained, 'After the defeat of the Alliance party, conspirators united to oppose the installation of a multiracial government. Raiwaqa, a neighbourhood in Suva, had become the strategic command centre of rebels led by hardliner ethnic Fijian politicians. An intelligence cable in late April 1987 had hinted that certain Fijian leaders were talking about protests and a possible coup against the government. It was proved, beyond doubt, that they were supported by the Fijians. Petitions were filed with the governor general Ratu Sir Penaia Kanatabatu Ganilau to dismiss the elected government. Violent protests were being organised by mushrooming Fijian civil society groups and associations against the government. The new born government, a true multiracial government, was in deep trouble.'

Not officially present in Fiji, the R&AW could do nothing but watch events unfold and send reports to the Indian government. 'So, what did the spies do?' I asked Shekhawat.

'About a week before the coup on 14 May, a report had forewarned the Indian government about the conspiracy being hatched by Sitiveni Rabuka who planned to justify the coup by arguing [that] it was done to restore law and order in the country,' Shekhawat told me. 'This was indeed true. Rabuka later contended that the coup was a matter of cultural survival for ethnic Fijians as Indians had become dominant in his country. He wanted the Indians practising Hinduism and Islam to convert to Christianity. And he wanted them deported. He wanted all the Indians out of the Fiji Islands. Bavadra pleaded with opposition leaders to give his government a chance to govern. But on 14 May 1987, Rabuka and ten soldiers entered parliament and announced a military takeover. The entire cabinet was bundled together in a military truck headed for the Royal Fiji Military office where they were held at gunpoint. They were released later, but kept under intense surveillance.'

When Rajiv Gandhi met the R&AW chief a week later, the discussion meandered between diplomatic pressure and covert action to help the Indians in Fiji. Gandhi was assured by a top spy that while they had not been able to stop the coup that day, the tradecraft they had earned in the last eighteen years gave them tremendous capability to effectively counter any political and terror threats. Over the next few days, Gandhi spoke to his counterparts in Australia, New Zealand and the UK for the restoration of the Bavadra government. A CIA report said Rajiv Gandhi had also sent two special envoys to Canberra, Wellington and London for the same purpose and the Indian special envoys demanded economic sanctions against Fiji's interim government headed by Rabuka.

A CIA intelligence cable said:

> The high level of racial tension is having an adverse effect on the Indian community. Militant Fijians have attacked ethnic Indians and their business and property. Fearing for their safety, financially established ethnic Indians have begun to emigrate in significant numbers. Fiji's Indian community is looking to New Delhi to help resolve the ethnic strife. In several instances, Indian support to Tamil separatists in Sri Lanka was cited as justification for Indian involvement in Fiji. According to the US embassy in Suva, Fiji's Indian leaders have also looked to the high commissioner to exert pressure on the US, Canada, Australia and New Zealand to relax immigration rules for Fiji Indians.

Shekhawat said Rajiv Gandhi's diplomatic niceties did not work. Australia and New Zealand publicly criticised the military takeover of Fiji, but they refused to intervene for the restoration of the deposed government. Meanwhile, Rabuka was planning a constitutional amendment barring Indians from contesting elections. Intelligence officers from the CIA believed that Gandhi would oppose any amendment that reduced ethnic Indians to second class citizens, but only through diplomatic leverage as Fiji, thousands of miles away, was beyond India's military reach. The CIA analysts said:

> Restoration of the deposed coalition is a moot point, but India will continue to support the restoration of democracy

> in Fiji to show the ethnic Indians that New Delhi has not abandoned them. Gandhi will probably raise the matter of Fiji in international forums and is also likely to maintain pressure on the issue to gain favorable domestic publicity by asserting India's role as protector of Indian communities abroad. Fiji's Indian population almost certainly will continue to count on New Delhi for help in protecting its rights. Constitutional changes depriving ethnic Indians of their rights would further erode confidence within the Indian community and trigger even more emigration. The departure of prosperous Indians from Fiji would eventually leave a poor Indian minority without political or economic clout.

Though Shekhawat had agreed with the CIA's assessment, he added that foreign powers like the USA had played a major role in installing Rabuka and their deafening silence after the coup was a clear indication of their tacit support to the military regime.

'We learned that Mahendra Chaudhary, who served as finance minister in the Bavadra government, had been arrested and grilled for hours by Rabuka's soldiers. Temples and Indian-owned shops were closed down and Rabuka had declared that Indians needed prior permission to hold prayer meetings. The life of the Indians in Fiji was caged,' recalled Shekhawat. 'We were forced to evacuate the R&AW agents including Kailash Singh from Suva sometime in August 1987 when violent protesters started targeting Indians.'

An earlier Indian intelligence report had noted:

> By and large, the people of Indian origin in Fiji, particularly those working on farms in the rural areas, were emotionally quite devoted to their motherland—India—and they have kept up the religious and cultural traditions of India insofar as it was practicable at such a long distance and after loss of contact with the country for generations. This emotional devotion was proved eminently by the sincere and instantaneous reaction and sympathy voiced by them in public meetings held on the

> occasions of the passing away of prominent Indian leaders. The Indian shops were all closed and condolence messages came pouring in—this in addition to the public meetings, held all over the islands. In fact, it is understood that several Indians here offered to join the army in defence of India at the time of the Pakistan aggression.

Shekhawat flagged an old secret report to argue why it was imperative for R&AW to act for Indians in Fiji. According to the report the Fijian Indians expected support from the Indian government in cultural, religious and educational matters. The report also said:

> The vested interests of Europeans and Australians who have in recent years gained the implicit confidence of the Fijians by the good old policy of divide & rule and by dangling before the Fijian community the dangers of Indian domination, are always extremely uncomfortable whenever the discussions in the United Nations take place regarding Fiji or when this international body passes resolutions with a view to furthering the cause of freedom and democracy in these islands. The natural mouthpiece of this group—*The Fiji Times*—goes into convulsions whenever United Nations criticizes the unreasonable and unfair features of Fiji's constitution and seeks to remedy the state of affairs here by sending a United Nations delegation or by demanding a target date to be fixed for the freedom of these Islands. People of Indian origin have really made a preserving and determined effort to educate their children and for this they have not spared any sacrifice or effort.

'Don't you feel as though this is a letter from an abandoned brother?' Shekhawat asked me. 'We launched some covert action immediately after the coup in 1987, but hardline Fijian groups accused us of meddling in Fiji's internal affairs and any covert action from our side at that moment could have gone against the interest of Indian community.'

Fiji's ethnic Indians weren't abandoned, however. The evacuation of India's spies was merely a tactical retreat. 'We did not protest when our officers were declared persona non grata in Fiji. We returned to India to plan something bigger, something spectacular,' said Shekhawat. 'In a meeting sometime in September, a decision was taken that the future spy operation in Fiji would not involve the external affairs ministry. We were planning to fight on our own, but reports from our informers in Australia were very depressing. A report sent to us with a newspaper clip of the *Sunday Telegraph* revealed that Indian women were gang-raped by the Rabuka led Fijian soldiers.'

The news report added that seventeen children from the sugar town of Ba had been beaten and made to eat cow dung for violating government edicts that banned picnics and swimming on Sundays and that villagers were forced to bathe in raw sewage. As the mood of Colonel Rabuka's regime darkened, there was mounting evidence of human rights abuses against the island's Indians.

While the spies in India planned their operation, Rabuka's opponents, the members of the deposed government and political parties, were re-arrested. Shekhawat said Timoci Bavadra; Jabir Singh, a lawyer; Bob Kumar, a Fijian politician; and Harish Sharma, who served for about a month as deputy prime minister of Fiji, had been picked up by the Fijian army along with other politicians and prominent figures. 'Our informer in Australia got in touch with human right groups to galvanise international pressure for their release,' he said.

In mid-September, fearing that some of his aides might attempt to reinstate democracy, Rabuka declared Fiji a republic. He took power away from all those he suspected of turning against him and installed Kamisese Mara as prime minister and Ratu Penaia Ganilau as president. Since these two were selected, not elected, actual power remained with Rabuka.

In early October 1987, Rabuka severed Fiji's ties with the UK, claiming in public meetings that he had no political ambition and his efforts were mainly focused on restoring Fijian culture and the Fijian way of life that had been threatened by the outsider Indians.

India's minister of state for external affairs, K. Natwar Singh, had been attending the United Nations General Assembly at the time of the Fijian crisis. Rajiv Gandhi asked him to make a statement on Fiji. In his address to the global community, Singh said: 'Attempts to deprive citizens of the country of their legitimate rights merely on the basis of their racial origin are against all tenets of democracy and human rights and are contrary to the UN charter. What is happening in Fiji has distinct and unacceptable racial overtones. This development is reprehensible. We believe that the path to peace and prosperity in Fiji lies in restoration of democracy and the rule of law.'

The Rajiv Gandhi regime refused to recognise Rabuka's military government and even warned him against depriving a majority of Fiji's citizens of their legitimate rights. Gandhi also decided to suspend all trade and technical cooperation with Fiji.

'Never mind Fiji, such statements are impotent against military governments anywhere in the world,' said Shekhawat. 'The very concept of military rule is exploitative and it was merely a coincidence that Indians were at the receiving end in Fiji.'

The news of increasing atrocities against Indians rattled Gandhi's administration. Rajiv Gandhi issued a statement flagging human rights abuse in the Fiji islands. He said:

> The South Pacific has long enjoyed a reputation for tranquility and friendship. It is unfortunate that this reputation has been tarnished by the military coup in Fiji. Different communities had lived together in Fiji in peace and harmony for more than a century. The special rights of the Melanesian Fijians were fully safeguarded. It is important to maintain racial amity. The current situation in Fiji is a matter of concern as it

> threatens human rights and human dignity. It is our hope that Parliamentary democracy will be restored in Fiji, promoting harmony and equality before the law for all it citizens.

'We were in the final stages of our planning when Rajiv Gandhi made this statement,' said Shekhawat. 'A special unit within the agency was created for the Fiji operation. The upper echelon of the government had given it complete operational freedom. It was composed of three fearless spies we fondly called "The Band of Three."'

Mavericks and Avengers

On a chilly afternoon on 20 March 1988, thirty-five-year-old Anupam Malik checked into a R&AW safe house south of Trafalgar Square in central London. He was ostensibly a jute exporter from India, but actually the senior-most member of 'the band of three'.

Malik was regarded as one of the agency's best spies. He had spent a month meticulously working on an operational blue print for Mission Fiji, which aimed to disrupt and dismantle Fiji's military regime. When the plan was finally discussed with top officials, there was a mixed sense of scepticism and awe. They were unsure whether the team was capable of conducting such a daredevil covert operation in two months.

According to Shekhawat, Malik had wanted six months to complete the operation. 'But his seniors wanted a feel of the wind in the first two months before allowing him to operate further,' said Shekhawat. 'Malik pleaded that if Rabuka was to pay a price for what he was doing to the Indians, the spies needed more time. But the decision had already been made; Malik was to fight Rabuka and time together.'

On 21 March 1988, Malik entered the Quo Vadis restaurant on Dean Street. He was ushered into a private dining room where

Samuel Cooper waited. Cooper flashed a broad smile and lunged forward to shake hands with Malik. Both said nothing until the attendant had left the room.

'Malik, you said something urgent has come up. I hope you are not going to ruin my lunch,' Cooper chuckled.

'How much time and money do you think it will take to activate your contacts in Fiji?'Malik asked.

'Oh!'Cooper was surprised by the subject of Fiji. He had thought Malik needed help in London.

'No, I need a safe house in Sydney,' Malik said. 'I also require your help with assets in Fiji. I believe you already know about the situation.'

Forty-five-year-old Cooper, born in Canberra, Australia, had inherited a sugar business from his father Oliver Cooper in the early 1980s. The senior Cooper had a limited line of sugar exports from Fiji to the UK. But Samuel Cooper had his eye on all of Europe.

During a dinner at the Australian embassy in London sometime in 1982, he had met Malik, a junior Indian diplomat. Malik promised to help Cooper however he could. In the next few months, Malik introduced Cooper to several import houses in Europe. Cooper's trust in Malik was organic and soon they became good friends. Good enough for Malik to reveal the true nature of his work.

'I'll repay you someday,' Cooper had told Malik when he opened a branch office of his business in London in 1983. The time had come to pay his debt.

'It will be done. Give me a few weeks. When are you planning to visit Sydney?' asked Cooper as he enjoyed his sumptuous meal.

'Next week. Can you also put me in touch with someone in Wellington?'

Cooper was silent for a moment. 'I think I can, but be careful, you are playing a dangerous game.'

That evening, Malik had a heavily-coded conversation with Sanjiv Sahgal, the second member of the band of three, who was in Delhi. Sahgal was told to prepare for a trip to Wellington, the capital of New Zealand. He was to receive the details for his stay via the diplomatic pouch in a couple of days.

Meanwhile, Kailash Singh, the third member of the band, was working on an alternate plan and safe house. Thrown out of Fiji by the Rabuka regime, Singh wanted revenge. He had arranged for a safe house in Adelaide, South Australia, through an old acquaintance named Max Hamilton and was scheduled to fly there the first week of April 1988.

Shortly before six p.m. on 11 April, a chauffeur driven car pulled into Wisdom road, Greenwich, a peaceful suburb in north Sydney. Kailash and Sahgal emerged to find Malik waiting at the porch. The redesigned colonial house with high ceilings and light filled interiors was going to be the control and command centre of Operation Fiji.

Meanwhile, at the R&AW headquarters, some of the agents believed that the coup and subsequent changes in Fiji were internal matters of that country, and any action by an Indian agency could very well harm and not help the ethnic Indians. Other agents countered that if India did not act for Fiji's Indians, there would be no Indians left there at all. 'In the long run, if India needed to exercise its influence in South Pacific countries, this covert conquest was our only available option,' said Shekhawat.

Malik was the best person to lead the operation because, according to Shekhawat, he loved action and hated paperwork. 'I don't remember if he ever said "no" to an operation,' Shekhawat laughed. 'Once, when he was informed that an enemy element was troubling our operatives in Europe, he only asked for two days to resolve the issue. "If you want to eliminate, just do it, don't make plans," was Malik's favourite line. He was the most charming and devil-may-care spy of our time.'

That April night when the band of three sat down to discuss the plan, the first thing they agreed was not to travel together. They would work alone and a pre-decided monthly meeting would be held at the Wisdom Road safe house. Sanjiv Sahgal was put in charge of PSYOPS (Psychological Operations), while Kailash Singh was handed the task of infiltrating the camps of Rabuka's opponents to ensure that the agitation against military rule continued with maximum efficiency. Malik was to supervise the entire operation besides helping the opposition in Fiji with finances and weapons if required. This was an exclusive operation. The band had clear instructions not to contact R&AW operatives working undercover in Australia and New Zealand.

Within a few days Sahgal activated his contacts in the media. The main task was to run a series of campaigns in Australia, New Zealand and the UK in support of democracy in Fiji. The long term strategy was to create international pressure to end military rule and hold general elections under the supervision of neutral countries. Sahgal quickly recruited local assets and paid them huge sums to gain space in influential publications. In the meantime, Kailash went to Wellington for a meeting with Benjamin Taylor, the owner of an electronics equipment company set up in the late 1970s and a man truly entrenched in his country's political system. Kailash's purpose, Shekhawat recalled, was clear: 'Generate support from New Zealand politicians for the deposed Bavadra government and hire those having even the slightest link with Fiji politicians. He was required to identify vulnerable politicians and Taylor was the man best suited to help.'

They met at a café on Brandon Street. Taylor was a bit puzzled. Kailash had asked for an urgent and important meeting. 'This is not his style. When it comes to a deal, he always takes it slow,' Taylor thought.

After the plan had been unpacked, Taylor was in a teasing

mood. 'You think money could buy you that support,' he told Kailash, amused.

'Of course. It is just a matter of identifying those greedy for money even if it requires an endless chase,' Kailash said.

'You'd better have bricks of gold because this is not easy. You are talking about politicians here and in Fiji. Don't blame me if you feel they have robbed you.'

'There is a war going on against Indians in Fiji and we need to do something soon to stop it,' Kailash said. 'I am sure that if money can buy a peaceful life for our brothers and sisters, we won't hesitate to provide truckloads of gold bricks for this operation.'

'I always keep my promises but this is the scariest thing you have asked me to do. I am suddenly feeling vulnerable,' Taylor said. 'I think I will be able to manage it but I need some time.'

When Kailash and Taylor met again two weeks later, Taylor told the Indian spy that he had set up a meeting with a popular politician sympathetic to the deposed Bavadra government. The politician codenamed ARC had criticised the coup engineered by Colonel Rabuka at numerous public appearances.

'ARC held Rabuka responsible for the exodus of ethnic Indians from Fiji. I think he is your guy. He has close links with Indian members of the Bavadra cabinet,' said Taylor.

Over the next few days, as Kailash met ARC on several occasions, Malik found himself faced with possible exposure. He had taken on one of the most difficult tasks—shipping weapons and money to a group of Indians in Fiji to help them protect themselves against continuing atrocities by Rabuka's soldiers. His well-placed network in Australia was ready to ship a consignment of small arms into Fiji but a leaking cell ruined the plan. Australian enforcement authorities were tipped off about the cargo and on 10 June 1988, an Australian newspaper suggested that India was involved in smuggling arms to Rabuka's opponents in Fiji.

The MEA had been dead against such an adventure against Rabuka, but was forced to issue a clarification denying India's role in the arms case:

> Our attention has been drawn to a report in the 'Australian' alleging that India was heavily involved in recent moves towards a coup in Fiji and that arms recently seized by the Australian authorities at Sydney were sent by India. We take this opportunity of categorically denying this report as baseless, mischievous and motivated. It appears to us that strenuous efforts are being made by some to spread disinformation. The acting High Commissioner of Australia in India has been informed of our concern in the matter.

The person who leaked the information turned out to be a double agent, said Shekhawat, and he was eliminated before more harm could be done. 'But within days a paranoid Rabuka came out with a new rule presented as an internal security decree. Basically, it aimed to terrorise Indians by arresting without a court warrant anyone in possession of arms. It gave extraordinary powers to the soldiers and listed very harsh measures against Indians. The Indian government was convinced by the spies to issue a statement against the rules to mount psychological pressure,' Shekhawat said. The Indian government statement said:

> While the ostensible reason for the decree is the seizure of illegal arms in Fiji, it is difficult to avoid the conclusion that the real motivation is political and that its provisions are likely to be used against the people of Indian origin as already evident from the individuals taken into preventive detention. The need in Fiji is for national reconciliation and promotion of harmony between the different ethnic groups in the interest of stability, peace and progress. The order should be rescinded, the political detainees released and civil liberty and democratic rights of all Fijians fully restored.

In July 1988, Malik and his team launched the second stage of the Fiji operation. A contact was developed in Australia's ruling Labour Party headed by Bob Hawke. The asset inside the government had close links with trade unions in Australia and Fiji. Malik and his band realised that Indian groups in Fiji at that time needed money more than anything else to fight Rabuka's oppressive regime.

'We give them what they want to start the massive agitation and mobilise support. We want Indians safe in Fiji. They have already suffered so much under the British. We need persistent protests to weaken Rabuka's position. We need to support Indian groups financially and by any other means required to fight the tyranny,' Malik told the asset.

The plan was carefully woven to ensure complete deniability. They wired the money through a front company to high profile political contacts, arms smugglers, journalists and powerful media barons. There was no absolute estimate of funds flowing into their kitty but Shekhawat admitted that the band never faced a financial crunch.

The Indian spies had spent almost three months in Australia and New Zealand, gathering support for Fiji's ethnic Indians. Malik returned to Delhi in late August 1988. He had been informed by a source that Rabuka was working on a new constitution for Fiji. He sought a three-month extension for the team to finish the tasks they were working on.

'The extension was granted. But Malik was warned that the situation in the islands was going out of control and wealthy Indians were leaving Fiji. Those in government services were being removed and farmers were charged exorbitant prices for the lease of agricultural land. Malik acknowledged the perils of living under a dictator but his team was trying to do all they could with accuracy,' Shekhawat said. He vividly remembered handing extra packets of freshly minted dollars to Malik. The operation was indeed off the book.

Upon his return to Sydney, Malik accessed the draft of the new Fiji constitution through a contact. The new constitution did not permit Indians to vote and curtailed other fundamental rights. It was horrifying. He sent a copy to New Delhi to generate international diplomatic pressure on Rabuka. The deposed prime minister Timoci Bavadra had already issued a statement which pointed out that the new constitution reduced the Indian people to third class citizenry in a country where they comprised almost fifty per cent of the population. Malik wanted the government of India to release a public statement criticising the move. The government complied. The official statement said:

> The draft reportedly contains several provisions that are undemocratic, discriminatory and detrimental to the interests of peace, stability and racial harmony, such as the adoption of a communal franchise for all elected seats in the Parliament. The government of India notes that the interim government has stated that a process of consultations will be initiated shortly on the draft constitution. It hopes that this process will be free and democratic to enable all sections of the population to participate in the formulation of a constitution acceptable to all.

Warfare Is Deception

As the ancient master warrior Sun Tzu said, hold out bait to entice the enemy, feign disorder and crush him and if his forces are united, separate them. Towards the end of 1988, Malik and his team used this strategy in the third stage of the operation. Dampening Rabuka's power without fighting meant the cultivation of assets within Rabuka's administration to collect intelligence and carryout sabotage. Sometime in November 1988, Sahgal and Malik met Eknoa in Wellington. The charming thirty-year-old worked in the foreign department of the Fiji government and her maternal relatives were settled in New Zealand. She was introduced through an asset cultivated by Kailash Singh over the years. Eknoa agreed to harvest and deliver intelligence but on one condition—she would work alone and the Indians should never try to contact her. When she needed to meet them, she would leave a message at a bookshop. Malik knew Eknoa possessed all the qualities necessary to entice high-ranking officials in Rabuka's government. Two days before her departure for Suva, he personally briefed her on the importance of the mission and her targets.

A month later, Kailash informed Malik about another potential recruit in the Rabuka administration. Filipe, a fifty-five-year-old civil servant surviving uncertain days under the military regime, had been planning to quietly move to Australia for good. Kailash had met him at a café in Adelaide. Over endless cups of coffee and discussions about Fiji's past and future, Kailash dropped an offer wrapped as a question.

'How much money do you need to settle in Australia?' Kailash asked.

'A very substantial amount,' Filipe whispered. 'But why do you ask?'

'I want you to do something for me,' Kailash said, elaborating on the tasks to make sure Filipe did not misinterpret his intentions. 'I need the best that you can provide between Fiji politicians and army officers. And I promise your worries about finances will be taken care of.'

Filipe nodded enthusiastically and to prove his worth, told Kailash that senior officials in the Fijian police force were about to be removed as Rabuka wanted a clean administration. This input from a civil servant was not gossip, thought Kailash, and minutes later a handshake between the two men sealed the deal.

In early 1989, Filipe delivered a package to Kailash containing the details of new appointments being made by Rabuka in the army and government departments. It contained the contact number and dossier of a powerful Fijian press baron who was ready to carry news and opinions on what Indians wanted. Filipe also offered to recruit some journalists in Suva on behalf of the band of three.

Shekhawat said: 'It was a terrific opportunity for the band. Both Eknoa and Filipe were new to the clandestine world and although there was a little apprehension about their loyalty, the band did not know any other way to make life miserable for Rabuka. During this entire event, officers from the MEA and other units of the R&AW in Australia and New Zealand were kept out of the loop. This arrangement protected the secrecy of operation. Despite the clampdown by the military regime in Fiji, protests and pro-democracy demonstrations were intensified. This was clearly the result of the band's great skill and resilience. But much more needed to be accomplished.'

The Betrayal

The most miraculous thing to ever happen to a spy would be the survival of an operation after a betrayal.

To access information, a spy has to betray someone. But being betrayed by a recruit always leaves a scar. It also endangers the operation. In the world of espionage, trust is somewhat like entering a village of cannibals. There is a high chance of being eaten with knives and forks made of deception. In early August 1989, the members of the band found themselves surrounded by cannibals.

While the R&AW spies were reviewing clandestine reports to make reasoned intelligence analyses on Fiji for the Indian government, Benjamin Taylor sought an urgent meeting. Eknoa and Filipe had betrayed the Indian agents, Taylor revealed. He did not know the background but confirmed that Australian counterintelligence had been informed about the presence of some foreign operatives and he feared the queries were about the band of three.

It was later learnt that Filipe had spoken to his young European mistress about his plan to settle in Australia. The unidentified young woman knew how to listen. And when Filipe disclosed the fact that he was being helped by the Indians, she made her move. Filipe had been picked up by Rabuka's soldiers the very next evening and he readily agreed to betray the Indian spies. This treachery bought him clemency.

The next few days for the three spies were full of sound and fury, said Shekhawat. 'Three officers from Rabuka's military landed in Sydney sometime in the second week of August,' he said. 'They had contacted Australian immigration to help them identify an Indian, Kailash Singh. Since Kailash was operating undercover, the Australians had no information about him. They placed a watcher at the Adelaide café where Kailash had recruited Filipe, but he never arrived. They sent an emissary to the Indian embassy in Australia, looking for Kailash, and were categorically told that the embassy was not aware of any such Indian in Australia. The band had shifted base to a safe house in Melbourne arranged by Taylor. But because of Filipe's betrayal, the operation lost a few precious weeks.'

The crisis, however, was not over. The three Fijian officers returned to Suva in late August to update the dictator about the blank they had drawn and to extract more information from Filipe, if he had held back any. They returned to Sydney around the second week of September 1989. By this time, the Indians were back in the game. They used Taylor and his network to inform the Australian authorities that Fijian soldiers were illegally hunting on Aussie ground. When the Australian intelligence operatives were unleashed on them, the Fijian soldiers disappeared. The Indian agents believed they had been neutralised before they could escape to Suva.

'The strongest emotion I have is the living pain of betrayal,' Kailash had told Shekhawat and other officials who were concerned about the future of the Fiji operation.

'You cannot separate spying and deceit; they complement each other,' Shekhawat recalled telling Kailash and Sahgal when they made a trip to India in September 1989.

That was a tumultuous period. Rabuka, facing bad press in the international media due to the R&AW campaign, had appointed a Constitutional Inquiry and Advisory Committee to review the draft constitution of Fiji that discriminated against Indians. The exercise, though, was a smokescreen. The deposed government of Timoci Bavadra had submitted a memorandum before the committee requesting it to weed out provisions which were retrograde, unfair, discriminatory and unjustifiable taking into account the legitimate concerns and aspirations of all sections of the people of Fiji. On 21 September 1989, the Indian MEA said:

> Reports from Suva indicate that the Constitutional Inquiry and Advisory Committee has not addressed itself to the Central issue of insisting on establishing Constitutional provisions, which are just, fair, equitable and racially non-discriminatory. It is the hope and expectation of the government that all responsible members of the Fijian society will continue to work for a genuine and constructive dialogue amongst themselves, for this alone can ultimately ensure peace, stability and racial harmony in the troubled Islands of Fiji.

Meanwhile the band of three received another extension in October 1989 for Operation Fiji. The fourth stage was now launched, aimed at the Fijian army. R&AW opened its bank vaults to senior officers of the Fiji armed forces who were ready to support democracy and a fresh election in the country. Malik had managed to cosy up to a Fijian politician with considerable influence in Rabuka's camp. What passed between Malik and the politician codenamed MCA remains a secret but a few weeks later, senior officials in the spy agency were shipped a dossier containing detailed profiles of four Fijian army officers. They studied the backgrounds of all four potential recruits carefully and picked the one they thought could become a super informer for India. MCA was asked to broker the deal between Malik and the army officer. The deal cost the Fiji operation big money, but Malik and his team were convinced that a mole deep inside the Fiji army could deliver priceless intelligence on Rabuka's intents and future moves. The band devised unique mechanisms to communicate with the super informer, and aside from shipping intelligence, he was asked to start psychological warfare within the army. Malik asked him to sell the theory among Rabuka's trusted lieutenants that if the dictator held elections, the move would boost his sagging image and popularity globally.

The super informer was a charismatic recruit and the R&AW made good use of his skills. During October 1989, the band of three concentrated on an information war in Fiji. Huge amounts of money were shipped to journalists and media barons to mount pressure on Rabuka's regime by carrying tailored stories and opinions.

The fiercely committed operation was interrupted briefly towards the end of October 1989 by a manufactured controversy. The Fijian dictator, facing criticism in the international media, had decided to expel T.P. Sreenivasan, the Indian ambassador to Fiji. Government insiders believed that this decision by the military regime was an afterthought. The Indian government had already announced Sreenivasan's transfer to headquarters in Delhi before Rabuka criticised the ambassador for meddling in Fiji's internal affairs. On 1 November 1989, the Indian government hit back at Rabuka with a warning that it would not close its eyes to the absolute need to maintain full support for the human and political rights of all the people of the island nation including, of course, ethnic Indians. The Indian government prudently argued that India also stood for the many people of Fijian origin who supported democracy. On the controversy around Sreenivasan, the official record of the MEA observed:

> The Fiji authorities have written to our Ambassador in Fiji, T.P. Sreenivasan, indicating their displeasure with his recent statements and actions and alleging apparent interference of the Indian government in Fiji's affairs. These pertain mainly to the Ambassador's efforts to calm the feelings of the people of Indian origin of that country, after some misguided Fijians had recently burnt a Sikh Gurdwara, a Muslim mosque and two Hindu temples. The government of India is surprised by what the Fijian regime has done. The government rejects these charges as totally baseless. Sreenivasan was trying merely to emphasize the need for measures for restoring inter-racial harmony in Fiji and showing respect for all religions. Principled opposition to racial discrimination, wherever it occurs, has been a constant feature of India's foreign policy. This cannot be deemed to constitute interference in the internal affairs of any country. The communication received from the Fijian authorities also conveys their decision that the Ambassador should leave Fiji by 3rd November 1989, and their view that India's future representation in Fiji should be at a lower level. This statement is not easy to understand, as the government of India had already announced its decision to transfer Ambassador Sreenivasan back to headquarters, after completion of his normal term of duty in Fiji.

India was soaked in election fervour when news of the diplomatic controversy spread like wildfire. The Rajiv Gandhi government, mired in the Bofors scandal, was facing a united opposition led by V.P. Singh. Only two days after the Rajiv Gandhi government made a strong statement against the Rabuka regime, the deposed pro-ethnic Indian leader Timoci Bavadra died in Lautoka, a port city of Fiji. He was only fifty-five. Najma Heptulla, then deputy chairman of the Rajya Sabha, was rushed to Fiji by Gandhi to attend the funeral and to meet Adi Kuini Bavadra, Timoci's widow. She wrote in the condolence book:

> Fiji has lost a respected leader on whom the people of Fiji had placed great trust and confidence. He in turn inspired them not only with democratic leadership, but with noble ideals of equality, justice and brotherhood, transcending the narrow barriers of race, colour and religion. For us in India, these values, fundamental as they are to the basic principles of life and governance, bequeathed to us by the father of our nation, Mahatma Gandhi, are of paramount importance. At this moment of national grief for Fiji, the one thought that I would like to express is that there can be no better tribute to the memory of the departed leader than to dedicate ourselves to the ideals for which he lived and died.

Closely watching the developments in Fiji and India, the band of three decided to fight the tyrannical regime with renewed fury and ruthlessness. Though a large number of supporters had turned up at Bavadra's funeral, creating a louder voice for the reestablishment of democracy, the spies knew Rabuka retained the upper hand in Fiji. They were able to recruit two more senior officers from Rabuka's army and now had three deep throats inside the Fijian army headquarters. These assets passed on vital intelligence on the activities of Rabuka's administration and by the early 1990s, the brutal attacks against Indians were controlled to a certain extent by the distribution of money among the lower ranks of the army. The instruction was to keep the bullet in its chamber.

But the band's persistent request to push for desired amendments in the draft constitution met fierce resistance. The Fijian recruits, though they were top level decision makers, expressed helplessness on the issue and admitted that Rabuka was under tremendous pressure from a powerful group of Fijian community leaders known as 'Bose Levu Vakaturaga,' who wanted indigenous Fijians to rule the country and all the rights given to ethnic Indians to be suspended.

An ethnic Indian political leader codenamed Laxman Prasad was paid a handsome amount of money by R&AW to exert pressure on Rabuka and his associates through agitations across the islands. The band delivered additional money to Prasad to procure support from Australian politicians, guided him to potential targets in the Australian political circle, and showed him when to operate and where to hunt. India considered the Fijian regime 'illegal' and the main focus in April 1990 was to drop the amendments in the proposed constitution that would alienate ethnic Indians. The next two months were therefore crucial for the band. They made every possible attempt to win support in Australia, New Zealand and the USA.

The MEA issued a strong statement:

> At a time when racism is on the decline even in South Africa, this institutionalization of racism, similar in character to the humiliating system of apartheid sets the clock back for human civilization. Institutionalized racism is a crime against humanity. It has not been tolerated in South Africa. It should not be allowed to rear its ugly head anywhere else in the world. We have nothing but goodwill for the people of Fiji. Nor do we see the issue solely as concerning Fijians of Indian origin. We wish all Fijians peace and prosperity, irrespective of race, religion or colour. We believe that this can only be ensured in a multiracial, just and equitable system. Our opposition is simply to racism. At this critical moment in the history of Fiji and in the battle against racism, we call upon all democratic forces in the world to condemn the promulgation of this constitution in Fiji. Indeed, the time has come to decide, in concert, on ways to isolate the illegal regime there and defeat its attempts to impose this new form of racism.

Even though the call was about justice and retribution, it did not find support from friendly nations. India felt deeply isolated on the issue. The band was summoned back to Delhi. Verma, the R&AW chief told them: 'You are here to tell me how this bloody constitution happened after all we did according to your operational requirements.'

The spies confessed to the disaster, but in an hour-long meeting, they also vehemently argued that all the assets on the ground were operating with maximum efficiency.

'Do you still think it is possible to neutralise the situation? I know you have done some spectacular work and are still doing everything possible, but the government wants the result sooner rather than later. Knock him down. We need a permanent political solution and please make sure your assets are satisfactorily assertive against Rabuka's hostility. Their efficiency must result in purging his support base.'

With that, the meeting was over.

For the men operating in hostile terrain, this was a new beginning. The operation had run into trouble because India's so-called friends had ignored the country's request to put pressure on racist regime. But the war waged by the spies in the shadows was making some impact.

'We could have done wonders if even the slightest over ground support had been provided to us by the other countries in the way of open international condemnation. But there is no measure to judge a spy operation and we set out to remind the Fijian regime that the game was still on,' Shekhawat chuckled.

Within days of arriving in Adelaide sometime in late October 1990, Kailash Singh made contact with Benjamin Taylor. Singh had so far shown persistence in dealing with Taylor and on this occasion, he asked him whether a disinformation campaign could be unleashed in Fiji for an early election under two neutral observer countries.

'Rabuka must be told that he would win with a thumping majority if he decides to contest the election. At least this will break the status quo and who knows, in future we could find a lone wolf with a steel frame,' Kailash told Taylor.

'All the ethnic Fijian community chiefs are supporting him. If there is an election, he is definitely going to win,' Taylor said, surprised by Singh's logic.

'Then we can play off one against another,' Singh said. 'There will be some battles lost but our focus is on tactical victory. We need to identify and engage with allies in Fiji if we plan to defeat and dismantle the military regime and get the Indians out of this nightmare scenario.'

Meanwhile, Rabuka made another shocking move. In a discussion with his army colleagues, the military ruler strongly favoured the possibility of deporting all ethnic Indians back to India. The band realised the importance of a political antidote. They pushed a top rung Indian leader in the Fiji Labour Party, one of their prized assets, to lead the party. Adi Bavadra, widow of Timoci Bavadra, had been controlling it since the death of the deposed leader in 1989. It took a couple of months and a spectacular operation from Sydney to win over the opponents of the Indian asset in the party. All sorts of ammunition were used to garner support for her. Once the Fiji Labour Party decided to appoint the Indian asset as its chief, the long and daring spy operation was called off and the band returned to Delhi.

Post-script

In Delhi, the band was now limited to desk jobs. In the vocabulary of espionage, they had been told to spend some time in the cold. But Malik, Singh and Sahgal continued to devote long nights reading cables from Sydney. Rabuka was turning democratic. In June 1991, he accepted the leadership of a new political outfit called Soqosoqoni Vakavulewani Taukei. He announced that elections would be held in 1992. Despite massive rigging by the military regime, Rabuka's party won only thirty out of seventy seats in parliament. As he desperately sought support from other parties to form the government, the Indian asset was activated. He told Rabuka that the FLP would support him on the condition that after forming the government, the racist constitution would be reviewed. Rabuka accepted the deal. But after assuming power, Rabuka kept postponing the review of the constitution and other laws that had been promulgated to deny the rights of Indians.

In December 1992, a top secret report landed on Singh's desk. The band of three was needed in Sydney. In a secret ceremony, the spies were felicitated and the Indian asset organised a private dinner to show them his gratitude.

Shekhawat said that after the band of three returned to India, the Fiji operation ran on auto mode. The agents and assets created by the band continued to work against Rabuka for the next couple of years.

Contacts within Rabuka's administration and in the media were successful in demonstrating his corruption and what was widely believed to be his weakness for European prostitutes. He was videographed in the act by Malik's recruit and copies were secretly circulated to ethnic Fijian leaders and senior military officers. By the mid 1990s, Rabuka was completely discredited. In 1999, his political career ended when, after the general election, the Indian asset occupied a high-level position in the government of Fiji.

The secrets of the band of three and their hired agents have always been kept under lock and key. To some veteran spymasters at the top of the Indian intelligence community, the band is the epitome of legendary espionage operations.

'The three brother spies were ready to die for the country. They should be declared national heroes. Unfortunately we cannot do it,' Shekhawat said. After all, he added, a spy would always prefer death to a life of public accolades.

Today, Indo-Fijians dominate the executive in Fiji. The present council has five ministers, six assistant ministers and five permanent secretaries of Indian origin. Indo-Fijians also dominate the island nation's foreign service. Fiji's permanent representative to the United Nations is a person of Indian origin. The country's missions in the UAE, China, Switzerland and Belgium are headed by Indo-Fijians.

3

A WARRIOR AND THE WARLORDS

'Aaiye, Ashfaq sahib (Welcome, Ashfaq sahib),' said a deep voice in the shadows of a luxury suite at Hotel Marmara Taksim in the heart of Istanbul. As Ashfaq Khan entered, a six foot tall Pathan with a Kalashnikov pointed the barrel at his chest.

'*Nahi, koi zarurat nahi. Yeh dost hai* (No need for that, he is a friend),' said the voice with a tinge of scorn for the Pathan, a thirty-four-year-old from Mazar-e-Sharif.

Clearly, Khan was one of a rare group of people permitted to enter Room No. 209 without a body search.

'How are you, Mirza sahib?' Khan gave his host a warm hug. The bulky man who had welcomed Khan so affectionately was the legendary Afghan warlord Mirza Murad Rustam. Today, he occupies prominent position in the Afghanistan government.

Mirza patted Khan on the back. '*Achha hai, humko thoda bahut Hindi aata hai, aap logo se hi sikha hai, ghabraiye nahi* (I'm very well. I learned a little Hindi from your people, don't worry).'

R&AW agent Ashfaq Khan had been chasing the elusive general since the first week of June 1997, when Mirza was forced to flee Mazar-e-Sharif after a betrayal by his own lieutenant general, Abdul Malik Pahlawan. Once his confidant, Pahlawan had quietly sold Mirza and his citadel to the Taliban's

Mullah Omar. The reason for the betrayal was personal. A relative of Pahlawan had been killed in suspicious circumstances and he believed that Mirza and his close aide Ismail Khan had been behind it. Mirza escaped death by a whisker when Taliban fighters were secretly allowed to march inside Mazar-e-Sharif on 25 May 1997. Although Pahlawan realised that he had made a mistake and ordered the execution of the Taliban fighters, it was too late for Mirza and his favourite city.

The Indian spy agency, which had recruited Mirza sometime in 1979 when he was just a middle rank army officer, was shocked by the development. An Indian spy codenamed S. Reddy, travelling to Prague around the time of Mirza's escape, was asked to establish contact. Assets were activated in Turkey to learn his whereabouts. A search within the community of Afghan migrants drew a complete blank. A few days later, Reddy heard that Mirza was staying at a five star hotel in Istanbul under a cover name. Ashfaq Khan, a seasoned operative in Frankfurt, was told to find him. Within hours, Khan was in Istanbul looking for the Uzbek warlord who had commanded a force of fifty thousand fighters and ruled a free territory in northern Afghanistan before Pahlawan's treachery destroyed his fortunes.

Ashfaq had earlier met Mirza in Afghanistan in 1996 after the fall of Kabul to the Taliban but the meeting had lasted for just about five minutes. His task then had been to deliver aid to Mirza. Once again, he was assigned to help Mirza as much as he could. The hour-long meeting between the spy and the warlord focused on the emergence of the Taliban and Pakistan's tacit support to them which threatened India's interests.

'You cannot trust anybody in Afghanistan,' Reddy told me. 'Nothing is hidden from the warlords. R&AW made two effective recruitments during the Soviet invasion, each in a different camp. While Mirza fought against the mujahideen, Ahmad Shah Massoud, a trusted aide of Burhanuddin Rabbani and key figure of the Jamaat-e-Islami, fought against the Soviets and the Afghan forces. Both were jewels in our crown despite being poles opposite.'

After a pause, Reddy added: 'Massoud was the only warrior in Afghanistan, all the others were warlords.'

The Beginning of the Afghan Rendezvous

A lot has been written about the exploits of the spies of the US's Central Intelligence Agency (CIA) and Pakistan's Inter-Service Intelligence (ISI) inside Afghanistan at the time the USSR occupied the troubled mountain country. But the R&AW also had its spies in Afghanistan, working to ensure India's security in a situation where the USA was frantically arming Pakistan with cash and sophisticated weaponry to stave off Soviet influence in the region and Pakistan was using much of those USA-provided resources to arm terrorist groups out to harm India.

But the R&AW had seen the threats emanating from Afghanistan months before the Soviet intervention in 1979 and it had duly stepped up its intelligence gathering apparatus in the region. The Indian agency needed allies to counter the unlikely partnership of the mujahideen and the ISI and ensure India's interests were not trampled in the war for control over Afghanistan. The ISI has always been an enemy and its partnership with the CIA had triggered serious concerns in the Indian establishment. The Pakistani agency harbored an abiding resentment of the R&AW, which it blamed for dividing Pakistan with the creation of Bangladesh in 1971 and also for interference in Balochistan. With the increasing interest of the Soviets, the Pakistanis and the Americans in Afghanistan, the only check on inimical elements had to be trusted assets behind enemy lines to access vital secrets and future plans.

The Indian spy agency had two objectives in Afghanistan. First, it needed a significant increase in human assets to fill intelligence gaps and widen engagement with pro-India elements to counter the influence of the ISI-backed mujahideen. Second, it needed sources in every powerful group in the mountain country.

Three R&AW officers, codenamed S. Reddy, Ved Asthana and Asthana's junior, Ashfaq Khan, played key roles in running assets inside Afghanistan. These assets were recruited at different stages of the turmoil in the troubled nation, but each had a prolonged lifespan. Besides numerous informers, the R&AW supported and in return received invaluable inputs from three key figures in Afghanistan—Ahmad Shah Massoud, Mirza Murad Rustam and Abdul Jaleel. This was an intelligence coup. But the real challenge arrived with the Taliban attack on Kabul in 1996 when the assets were in disarray. The rise of the Taliban had devastating consequences for the R&AW's effort to gather intelligence to help coalition forces formulate a successful counterinsurgency strategy.

The biggest driver for R&AW involvement in Afghanistan was the history of the extreme hostile region and Pakistan's tried and tested method of using non-state actors against India. It is worth going back in time to fill in the blanks of the spectacular espionage operations the R&AW carried out in Afghanistan.

A significant event long before the arrival of the spies was the demand for a separate Pakhtoonistan. The movement aimed to create either an autonomous or an independent state for the Pakhtoons, the tribal people who speak Pashto and inhabit the borderlands of Afghanistan and now Pakistan. The geographical area claimed by the movement varied from time to time. Originally the three princely states of Chitral, Pir and Swat and the six agencies of tribal territory between the North West Frontier Province and the Durand Line, which constituted the boundary between British India and Afghanistan, were included in the proposed state. After the emergence of Pakistan as an independent state in August 1947, Pakhtoonistan became a matter of dispute between the Pakhtoons, Afghanistan and Pakistan.

At a conference held in Karachi between representatives of Afghanistan and the new nation of Pakistan, the Afghans made no territorial or population claims, but demanded that the frontier Pathans should be given the right of self determination. Meanwhile Khan Abdul Ghaffar Khan, also known as 'Seemant Gandhi,' formed the Pakistan People's Party in March 1948 and one of its objectives was an autonomous Pakhtoonistan within Pakistan, giving up the demand for independence.

The premier of the frontier province arrested Ghaffar Khan in June 1948, although the governor had reported that at that time, Pakhtoonistan had not been mooted as a serious demand by anyone in the frontier. The only sense in which the movement had any reality seemed to be a disinclination of the people to be linked with Punjab. The Afghan government openly sponsored the cause of Pakhtoonistan and as the agitation gathered support, made finances available to the movement as well.

The1955 merger of the North West Frontier Province (NWFP), Sindh and Punjab into one unit was also considered by the Afghan government as an effort by Pakistan to destroy the independent identity of the Pathans. Attempts by the Afghan government to negotiate a solution with Pakistan fell through in 1959. As relations between Pakistan and Afghanistan deteriorated, Pakistan withdrew its mission from Afghanistan in 1961. However, two years later, in view of heightened tensions with India, Pakistan reconciled with Afghanistan with the intervention of the Shah of Iran.

Within Pakistan itself, those demanding Pakhtoonistan were divided. The National Awami Party led by Abdul Wali Khan sought regional autonomy for Pakhtoonistan, while other leaders, such as Mohammed Ayub Khan and Abdus Samad Achakzai, demanded independence instead. Abdul Ghaffar Khan supported autonomy but stressed the importance of Pashto and Baluchi speaking regions remaining together. Coordination between

Pakhtoons and Baluchis would give Pakhtoonistan an outlet to the sea, offering a prospect attractive to landlocked Afghanistan.

When the Pakistan government launched its campaign against the Awami League in East Pakistan in March 1971, some of the Pakhtoon leaders considered it an opportunity to press their claims. The Afghanistan government, however, felt that no real movement was possible for Pakhtoonistan. In January 1972, the Pakistani leadership paid a surprise visit to Afghanistan to request the government not to step up propaganda for Pakhtoonistan. They received a non-committal response that worried them. The loss of East Pakistan in the creation of Bangladesh had created a new geo-political situation in the Indian subcontinent and Pakistan was anxious to preserve its integrity, stability and unity. This found support from the USA as well as neighbouring Iran. In May 1973, the Shah of Iran stated that Iran would not permit any further dismemberment of Pakistan, leaving the world to understand that Iran would not hesitate to cooperate with Pakistan to suppress any separatist movement that might raise its head in Balochistan.

But the new republican government of Afghanistan, following the military coup in July 1973, showed a renewed interest in the Pakhtoonistan movement. While Pakistan considered issues relating to the NWFP and Balochistan domestic matters, at the non-aligned conference held at Algiers, Afghan delegates raised the issue of Pakistan's arrests of Pakhtoon and Baloch leaders.

The Afghan leaders knew that if Pakhtoonistan merged with Afghanistan, the landlocked country's dependence on Pakistan for transit to and from the sea would end. India tacitly supported such a move, but Afghanistan in the late 1970s was economically and militarily not strong enough to pull off liberating a part of Pakistan the way India had done in the east. Also, the USA and the Soviet Union, who were both interested in the region, let it be known that they would not endorse such a step. In the absence of external support and internal cohesion, the chances of the Pakhtoonistan movement realising its aspirations were not very bright, but it survived because of a cultural and linguistic consciousness and a little support from Afghanistan and India. The Indian government knew the advantage of having eyes and ears on the ground and to ensure that the R&AW became a formidable intelligence organisation in the region, hundreds of informers and field agents were hired. According to R&AW documents, when Afghanistan's Khalq Democratic Party celebrated its fourteenth anniversary on 1 January 1979, the Indian spy agency's chief N.F. Suntook decided to step up operations in the region and R&AW officers were told to recruit Uzbek and Shia warlords. They spotted Mirza, who was then deployed in an Afghan army battalion at Jowzjan province in northern Afghanistan, and noted his hunger for power. 'He is a bird on the wing, encage him,' the Indian spies were told.

Reviewing the performance of his government, Afghanistan's president, Nur Muhammad Taraki, was satisfied. He was consolidating state power with the expansion of party cadres and he was able to legislate a thorough socio-economic programme despite some turbulence. The R&AW supported Taraki but to ensure a wider base of assets, the agency recruited key figures from other factions as well. Taraki was unaware that a bloody war was lurking on the horizon. A R&AW dispatch revealed that on 14 February 1979, the first sign of the war arrived with the assassination of the USA ambassador in Kabul, Adolph Dubs. R&AW spies said Dubs was apparently killed in crossfire between the urban guerrillas who had abducted him and the Afghan security forces. There was good reason for the Indians to believe that the Afghan security forces had used maximum force without adequate consideration for the life of the USA ambassador.

January and February 1979 had seen both Shia and Sunni mullahs arrested throughout Afghanistan. Important amongst those arrested were Ibrahim Mujahidi alias Hazrat Sahib of Shor Bazar, a top Sunni leader. R&AW field agents reported that about forty of his disciples, including Mir Yusuf, Abdur Rehman and Noor Iqbal, had also been rounded up. Amongst the arrested Shia leaders were Syed Kiyan, Sheikh Mohammad Waiz, Yusuf Binish and Majeed Riasi. The inevitable result of these arrests had been grave discontent and frustration amongst conservative sections of the population.

While the Indian spies flirted with warlords, a large number of Afghan politicians and activists were arrested and jailed on charges of conspiring against the government. More than two hundred anti-Taraki elements including Nizamuddin Tehzib, the former minister of frontier affairs, Usman Rasikh, the former governor of Badakhshan and Dr Farooq, the former president of public health, were also taken into custody in February 1979. According to the spies, clashes between Taraki and anti-Taraki army officers in and around Kabul had become a routine affair. The president was forced to order an overhaul of Afghan intelligence to gather inputs on his enemies' moves. In March 1979, the intelligence gathering units of Afghan civil and military setups were merged to form an organisation known as AGSA (Department for Safeguarding Interests of Afghanistan). Major Assadullah, a former air force pilot and a Taraki loyalist, was appointed as head of this new omnibus intelligence organisation.

To protest the abduction and assassination of the US ambassador, US aid to Afghanistan was reduced to approximately $3 million, from the previous annual figure of approximately $15 million.

Indian agents on the ground reported that the Taraki government's various social measures were moving swiftly and a crucial land reform was being implemented more rapidly and with greater success than even the government had dared to expect. But the left-wing People's Democratic Party of Afghanistan (PDPA) was split into two factions—Khalq and Parcham. Taraki headed Khalq and Parcham was led by Babrak Karmal. Each faction strongly resented the other.

'When Indian intelligence was hunting for assets inside Afghanistan, they saw that the government was pushing for several reforms, including literacy, in most parts of the country, and an academy of sciences was inaugurated in Kabul on 21 February 1979. A delegation led by Vasili Arkhipov, Soviet first deputy premier, paid a brief visit to Kabul from 27 February to 1 March 1979 and several agreements for economic and technical cooperation were signed. There were increasing indications, however, of the Afghans displaying an independent, even somewhat pugnacious attitude, vis-à-vis the Soviet Union with regard to the overall economic and commercial relations between the two countries. But perhaps our assessments were wrong,' Reddy said.

The Indian agents' dispatch for Indian decision makers in March 1979 suggested a deteriorating situation for Taraki. The anti-government insurrection had slowly but surely expanded over the last few months. By mid-March, almost all the provinces had witnessed serious, extensive and violent anti-government uprisings. This situation culminated in a sudden conflagration on 15 March 1979 in the western city of Herat. What began as a peaceful demonstration by a large number of townspeople against the government's repression of religious elements quickly blew up into a generalised insurrection in the city and its environs. The city of Herat remained in the hands of the rebels for a good thirty-six hours. Massive reinforcements had to be rushed there by the Afghan government to control the situation. These included Soviet aircraft from across the border. With the USSR's help, the regime was able to restore formal control over the city by 20 March. Between four thousand and ten thousand people were killed during this uprising and about three hundred

Soviet men, women and children were casualties. Even at the end of the month, the situation in and around Herat remained tense and abnormal, despite the restoration of the government's authority.

After the uprising, the Afghan government was forced to make several changes at the top. The most important was the creation of the Homeland High Defence Council (HHDC) that promised to act as a government within Taraki's government. All substantive power was vested in President Taraki and First Minister Hafizullah Amin, who was also designated as the vice president of the HHDC. The Indian spies of R&AW were informed by Mirza and a few other assets that these constitutional changes had been made by Taraki on the advice of the Soviet Union. There was an obvious attempt to confine Hafizullah Amin's power and influence to civilian and administrative matters. And it was widely reported that the Taraki regime's counterinsurgency measures were harsh and repressive. An intelligence dispatch said:

> What began as a revolution in [the] 70s in Afghanistan, has by now become a mindless tyranny. The rulers had perhaps expected this policy of maximum punishment to cow down the populace, but this policy has toughened the resolve of the insurgents and led to more violence rather than leading to submission. With the increasing tempo of internal opposition to the regime, there has been an increase in the anti-Pakistani statements of this country. For the first time, they are now alleging openly that Pakistan is fomenting internal opposition in this country, and interfering in their internal affairs. With the deterioration in the internal security situation in the country, the Soviet Union has cautioned the US, China, Iran, and Pakistan against intervention in Afghanistan. There were indications during the month of increased tempo of arms supplies to Afghanistan from Soviet Union.

The R&AW in April 1979 cautioned the Indian government that the insurgency in Afghanistan had assumed serious proportions. Disturbances were taking place in most provinces of the country, with reports of desertions from the armed forces and an obvious erosion of morale. The Taraki regime was roping in civilian party cadres and teenage schoolchildren for crash courses in military training as they apprehended increasing aggression by Pakistan into Afghan territory.

Reddy said the Pakhtoons in Pakistani territory were unhappy with Taraki for two reasons—they were not getting vocal support from the government and the religious persecution of tribal leaders by the Afghan authorities was triggering a migration to Balochistan. This was an ideal situation for Pakistan, which had decided to use the Afghan migrants flocking to its soil against Taraki. Pakistan had not forgotten or forgiven Afghan leaders for supporting Pakhtoonistan and therefore another division of Pakistan. It had earlier warned Afghan leaders not to intervene in its domestic affairs and now it was Afghanistan's turn to complain about Pakistan's growing interference in its internal situation.

On 27 May 1979, President Taraki decided to hold a meeting with the Afghan ulemas to soothe religious nerves. Reddy said the discussion was primarily a message to Pakistan that it should not interfere in Afghanistan's internal affairs and must stop the infiltration of mujahideen who attacked villages, massacred the inhabitants and subsequently gave the incidents an Islamic colour.

In June 1979, after the visit of Abha Maiti, India's minister of state for industry, India intensified cooperation with Afghanistan. Specific fields in which India offered assistance and cooperation included quality control, steel projects, the silk industry, the paper and pulp industry, cement and cement products, rural energy systems, small industries development, a manufacturing complex for agricultural and irrigation aids, fumigation centres, rice milling and solvent extraction, and the set up of industrial estates. Maiti also had meetings with President Taraki and his deputy, Amin, who had visited New Delhi earlier that year to attend India's 30th Republic Day ceremonies.

Meanwhile, as India worked in the shadows to lure warlords to counter Pakistan's influence, the relationship between the Soviet Union and Afghanistan took a new turn. A diplomatic dispatch said that around June 1979, Afghanistan began leaning heavily on the Soviet Union and four key agreements were to be signed.

1) To establish direct telephone and telegraph links between Kabul and Moscow. Under this agreement a complete wireless station including transmitters, receivers and four-channel telegraphic link was to be set up. Expenditure for the entire set-up was to be borne by the Soviet Union.
2) 'Mutual cooperation' between the Afghan ministry of planning affairs and the Soviet Union's state committee of planning affairs.
3) The construction of an Afghan-Soviet friendship house in Kabul.
4) To jointly construct a fifty-three kilometre long gas pipeline from northern Afghanistan to the Soviet border. The Soviet Union had also agreed to construct a compressor project in Khwaja Gogardak. The total cost of these two projects was estimated to be twenty million Russian rubles.

On 12 June 1979, when Indian Prime Minister Chaudhary Charan Singh was in Moscow, Soviet President Leonid Brezhnev expressed his concern about Pakistan's growing interference in Afghanistan. In a closed-door meeting with Charan Singh, Brezhnev made it clear that the Soviet Union had no desire to leave Afghanistan to fend for itself.

This alarmed the R&AW spies who, one month later, found President Taraki's tone towards Pakistan a bit aggressive.

Visiting Farah and Nimroz provinces on 19 July 1979, Taraki said that Pakistan was doing the dangerous act of interfering in Afghanistan's internal affairs, which in fact meant playing with fire that would burn not only Pakistan and Iran but also 'Put to flames all the world'.

'We have no choice if war is forced on us,' Taraki said. This statement was followed by a direct attack by Amin on Saudi Arabia, the USA, China and Iran for arming Afghan refugees who had taken shelter in Pakistan.

Vodka and a Coup

Reddy told me that people in Afghanistan hear the truth only if it is shouted from the top: 'Whatever is being said is true because only truth can be so loud.'

The truth was positively deafening on President Taraki's birthday. A July 1979 intelligence dispatch sent to New Delhi revealed that a special Russian vodka labeled 'Long Live Soviet-Afghan Friendship' had been served at the reception to celebrate President Taraki's birthday, and that days later the Afghan regime paraded Syed Siddiqui Shah, a Pakistani embassy official described as a diplomat, announcing that he was seeking asylum in Afghanistan. Shah was made to disclose on television and radio that he was voluntarily seeking Afghan citizenship because of the country's progressive class revolution and eye catching achievements as against 'Pakistan's direct interference in the internal affairs of Afghanistan through espionage, subversion and armed aggression.' He said he had been posted in Kabul to collect intelligence information and also named other Pakistani diplomats engaged in intelligence work.

This was followed by another astonishing move by the Taraki government. It asked the USA government to recall USAID employees stationed in Kabul. At about the same time, Afghanistan signed an agreement with the Soviet Union according to which the Russians were to provide technical assistance for civil aviation forecasting stations and the sound quality of radio stations in Kabul and elsewhere in the nation.

Taraki did not know that the Soviet Union, behind the scenes, was preparing to crucify him. He returned from Moscow on 13 September 1979 and was virtually confined to the presidential palace. Three days later on 16 September, Shah Wali, secretary of the politburo, announced that Taraki wished to step down due to poor health and that Hafizullah Amin had been unanimously elected as general secretary of the party and president of the country. A day later, the newly elected President Amin dissolved AGSA and formed a new spy unit called KAM (Kargari Astekhabarati Muassessa).

Amin told the agents that as long as imperialism existed, every government would have to rely on its armed forces, consisting of the army, the intelligence agency and the police, and this was especially important in Afghanistan where a revolutionary workers' regime would be unimaginable unless supported by strong armed forces.

According to a R&AW dispatch, Amin held a closed door meeting with the spies where he told them: 'Though your past role in detecting the conspiracies of the enemies has been very well, the errors and mistakes of the previous authorities have left some unfavourable memories in the minds of our compatriots, who, now, should not worry about your patriotic work of eradicating the invisible influence of our enemies and guaranteeing the democratic rights and liberties of our people in the best way.'

The New Delhi headquarters of R&AW, however, had been informed that Taraki had been killed a day before Wali's announcement and media reports about his ill health was false propaganda.

According to Ashfaq, Taraki's secret execution was the beginning of the end of peace in Afghanistan. Within months it became clear that the Russians were unhappy with Amin and had begun preparing for an assault. Reports from the R&AW spy station in Kabul suggested that in approximately two hours, beginning from 7.10 p.m. on 23 December 1979, Soviet combat troops flew to Kabul. On 27 December, they killed President Hafizullah Amin and a few members of his family. A day later, Babrak Karmal, leader of the Parcham faction of the PDPA and one time deputy prime minister in Taraki's government, became president.

According to Ashfaq, just a month before the Soviet coup, Amin had given about half a dozen interviews, mostly to Western correspondents, about his desire to execute a new Afghan constitution by April 1980 with the approval of the Loya Jirgah (tribal parliament) to ensure the establishment of a socialist society. Amin also said the Afghan refugees in Pakistan were a handful of terrorists who had fled the country and were now being assisted by Pakistan and the US, and added that the Soviet Union would support his government if the country were be attacked from Pakistani soil.

Amin was so confident of his longevity as Afghanistan's president that on 3 November 1979, he and the council of Afghan ministers approved agreements with the Soviet Union for the purchase of equipment to drill oil and gas wells as part of the Jarqudug project. Before the project could be inaugurated, President Amin was dead.

An Indian dispatch revealed that the coup had been very carefully planned. Amin's Soviet advisors had persuaded him to shift to Darulaman Palace, where he was effectively isolated. Whatever was left of the Afghan army had been deployed in areas far from Kabul and some units had been disarmed or confined to barracks. The Soviet Union justified this massive military intervention on the grounds of a specific request made by the Afghan leadership under the Soviet Afghan treaty of friendship, good neighbourliness and cooperation signed on 5 December 1978.

The Soviet army took charge of all the important places in Kabul as a sense of calm slowly returned to the city after a period of fear and tension made worse by a brief round of firing on the night of 30 December. However, it was clear that the Afghans harboured a strong feeling of resentment against the Soviet troops. Meanwhile, more Soviet troops began spreading all over Afghanistan, ostensibly to launch an attack on Muslim rebels as the revolutionary council headed by Babrak Karmal announced that Amin had been executed by the revolutionary tribunal for the crimes he had committed against the noble people of Afghanistan.

Days later, Babrak Karmal called Amin a CIA agent and a scheming spy of American imperialism; a traitor who did not have pity even on Taraki. He also promised to release all political prisoners and abolish all anti-democratic and anti-people regulations and support respect for the sacred principles of Islam.

The Afghan armed forces, demoralised and divided, remained practically inactive during the Soviet army's December 1979 operation. Though some units around Darulaman Palace resisted the Soviet troops, they had been quickly subdued. The following day, as Soviet T-55 tanks guarded the entry points to Kabul and fighter planes exercised surveillance, the Afghan army in and around Kabul was made to surrender and was later disarmed. Fuel and other essential supplies were withheld to prevent resistance. Indian intelligence operatives reported that reactionary circles in Pakistan, China, Saudi Arabia and Egypt, supported by the Americans, were training and arming mercenaries in military camps beyond the Afghanistan border. These mercenaries were called mujahideen and, accompanied by ISI agents, they aimed to enter Afghanistan.

On 27 January 1980, *Kabul News Times* reported that in training the mujahideen, Pakistan planned to kill three birds with one stone: first, show its irreconcilable enemy, India, that it could use the Islamic block as global leverage to achieve its long held desire to annex all of Kashmir; next, acquire arms and funds to strengthen itself against India and Afghanistan; and finally, threaten Moscow and entertain China.

President Karmal later disclosed that the unfaithful Amin had been killed because he had been working with the CIA and trying to nullify Afghanistan's progressive ideas by planning a bloody coup together with Gulbuddin Hekmatyar, leader of the Hizb-e-Islami, an ISI sponsored terror group that wanted to establish sharia rule in Afghanistan.

On 12 January 1980, Karmal abolished the KAM and set up a new intelligence service called KHAD that aimed to protect democratic freedoms, national independence and sovereignty and the interests of revolution, the people and the state, and to neutralise plots hatched by external enemies.

In an editorial dated 2 January 1980, *Kabul Times* wrote that the US president James Carter had wept for Amin despite the fact that he had killed President Taraki and other opponents. The editorial also said that the US criticised the Soviet Union for sending troops to Afghanistan, although the US itself had violated international law and the principles of the UN charter no less than forty-eight times since 1950 by landing troops in several countries.

For those who loved their spycraft, Kabul was the best place to be in early 1980. In February, residents of the city secretly organised an unarmed resistance by distributing 'shabanams' (night letters) against the Soviet military presence in Afghanistan. Days later they loudly chanted 'Allah-hu-Akbar' from their rooftops. The Karmal government retaliated with a massive show of force. For two days, four MIG fighter planes and half a dozen armed helicopters manned by Soviet pilots remained airborne, making low passes over Kabul. Arms were issued to party workers. The government accused British, American, Pakistani and Chinese spies of murder, looting and arson. Seventeen suspected agents—sixteen Pakistanis and one American—were arrested for causing law and order problems.

The unexpected success of the agitation was due to the traditional hostility of Afghans to the presence of any foreign troops in their country. There was also a general feeling that Babrak Karmal was no better than his predecessors Hafizullah Amin and Nur Taraki.

India was active in the grey world of Afghanistan, but overt activities were carefully crafted to suit strategic ties with all the countries overwhelmingly interested in Afghanistan. In February 1980, Prime Minister Indira Gandhi sent a message to Karmal through S.K. Singh, India's special envoy to Afghanistan. Indira believed that China's and the USA's arms support to Pakistan meant that they wanted to interfere in the affairs of Afghanistan in the same way as the USA had done during the now deposed Shah's regime in Iran. The R&AW helped Afghanistan's fledgling security apparatus launch a counteroffensive against ISI agents operating in the region. Behind the scenes, the R&AW network provided accurate inputs on arms smuggled from Pakistan to insurgents in Kandahar.

'Not a single raid was unsuccessful,' Reddy said about the operation that the Afghanistan army carried out based on R&AW information to KHAD. Between a thousand and twelve hundred armed Afghan insurgents infiltrated Kandahar and its neighbouring areas, Kars, Balakarz and Malajat, to train and arm locals against the Soviet army. On the basis of R&AW inputs, the Afghan army launched a spectacular offensive. Sometime in April 1980, the Indian government was pressured by Americans to openly criticise the presence of Soviet troops in Afghanistan, but Indira Gandhi refused to yield. However, the CIA observed that Indira was disturbed by the Soviet occupation of Afghanistan. It said in a report:

> She [Indira Gandhi] believes that Afghanistan falls within Moscow's sphere of influence and Soviet intervention must be accepted as a fait accompli that will be sustained on Moscow's terms and that the sooner the Soviets consolidate their control, the sooner they will substantially reduce their military presence. If Pakistan continues to support the Afghan insurgents, New Delhi believes the Soviets, at a minimum, may try to undermine President Zia's government and replace it with a pro-Soviet regime. Gandhi also fears that the Soviets and their Afghan puppets may move against rebel sanctuaries on Pakistani soil and that the situation would then quickly deteriorate. New Delhi might be forced to accept or even participate in a Soviet takeover of Pakistan.

It became clear on 14 May 1980 that the CIA assessment had not been fully accurate. Afghanistan announced a seven-point political settlement programme that included a proposal for direct bilateral negotiations with the governments of Iran and Pakistan to promote friendly relations, discuss bilateral issues and provide immunity from prosecution to all Afghans who had left the country for various reasons and were now willing to return. The Karmal government also emphasised that the bilateral accords should be backed by appropriate political guarantees by the Soviet Union and the United States not to wage subversive activities against Afghanistan. As far as the withdrawal of Soviet troops from Afghanistan was concerned, President Karmal said the issue should be resolved within the context of the proposed political settlement and moreover, it would depend on the effective guarantees.

According to Reddy, this statement had had the prior approval of the Soviet leadership and it was obvious that they were in no mood to leave. Just before the announcement of the withdrawal of troops, fresh Soviet troops and equipment came into the country and therefore there was no net reduction of Soviet forces in Afghanistan. The withdrawal and its announcement was thus a military move camouflaged as a political settlement of the Afghan crisis. Afghan officials commented that it was now for Pakistan, Iran and the West in general to react to the announcement.

In an attempt to seal the border against infiltration from Pakistan, Soviet troops in the mid 1980s launched a major operation in Paktia province. India's concerns related to Afghanistan were manifold but at least two issues agitated the spies: the training of mujahideen that could be used by Pakistan against India and the unhindered arms supply by the US to the Pakistan army, which was virtually part of its intelligence unit, the ISI.

Zia and the USA Nexus

Pakistani dictator Zia-ul-Haq, who supported the USA's arms supply to Afghan mujahedeen, met Soviet ambassador Vitaly S. Smirnov in Islamabad on 1 January 1981. The two of them sent a letter to the United Nations (UN) asking for the nomination of a special emissary to conduct a dialogue on the Afghanistan issue. India believed that this move was a smokescreen: there were some differences between Pakistan and the Soviet Union, especially on Pakistan's insistence on a trilateral framework consisting of Pakistan, Afghanistan and Iran, and the role of the special representative appointed by the UN secretary general. But a month later, events took an unexpected turn. On 2 March 1981, a Pakistan International Airlines Boeing on its way to Kabul and subsequently Damascus was hijacked, causing a great deal of political drama in Pakistan. The hijacked plane had a hundred and forty-eight people on board. On 6 March 1981, in Kabul, the hijackers killed one of the hostages, a Pakistani diplomat who had been an aide de camp to Zulfikar Ali Bhutto. The hijackers identified themselves with an organisation called Al-Zulfikar and claimed that Zulfikar's son Murtaza Bhutto was its secretary general. The original demand of the hijackers was for the release of ninety-two people from prison in Pakistan. The Pakistani government offered the release of only fifteen of these prisoners. The hijackers refused the offer and on 9 March, took the plane to Damascus. There they demanded the release of fifty-five persons by 12 March. Zia finally conceded to the demands of the hijackers and announced the release of the prisoners before the deadline. In his broadcast, he referred to the prisoners as rotten eggs. While Pakistan publicly criticised the Afghans, accusing them of collusion with the hijackers, they praised Syria for the sake of the record.

Now Zia had a four-point programme for the resolution of the Afghanistan crisis: the withdrawal of Soviet troops; the maintenance of Afghanistan as an Islamic country; the repatriation of about two million Afghan refugees in Pakistan; and the provision of an opportunity to the Afghan people to have a system of government of their choice.

At around the same time, the USA President Ronald Reagan, elected with a huge margin on 4 November 1980, decided to give Pakistan substantial military assistance. Although the ISI's original demand was to the tune of $4 billion, Reagan agreed to $2.6 billion worth of arms for the Afghan mujahideen. This provoked the Soviet Union. The Soviet ambassador protested to Pakistan's foreign minister Agha Shahi about the use of Pakistani territory in the supply of arms to the Afghan rebels and warned him that should this happen, Afghanistan and its friends would take appropriate measures.

The USA knew about Indian activities in Afghanistan and used the media to launch propaganda against the Indian intelligence agency. Reports about internal strife in the R&AW appeared in

Washington. Pakistan too launched its propaganda machinery and two pre-recorded cassettes containing satirical references to Indira Gandhi were circulated within Pakistan and exported to other countries, particularly in the Middle East. These audio tapes were recorded by Shalimar Recording Company Limited, Islamabad, which was a government owned entity. Mirza, who was fighting the mujahideen, warned India that the USA would never stop supplying arms to Pakistan and the Indian government must initiate a dialogue with the US on the matter. A report prepared by the diplomats in the Ministry of External Affairs (MEA) in early 1981 said the Indian government had not been consulted by the US on the arms sales to Pakistan and indications were very clear that the Americans would not allow India's opposition to control the amount and type of military assistance flowing to Pakistan. The note said:

> In our meeting with US officials, we have stressed the need for defusing the situation in order to avoid great power confrontation. While indicating that we were in favour of the withdrawal of Soviet troops from Afghanistan, we have maintained the view that a political and negotiated way must be found to facilitate the Soviet withdrawal. We have also made it clear to the US that further induction of arms into Pakistan would only aggravate tensions in the region. The US administration has even acknowledged that its assistance for Pakistan should be seen only from the point of view of Soviet presence in Afghanistan and bears no relevance to India-Pak relations.

Geoffrey Kemp of the US National Security Council was a staunch supporter of the USA arms shipments to Pakistan. In a meeting of the India–USA business council in June 1981, Kemp said the USA was increasing its defence expenditure to protect western interests in southwest Asia. He hinted at a continuous arms supply to the Afghan mujahideen through Pakistan. On 9 July 1981, the

Berne based newspaper *Neue Zurcher Zeitung* carried a front page story with a Washington dateline suggesting that the USA arms supply to Pakistan was a sort of punishment to India for failing to oppose the Soviet Union on Afghan soil and the Soviet–Vietnam interference in Cambodia. A month later the Indian government refused to accept George Griffin as the political counselor at the US embassy in New Delhi. This was an unprecedented move. It was alleged that Griffin was leading the CIA operation against the Afghanistan government.

Meanwhile, insurgency powered by American weapons increased during the first fortnight of January 1982, with the rebels dominating the main market areas of Kandahar. Besides attacking the corps HQ, the rebels attacked the governor's office on two occasions, killing five guards on duty near the outer boundary wall. They also attacked the Kandahar radio station with rockets on 14 January, effectively closing the station from 14 to 17 January 1982. On 16 January, the mujahideen active in Kandahar city fled from a Soviet onslaught, retiring to the rural parts of Kandahar and Panjawai districts. They did not return to the town till the end of January. Some mujahideen had approached the locals for donations, but in contrast to their actions in the past, the locals told the mujahideen that they were still grieving the loss of family and property and so could not contribute monetary help. General Abdul Qadir, acting defence minister of Afghanistan, synchronised his visit to Kandahar city with the Russian action against the mujahideen, which indicated that the Soviets had the approval of the defence ministry. In February, the Soviet offensives in Kandahar, Herat, Lashkar Gah and other regions of southern Afghanistan caused the leaders of the mujahideen to flee to Pakistan for consultations, while the rank and file were told to assemble in Zhanjawat in Kandahar, where they dug trenches for their safety.

Obviously the rebels were neither capable nor prepared to face Soviet action and the heavy Soviet blow left them unable to react. A R&AW dispatch said that residents of Kandahar had seen reports about the misery of Afghans in Pakistan refugee camps, where they did not even have the minimum necessities of life.

The Afghanistan government continued to mobilise the support of tribal chieftains and the clergy by various incentives, monetary and otherwise. Dr Najibullah, the chief of the Afghan security agencies, and Suleiman Laiq, the minister in charge of tribes, visited important tribal areas. The mullahs were won over by material goods, including the repairs and renovations of old mosques and the construction of new ones. In January 1982, J.N. Dixit succeeded J.S. Teja as India's ambassador in Kabul. He arrived in Kabul on 15 January.

Sometime in August, Soviet troops conducted a major anti-insurgency operation in the Pashmool, Malajat and Sanzari areas of Kandahar province, with the help of about two hundred and fifty tanks and three hundred vehicles. According to government reports, the Afghans now had a hold over the major towns, but the rebels still dominated the rural areas. A R&AW dispatch to New Delhi noted:

> The rebels were not in a position to dislodge Soviets from Afghanistan and the Soviets on their own have not shown the least intention to move out of Afghanistan in the very near future. The rebels enjoy sympathies of more than 90% of the local population who do not want the presence of Soviet troops in Afghanistan but they have not been able to channelise this discontentment properly and are frittering away their energies in inter-group fighting.

In his address on 5 September 1982 to soldiers of the 37th para-commando regiment which had returned from Panjshir, Babrak Karmal claimed that the party's programmes and policies were at last being accepted by the religious and tribal elders in areas where opposition had been most vocal. The misunderstandings created by the policies of Taraki and Amin were being clarified. Karmal also addressed a series of meetings in the presidential palace where representatives of different tribes and nationalities from all over Afghanistan were gathered. He declared that the party and the government intended to actively encourage the revival of the tribal jirgas at the district and sub-district levels to ensure the extensive participation of representatives of different tribes and nationalities in the process of administration. In a message to the nation, Karmal called upon all Afghans living abroad to return to their homeland without fear of reprisals for past misdeeds, subject to the condition that they would no longer indulge in subversive activities.

The first week of October was marked by some reverses for the government in the Kunar province, which ultimately led to the suicide of the Central Corps commander, Major General Wadood. Since Wadood was a leading figure in the Khalq faction of the PDPA, it was feared that his death might lead to a further spate of violence and confrontation between the Khalq and Parcham factions.

There were intelligence reports about the increased flow of arms from Pakistan to the insurgents and the possibility of some insurgent leaders crossing to Afghanistan to provide active leadership to the rebels. According to reliable sources quoted in the reports, Soviet troops were deployed at the northern and southern ends of the Panjshir valley to spearhead attacks against insurgent forces.

In October 1982, the chief of KHAD, Dr Najibullah, sent the intelligence agency's spies to the villages to educate the people in favour of the government's programmes and policies. Insurgent activities continued unabated all over the country throughout November and December 1982, affecting Herat, Kandahar, Jalalabad and Mazar-e-Sharif in particular. There was an increase in violence in urban centres including Kabul and frequent attacks by rebels on convoys on the highways. Reports indicated that the rebels had acquired more sophisticated equipment as well as better medical supplies. According to Afghan intelligence sources, the total number of insurgents was about one lakh and twenty thousand, half of whom were operating from Pakistan where the number of training camps had gone up from eighty to a hundred and six. Due to unabated violence, the country lived in an atmosphere of unease and apprehension. Both Afghan and Soviet officials at the middle and lower ranks gave the impression of being impatient at their inability to put an end to the violence.

An intelligence report circulated among top Indian officials said: 'The efforts of Afghan government to woo and win over the tribals by distribution of arms and financial doles met with little success. The changes in the council of ministers and various party organs have also not been able to create any perceptible impact. While the resentment against presence of Soviet troops as well as the Karmal regime has continued.'

The spies also found the Afghan forces inefficient. In an elaborate description sent from the war zone they noted: 'The present Afghan army by itself is not in a position to deal with insurgency situation because neither they have the strength nor the capability to do so. Therefore, as long as the Mujahideen are supported from outside, the Afghan army will continue to depend on the help of the Soviet Army.'

The Terrorists Pakistan Helped to Grow

A Joint Intelligence Committee (JIC) report sent to the cabinet secretary and principal secretary to Prime Minister Indira Gandhi on 25 November 1982 noted that at least six terror outfits had been raised by Pakistan to fight the Soviet forces in Afghanistan.

All were headquartered in Peshawar, an ideal launch pad. At the top was the Hizb-e-Islami led by Gulbuddin Hekmatyar. The JIC report said Hekmatyar wanted Afghanistan to become an Islamic state. The Hizb-e-Islami maintained offices in Afghanistan, the UAE, Iran, Jordan, the UK, the USA and West Germany. The JIC report observed:

> Though its present strength is approximately 20,000, it claims to have the following of a million people mostly in Northern and Eastern provinces. It is most active in Pakhtoon areas and provinces around Kabul. This group maintains liaison with other groups for tactical and operational reasons at the local commander's level. It was believed to be behind the large scale civil disobedience movement in Kabul during February 1980.

The second terror outfit raised by Pakistan was known as Hizb-e-Islami Khalis, which was led by Maulvi Yunus Khalis and was mainly active in Kabul and Nangarhar areas.

The third and most important group, which the R&AW had been trailing for a long time, was Jamaat-e-Islami. The outfit headed by Burhanuddin Rabbani had an estimated strength of ten thousand guerrillas active in Nuristan, Paktia and Nangarhar areas. It was recruiting young Afghans in Panjshir with the help of Ahmad Shah Massoud, who was adored by the general public.

According to the JIC report, Pakistan was providing small arms to the rebels, including manually operated rocket launchers, mines, and infantry weapons including hand-grenades and light mortars. Ammunition without numbers and markings was being manufactured in Pakistan, including 9 mm and 7.26 mm bullets and hand grenades number 36. The intelligence report added:

> There are various training centres in Pakistan, where training is being imparted by Pakistan army and Para-Military instructors to Afghan insurgents. Each training Centre has

> 500-600 trainees. These training centres are located at Chitral, Cherat, Attock, Wardak, Jamroud, Parachinar, Miran Shah, Shagai Fort, Dargai, Nowshera, Quetta Tangi fort, Peshawar, Sialkot and Sargodha. Pakistan territory is thus being used by Afghan insurgents as a base for conducting operations into Afghanistan.

Attempts were made to establish unity among the various terror groups so they could offer effective resistance to the Soviets. But the Indian spies felt that these groups were genuinely not interested in a united front since that would affect the financial and material aid each received from their respective patrons. The Americans tried to mobilise some outfits by pumping in huge sums of money and a group of insurgents called Ittehad opened an office in the USA sometime in August 1982. Indian spies said Pakistan exploited the Afghanistan situation to its own benefit by securing economic aid and obtaining sizeable amounts of sophisticated military equipment from the USA. Pakistan also received financial assistance from Islamic countries like Saudi Arabia and had been able to intensify its links with West Asian countries in the fields of defence and security. With Zia at the helm, Pakistan was trying to become a champion of the Muslim cause by seeking to restore the Islamic character of the Afghan government, which enhanced its stature among Islamic countries. On the other hand, the USA looked at Pakistan as a frontline state that could help achieve its objective of checking the further advance of the Soviets. In the process, Pakistan cornered a large chunk of money and arms that it intended to use later against India.

Intelligence inputs pointed out that assistance from Saudi Arabia had also intensified. The Saudis provided money and arms to the Afghan rebels through the Pakistani government. While the exact quantum of Saudi financial and military assistance was not known, it seemed that Afghan insurgents were procuring light infantry weapons clandestinely from the countries of the Gulf and Middle East. Egypt had opened centres in Pakistan to facilitate Afghan insurgents and small arms were airlifted from Egypt to Pakistan on a regular basis. Interestingly, these arms had been procured from the Soviet Union by the Egyptian government. Afghan insurgents were fighting the Soviets with weapons made in Moscow!

The R&AW operatives worried that the intense indoctrination, the huge cache of arms and the vast army of terrorists in Pakistan and Afghanistan could be a security nightmare for India when the war in Afghanistan ended. According to Ashfaq, the Soviet intervention in Afghanistan not only brought a threat close to India's border but also initiated the process of producing more terrorists than ever. The JIC stated that there was no possibility for a proper lasting peace in the strife-torn region. The report said:

> The Soviet appears willing to maintain a prolonged military presence, despite adverse international reaction and believe that a policy based on attrition, force, steady indoctrination and incentives would eventually achieve their objectives. The Soviets have been trying to change some aspects of Afghan society on the Soviet model e.g. military, government, party cadres, and economy. If things become difficult for the Soviets, there are other options open to it including that of crushing the insurgency with a vastly enhanced military strength, and if necessary to use the Balochistan card at an appropriate time, should Pakistan go beyond limits of tolerance. There appears to be no likelihood of the withdrawal of Soviet troops unless a pro-Soviet regime is firmly established in Kabul, which can sustain itself.

The Indian intelligence report went on to perfectly describe the USA intervention, calling it a strategy to reaffirm American hegemony in this part of the world.

> The sharp initial US reaction to Soviet military intervention in Afghanistan has been followed by open declarations by the new US administration to help the Afghan rebels with arms and also to keep the Afghan issue alive as long as Soviet forces continued to be in Afghanistan. The US stand is obviously motivated by its keenness on repairing the damage done to its interests and credibility in the region. US perceive Soviets armed intervention into Afghanistan as part of long term Soviet plans to eventually gain access to the warm water ports. The US has advocated the idea of strategic consensus, in conjunction with other allies, increased its presence in the Indian Ocean. The offer of massive arms and economic aid to Pakistan needs to be viewed in this context. The US could well be aiming at acquiring military bases and logistic support facilities in Pakistan as in some other countries to counter-balance the Soviet presence in Afghanistan, and thwart the advance of Soviet influence in South and West Asian region. No doubt the string bases along cost-line (sic) of Indian Ocean and presence of western fleets is one of the responses to this situation. However, it appears that having not succeeded so far in securing withdrawal of Soviet troops by exerting economic, political and diplomatic pressure, the US may sooner or later seek a political solution of the Afghan question as part of its overall approach towards Soviet Union in global context. China perceives Soviet intervention in Afghanistan as a step towards its further encirclement and hence it has been very vocal in criticising the Soviet action. It has also tried to persuade Pakistan to continue status quo vis-à-vis the Afghanistan question so that the pressure of resistance movement could be maintained on the Afghan regime. It is to be noted that withdrawal of Soviet troops has been made by China as one of the pre-conditions for improvement of bilateral relations with the Soviet government.

R&AW's worries related to armed non-state actors were shared by the MEA, which observed that the USA would not be able to control the use of arms by Pakistan. S. Jaishankar (India's current external affairs minister) serving then as the under secretary in the MEA, with his experience as former foreign secretary said in a note that India should keep in mind that the USA could have the impression that India's opposition to its supply of arms to Pakistan could be neutralised by a mere assurance that those arms would not be used against us. He wrote:

> Such an impression would be particularly dangerous because it does seem unlikely that the US would actually be able to control the use of arms by Pakistan. Therefore, while welcoming US assurance, which could one day serve as a marginal constraint on Pakistan, we would have to take the position that an assurance by itself is not an adequate gesture towards India.

The American intelligence community on the other hand was deeply worried about India's growing influence in the region. The CIA was literally bitter when it drafted a report in December 1982 suggesting that India eventually wanted to usurp its smaller neighbours. The CIA felt New Delhi's record of building solid and constructive relationships with its neighbours had been spotty at best. The American intelligence assessment further noted:

> Since independence in 1947, India's relentless and often heavy handed pursuit of leverage over its far weaker neighbors and its insistence on a benign hegemony over the subcontinent, in our view, have created a series of adversarial bilateral relationships and have poisoned the atmosphere for a regional approach to common problems. We believe that both Bhutan and Nepal continue to worry that Sikkim's fate may someday be their own. New Delhi remembers the secret US air facility at Peshawar and has publicly voiced its suspicion that the new US security relationship with Pakistan provides similar privileges. India insists on dealing with each of its neighbors

> on a bilateral basis—a form of 'divide and rule.' This policy enables New Delhi to enjoy the benefits of its size and power without the risk of being chastised or outvoted at multilateral regional meetings. It is also meant to discourage the smaller states from working in concert against Indian interests, a tactic the Indians term encirclement.

The CIA also worried that increasing the USA arms supply to Pakistan may foment trouble in the region and in case of a war between India and Pakistan, the Soviets would support New Delhi. US intelligence officials believed that India would welcome the withdrawal of Pakistani support to Afghan resistance. But the Americans were in no mood to do so.

In December 1982, a group of R&AW operatives, facilitated by Mirza to set up safe houses and listening posts in two unidentified yet sensitive provinces, quietly entered Afghanistan. Later, two members of Parliament from the Congress party, Y.S. Mahajan and Saminuddin, landed in Kabul on 24 December to meet President Karmal. The Afghans were apprehensive of a meeting between Indira and Zia and had cautioned the Indians about Pakistan's unreliability. On the other hand, Zia worried that the Soviets and India were conspiring to break Pakistan into several states including Pakhtoonistan, Balochistan, Sind and Punjab and therefore allowed his country to be used as a supply base and sanctuary for terrorists.

Meanwhile, a R&AW operative Ved Asthana, who had established contact with Massoud at Panjshir in northern Afghanistan in 1983, had advised him to enter into a temporary truce with the Soviets. Massoud was also warned against Jamaat-e-Islami leader Rabbani, who the R&AW insisted was playing by Pakistan's rules. He was advised to mobilise the local commanders under a new council outside the influence of insurgent groups operating from Pakistan, and while admitting Rabbani's treachery, he promised to rebuild the units under his command.

Ashfaq said Indian intelligence provided Massoud with some financial support but that was not enough. He maintained his army of five thousand guerrillas with his own resources and was able to capture several northern provinces over the next few years, defeating the combined forces of the Soviet and Afghan armies. By the end of 1983, Ashfaq said, the resistance powered by American arms had become a formidable force against the Soviets. According to Indian intelligence estimates, the Afghan government backed by Soviet troops was in control only of about thirty per cent of the region.

> In 1984, the insurgents were provided with more sophisticated weapons to shoot down Russian jets and attack helicopters. There was also some sort of unity among various insurgent factions, which was not visible earlier. Although Soviets and Afghan intelligence tried to encourage defections, it was a complete failure.

Ashfaq told me that India was becoming a bit uneasy about the ongoing conflict because the ISI led by Lt General Akhtar Abdur Rahman was preparing a force of terrorists that they intended to use in Kashmir once the Afghan insurgency ended. The new prime minister, Rajiv Gandhi, wanted to strengthen ties with Western countries, especially the Americans, and he knew such a move would sour India's relationship with Moscow.

The R&AW by this time had developed a formidable capability for collecting and evaluating intelligence streaming in from abroad. Reddy said Rajiv Gandhi was suspicious of KGB activities in India and though he held a meeting with Mikhail Gorbachev in Moscow in 1985, he quietly directed the domestic spy agency, the Intelligence Bureau (IB), to take out a Russian trojan horse that may have infiltrated the Indian government machinery.

'Rajiv wanted to balance the ties between Moscow and Washington and he was right in a sense. You cannot put all your eggs in one basket and since he was focused on empowering India's technical sector, it was impossible to avoid the USA. The strain between New Delhi and Moscow now became too obvious,' Reddy recalled. He added that the R&AW's sole focus during Rajiv's term in office was terror outfits and training camps. There were estimated to be around one hundred and twenty Markazud Dawah (learning centres) based in various parts of Pakistan. On the other hand, Afghan president Babrak Karmal was persuaded by the Soviet leadership and the KGB sometime in mid-1986 to step down and hand the presidency to Dr Najibullah, the Afghan intelligence chief.

The CIA observed that Rajiv Gandhi's government felt that the regional repercussions of the Soviet invasion posed a direct threat to India since it had introduced increased superpower competition to a region where India aspired to be an unchallenged military and political power.

The American assessment was true to a certain extent, believed several R&AW officials who spoke to me. They argued that as the Indian government was getting increasingly involved in Sri Lanka, they did not want another vulnerable front on the Pakistani side.

A declassified CIA report dated 9 October 1987 noted that Rajiv Gandhi felt the Afghan issue was an irritant in India's relations with the Soviets and the USA, but he did not believe India could do anything to significantly influence the outcome of the Afghan conflict. A CIA report said:

> He (Rajiv Gandhi) is likely to be receptive to US agreements that India encourage a role for former Afghan King Zahir Shah or non-sectarian political parties in an interim and post-settlement government. Gandhi is also interested in limiting Islamabad influence in a post-withdrawal Afghanistan so that a Pakistani-backed Islamic fundamentalist regime in Kabul does not cause problems for India. His concern is that India's

> 90 million Muslims could be more susceptible to the influence of an Islamic-ruled Iran, Afghanistan and Pakistan after what could be perceived by Indian Muslims as an Islamic victory over the Soviets in Afghanistan.

Reddy and Ashfaq, however, argued that Indian Muslims had no traction with Pakistan and Afghanistan Muslim outfits and moreover the R&AW had informed Rajiv Gandhi that Moscow under Gorbachev was already looking for a political settlement for the Afghan issue.

'We were more worried about Lt General Hamid Gul's rhetoric against India than some mundane diplomatic issue. The Pakistani general had taken over as the new ISI chief in March 1987 and our agents had confirmed that General Gul was preparing a separate batch of terrorists to be launched in Jammu and Kashmir, armed with weapons provided by the USA for Afghan mujahideen. The USA had started supplying deadly missiles to Pakistan for the Afghan insurgents and the fear of them being used against India during any future conflict was heightened,' Reddy told me.

A Pashtun, General Hamid Gul hated India's military dominance in South Asia. Gul's first move as ISI chief, Ashfaq said, was to provide massive finances and weapons to Gulbuddin Hekmatyar to launch an offensive against the Soviet troops and help the ISI run agents in Afghanistan for subversive activities. Gul also tried to get cosy with Massoud, but the warrior, faithful to the Indian intelligence agency, snubbed his overtures.

'As a matter of policy, we did not try to recruit Hekmatyar, who was ready to sell himself to the highest bidder. We had told the R&AW chief, A.K. Verma, that Hekmatyar, a Salafi, wouldn't be loyal to us. We could do things in Afghanistan without Hekmatyar and had developed a wide network by mid 1987,' Ashfaq said.

The General and the Holy Warriors

Since the beginning of the bloody war in Afghanistan various mujahideen factions operating from Pakistan had tried in vain to unify the so-called holy warriors into a single organisation. Sometime in 1986, fresh attempts were made by Sibghatullah Mojaddedi, leader of the Jabha-e-Najat-e-Milli Afghanistan, to create an alliance between seven parties with the help of the ISI. Mojaddedi and several others refused to acknowledge Dr Najibullah's government and wanted to form an Afghan government in exile before launching an all out attack on Kabul. Although Mojaddedi was named spokesperson of this seven-party alliance that included the Hizb-e-Islami led by Hekmatyar, the Hizb-e-Islami Khalis of Yunus Khalis, the Jamaat-e-Islami headed by Burhanuddin Rabbani, the Harkat-e-Milli-e-Afghanistan led by Nabi Mohammadi, the Ittihad-e-Islami Barai Azadi Afghanistan led by Abdul Rasul Sayyaf and the Hizb-e-Inquilab-e-Islami led by Syed Ahmed Gilani, both the ISI and the CIA believed they lacked solidarity. One of the reasons for friction, Reddy argued, was the fundamentalist approach of Hekmatyar, Sayyaf and Rabbani. Mojaddedi was moderate and he worried about funds from Saudi Arabia for fundamentalist units that desired sharia rule in Afghanistan. Mojaddedi also did not like ISI interference in the alliance's politics and in turn the Pakistani agents hated him for being too moderate.

The possibility of a formidable force in the form of a united alliance was renewed with ferocity by General Hamid Gul after he took charge of the ISI. Gul met all the terror outfits' leaders separately in early 1988. Individually, each agreed that they needed a faster and more sophisticated army of insurgents to mount a coordinated attack on the Najibullah government.

Meanwhile, Soviet troops began withdrawing from Afghanistan in May 1988, after the Geneva Accord signed by the

Soviet Union, the USA, Pakistan and Afghanistan. But the war was far from over. Pakistan was still not ready to accept the interim government of Najibullah and Zia gave Gul complete freedom to prepare a strong force of mujahideen. Though Zia died on 17 August 1988 in a Hercules C-130 crash near Bahawalpur, his death only slowed Pakistan's plan to depose the Najibullah government, it did not end it. According to Ashfaq, after Benazir Bhutto came to power as prime minister of Pakistan in the first week of December 1988, Gul convinced her to continue the operation.

'Gul told her that since the withdrawal of Soviet troops the insurgents had captured major Afghan provinces, so if a Pakistan backed operation was launched quickly, the Afghan regime would fall to its knees. He was correct to say that the insurgents had captured Takhar, Paktika, Bamiyan and some border areas as well, but the Afghan forces trained by the Soviets were fighting to the hilt. Gul was asked by Benazir to move slowly and wait for the total sanitisation of Soviet troops from Afghan soil,' Ashfaq told me.

The R&AW spies revealed that in late February 1989, Benazir Bhutto and Gul decided to capture Jalalabad city to establish the seven-party alliance government. The idea was to make Jalalabad the capital of the government of the holy warriors.

'We forewarned Najibullah's government and shared a report with the Afghan army which noted that about six thousand mujahideen may attack Jalalabad. Gul and his trusted friends in the CIA had promised Hekmatyar that he would become prime minister of Afghanistan after Jalalabad was captured. Though it could not be verified as a fact, our agents in Peshawar reported that the US ambassador to Pakistan, Robert B. Oakley, had been present at a high-level meeting of Pakistani officials where it was decided to besiege Jalalabad,' Ashfaq said.

The R&AW intelligence was not a hundred per cent accurate as far as the strength of insurgents was concerned, but the attack on Jalalabad in the wee hours of 5 March 1989 duly took place.

The forces led by the Hekmatyar faction captured the Jalalabad air base the same day. Afghan soldiers surrendered and were executed by the mujahideen. However, Najibullah's government had been prepared for this. It was not going to be an easy battle for the holy warriors. The Afghan army retaliated and the siege ended two months later in a humiliating defeat for the fighters of the seven-party alliance.

A Marxist newspaper called *Spartacist Canada* published an eye-grabbing headline on 12 May 1989: 'Afghanistan Smash CIA's Cutthroats!' The paper quoted various sources in its report that Afghan government troops had broken out of the besieged city of Jalalabad and were recapturing positions taken by the mujahideen, whose strategy was in disarray. It said: 'For Washington and its allies, this is a humiliating setback to their plans to rout the Soviet-backed Afghan government and re-impose a regime of Mullah, Tribal Chiefs and landlords on the long-suffering peoples of this country. But, the danger is far from over. While the rebels' morale is flagging, their paymasters in Washington want more blood.'

Benazir Bhutto blamed General Hamid Gul for the debacle and unceremoniously removed him from the post of ISI chief, replacing him with Lt General Shamsur Rahman Kallue, a retired army officer. But there was no change in the policies of either Pakistan or the US to dislodge the Najibullah government by force.

Around September-October 1989, R&AW officers armed with evidence of terror training camps confronted US officials, Ashfaq told me. The Americans were told that Pakistan was not preparing holy warriors for Afghanistan but terrorists who would haunt the Western powers in future. The Indian agents were rebuffed. A CIA note prepared on 13 November 1989 said the American intelligence community believed that the Afghan insurgents would prevail over time but continued USA support would be essential.

> The Mujahideen are employing the right tactics—attacking lines of communications, airfields and trying to mount small scale military attacks throughout the country. The war may well continue several more years and there will be no significant changes in the military balance of power through this winter. Najibullah's Kabul regime survives because of massive Soviet support. It has surprised everyone by its military performance but remains unacceptable to the vast majority of Afghans. It is torn by factionalism and will not extend its control outside the urban areas. Certain of the important Mujahideen commanders must become more assertively engaged, particularly those in the north such as Ahmad Shah Massoud and Ismail Khan, to bring additional pressure to bear. A US disengagement at this point would be the worst possible alternative for US interests because this would cause the levels of fighting to immediately drop off, lowering the pressure on Najibullah, and would threaten the stability of Pakistan. The decision to disengage would also leave the Mujahideens feeling betrayed and risk an eventual anti-American government in Afghanistan. Mujahideen military pressure has already forced extensive change and compromise on the Kabul regime. Continued pressure eventually will either defeat the regime militarily or will reach an accommodation with whatever is left in Kabul. Najibullah probably must depart under any scenario.

Two American intelligence organisations held differing views about the tactics of the mujahideen. The Defence Intelligence Agency (DIA) felt that the low-level harassment tactics of the mujahideen would not threaten the Najibullah regime in the foreseeable future and in fact Najibullah was stronger and with higher morale today than six months ago because of the surprising performance of the Afghan army and the dependable high level of Soviet support. However, the CIA felt that the mujahideen were following the same harassment tactics that succeeded against the

Soviets and sufficient pressure was being generated to force the collapse of Najibullah's government.

The Final Assault

Ved Asthana met Massoud sometime in September 1990, a month after the fall of the Benazir Bhutto government in Pakistan. The Gulf War had already set the Middle East on fire and R&AW intelligence reports had suggested increasing terror activities in the Pakistan–Afghanistan border area. Najibullah was trying to rebuild the Afghan army but consistent attacks by resistance forces had reduced government influence to merely ten per cent of the region. Above all, Najibullah had decided to oust all militia groups from Kabul including the Juzjani militia headed by Mirza, who was once considered close to the Afghan government. This was an unexpected development and in late 1990, an Indian intelligence operative was sent to develop contact with Abdul Jaleel, a commander of Hizb-e-Wahdat Islami Afghanistan, which had excellent influence over the Tajik and Hazara communities. Jaleel was paid a handsome amount and the R&AW later used his network for operations in Tajikistan and Iran. But among all the warlords in the network of Indian agents, Massoud, despite meagre support, was the most reliable and extremely powerful.

'He always wanted to attack from the front. I cautioned him about the increasing casualties among his forces and he smiled and said, "Ved sahib, we are born to fight, don't worry about the casualties. We are going to rule Afghanistan soon,"' Ved Asthana recalled.

After the dissolution of the Soviet Union on 26 December 1991 and the subsequent decision of the Russian government to stop the aid to Afghanistan, Najibullah was left to fend for himself. In March 1992 he offered to resign and in April he quit. Later he was forced to take refuge at the UN office in Kabul.

The Afghan Justice Project, which prepared a report on Afghan war crimes, said that within a few months of the collapse of Najibullah's government, Kabul was engulfed in a civil war. During this conflict, the multiple factions that had participated in the struggle against Najibullah's regime and the Soviet occupation fought together with various militias for control of territory within and around the capital, as well as elsewhere in the country. Despite intermittent efforts by the United Nations, it proved impossible to win sufficient support for any political agreement on power sharing for the sake of stability. Following negotiations with some of the commanders formerly allied with Najibullah, the forces of Ahmad Shah Massoud entered Kabul. Other mujahideen forces also entered the city and claimed control of institutions and neighbourhoods. A number of units from Najibullah's government joined Massoud's forces. Fighting began almost immediately between Massoud's forces and Gulbuddin Hekmatyar's Hizb-e-Islami. Massoud's forces, together with Mirza Murad Rustam's umbrella group popularly known as Junbish-e-Milli, launched rockets and artillery at Hizb-e-Islami strongholds while Hekmatyar's forces mounted attacks on the airport and areas around the palace, killing hundreds of civilians.

Asthana said, 'Massoud was a true warrior but too shy to become a political leader. At one point he was reluctant to become the defence minister but we persuaded him to accept the position as we wanted someone who was on top of Afghan policy making.'

The Afghanistan Justice Project report, however, said Massoud's objective during the tenure of the Islamic State of Afghanistan headed by Burhanuddin Rabbani was to defeat the forces fighting against him. Besides Hekmatyar, his force had to also fight the Hizb-e-Wahdat and later, even Mirza's Junbish forces.

According to the report, during the first year of the tenure of the Islamic State of Afghanistan in 1992, 'His (Massoud's) principal foe was Hizb-e-Islami, whose rocket attacks killed thousands of civilians between 1992 and 1995, according to humanitarian agencies working in the city. However, Hekmatyar was not the only leader ordering such attacks: every major armed faction in Kabul had an arsenal of heavy weaponry that they used in battles that raged in the streets of Kabul during this period. Those with planes, including Massoud's forces and Junbish, bombarded particularly the south and west of Kabul during different periods of the war. Hizb-e-Wahdat also used heavy artillery in its battles with Ittihad and Massoud. All of these attacks, the vast majority of which were indiscriminate and resulted in tens of thousands of civilian casualties, represented grave breaches of the laws of war.'

Ashfaq said that since late 1993, the R&AW had been warning Massoud that the fundamentalist Taliban was being propped up by Pakistan and it was just a matter time before they would arrive in Kabul. In 1995, the Taliban, powered by the ISI, took control of Kandahar and subsequently Helmand and Wardak provinces and sharia (Islamic rule) was imposed. Taliban leader Mullah Omar, who headed a twenty-two member council (shura) now decided to capture Kabul and the first attempt was made in late 1995. In early 1996, the Taliban also targeted Jalalabad and gained control of the city on 11 September 1996. On 26 September, Taliban forces entered Kabul.

Ashfaq said, 'The Taliban takeover of Kabul forced all our three assets—Ahmad Shah Massoud, Abdul Jaleel and Mirza Murad Rustam—to join hands. They formed a new alliance and we provided whatever we could to help them fight against Taliban expansion. Abdul Jaleel once told me that Pakistan is openly supporting the Taliban with money and weapons. Can you do the same for our forces? If you can do that we will wipe Pakistan off the map."'

Ashfaq was shocked by Jaleel's words, but he understood the deep anguish the Afghan had about the USA–Pakistan nexus that was tearing down their country. 'I told him we cannot do that because we are a responsible, democratic nation and not a rogue country like Pakistan,' said Ashfaq.

Even the DIA had acknowledged the role of Pakistan in sowing the seeds of the Taliban. In a report, it said the Taliban in the early 1990s began as a group of religious students who rejected the mujahideen takeover of Afghanistan. Due to Pakistani support, they became militarily powerful and at one point controlled approximately ninety per cent of Afghanistan. The report said:

> Many Afghan opposition forces were outnumbered and outgunned by Taliban forces and could not fight the Taliban forces directly. The former Mujahideen Commander Ahmad Shah Massoud managed to form the Northern Alliance Forces (NAF) and continued his fight against Taliban forces in northern Afghanistan. Through Northern Alliance's Intelligence efforts, Massoud gained limited knowledge regarding the intentions of the Saudi millionaire Osama bin Laden and his terrorist organization Al-Qaeda to perform a terrorist act against the US.

The Indian spy agency feared that the Taliban would not waste time in killing Najibullah once they gained dominance in the war. Ved Asthana recalled the message the R&AW sent to Najibullah, who was staying at the UN mission in Kabul, to leave the country protected by the R&AW. The former president refused outrightly. Another effort was made through a reluctant Massoud, but Najibullah rejected the offer once again, arguing that the Taliban may not attack him.

'Despite our insistence and warnings about the Pakistan-Taliban trickery, Najibullah waited for some kind of miracle to happen. It did not happen and he was brutally executed by the Taliban,' said Asthana.

The Indian diplomatic mission in Kabul was closed after the Taliban takeover on 27 September 1996 and Massoud and other warriors retreated to northern Afghanistan. In an official statement, India made it clear that the situation had been further exacerbated by the direct interference of Pakistan and more so through its creation, the Taliban. The R&AW report said the Taliban militia had received the active support of Pakistan army regulars while attacking the Afghan capital. On the diplomatic front, the Indian government continued to recognise Rabbani's rule in Afghanistan but in the world of shadows, there was significant apprehension since the Taliban in early 1997 was making advances against the combined forces of the Northern Alliance consisting of Mirza, Massoud and Jaleel, the three R&AW assets. Months later Mirza found himself helpless and homeless.

Igniting the Flames

Ashfaq's meeting with Mirza that fateful day in Istanbul was a revelation about Pakistan's unflinching support to insurgents operating in Afghanistan. Mirza revealed Pakistan's plan to foment terrorism and prop up fundamentalist forces.

'The R&AW should have known about the ISI and the entire terror plot.' Mirza looked at Ashfaq in surprise.

'We know raising jihadis is still a standing order for the ISI and they are making every possible effort to take over Afghanistan through terror proxies, but we are doing whatever we can by providing evidence to the US and other countries,' said Ashfaq.

'Do you think these countries even care about the Afghan people?' an angry Mirza shot back.

Ashfaq was silent. Within the Indian intelligence community was a prevailing view that while the R&AW did a fantastic job in Afghanistan, it was not able to provide as much support as it should have to the Afghan warlords and provincial leaders who were trying to save the country from terrorist outfits.

'Even Mirza had so many grouses. He told me that he has done so much for India but Indians did nothing for him. Look at how Pakistan treats the assets and outfits it helped to grow, he said. I couldn't contest his argument because he was, in a sense, absolutely right. Our financial support to assets like Mirza was miniscule. I promised to pay his dues. Around two weeks later I requested a meeting with one of his close aides in Prague and gave him a substantial amount of money to deliver to Mirza,' Ashfaq said.

Sometime in October 1997, Mirza established contact with Ashfaq again. The Indian spy was in Madrid to complete some business. 'Mirza wants a favour, his emissary told me. A distant relative of Mirza is struggling to get Turkish citizenship. Can you deliver this for him? He would really be grateful,' Ashfaq recalled.

It took Ashfaq a couple of months to activate contacts in the Turkish establishment. They were told it was a huge favour for a loyal friend. 'I somehow managed the citizenship and Mirza was very happy. He visited me in Madrid to express his deep gratitude and promised to connect me to the formidable Uzbek intelligence collection operation active on the Afghanistan–Pakistan border. And he delivered. By early 1998, we were given unhindered access to the sanctum sanctorum of the network, which later helped us develop contacts with at least three powerful Baloch leaders. I recruited all three assets for future usefulness. We found a way to gain a foothold in the region and when the opportunity arose later, we successfully planted our listening posts at key locations,' said Ashfaq.

'But did we really achieve our aim in Afghanistan?' I asked Ashfaq over a few drinks at a bar overlooking the Dhauladhar hills.

'To a certain extent. I will not claim that we got what we wanted. It was also due to the US. Look, the Americans have had a theatre in Afghanistan since the Soviet invasion, which they want to use for a long time. I would say Afghanistan has become an American ammunition testing lab,' Ashfaq smiled. 'That was the reason for our panic.'

The R&AW's fears came true on 24 December 1999 when ISI backed Harkat-ul-Mujahideen terrorists hijacked Air India flight IC-814 with one hundred and sixty passengers on board. The ill-fated flight that ultimately landed at Kandahar was guarded by Taliban militants carrying USA supplied stinger missiles on their shoulders. India did not recognise the Taliban regime but the hijacking and the presence of a R&AW officer on board the flight forced the Atal Bihari Vajpayee government to strike a deal with the militants. Later, the MEA issued a statement to salvage the situation.

'Notwithstanding our lack of recognition of the Taliban, our strong reservations about its obscurantist ideologies and our opposition to the manner in which it has permitted itself to be manipulated by Pakistan, we established direct contact with the Taliban during the hijacking of Indian Airlines flight IC-814. The role played by the Taliban during this crisis was noted but we made it clear that the fundamentals of our Afghan policy would not change.'

The R&AW did not forget the humiliation. In 2000, the Indian spies converged on Afghanistan with ferocity. While the Taliban took over town after town including cities in Baghlan, Takhar and Kunduz provinces, the Indian espionage network was quietly working out a strategy with Massoud to launch a counteroffensive. Sometime in October 2000, R&AW recruits in the Afghan areas of Hazaribagh, Khajaghar and Imam Sahib helped Massoud's forces build up a massive attack on Taliban strongholds. By the end of October 2000, the R&AW revenge was complete. All the major towns that had been ruled by the Taliban were recaptured by Massoud's warriors.

'Although we had a wide network in Afghanistan, Massoud was the best asset we have ever had. When he was killed in

September 2001 by Osama bin Laden's terrorists, the R&AW was working on several important missions with his forces in Kunar, Laghman and Bamiyan provinces. We airlifted him to our field hospital at Farkhor in Tajikistan but he didn't survive the deadly attack,' said Asthana.

Two days later, Osama's terrorists inflicted a massive attack against the USA, bringing down the twin towers of the World Trade Center in New York. Asthana said the CIA had sought R&AW help in tracking down the Taliban and Al-Qaeda's terror havens in Afghanistan, and the Indian agency opened its secret vaults to share whatever dossiers it had on terrorist hideouts and leaders. The CIA was categorically told that the real fountainhead of terror was Pakistan.

'The Americans refused to accept it then. It was a big mistake and they acknowledged it during our closed-door meetings in early 2002. But during the chaos in the immediate aftermath of the 2001 attack, they misjudged the ISI as a great partner in its war against terror,' said Asthana.

The R&AW spy also recalled his meeting with General Hamid Gul sometime in 2002 at an undisclosed location in an European country. It was a chance encounter, revealed Asthana. He was pacing around the reception area and General Gul, well dressed in a black coat, appeared out of a lift in the hotel lobby and walked to him.

'I told him, "General saab, you keep harping about India, do you think Pakistan can really conquer our country?" He was dumbstruck for few seconds and said, "No." Then I fired another question. "Do you think India wants to conquer Pakistan?" General Gul smiled this time and said, "Yes." Then I said, "General saab, this is your real problem, you have a sense of insecurity." Gul got a little agitated and whispered to me that Pakistan would bleed India in Kashmir. I said, "General saab, you have no sense of history. A nation has a long life, don't forget that."'

This verbal confrontation left General Gul hugely embarrassed and he retreated.

The attack on the USA in 2001 had changed the security and strategic dynamics in this part of the world. The ISI and the Pakistan army made a tactical retreat to show they were siding with America and its allies to fight terror but they were recalibrating their next moves, targeting the Afghan and Indian theatres. The R&AW spies had served India well. At least in the Afghanistan–Pakistan border area, they had raised a good number of covert operators and within the Afghan boundary, the Ashfaq and Asthana-led team had dependable hunters.

'Despite having the best operatives, we have avoided certain covert actions against terror outfits at the Afghanistan–Pakistan border. It has to be done internally. We have to keep in mind the pressure from the global community. They may question our outings in the region. The big question is whether the Indian establishment can take the international pressure,' Asthana said.

A confident Ashfaq couldn't agree more with his senior. He candidly said that whichever government comes to power in Afghanistan, the R&AW will certainly have its own people in powerful positions.

4

SRI LANKAN AFFAIRS

Avinash Sinha arrived at Colombo Fort Café on the morning of 3 December 2005, looking forward to what he had been told was the best Sri Lankan breakfast in the city. The blue-yellow restaurant in the Dutch hospital complex at Echelon Square had an excellent reputation and Sinha was hungry.

As he scanned the menu greedily, a grey haired man in his early fifties chuckled at the sight of the person he was looking for so engrossed in deciding what to eat. The grey haired man marched to the red table and said, 'I am so glad to see you, Avinash.'

'Kosala! It's been a long time, my friend. Look at you. You are as ready as a lion in the morning.'

The two men chatted in this quiet corner of the café. Avinash, a R&AW operative, perhaps a few autumns younger than Kosala Ratnayake, had returned to Colombo that October after three years. He had recruited Kosala, a top functionary in the Sri Lankan government, over several wet evenings in January 2002. That was when the Sri Lankan regime had been seriously engaging with the Liberation Tigers of Tamil Eelam (LTTE) for peace talks. LTTE, an armed guerrilla group, had been fighting for an independent Tamil state in the northeastern part of Sri Lanka for the last twenty-five years. The months before 2002 were a turning point in the civil war when a ceasefire agreement was reached between the two sides owing to international pressure and diplomatic manoeuvring. The insurgent organisation formed in 1976 by Velupillai Prabhakaran had begun to wage a guerrilla war against the Sri Lankan government in the early 1980s. Prabhakaran had been well trained by the R&AW at undisclosed locations in Uttar Pradesh. When Kosala became one of the most prized assets of the Indian spy agency in 2002, Prabhakaran's era was drifting into darkness. But Kosala had warned Avinash that Prabhakaran was not pleased with the peace negotiations, believing the Tigers had been given a raw deal. He predicted that the LTTE would be back with yet another long, bloody battle within a few years. It was a prophetic statement and the only reason Avinash was back in the Sri Lankan capital.

'LTTE is not very comfortable with President Mahinda Rajapaksa. I should rather say Prabhakaran doesn't trust the president and the president doesn't want Prabhakaran to live even for a minute on Sri Lankan soil. They hate each other and the peace talks in Norway will ultimately fail. Prabhakaran will never join talks with the Rajapaksa government,' Kosala said calmly over a cup of coffee.

Avinash laughed. 'So do you think an all out war is the only option?' he asked.

'The president thinks so. Though he may give the LTTE another chance under pressure from the international community,' Kosala smiled.

Months later, war had returned. Kosala was the first to inform Avinash about an attack in April 2006 targeting the Sri Lankan army chief Sarath Fonseka. The LTTE denied the suicide attack which had badly injured the army chief, but President Rajapaksa squarely blamed the Tigers for the act of terror and the air force was ordered to carry out intense strikes against the LTTE's strongholds. The strikes lasted for two days. But more was to come. Avinash and Kosala watched the LTTE mount yet another offensive in May 2006, this time against the Sri Lankan navy. A vessel was destroyed and the Tigers fired upon other patrolling units, making the sea a new theatre of civil war. Kosala said that the European Union agreed with the Sri Lankan government's demand to declare the LTTE a terrorist outfit. On 19 May 2006, LTTE assets on foreign soil were frozen on the grounds that the terror outfit did not represent Tamils in Sri Lanka.

Running out of Time

The R&AW was increasingly worried over the safety of Tamils who had made Sri Lanka their home for the last many decades. In late 2006, a diplomatic dispatch from Colombo put the number of ethnic Tamils at thirty thousand while the R&AW told their chief P.K.H. Tharakan that at least one hundred and sixty thousand Tamils were caught in the crossfire. Avinash said that the R&AW had penetrated Sri Lanka's northern province deeply, especially districts like Jaffna, Vavuniya, Kilinochchi and Mannar.

'Our assessment was solid and as the war loomed large over the horizon, our primary objective was to evacuate as many Tamils as possible. But that was just a foggy dream. Under tremendous pressure from the Tigers, the Tamil populations had decided to remain and we couldn't do anything about it,' said Avinash.

The Indian government had taken a principled decision to support the Sri Lankan army offensive because the entire international community had been outraged by the LTTE's string of suicide bombings. According to Avinash, between late 2007 and May 2009 when Sri Lanka declared total victory against the LTTE, the R&AW provided satellite imagery of all the Tigers' camps in the north and east provinces to the Sri Lankan military. The intelligence included the Tigers' military formations as well as civilian populations so as to avoid casualties.

'If it hadn't been for R&AW's technical support, the Sri Lankan army would not have defeated the LTTE,' said Avinash. 'The Tigers were better trained than many Sri Lankan army units. Besides training the LTTE's top leadership in India during the Indira Gandhi government, the Indian agents had helped raise massive infrastructure in Jaffna. The success of the LTTE's naval wing could be gauged from the fact that three swimming pools, each the size of a football stadium, had been created in Jaffna for underwater training. The depth of these pools was approximately one hundred metres.'

Even the CIA had acknowledged way back in 1986: 'LTTE is capable of fighting government troops without Indian support and probably would continue operations even if other groups agreed to a negotiated settlement. LTTE has developed a disciplined fighting force of about 3,000 members and may be training some of its cadres in Nicaragua and Cuba.'

Avinash thought the CIA's assessment was wrong. He said the LTTE cadres had been made battle-hardened in the jungles of Uttar Pradesh and while they may have received arms and ammunition from abroad, their skills had been earned in India.

According to Avinash, there had been two factions in the R&AW during the 1980s: one supported the LTTE and their demand for a separate Eelam and the other opposed any kind of meddling in Sri Lanka's internal affairs. 'The group in support of the LTTE was much stronger and that was why we decided to support the insurgents at the cost of straining our relationship with the Sri Lankan government,' said Avinash. 'But there are no permanent enemies and friends in the grey world. By 1987, all the outfits demanding a separate Eelam had become the enemy and we faced humiliation by sending in the Indian Peace Keeping Forces (IPKF). We were drawn into the war and had to suffer huge casualties at the hands of the very organisation we had trained, forcing us to withdraw within two years. But 2006 was different ball game altogether. It was the conscious decision of the Indian government headed by the Congress party to finish the LTTE.'

The IPKF was launched during the tenure of the then R&AW chief A.K. Verma. He had expected the IPKF to weaken the LTTE so that later, with the help of the Sri Lankan army, provincial council elections in the Tamil dominated northern and eastern provinces could be held for long-term peace. The IPKF's first offensive started in October 1987 in Jaffna when the operation to capture LTTE chief Prabhakaran went haywire due to a massive intelligence failure, resulting in heavy casualties.

Serving R&AW officer Pawan Arora believes that signing the peace accord with Sri Lanka and launching the IPKF was a political blunder. The time was not ripe for an IPKF kind of operation in Sri Lanka as the LTTE, just a year earlier, had been trained by India. 'It was like fighting your own recruits,' Arora said. 'Moreover, groups like the LTTE were pressure groups for the Indian government against Sri Lanka.'

A CIA report in November 1987, a month after the offensive, said:

> Over the short term, Indian Prime Minister Rajiv Gandhi still hopes that he can sufficiently weaken the main Tamil insurgent group LTTE, to force them adhere to the peace accord. At the same time, we believe he does not want to weaken them so much that they cannot be used as an Indian lever against the government in Colombo in the future. New Delhi therefore almost certainly will remain open to the possibility of resuming a political dialogue with the tigers. Over the long term, we believe Gandhi anticipates he can extract Indian troops from their difficult peacekeeping mission after implementing the accord. There would be more widespread outbreaks of violence between Tamils and Sinahalese, and India may conclude there is little chance to settle the Island's ethnic problem. Gandhi would then begin to look for face-saving ways to

> withdraw Indian troops, possibly arguing that India faced more compelling national security threats such as renewed tensions on the Indo-Pakistan or Indo-Chinese border.

The complete withdrawal of the IPKF from Sri Lankan soil was indeed a face saving move, but one that was made by Gandhi's successor V.P. Singh, who won the 1989 elections promising a corruption free government.

But the planning in 2006 was different. The R&AW had learnt from the mistakes of 1987 and both human intelligence (HUMINT) and technical intelligence (TECHINT) used their assets to defeat the mighty Tigers. According to Arora, the Sri Lanka army would have been completely blinded without the support of the R&AW. The Indian agency, however, had to quietly bear the loss of four assets who were recruited to continue providing HUMINT.

'It was not LTTE alone that killed our assets,' said Arora. 'We later learnt that the Sri Lankan army had also been involved in hitting our informers. Just before the final and massive offensive in April 2009, some important assets were evacuated from Jaffna on a ship headed to the Maldives. A month later, the R&AW team hired several safe houses in Cambodia to provide them with security. In subsequent months, all the assets were strategically relocated to European countries.'

The need to get the Sri Lankan informers out of the country had been vital, said Avinash. At Kilinochchi in the northern province of Sri Lanka, he revealed, a compound that housed some R&AW informers had had just one survivor that month—a white cat.

The Price of Loyalty

Lasantha Wickrematunge, the fearless editor of the Sri Lankan newspaper *The Sunday Leader,* was shot dead on 8 January 2009 at around 10.15 a.m. The murder on Attidiya Road, Ratmalana, in Colombo south, executed by two gunmen in broad daylight, panicked the R&AW. Lasantha was not only an excellent journalist, he was also a loyal friend of the Indian spy agency. Javed Faridi, a R&AW officer who had befriended Lasantha even before the civil war had started, was dumbstruck. Faridi said Lasantha had been threatened by government-backed groups for several months and that he had had several rounds of meetings with the newspaperman to discuss who might want to harm him. 'Lasantha suspected Mahinda Rajapaksa and his younger brother Gotabaya Rajapaksa because his newspaper was not only critical of the government, but they were also exposing massive corruption in the defence ministry,' said Faridi.

After Mahinda Rajapaksa's electoral victory in 2005, Gotabaya Rajapaksa had been made secretary of the Sri Lankan defence ministry. A month before he was killed, Lasantha had told Faridi that he was working to unearth a defence scam involving Gotabaya. Always protective of its assets, the R&AW had warned Lasantha that the Sri Lankan regime might strike back. Lasantha told Faridi that he felt the same. 'His apprehension was right. Just a few days before he was murdered, I had told him to avoid going out. He called me a day before he was killed to say that he was feeling suffocated at home and could not live in fear of government threats.'

The day Lasantha decided to go to his office, he phoned Faridi, who warned him not do so for the next couple of days at least. 'But he laughed,' said Faridi. 'I was talking to him on the cell phone when he told me that two persons on a motorcycle were perhaps following his car and two others were backing them in another vehicle. I asked him to drive towards any police picket in the area. He couldn't find one and kept repeating that he might be killed today. He shouted many times: "I can't see a police station, what should I do now?" I tried to pull out details of the area to guide him towards a police station but then I heard his voice for the last time. He said, "They are here." I froze. I knew that very moment that I had lost Lasantha,' Faridi told me.

A day after Lasantha was killed, opposition leader Ranil Wickremesinghe alleged that the Sri Lankan intelligence service was responsible for assassinating Lasantha and that they reported to Gotabaya. Although this was a mere allegation from a political leader, international intelligence agencies operating in Sri Lanka were certain that the order to eliminate the journalist-editor had come from Gotabaya. The murder of Lasantha hit the headlines all over the world and reminded the global community about the decades-old civil war in Sri Lanka.

The Beginning

The indigenous population of Sri Lanka (formerly Ceylon) consists largely of elements that had migrated from India over various periods of the distant past. However, in modern times, systematic labour migration from India to Sri Lanka began in the 1830s. Yet, the stream of workers from south India, which greatly increased between the 1830s and 1880s, was never assimilated into the island's permanent population. The collapse of the coffee industry in the 1890s led to a sharp decline in the migration of labour from India and during the period 1931 to 1946, the Indian labour population registered a sharp decrease following a 1939 ban imposed by the government of India on the emigration of unskilled labour. The majority of the Indian labour, which overwhelmingly came from south India, was concentrated in the tea and rubber estates. The proximity of the migrants' homes in India and the lack of contact with the local population resulted in the emergence of an immigrant Indian community as a separate part of the Ceylonese permanent population, but at the same time as an unassimilated minority. This had political consequences when Ceylon gradually acquired responsible and elected government under British administration, long before the country became independent in 1948. After independence, the Ceylonese government took several administrative and legislative measures to regulate and control the rights of the Indian population.

The question of the status of Indians in Ceylon became a matter of negotiations between the independent governments of India and Ceylon. Discussions between the two sides in 1947–48 did not yield concrete results. After several years of negotiations, the two countries concluded an agreement in 1964 regarding the status and future of persons of Indian origin in Ceylon, accepting a formula based on what the Ceylonese government considered 'the absorbable maximum' to which it could accord the Indian migrant community citizenship of Ceylon. The island country agreed to accept up to three lakh of the more than nine hundred and seventy-five thousand workers of Indian origin while India agreed to accept five hundred and twenty-five thousand of the migrants as Indian citizens, to be repatriated over a period of fifteen years. In 1974, the two countries agreed to share the remaining one hundred and fifty thousand Indian migrants between them. But the situation changed in 1978 when J.R. Jayewardene was elected president on 4 February and made important changes and developments in the constitutional, political and economic scenes of the country. Discarding the Westminster type of constitution under which the country had functioned since independence, a presidential form of government was ushered in, with vast executive power for the head of the state. The problem of the Tamils continued to elude a solution, but the government isolated the Tamil dominated eastern province by winning the sympathies of the members of parliament from there. By appointing S. Thondaman as the cabinet minister representing the Indian estate workers, the government separated the Indian Tamils from the Ceylon Tamils. However the law and order situation in the north of the country continued to cause anxiety. The local population refused to help police investigations into cases of robbery, bank hold-ups, murders and so on that were perpetrated by young terrorists who styled themselves the Tiger Liberation Movement.

As far as the economy was concerned, Sri Lanka was receiving aid from around the world. A secret report from Colombo in 1981 suggested that the country had received 17,222 million rupees of which 14,246 million was in the form of loans while 2,975 million was from outright grants. Japan had donated 756 million rupees for a hospital while the USA had earmarked Sri Lanka as one of the chosen few in its new private enterprise linked aid package. The USA opened a new office in Colombo known as 'Bureau of Private Enterprises,' which the R&AW suspected was a front for espionage activities. On the face of it, the American bureau was to create a climate for private investment and also assist the American private sector to identify new projects in Sri Lanka and finance them. Agro-business projects and financial intermediaries who could serve as mid-sized entrepreneurs had been identified as the ideal investment opportunities for Americans in Sri Lanka.

But on the security front, Sri Lanka was losing its grip.

Tiger Liberation Movement

Alarmed by increasing terrorism that culminated in the murders of five senior police officials in north Sri Lanka, the government passed two extraordinary laws. The first proscribed the Tiger Liberation Movement and the other authorised the courts to refuse bail to any person accused of committing certain specified offences until the trial had been completed. The debate that ensued after the bills were introduced once again highlighted the antipathies between the Tamils and the Sinhalese.

The Tamil United Liberation Front (TULF) was the dominant voice of the Tamils and it rose to prominence after promising a separate independent state consisting of the predominantly Tamil speaking areas of the northern and eastern provinces in Sri Lanka. However, after elections, the TULF lost its monolithic unity when leaders from the eastern province differed on major issues with the leaders from the northern region.

Jayewardene's government repeatedly promised fair treatment to all communities irrespective of language, race or religion. Against this background M. Canagaratnam, member of parliament from Pottuvil in the eastern province, crossed to the treasury benches. Subsequently an attempt was made on his life, presumably by Tamil terrorists. On 7 September 1978, an hour before the formal promulgation of Sri Lanka's new constitution, the youths of the Tiger Liberation Movement blew up an Avro aircraft belonging to Air Ceylon at Ratmalana airport near Colombo to protest the lack of independence to a Tamil Eelam. The act was allegedly carried out by two Tamil youths who had travelled by the same aircraft from Jaffna.

Anyone suspected of having helped the police was brutally killed by the young terrorists. The TULF officially disowned any responsibility for these violent acts and also declared that they had nothing to do with the terrorist movement. The youth wing of the TULF however, was increasingly restive over the slow pace towards the achievement of an independent Tamil Eelam. Though the senior leadership argued that nothing could be achieved by violence, the young Tamils were impatient. India watched the developments cautiously. In 1978, the Indian High Commission with Thomas Abraham at the helm of affairs had thirty-nine Indian staff and seventy-two locals. On 17 August 1981, an emergency was imposed on the country following violent attacks on Tamils in the estate areas. The emergency lapsed on 16 January 1982. Some pro-Tamil leaders believed that a lasting Eelam could not achieved by fireworks set off in London. In February 1982 the dissidents of the TULF group christened themselves the Tamil

Eelam Liberation Front. The leaders of the group said that the TULF leadership had once craved Eelam but today were slaves of the Sinhalese in parliament. The bitterness between the two groups was so strong that they started targeting each other to assert supremacy. Amid the growing animosity between the Sinhalese and the Tamils, Indian President Sanjiva Reddy visited Sri Lanka between 2 and 7 February 1982. Reddy was the guest of honour at the 34th anniversary celebrations of Sri Lanka's independence held at Anuradhapura. There, the Indian president remarked that prosperity for people of Indian origins lay in the prosperity of their adopted country and he was happy to note that the those who had decided to make Sri Lanka their home were making significant contributions to the country. Reddy said:

> Our two countries have remained close to each other throughout history, sharing a common culture, inheriting a common civilization. We are convinced that these ties which have withstood the vicissitudes of time and foreign rule will grow even stronger in the years to come.

Just a week after Reddy's visit, on 13 February, the Tigers allegedly shot an army driver in the north of the island, threatening the fragile peace in the region. The official statement issued by the Sri Lankan government said the objective of the terrorists had been to provoke the security personnel stationed in Jaffna to retaliate and to cause further estrangement between the army and the public. Although the Sri Lankan army had taken special care to prevent souring its relations with the civilian public, there were complaints from political leaders against the rough handling received by Tamil residents during the searches.

Sri Lanka feared that the Indian establishment was training the Tigers. On 1 June 1982, R. Rajasingham, a top intelligence officer in Sri Lanka, said there were about thirty Tigers still at large in India. He told President Jayewardene about the arrest of five Tigers in Madras, now known as Chennai, on 19 May. The Sri Lankan government-controlled newspaper *The Daily Mirror* reported that fringe Tamil groups like the Nava Sama Samaja Party had requested political asylum in India for Tigers like Uma Maheswaran and Prabhakaran.

Phase two of the Tiger Liberation Movement began in July when the pro-Tamil state leaders decided to set up a government abroad. The world Tamil Eelam Convention held in New York on 3 and 4 July was widely considered a diplomatic triumph for the TULF when it passed the resolution to install an interim government on foreign soil. TULF Secretary General A. Amirthalingam made an appeal in New York, requesting the audience not challenge his motives or his bona fides. He said:

> If at any stage I feel that I have lost the confidence of the Tamil people, we would step down and hand over the reins of office to whosoever has the confidence of the Tamils. Tamils should unite in achieving two objectives—first, Tamil territory should be safeguarded and Tamils of other parts of Sri Lanka should be persuaded to settle down in northern and eastern parts of the country. Secondly, Tamils should seek international support for the cause of Eelam.

As the resolution was being made in New York, the Tigers gunned down four policemen at Nelliady in Jaffna, triggering panic in northern Sri Lanka. A newspaper called *The Island* wrote: 'The moment the terrorists strike there is a backlash from the security forces. Official searches and interrogations are combined with acts of harassment and arm-twisting and a howl goes up that the civilian population is being punished for the acts that have been committed by a handful of terrorists.'

As a result of the Nelliady attack, it was decided that patrolling in Jaffna district was to be undertaken jointly by the police and the military. A statement issued by the Sri Lankan security forces on 25 July said that an all-out offensive to wipe out terrorism in the north would be mounted and top priority would be given to flushing out terrorists in Jaffna.

A report dated 11 August 1982 said: 'Parcels of explosives have been found in railway wagons and carriages—some of these parcel bombs have been addressed to Ministers in the government, such as the Minister of Home Affairs and Minister of Posts and Telegraphs, as well as top police officers.'

On 27 August, Jayewardene sought a mandate from the people through a presidential election. Tamil leaders, however, were wary of the president's move. Speaking in Trincomalee on 30 August, TULF president M. Sivasithamparam said: 'Tamils have no interest in the Presidential election because it will be a poll to elect a person who will rule Sinhala people in a Sinhala country. The Tamils have no interest in the election of a Sinhala ruler.' He defended TULF's dialogue with the government and said that Tamils were being harassed and had no alternative but to complain to the president of the country.

'Three million people were massacred during the independence struggle in Bangladesh. A similar sacrifice could not be made here because then there would be no Tamils left to form Eelam. It is therefore the desire of the TULF to ensure the safety of Tamils while fighting for Eelam,' he said. A. Amirthalingam said that he had spoken to Tamil Nadu Chief Minister M.G. Ramachandran to ensure better protection for the Sri Lankan Tamil youths who had been arrested there recently and disclosed that the discussions had been successful. 'Tigers are in safe hands,' Amirthalingam told the Tamil population.

A TULF spokesperson said that the fragmentation of the Tamil community was sapping its strength and they were making attempts to tie up with Muslim organisations in the eastern province, comprising districts like Ampara, Batticaloa and Trincomalee. On the question of whether the TULF should contest the election, there were differences of opinion. India's Ministry of External Affairs (MEA) note dated 12 November 1982 said:

> The TULF has not come out particularly well from the Presidential elections with its call for boycott being ignored to a very great extent. If the hold of TULF, which is currently moderate in its leadership, slips then one cannot discount a further fillip to extra constitutional activities by the Jaffna Tamils.

Nevertheless, Sri Lanka went to the polls on 20 October to elect an executive president and Jayewardene won an outright majority with 52.91 per cent of the votes cast. Indian analysts believed the Tamil factor was also responsible for Jayewardene's victory. Approximately two hundred and eighty thousand Tamils were registered as voters. The Ceylon Workers Congress, the largest organisation representing plantation labour, threw its weight behind Jayewardene. He also benefitted because TULF, which represented the Sri Lankan Tamils who constituted about eleven per cent of the population, had decided to boycott the polls. Despite TULF's decision, the voter turnout in Jaffna was as high as 46 per cent.

Indian government spies closely monitored global dynamics that might have a bearing on Indian security. A note prepared by the MEA's analysis unit said:

> The security environment around India has undergone a considerable change in the last one year. It is a matter of great concern to us that the change effected has been negative in so far as it has enhanced tensions, aggravated insecurity and heightened the possibility of global conflagration. Several regions of the world of particular interest to India are already embroiled in conflict: Afghanistan, Iraq, and Lebanon etc. The rivalry between superpowers has become more intense.

The mushrooming of the area of tension around the world with large-scale induction of US arms is a fall-out of the confrontationist policies advocated by the Ronald Reagan administration and aimed at stemming what it perceives as the progressively enlarging Soviet sphere of influence and its determination to negotiate from a position of strength. The main cause for concern for India is the spectre of big power conflicts near our thresholds, which could embroil the country in a hot war by proxy or envelope it in the freezing embrace of cold war. The confrontationist US policies and the corresponding riposte of the Soviet Union have dealt a severe blow to détente between the superpowers. Attitudes towards détente and disarmament have been hypocritical and discriminatory and attempts to achieve the end halfhearted and deceptive. The arms aid policy of the Regan administration marks a shift from the previous US policy in that it does not take into consideration the human rights aspect. The sole criterion for a country to be entitled to US arms assistance is its friendliness to the US and its subscribing to its strategic obligations. Subject to these criteria, the US government has made it explicit that its arms sales policy would not suffer any limitations and that arms transfers to friends and allies complement US security commitment and serve important political objectives. The US on its part has made it known that its policy of economic assistance to third world nations will be linked to US political and foreign policy objectives. Even food aid is made conditional on these factors. Such a linkage will spill into the third world the rivalries and tensions of the big powers and is a negative factor. The international situation both economic and political in our region is made worse by military conflicts. In such an environment, while we need to exercise moderation and keep our options towards various possible developments open, we must, in the final analysis, depend on our own political, military and economic strength while making sure that the demands on our security do not gather from more than one front at a time.

An MEA note said that in 1982, the Indian government was a little cautious about openly supporting the Tamil cause.

> A minor, if sometimes intense, irritant has been the demand of Sri Lankan Tamils for Tamil Eelam—a separate Tamil state in Sri Lanka. Though the moderate Tamil leadership, led by the TULF, has been willing to go along with Jayewardene's reforms to usher in greater regional autonomy, the hardline Tamils have taken the view that they should fight for a separate state. The government of India's position on this question has been unequivocal. We have scrupulously treated this as an internal problem for Sri Lanka to resolve. In view of the recent political agitation within Tamil Nadu on this question the Indian government would have to take even greater care that it is in no way perceived by the Sri Lankans as endorsing the separatist movement. Any ambivalence on this score would not only undercut Jayewardene's position and weaken his hands vis-à-vis the hardliners within his own party and Sinhalese chauvinist groups in general but would also affect the overall tenor of our relations with Sri Lanka.

The MEA believed that relations with Sri Lanka would continue on an even keel and at the moment no major problems existed. The only outstanding problem, it believed, was the question of stateless persons of Indian origin, as a certain number of persons who were to be covered under the agreements signed in 1978 still remained stateless.

In 1983, the R&AW trained and financed Prabhakaran's LTTE that was fighting the Sri Lankan government in the north and east of the island to establish a separate Tamil state. Prabhakaran, then 31, was authoritarian. He headed the insurgent force of three thousand cadres which sought to portray itself as a guardian of the Tamil interest in Sri Lanka. CIA intelligence operatives believed that the most important Indian aid was the grant of sanctuary in Tamil Nadu to train the insurgents and maintain a smuggling operation to finance terror activities. The American agency also remarked that each main Tamil insurgent group of Sri Lanka enjoyed close ties to ministers in the Tamil Nadu state government. The Americans were wary of extending support to the Sri Lankan government against the Tigers, as they believed India had invested heavily in brokering peace between the Tamils and Sri Lanka. It maintained however, that New Delhi's policy under the leadership of Indira Gandhi to provide arms and sanctuary to Tamil insurgents was becoming futile. A CIA report said:

> Prime Minister Indira Gandhi believes ethnic violence in Sri Lanka can have serious repercussions for India as well as her own political future. We believe New Delhi seeks stability in Sri Lanka and at the same time is under pressure from the Tamils in the Indian state of Tamil Nadu to protect Sri Lankan Tamils. Although Prime Minister Gandhi has used her good offices to bring together representatives of the Tamil separatists and the central government, New Delhi is also granting sanctuary to Sri Lankan Tamil insurgents in Tamil Nadu and has permitted the creation of numerous training camps near New Delhi, Madras and elsewhere in the country. We believe New Delhi's support for Sri Lanka's Tamil separatists probably is an effort to control a movement it cannot eradicate. Gandhi cannot move against Sri Lankan Tamils in Tamil Nadu without risking the loss of Indian Tamil voters in the election. Moreover, New Delhi sees its involvement with Tamil insurgents as an important adjunct to India's diplomatic and military options. Gandhi wants to forestall intervention in Sri Lanka by the superpowers. Indian officials reacted with dismay last summer after hearing of Sri Lanka's thinly veiled pleas for security help from several countries, including Pakistan, Bangladesh, the United Kingdom and the United States. Sri Lanka's Foreign Minister had asked for US support for the Jayewardene government, including weapons, training in anti-guerrilla techniques, and

> a show of force by the US Navy. Washington rejected each of these suggestions, and Jayewardene subsequently denied ever having made them. The likelihood of peaceful resolution of the tensions that divide Sri Lankan society is rapidly diminishing. Younger and more militant communal leaders of both the communities, raised in a post-colonial atmosphere emphasizing ethnic differences, are less ready to compromise and more prone to violence.

Faridi said the American intelligence was right. We had high stakes involved in Sri Lankan affairs. Indira and subsequently Rajiv Gandhi would not have imagined letting go of this massive investment in regional dominance. Rajiv Gandhi, Faridi clarified, was not very confident about a separate Tamil state in Sri Lanka and during the discussions with then R&AW chief Girish Chandra Saxena, he made it clear that India should act like a negotiator but maintain its leverage over the Sri Lankan government and Tamil groups.

The R&AW was also unhappy over the growing relationship of Sri Lanka with Pakistan and China in its quest for arms and ammunition. The Jayewardene government had quietly forged ties with the two countries India was most uncomfortable with. The spies believed that the1987 peace accord with Sri Lanka to end the violence though non-military means was an effort to neutralise Islamabad's and Beijing's growing influence in the island nation. While playing peacemaker in 1987, India also helped insurgent groups including the LTTE to set up Tamil peace societies in Moscow, East Germany, Singapore, Cambodia and Cuba with the help of the KGB, the Soviet intelligence agency. These organisations were primarily used to channel funds and carry out propaganda in support of a separate Tamil state as demanded by insurgents and moderate Tamil groups.

The growth of Singapore into a centre for the entire southeast Asian region had attracted a large number of Indian migrants, mostly from the merchant communities. While the Parsis, Punjabis, Marwaris and Bengalis were mostly engaged in wholesale and import-export trade, there was also a large number of South Indians mainly engaged in retail. Singapore, as one of the few well developed urban centres of Malaya, had an Indian population constituting between seven and nine per cent of the total population. With the help of the R&AW, the LTTE managed to recruit several assets in the region. A US embassy cable of 1987 later made public by Wikileaks said the LTTE at that time was indisputably the predominant Tamil separatist organisation, having cowed rival militant groups, supplanted the moderate groups as the leading political light of the Tamil cause, slipped the bonds of Indian tutelage and established a functioning, even though limited, civil administration in territory under their control. Prabhakaran had returned to Jaffna after three years of exile in Tamil Nadu and revamped the politico-military structure of the group. The cable said:

> LTTE has divided the north and East into 5 regional command structures, each with an overall regional commander who reports directly to Prabhakaran. Each of the 5 regions is further subdivided into smaller areas, with a designated local leader, who reports to the regional commander. The 5 regions were Jaffna, Mannar, Vavuniya, Trincomalee and Batticaloa. The number 5 is considered to be very lucky in Tamil Nadu mythology, and one military contact says Prabhakaran set up 5 regional commands for this reason. The LTTE operational command structure is highly centralised and is dominated by Prabhakaran. Jaffna plays the key role overall, both because of the LTTE control and freedom of operation there, as well as the fact that Jaffna Tamils dominate the LTTE's ranks. The tigers run a sophisticated radio communication network between the regional commands and Jaffna, a system which many claim is a primary reason for the LTTE's centralised

> coordination, discipline and effectiveness. The regional commanders establish and maintain their authority by means of strict control of all munitions and supplies distributed through the LTTE structure. Sub-regional commanders have guns, ammo, and other supplies doled out to them by the regional commanders. One Police contact claimed that the substantial ransom collections made by the LTTE are all immediately sent back to Jaffna for later distribution for the whole organisation as Prabhakaran sees fit. Everyone is required to take an oath of allegiance to Prabhakaran. The regional leaders are handpicked by Prabhakaran himself on the basis of trust, loyalty and experience.

Faridi explained how the R&AW balanced India's need to support both the Tamil insurgents and the Sri Lankan government. 'We provided the LTTE with missiles like the SA-7 just before the peace accord was signed, but avoided arming them with more sophisticated weapons,' he said. 'However, we received regular intelligence inputs that LTTE assets abroad had managed to establish links with the international arms market to procure advanced weaponry. At one point in 1986 we received real time intelligence that arms dealers with links to the Soviet Union were supplying weapons to the eastern provinces. It was actionable intelligence, but we took a conscious decision to keep alive the illegal supply route to maintain balance as the Sri Lankan air force had increased attacks on LTTE's suspected armouries and the ultras were desperate to retaliate.'

In those tense days of the cold war, the US and the Soviet Union played out their relationship via hostile interventions in countries that could easily be manoeuvered. A secret note said:

> Any balanced account of the events in the last decade would concede that the Soviet Union took advantage of the post Vietnam political problems in the US to make a series of moves, particularly in Africa and Asia, which gave them major political

> advantages. Yet to see the Soviet hand in all anti-American developments, whether in Africa, South East Asia or Central America, is a deliberately simplistic analysis of International reality. The Ethiopian revolution or the defeat of the Portuguese colonialism in Southern Africa were determined more by the indigenous developments in those countries than by Soviet instigation. The major question, now, is whether and how long the mood of confrontation, which has produced the largest US defence budget in history, would last. It is argued, not without reason, that the internal logic of US President Ronald Reagan's economic policies would eventually defeat the very objective of these policies. While the ability of the Soviet society to accept hardships in the face of external threats is far superior to that of the US, this is to an extent compensated by the limited resources which the Soviet economy would be able to muster as against that of the United States. Thus is the balance between the relative strength of the two superpowers' economies, which is compensated by their inverse ability to make sacrifices, to determine the course of international events in the decade. On both sides there have been groups, which have argued publicly against a return to the limited understanding of the early 70s. Yet it would be reasonable to expect that for all the inherent contradictions between these two powers, in the long run eventually a return to a limited understanding in inevitable.

The Indian spies were also worried about Chinese covert interference in Sri Lanka with the help of the US as the two countries were coming closer. China's value as an ally to the US in its anti-Soviet crusade had earned it the qualification of a friendly country entitled to the US export of lethal weapons and the privilege of the exchange of strategic intelligence on a global scale. The intimacy of the China-US relationship was reflected in the permission accorded by the Chinese in 1981 to the US to set up a joint surveillance facility, manned by Chinese technicians, at Xinziang near the China-Soviet frontier. The China-US differences over the Taiwan issue, to which China was very sensitive, was somewhat smoothened with the announcement in August 1982 that American arms sales to Taiwan would be reduced collectively and quantitatively and finally stopped within a fixed but unspecified period. This growing partnership was a cause of concern to South Asian countries. India had taken cognisance of this cooperation since it had the potential of adversely affecting its hold over neighbouring countries. The Chinese obsession with Soviet hegemonies had prompted the country to reiterate its desire to improve relations with South Asian countries and that was the thrust of the Chinese premier Zhao Ziyang's visit to South Asian countries. The Chinese approach towards the third world was a clear desire on Beijing's part to appear not merely a friend and ally but a full-fledged member of the third world.

Citing several reports, Pawan Arora said the situation around the globe, especially in East Germany, Afghanistan, Angola, Mozambique and Cuba, kept the major players away from Sri Lanka to an extent. The Russian view, Arora said, was to extend limited help to the LTTE covertly, not any kind of ideological support for a separate Eelam in public. On the other hand, the Sri Lankan government's foreign policy thrust was to secure maximum assistance from the West for economic development. Economic difficulties had forced Sri Lanka to formally apply for membership of the Association of South East Nations (ASEAN). Because of its pro-West posture and its approval to the Coast Corporation of America for the set up of an oil storage terminal at Triconamalee, this was a serious concern to India and the Indians decided to silently oppose the terminal project.

Though he cited foreign intelligence analysts, Arora made it clear that India's policy in Sri Lanka was not feasible. He argued that the Indian military intervention lacked foresight and that fighting a guerrilla war in foreign terrain was a big mistake. In a situation like Sri Lanka where stability was important for a peaceful neighbourhood, insurgency was not a viable option, he said. While the situation definitely provided India with a certain advantage in establishing strongholds in Sri Lanka, we had to pay a heavy price for it when, years later, the LTTE assassinated Rajiv Gandhi. The CIA had said:

> There are two possible scenarios. In the more likely scenario, the Sri Lankan military's increased training and experience in counterinsurgency would eventually yield significant gains against insurgent strongholds and stem the rate of terrorist attacks in Colombo. Under these circumstances, President Jayewardene would be more likely to offer concessions on Tamil autonomy—including greater provincial control of police forces and land settlement policies—and negotiate a settlement with some Tamil groups. An Indian crackdown would not be sufficient to contain LTTE. We believe LTTE could re-establish its operational headquarters and training camps on the Jaffna peninsula within several weeks and would absorb members from other groups. The crackdown would probably force LTTE to seek additional funding from narcotics trafficking as well as possible increased training from abroad. In the second scenario, LTTE could use its assets among radical Sinhalese Marxists and its own disciplined ranks to terrorize Sinhalese urban centres, target foreign facilities and personnel, and cripple transportation links and economic installations including tea estates. We believe an Indian military intervention could cripple Sri Lanka's prospects for maintaining a multi-party democracy. Widespread LTTE attacks in the Eastern province could bring Sri Lanka's 1 million Muslims directly into conflict with Tamil civilians, accelerating the collapse of civil order. An Indian troop presence in Sri Lanka would underscore the weakness of the Colombo government, deterring foreign investment and making Sri Lanka militarily, politically, and economically dependent on India.

The CIA assessment was also prophetic about Indian army operations inside Sri Lanka, suggesting that the Indians would be ill prepared for the insurgency in the island nation. The assessment said:

> Indian army has gained some counter-insurgency experience in operations against tribal separatists in India's north-eastern states. In Sri Lanka, however, it would be a foreign presence not tolerated by an armed, organized enemy—Sinhalese or Tamil. Indian conventional forces trying to hold territory and maintain peace would be a welcome change for Colombo's military. If New Delhi continued to oppose a separate Tamil state, we believe Tamil insurgents would resist the Indians as they now do the Sinhalese. In our view, if Indian intervention were not soon followed by a settlement between Colombo and the insurgents, violence would again flare between the Island's communities, but this time with Indian forces caught in the middle.

Most Disastrous Spy Operation and Saving Grace

Sri Lanka remains one of the R&AW's most disastrous espionage operations ever. The political decisions to first support the insurgents and subsequently turn the guns against them had little gains for India besides holding onto influence in the neighbouring country for a few decades. The spies believe India's reaction in 1983 had been appropriate when the decision to support the insurgents was taken, as the country could not remain unmoved by atrocities against ethnic Tamils. But the battle was too long and arduous. Sustaining a covert operation for more than two decades doubled the danger. Plus, international community pressure was clear—terrorism in Sri Lanka must stop. The UPA thus gave its support to Mahinda Rajapaksa and so did its ally, the DMK, and Tamil Nadu Chief Minister M. Karunanidhi.

Any debate over the DMK's support to Rajapaksa against the LTTE was clarified by a US embassy cable dated 27 October 2008 titled 'Karunanidhi concern mostly political theatrics,' based on a conversation between the US ambassador to Sri Lanka and the Sri Lankan president. The cable said:

> Ambassador asked for the President's views on how far he expected Tamil Nadu Chief Minister Karunanidhi to press the Indian government on Sri Lanka. The President responded that Karunanidhi's recent tough line was mostly to keep his opponents in Tamil Nadu off balance. Rajapaksa even admitted he had received word from Karunanidhi that as long as Sri Lanka took care of the civilians, spoke of a political solution and did not criticize Karunanidhi, he would be satisfied. With fewer demands from Tamil Nadu, continued good humanitarian resupply, and care for low civilian casualties, President Rajapaksa thought he would likewise be able to keep the Indian government happy.

Around the same time, Mahinda Rajapaksa sent his younger brother Basil Rajapaksa to New Delhi as a special envoy. It was a political gesture and India conveyed its concerns over the humanitarian situation in the northern part of Sri Lanka, especially the civilians and internally displaced persons caught in the crossfire. In the background, Sri Lanka knew the power of the R&AW and under the cover of the civil war, they covertly worked to neutralise the spy agency's influence and network.

Avinash said that between 2006 and 2009 when Sri Lanka waged an all-out war against the Tigers, a Tamil boat owner and a maid were the R&AW's only effective arsenal in the island nation. There is no single documented account of Operation Satori carried out with the help of an Indian maid named Sundari. The fifty-five-year-old Tamil and Sinhalese speaking woman worked to rescue and evacuate R&AW sources when the Indian spy agency stopped personal meetings with local informers to ensure their safety.

Avinash said: 'We were scrambling to find innovative means to communicate with our informers and assets caught in the crossfire when one officer suddenly looked at Sundari, who was serving us tea. The most frightening aspect of the operation was to maintain utmost secrecy about the movements of the assets, which were more or less banned. We had to save the assets from both sides and also assess the strengths and weaknesses of the intelligence services of Sri Lanka and the LTTE's espionage network to carry out the operation.'

The government had restricted the movements of people in the battle zone and assets were stranded. Informers were being hunted by both the Sri Lankan government and the Tamil Tigers. The LTTE espionage network was quite strong and there was a standing order that any leader leaving the battle zone must be shot dead. Although the R&AW knew the weaknesses of Sri Lankan intelligence, they realised that Rajapaksa's spies were also keeping an eye on the northern and eastern provinces, scouting for prize catches. Within a week fictitious papers were arranged for Sundari through Kosala that would allow her to travel inside the battle zone freely to help the badly wounded in their makeshift hospitals. There was hopelessness and misery all around Jaffna and Sundari was trained to deal with this anxiety while on her rescue missions.

Sundari was pivotal to Operation Satori. Though she was not a conventional spy, she was a thorough professional. With the help of Asanka, an ambulance driver, and Ramanuj, an animal activist, she managed to rescue several leaders who were R&AW recruits and thus on Gotabaya Rajapaksa's hitlist. On the one hand, the R&AW was providing satellite imagery to the Sri Lankan army to help neutralise the LTTE, and on the other hand, Sundari, Asanka and Ramanuj had the task of evacuating Indian informers and political assets from Jaffna. The area where Sundari operated was darkened via PhotoShop before images were shared with the Sri Lankan army and its intelligence unit, and Kosala had bribed certain senior personnel in the army so that people could safely be smuggled out of the war zone. Avinash, Kosala's official handler, provided reports of the evacuation to Indian spies stationed in Singapore, Cambodia, Maldives and New Delhi. Although Avinash had dark thoughts about Gotabaya Rajapaksa and his scheming followers, he believed the Indian network with Kosala's help would save the day.

'Gotabaya had the unique distinction of torturing those he considered the enemy, including suspected informers. We had never witnessed such brutal killings in our careers,' Arora told me.

As an ambulance driver, Asanka witnessed dangerous and dirty games orchestrated by political leaders. In 2006, when the war started, he had been involved in rescue operations in the southern provinces, where the Sri Lankan Air Force kept LTTE targets to keep the Sinhalese population happy. A Sinhalese himself, Asanka knew human rights violations were a reality and that Mahinda Rajapaksa's assurances that his forces were trained to prioritise human rights were merely lip service. He was privately furious but continued to work in the army's medical unit, waiting for a day of redemption.

Sundari and her team let the rescued assets and leaders know that Gotabaya Rajapaksa was targeting them and that their evacuation was being done in complete secrecy. According to Arora, Mahinda Rajapaksa claimed on several occasions that his intelligence operatives had accurate information about Prabhakaran's whereabouts but in reality they were dependent on Indian sources to supply information about the Tigers' positions.

The guns fell silent in May 2009 and Rajapaksa announced the victory in parliament on 19 May. Although he announced development programmes for the Tamil and Muslim minorities, he also said that the Tamils had been reduced to misery by the LTTE's terrorism and the Tamil diaspora that supported the insurgents must stop such assistance for a separate Eelam. In Rajapaksa's view, the victory of the Sri Lankan army in the civil war was in fact the victory of the Tamil people, as they had gained nothing from the years of bloody war. He argued that the LTTE had falsely promised Sri Lankan Tamils a separate autonomous state via terror activities against the government. This stalled development in LTTE dominated areas and the large Tamil population had had to suffer because of that. In his view Tamils were victims of the insurgency and the victory would ensure that they became part of mainstream society.

Rajapaksa knew the international community was readying itself to criticise the Sri Lankan army for war crimes and he launched a major offensive immediately after the Sri Lankan television channels beamed images of Prabhakaran's dead body. Without naming any particular country, Rajapaksa said Sri Lanka had cared for and sustained all its people, including the Tamils, throughout the two decades of the LTTE's violence and terrorism and he needed no advice on better treatment for the Tamils.

According to Arora, in April 2009, before Prabhakaran was killed, India had requested the Sri Lankan government to stop the attacks on LTTE strongholds. National Security Advisor M.K. Narayanan and Foreign Secretary Shivshankar Menon had travelled to Colombo on 24 April, focused on ensuring the cessation of the war on the Tigers. Their visit coincided with the Sri Lankan army's operation in Mullaitivu. The army's intention was to capture Prabhakaran alive. Narayanan promised Rajapaksa that India had plans to provide assistance and rebuild Sri Lanka's strife-torn regions after the end of the war. In return, Rajapaksa promised to silence the guns, but he did not do so till his army chief Sarath Fonseka confirmed that Prabhakaran and thirty of his trusted aides were dead. After the war ended in May, Gotabaya Rajapaksa claimed that the LTTE had developed a strong base in Eritrea, complete with boat-building operations, and that LTTE operatives had employed middlemen in India, Philippines, Thailand and Malaysia. He also admitted to some diplomats that the R&AW had supplied information on suspects infiltrating Sri Lanka and that Sri Lanka had carried out a few operations with the help of the Indian spy agency. This was enough to show the deep relationship between the two countries and the sharing of actionable inputs with each other.

Arora argued that while the UPA government invested the maximum in Mahinda Rajapaksa, it was only able to extract the minimum. The Indian mission in Colombo after the civil war had become completely ineffective and inefficient in maintaining a hold over the Sri Lankan government. A top official of the Indian embassy was in fact leaking information harvested by the R&AW and he could only be removed after persistent protests by K.C. Verma, the then spy chief. His predecessor, Ashok Chaturvedi, had not been very interested in Sri Lanka, but Verma wanted to keep the island nation in the R&AW's control. The agency had warned of growing Chinese penetration but the Indian diplomats were busy elsewhere. Sometime in 2010, the diplomats' indifference towards the Chinese presence in Sri Lanka triggered a storm in New Delhi. The Chinese were about to grab a mega contract to build massive highways in the country, but the Indian diplomats were certain Colombo would ultimately pass on the contract to the Indians. A document revealing the contract was faxed to the Prime Minister's Office (PMO) by a R&AW agent when a delegation from the MEA was meeting Prime Minister Manmohan Singh. Foreign Secretary Nirupama Rao was furious and pulled up the officials posted in Colombo. The UPA had returned to power a year earlier and Prime Minister Manmohan Singh told Rajapaksa that his victory in Sri Lanka's January 2010 elections provided a historic opportunity for the country's leaders to address all outstanding issues in a spirit of understanding and mutual accommodation and to work towards genuine national reconciliation. Rajapaksa expressed appreciation for India's substantial and generous assistance including a grant of five hundred crore rupees for the humanitarian relief, rehabilitation and resettlement of Internally Displaced Persons (IDPs) and assured Singh about the rapid and sustainable resettlement of the bulk of the IDPs. Though polite words flowed from both sides, the R&AW spies knew the relationship between the two countries was not as cosy as it appeared in the beautiful pictures immortalised at Hyderabad House in New Delhi. Rajapaksa was coldly cunning and was flirting with China and Pakistan to counter India. The R&AW was aware that Rajapaksa would land in Beijing within no time to start a renewed relationship with the Chinese.

Now the RA&W agents began to enquire in Beijing and Islamabad about Colombo's plan. The liaison unit, working with friendly foreign intelligence agencies, reported that China had secretly provided arms and ammunition to the Sri Lankan army during the civil war and was now ready to invest more than $2 billion in Sri Lanka. The civil war had provided Beijing with an opportunity to considerably expand its footprint in Sri Lanka. China had not only provided fighter jets to the Sri Lankan army, it had also trained the pilots with the help of Islamabad.

Avinash said: 'When we warned the India foreign service about the Chinese, a senior officer told me not to worry. Let the China build the roads, he said, and we will ply our buses on those roads. When we complained about him, he was immediately removed and shifted to some insignificant position at the Delhi headquarters.'

The officer codenamed 'PAS' was fond of scotch and the Indian spies had reported on various occasions that he was more interested in attending high-spirit parties than protecting and preserving India's interests in Sri Lanka. 'Once he was trapped by our spies and subsequently confronted with the evidence, we wanted him out of Sri Lanka. He was a compromised man,' Avinash said, quoting a report that the R&AW had ciphered to New Delhi.

In January 2012, the then foreign minister, S.M. Krishna, landed in Colombo to strengthen ties with Sri Lanka and announce enhanced cooperation as a counterweight to China. He also handed over the first lot of housing units at Ariyalai and Jaffna and visited Galle in southern Sri Lanka where he inaugurated a segment of the Southern Railway Project implemented under the Line of Credit extended by India. But it was too late. The Chinese had already started massive operations in Sri Lanka.

LTTE 2:0?

What will emerge from the ashes in Jaffna? The regrouping of the LTTE and a renewed uprising against the Sri Lankan government? The spies who have been monitoring the situation in Sri Lanka and LTTE's remnants in foreign countries believe LTTE 2:0 is a possibility, though on a smaller scale. Since the insurgent organisation's elements are active in Singapore, Cambodia, Canada and coastal areas of Tamil Nadu, they may generate psychological warfare for a Tamil Eelam but not enough to pose a threat to Sri Lanka's internal security. After the elimination of Prabhakaran and the arrests of approximately twelve thousand LTTE cadres, there were whispers that the Tigers' movement may emerge from Cambodia and Canada with Singapore based sympathisers providing much needed financial help for the guerrillas.

A spy codenamed Ajeet Shah travelled to Cambodia in 2015. He was a seasoned operative and had closely monitored the massive purging of the LTTE's leaders after the civil war. Some LTTE remnants, which were settled in the southeast Asian country, were making efforts to start a new life, though the schools they ran taught children about the lost nation of the Tamil Eelam. Shah said the LTTE had become history and within six years of its complete annihilation in Sri Lanka, it was now merely part of textbooks.

'They are not capable of engineering an uprising. The attempt is to keep the Tamil Eelam issue alive socially and politically. These elements are no real threat to Sri Lanka,' Shah told me.

Politically, there is a strong international lobby known as the Transnational Government of Tamil Eelam (TGTE) which aims to win freedom for Tamils on the basis of the fundamental political principles of nationhood, homeland and right of self-determination. The group operates from New York and claims to fight for justice for the Tamil population in the north and east parts of Sri Lanka, including punishment for those who committed genocide, war crimes and crimes against humanity. Formed after the 2009 civil war, the TGTE is a democratically elected government of a million strong Tamils from the island of Sri Lanka living in several countries around the world. According to one of its publications, 'TGTE twice held internationally supervised elections among Tamils around the world to elect 132 Members of Parliament. It has a bicameral legislature and a Cabinet. It held its Parliamentary sittings among other places in the British and French Parliaments. The Constitution of the TGTE mandates that it should realize its political objective only through peaceful means. The Prime Minister of TGTE is Visuvanathan Rudrakumaran, a New York based lawyer.'

Shah said the TGTE works as a pressure group demanding justice for atrocities committed by Mahinda Rajapaksa and his government against Tamils between 2006 and 2009. At best, the hardcore elements among the remnants of the LTTE could become irritants involved in low-level operations. But they may never dominate a territory again.

5

SHADOWY WAR IN WASHINGTON

One fine spring morning in 1988, Dinesh Mathur slammed shut the door of his Georgetown residence and rushed towards a waiting taxi. He needed to get to a very urgent meeting in Wesley Heights, just two and half miles away. Luckily the driver was South Asian because, lost in his thoughts, Mathur spoke to him in Hindi.

Within ten minutes he was at the Methodist Church in Wesley Heights, the place his friend had recommended for their meeting. As he paid the cabbie, Sartaj Singh, standing quietly at the street corner, waved to him. Mathur grinned. Finally, his most daring operation in the USA would begin.

At thirty-eight, Mathur had been a R&AW operative for almost a decade, travelling across the world to carry out the tasks assigned by his bosses. His ability to infiltrate unknown territories in foreign lands, track down targets and sniff out information without inviting attention seemed almost inborn. He was straightforward, avoided using the jargon of espionage and had a knack for thinking on his feet that made him one of the agency's most revered figures. On his arrival in Washington that January, Mathur's first task was to track down Jagjit Singh Chohan, a former Punjab politician and the face of the Khalistan movement abroad since the 1970s.

Sartaj, a long time R&AW informer, had been horrified when Mathur asked him to set up a meeting with Chohan. He warned Mathur that it would be a bad idea for him to openly meet the fifty-nine-year-old militant leader who had a free run in the USA and was famous for his ruthlessness. But Mathur did not care about possible personal repercussions. Washington was becoming a haven for fleeing Sikh militant leaders and Mathur had been told by his bosses to make direct contact with them without concealing his identity. In an operation where no cover is provided, the risks are great.

Mathur patiently waited for two months before Chohan agreed to meet him. When Sartaj finally phoned him that morning, it had been out of the blue. Mathur had not planned his agenda for the meeting and the prospect of a disaster shadowed his thoughts.

When Mathur and Sartaj were ushered to the drawing room where Chohan was sitting on a corner sofa, surrounded by armed bodyguards, he noticed a sardonic expression on the militant leader's face. Sartaj was expressionless.

'Kaka, this is Dinesh Mathur. He wanted to see you,' Sartaj said.

'I don't understand why you want to see me. I am the most wanted enemy of your country,' Chohan said after Mathur had been seated.

'Your country too, sir,' Mathur replied warmly.

'It is not my country. I promise you, there will be a Khalistan within a year and that will be my country. We will defeat you and free Punjab from India and Sikhs will rule a prosperous Khalistan together,' Chohan smiled.

Mathur laughed. 'You will not be able to do that,' he said, trying to quell the sarcasm in the tone of his voice.

'How can you say that?'Chohan said.

'Because Sikhs are patriots and they will not side with Pakistan. I have Sikh friends and I trust they will never leave me,' Mathur said passionately.

'And what about the atrocities you committed on our community?' Chohan asked angrily.

'Sir, I don't want to get into history and debate on issues. But I can tell you that you will not be able to sustain this violence for long,' Mathur said.

'What do you mean?' Chohan was highly displeased.

'Sir, I came here with a request to stop this violence and all militant activities in India. Innocents are dying. I also want to tell you that Pakistan is not your friend. They are using you as a weapon to bleed our country,' Mathur said softly but firmly.

The conversation continued for more than half an hour. Chohan boasted to Mathur about the support for Khalistan from more than twenty lakh Sikhs settled in countries like the UK, the USA and Canada. These internationally-located pro-Khalistan groups, he said, managed to maintain close contacts with militant cadres in India. Sikhs in the USA, Thailand and West Germany had also set up financial hubs and safe houses to continue the operation till the goal was achieved, he said.

'We already have a republic of Khalistan abroad and not just one organisation but hundreds are working together,' said Chohan. 'Here in Washington we have a strong network working closely with the US government to achieve an independent Sikh state. And don't forget, I am capable of launching attacks anywhere in India from right here in this house. Don't forget what we did in 1986 against the policeman who tried to counter us.'

For a moment, Mathur was puzzled, but he quickly remembered the assassination attempt on Punjab's director general of police, Julio Ribeiro, in which serving policemen were alleged to have been involved. They had been brainwashed, recruited and trained to penetrate a highly secure police compound to carry out the attack. Ribeiro survived but the event made headlines worldwide. Pro-Khalistan groups based abroad wasted no time to use the attack as a propaganda tool to generate more funds and cannon fodder for the militants.

'Things are changing, Chohan sahib. Please give peace a chance,' Mathur said.

'It was nice meeting you, Mathur,' Chohan said abruptly, indicating that the meeting was over.

Years later, recalling the encounter at a quiet café in Delhi, Mathur told me he had been nervous before the meeting but as he left the building, he realised that a man running a militant campaign from a safe house in Washington was as vulnerable from the inside as any other human being.

'His image of a tough warrior was the creation of propagandists and partly the media. I would not say he was affable, but he was normal. We exchanged phone numbers and promised to keep in touch. For me, the primary task was to convince him to stop playing Pakistan's game and I had a feeling that my first meeting was impressive. The government was working hard to end Sikh militancy and the R&AW's job was to persuade and neutralise the pro-Khalistan elements abroad by any means,' Mathur told me.

Around a week later, Mathur received a call. Jagjit Singh Chohan had something important to share. Rakesh Nagar, a junior R&AW officer who was part of Mathur's team in Washington, made every effort to dissuade him from meeting Chohan again.

'Nagar was really worried. He thought it was a trap to abduct and kill me to grab international headlines. He offered two bodyguards for my security, but I insisted on meeting Chohan alone. I had a feeling that Chohan was powerful and vulnerable at the same time. If I played my games perfectly, Chohan's downfall was imminent,' Mathur said.

The meeting took place at a pre-decided nondescript location. Unarmed and defenseless, Mathur was ushered into the room where Chohan was sitting, protected by his armed bodyguards.

'What is the pressing matter for this urgent meeting,' Mathur asked before taking a seat next to a person who was supposedly one of Chohan's advisors.

'We are going to carry out some attacks in India,' Chohan said in messianic tone.

'Why are you telling me this?'

'Because I think your job as a spy is to collect intelligence about an event and warn security agencies in advance. I am doing you a big favour and you may get some reward.' Chohan was a little amused.

'No, Chohan sahib. I don't need this information. My meeting with you is not about gathering intelligence. It is about a request. At the cost of sounding repetitive, let me ask you again—please stop this terror support to the Khalistan movement. We are Indians first and I must tell you that it will be a great service to all the innocent people of our country. Chohan sahib, mark my words, Pakistan will use and discard you,' Mathur said briskly.

The meeting ended on a sour note. But Mathur was pleased. He had shown Chohan that he was in command of the situation. Of course, he also immediately ciphered the intelligence he had received to New Delhi.

'Some militants were arrested and a terror blast in Delhi was averted due to my report. But my sole intention was to penetrate Chohan's terror haven and not pick up the pieces of intelligence he was deliberately throwing at me,' Mathur said flatly.

About a month later Sartaj informed Mathur that a person close to Chohan was keen to meet him. His name was Suchcha Singh, said Sartaj, and he was a Canadian citizen of Indian descent. Mathur agreed. They decided to meet at Martin's Tavern in Georgetown for lunch.

When Mathur saw the strongly-built man striding to the table where he and Sartaj were chatting, he was stunned. Suchcha Singh was none other than the man who had sat beside Chohan just a month ago, supposedly one of the leader's key advisors.

'Although I greeted him with a smile when Sartaj introduced us, questions just rained in my head,' Mathur said. 'Was he here as a messenger for Chohan? Why did he want to meet me outside Chohan's orbit? Was this some kind of plan devised by Chohan to lure me into a trap? He had told Sartaj that he had already met me once, though we had not been formally introduced. Now I was looking at the prospect of building a contact inside Chohan's network.'

While Sartaj ordered the food, Suchcha Singh told Mathur in chaste Hindi that he had been impressed with his interaction with Chohan the month before and had been planning to meet him since then. As the conversation continued, Mathur learned more about his surprise guest. Suchcha had been a civil engineer at a private firm in Vancouver when Operation Blue Star, the military operation on the Harmandir Sahib Complex in Amritsar in June 1984, turned his life upside down. He turned naturally towards the Khalistan movement and his educational and professional qualifications catapulted him into Jagjit Singh Chohan's network. In March 1985, he became Chohan's closest advisor. Suchcha's other job was to coordinate and maintain the relationships among the various militant Sikh factions in the USA, the UK and Canada. Between 1985 and 1988, Suchcha planned and executed several operations for the Khalistan movement that included indoctrination, recruitment, fund raising and orchestrating terror in Punjab while sitting safely abroad.

'It felt as though he was sitting in a confession box and that made me a little cautious about his intentions. I listened to him but tried hard not to believe what he was saying. He sounded like a possible defector and just the thought was overwhelming. The prospect of having a mole inside Chohan's operational network was exciting. My only worry was whether this man could give the agency his unswerving loyalty,' Mathur recalled.

Mathur did not realise that Suchcha Singh had already made up his mind to turn and this meeting was the result of weeks of soul scorching introspection about his present and the future.

'"*Mathur sahib, main ghumne nahi aaya, aap ke liye kaam karne aaya hu. Mujhpe bharosa rakhiye* (Mathur sahib, I am not here to sightsee. I want to work for you. Trust me)." I was amazed that he was reading my mind. He was at the top of the Khalistan movement's chain of command and I saw this as a golden opportunity for a ringside view of the militant groups' activities in the West, and the possibility of dismantling them with his help. I was on the edge and needed to make a fast decision. So I asked him bluntly what he could offer me. He smiled and said, anything within his reach. My next question was whether any trained militants were travelling to India this month, or any terror facilitators. He went silent and his face turned red. A few seconds later, he asked for two days' time. When we parted, I prepared myself for the probability that he would not turn up ever again. But I was wrong,' Mathur said.

Exactly two days later Suchcha contacted Sartaj for another meeting. They met at the same restaurant and Suchcha handed him a brown envelope.

'These are the names and photos of people travelling to India this month. They are our guys,' he said calmly.

Mathur couldn't believe his luck. Suchcha had passed the loyalty test. He told Suchcha that Sartaj would be in touch with him soon and they would never again meet at this restaurant. The next day Mathur dispatched the envelope through a diplomatic pouch and waited for good news from Delhi. The security agencies had no records of the suspects provided by Suchcha. Several copies were made and various airports were put on high alert. The intelligence helped arrest at least six militants. They were whisked away from the media glare to an interrogation centre in South Delhi. Mathur was informed that his asset was gold. Suchcha was given a source number in the spy files. He was codenamed Blue Sky.

In the next few months, Suchcha provided not only the names of militants travelling to India but also of financiers of the

Khalistan movement in the US and Canada. He had also revealed the name of a leader who was coordinating with Pakistan's Inter Service Intelligence (ISI) and was said to have a hotline with its chief, Lt. General Hamid Gul. Mathur and Sartaj had pulled off a brilliant coup, which inflicted serious damage to Chohan's network in US.

The Khalistan movement has a long and complex history. In 1966, after the formation of Punjab as a state meant for Punjabi speaking people, political and religious leaders sought more autonomy for the state. The agitation and propaganda remained local till 1970. It became global in 1971 when the Sikh extremist leader Jagjit Singh Chohan called for an independent Punjab that would be called Khalistan, with Nankana Sahib in Pakistan as its capital. Although it received moderate support among the Sikh diaspora, the Sikh leaders in India did not endorse such a move. However, the movement gained momentum among certain sections of the Sikh population in 1972 and 1973 when Pakistan, recovering from their humiliating defeat in the Bangladesh liberation war, started funneling money to Chohan and other leaders to recruit cadres in Punjab in order to wage a war against the Indian establishment. Any separatist movement requires three things—money, arms and publicity. In the late 1970s, Pakistan started shipping guns and explosives to extremists in Punjab while financiers based in foreign countries diverted Pakistani money through the hawala (money-laundering) system to help cadres in the state sustain the movement. The political reverberations of the propaganda in India and abroad generated sympathy and loyalty for the cause among hardcore groups. The Khalistan movement found a local face in 1981 when Jarnail Singh Bhindranwale openly sided with Pakistan to launch an armed revolution for a separate Sikh country. Although the Congress party had nurtured him in the late 1970s, Bhindranwale distanced himself from politics after his transformation as the poster boy of Khalistan. He had a massive following among radicals and was instrumental in killing several influential Hindus, including Lala Jagat Narain, the founder editor of the *Punjab Kesari* newspaper in September 1981. Bhrindanwale was killed in June 1984 during the army assault on the Golden Temple known as Operation Blue Star. His death intensified the Khalistan movement: even moderate Sikhs in India and abroad were angry with government decision to attack a sacred site. Months after Operation Blue Star, the then prime minister of India, Indira Gandhi, was assassinated by her Sikh bodyguards. This was followed by anti-Sikh riots in Delhi and targeted attacks by Khalistani extremists. The biggest attack was mounted in June 1985 when an Air India flight from Toronto to London was bombed, killing 329 passengers.

Desperate times need desperate measures and the R&AW launched a manhunt to track down suspected radicals holed up in the UK, the USA, Canada and other places. Many of these extremist leaders were getting active support from the ISI and the R&AW operatives were directed to choke the supply lines and counter the growth of armed terrorist groups. Despite R&AW efforts, several targeted killings were executed by Sikh extremists in 1986–87 including the killing of Hindus in Hoshiarpur and Mohali. Another objective of the R&AW was to counter the influence of the radical leaders on the younger generations of Sikhs abroad. The Indian intelligence agency analysed the strengths and weaknesses of key figures backing the Khalistan movement before coming up with an operational plan with superb tactics and matchless tradecraft. Today, with real-time digital intelligence, the R&AW has been warned of Sikh extremists abroad who are trying to resume the Khalistan movement by launching a referendum in 2020.

Americans Knew

The R&AW tried to understand why America allowed Khalistani forces to use its soil against India. Mathur said he had once told a Central Intelligence Agency (CIA) officer about Khalistan militants in the US national capital, but was bluntly informed that they were no threat to America. When Mathur provided files on several high profile militants that had been provided by Suchcha Singh, the Americans reluctantly arrested some of them, which Mathur thought was merely a gesture to show that the USA was concerned about terrorist activities in Punjab.

As early as 1971, USA-based R&AW operatives informed the Indian government about increasing activities by the Khalistan movement in the North American continent. These notes were shared with the domestic spy agency, the Intelligence Bureau (IB), which was watching extremists within the country. On 12 October 1971, *The New York Times* carried a half page advertisement captioned 'The Sikhs demand an independent state in India—the only guarantee for peace in the subcontinent.' On 13 October, a R&AW agent sent a coded report to New Delhi. The R&AW note said:

> The Advertisement was issued under the name of Dr. Jagjit Singh Chohan, Former Finance Minister of Punjab and General Secretary Shiromani Akali Dal, whose address was given as Hotel Commodore, New York. The advertisement after tracing the history of the Sikhs alleged: 'A planned racist offensive against Sikhs has been in operation. Their religious places have been defiled and taken.' It further announced that a demonstration would be held in front of the United Nations on Wednesday October 13, 1971 at 11 AM. One Surjit Singh Bhullar from London now on a visit to New York is reported to be working actively for the purpose. He is reported to have promised to incur all expenses in this regard. He further said that just as India was supporting Bangladesh Movement,

> Pakistan would support their demand for an independent nation. Further details are awaited.

The spies watched Chohan and the proposed demonstration. On 14 October 1971, they told New Delhi that it had been a flop. Only half a dozen Sikhs were visible outside the United Nations building and they mainly distributed copies of the advertisement in *The New York Times*. The R&AW officers and Indian diplomats had informally advised leading members of the Sikh community in New York to dissociate themselves from this irresponsible demonstration which was inspired and financed by Pakistan.

This is what Chohan had written in *The New York Times* advertisement:

> The world has been oblivious to the fate of 12 million Sikhs living under political domination in India and in constant fear of genocide. Another 6 million of us live abroad in alienation and exile waiting for the day of deliverance. An independent Sikh state in the Punjab is the only guarantee for peace in the sub-continent. This is a fact, which the United Nations must recognize. An independent Sikh state will act as a buffer between India and Pakistan. It will be a restraining influence on the two countries. It is the only solution, which can prevent a holocaust on the sub-continent. There will always be a Sikh nation. There always has been. Let the Hindu rulers in Delhi understand this because if they persist in their treachery and deceit, the sub continent will be engulfed in a war the like of which the world has never seen. The clock has come full circle. No longer can we wait in silence for the Indian government to wipe us out. We have decided to rise and proclaim to the world that we are an undivided nation prepared to fight till the bitter end for an independent Sikh homeland in India.

Days later, on 18 October 1971, an intelligence report from Washington said Pakistani agents were pursuing and persuading thousands of Sikhs settled mostly in the west coast, a majority of whom were unsuspecting farmers, to join the Khalistan movement. The propagandists claimed that the Indian government was usurping the power of gurudwaras, a focal point of Jagjit Singh Chohan's advertisement, and intelligence officers believed that was the only issue which could find traction with Sikhs otherwise loyal and devoted to India.

Analysts in the Ministry of External Affairs (MEA) felt that Jagjit Singh Chohan need not be taken too seriously as his advertisement was denounced by Sikh leaders in the UK, many of whom were his close friends and associates. The MEA said:

> We have reliable information that his trip has been sponsored and financed by Pakistan for its own purposes. He has recently written to some people of that Akali Dal here and we find that he has not mentioned his independent Sikhistan idea at all to them. As you have indicated in your telegrams one need not, therefore, take him seriously. However, we must prevent his making a nuisance of himself either in London or in New York or Washington during PM's visit there. Kindly take all necessary steps to ensure that no demonstration takes place while PM is there. PM's presence will naturally be sought by mischievous people to get a certain amount of publicity for themselves and their activities. Our objective has to be to ensure that they are not successful in this.

There were hectic activities within the R&AW to find out in what circumstances Chohan had left India and whether his adventurous trips had been planned and sponsored by the ISI, then headed by Major General Mohammad Akbar Khan. Their enquiries revealed that Chohan had been issued a passport on 20 August 1969, endorsed by the USA. On 30 June 1971, Chohan left India for London. Months later, in a press interview in London sometime in September 1971, Chohan raised the demand for Khalistan and said a rebel government would be formed with its headquarters at Nankana Sahib in Pakistan. Subsequently Chohan made wild allegations about the oppression of Sikhs in India. He said that gurudwaras in India had been razed, the Guru Granth Sahib burnt, that India wanted to destroy the Sikh religion, that there was economic discrimination against the Sikhs, and that India was planning a racist offensive against the Sikhs. He and his cronies claimed that the establishment of an independent Sikh state was essential to preserve the Sikh community and for the sake of peace in the subcontinent. In early October, Chohan went to the United States and issued his half page advertisement. Although there were over a thousand Sikhs in the USA, he could muster only five for the demonstration. On 31 October, Chohan, accompanied by a few other Sikhs—significantly, none from India—went to Pakistan to attend the birth celebrations of Guru Nanak at Nankana Sahib. During his visit to Pakistan, he spoke of arms being collected to fight for the Sikh homeland and of plans to form a Khalistan Liberation Army consisting of volunteers from all over the world. He argued that Sikhs and Muslims should fight hand in hand with China to achieve this objective. Chohan complimented the Pakistan government on the manner in which they maintained Sikh gurudwaras and made much of the Pakistan government's meaningless gesture of handing him the keys of the Nankana Sahib. He closed his eyes to the fact that the Pakistani government had, over the years, dissociated the Sikh community from the management of gurudwaras, used the assets of the gurudwaras for other purposes and expelled almost all the sewadars.

The severest condemnation of Dr Jagjit Singh's activities came from the Sikh community itself. In London, the Shiromani Akali Dal whole-heartedly condemned his activities and said he was acting in collaboration with Pakistan. In a resolution issued on 28 November 1971, the Akali Dal called upon the Sikh masses in the UK not to allow 'these traitors' to speak on gurudwara platforms and demanded that Dr Jagjit Singh Chohan should be asked not to allow the use of the holy book (which he had brought from Pakistan) for his 'political treacherous stunt.' The resolution said:

> We are aware that Dr. Jagjit Singh has been receiving financial and other assistance from Pakistan in his anti-national activities. For example, Pakistan government financed his visit to the US and the expenses of the advertisement in the *New York Times*. The Pakistan embassy in Washington also arranged for him to call on certain high officials of the State Department. The doings of Chohan and his utterances are being regularly purveyed by Radio Pakistan, which shows that he maintains close and continuous contacts with the Pakistanis. It is quite likely that he may continue to travel in foreign countries on papers provided by Pakistan. His plans, as stated by him, include the holding of demonstrations in front of Indian missions abroad.

Chohan's passport was supposed to expire on 20 August 1972, but after the R&AW reports on his activities, it was revoked by the government on 11 January 1971. The most difficult task for Indian agents in New York was to track Chohan's movements since he had started travelling on papers provided by Pakistan. The US agencies, including the Federal Bureau of Investigation (FBI), were not enthusiastic about chasing a radical Sikh preacher who they believed was not a threat to the USA security.

Years later when the CIA made a secret report on the Punjab militancy public, it became clear that some kind of tacit support had existed for Chohan since the beginning of the Punjab militancy. The CIA report said:

> The presence abroad of more than 2 million Sikhs has given Sikh extremism an international dimension. Nearly one-third of these expatriate Sikhs are in the UK, Canada and the US. According to Immigration and Naturalization Service (INS) reporting, Sikh extremists frequently travel between these three countries and probably maintain contacts with extremists in India. Some Sikhs apprehended in the US on immigration

> charges have admitted plans to recruit Khalistan sympathizers and to set up safe houses for Sikh militants wanted for crimes committed in India. According to the INS, the Bahamas, Mexico, Thailand, and West Germany serve as way stations for illegal Sikh immigration to the US. The explosion that downed an Air India 747 flying from Canada to India was probably executed with the help of Canada-based Sikh extremists. They have developed an extensive overseas network. Jagjit Singh Chohan has declared himself the leader of the 'Republic of Khalistan.' The International Sikh Youth Federation, the international wing of the All India Sikh Students Federation, is especially active in Canada and the UK. Press reports indicate other Sikh groups, such as the World Sikh Organization based in Washington, lobby democratic countries for support for an independent Sikh state. We believe that India faces a long-term terrorist threat from Sikh extremists that the government probably cannot eradicate. We expect resentment of New Delhi and fears of Hindu domination to linger among a majority of Sikhs, allowing the extremists to retain at least some popular support. The enduring differences between India and Pakistan suggest Islamabad will continue to provide sanctuary and limited aid to Sikh extremists. We believe Pakistan would significantly increase its support to Sikh extremists only if hostilities were breaking out with India over other issues, such as Kashmir. In this case, Pakistan would see Sikhs as a potential fifth column that would carry out terrorist activities in India and interfere with Indian military efforts. Sikh extremists will remain capable—without outside support—of significantly increasing terrorist operations in Punjab, elsewhere in India, and overseas. Contributions from Sikh temples, profits from narcotics trafficking, and remittances from pro-extremist Sikhs overseas will ensure enough financial support to enable the extremists to continue terrorist activity.

There was also a candid admission in the CIA report that the relationship between the USA and India could suffer because of the presence of Khalistani elements on the USA soil and their continued support to Sikh militancy in Punjab. It said:

> India views US policy toward Sikh extremists in the US as a major element in bilateral relations. The presence in the US of 1.5 lakh Sikhs—some who send funds to extremist organisations in India—has made New Delhi eager to see the US act against Sikh extremist activity within its borders. Senior Indian officials—including Prime Minister Rajiv Gandhi—credit Washington for the arrest of several Sikhs in the US on conspiracy charges and welcome repeated US statements supporting Indian unity, according to the US embassy. On the negative side, the government's accusations of Pakistani support for Sikh extremists have fuelled Indian press and parliamentary speculation of US complicity. We believe Soviet disinformation [on an increase] in extremist activity would prompt fresh accusations of foreign intervention in Punjab to deflect domestic criticism. Even if Gandhi discounted allegations of US involvement, pressure from his Hindu constituency, in the face of increased extremist activity, would probably force him to slow improvement in Indo-US relations. Unless Pakistani aid to Sikh extremists increases significantly, New Delhi is unlikely to seek Washington's aid in pressing Islamabad.

Many R&AW spies today are genuinely surprised to discover that the CIA became interested in Punjab as early as the mid-1960s and that its agents had begun forwarding intelligence reports to Washington on Sant Fateh Singh, the most influential Sikh leader of the time, who insisted that New Delhi should either make Punjabi the sole official language of Punjab or create a separate Punjabi-speaking state. CIA operatives on the ground predicted that efforts to find a solution were not necessarily doomed to failure, but great ingenuity would be required and time was running out for the Indian government.

Mathur later told me that the Americans did not intervene much in the activities of the Sikh militants inside the USA until they were provided with evidence and pressured to take concrete steps against the financiers and ring leaders of the separatist movement.

Political Challenges

Back home, the Indian government was fighting a psychological battle to win the hearts and minds of Punjab youth. Unfortunately, this battle wasn't free from the political games that have long dominated governance in this country. In October 1986, Congress leader Ajit Jogi drafted a note for Prime Minister Rajiv Gandhi, suggesting the hire of pro-Congress non-governmental organisations in Punjab to carry out constructive programmes for the youth. The idea, it appears from his note, was to ensure political dividends for the Congress. The note said:

> During the most impressionable period in their lives, they saw the cult of Jarnail Singh Bhindranwale at its peak and imbibed the feeling of the superiority of Sikh race over all others just as the Germans under Hitler were led to believe about the Aryan race. They also witnessed 'Operation Blue Star' which intensely hurt their ego and filled them to the brim with a bitter sense of vengeance. Relative affluence, availability of cheap labour from other states and optimum level of mechanization in Agriculture leaves the uneducated amongst them almost free and idle. Growing unemployment, similarly, leaves them educated, frustrated, idle and full of excess energy. As a consequence, new terrorists are being born every day. Thanks to Julio Ribeiro a large number of them get killed or captured but a larger number join the ranks of terrorists every day.
>
> Obviously bullets alone is not the answer to this gravest ever danger faced by our body politic. The limitless energy of the youth of Punjab, therefore needs to be directed in

> constructive channels so that they do not get attracted/diverted towards the adventure of terrorism.

American intelligence, it appears, was closely monitoring the situation in Punjab. Before Rajiv Gandhi's attempts at confidence building measures, the CIA had predicted that he would probably take several steps to resolve Sikh discontent. The American intelligence report, however, cautioned that his efforts would bear fruit only if he ordered an impartial investigation of the anti-Sikh riots and placated moderate Sikh leaders for peaceful talks.

Gandhi was not averse to the idea of placating the youth and moderates and on 5 November 1986, the Prime Minister's Office (PMO) asked the Ministry of Human Resource Development (HRD) to examine the suggestions forwarded by Jogi. Other government arms launched programmes to mobilise youth activities in Punjab and coordinate development measures at grassroots levels. But as far as Prime Minister Gandhi was concerned, these attempts to engage the youth of Punjab were half-hearted. A note from Sarla Grewal, secretary to Prime Minister Rajiv Gandhi, to R. Gopalaswamy, secretary of the Department of Youth Affairs and Sports, on 4 March 1987, was self-explanatory:

> The position as reported in your letter was submitted to the Prime Minister (Rajiv Gandhi). Prime Minister was not happy with the progress achieved and felt that a more concerted effort ought to be mounted. It was in this context that I had scheduled a meeting on 3rd March, 1987 to discuss various aspects thoroughly. It is indeed unfortunate you could not find it convenient to attend this meeting. The consensus reached at the meeting was that an inter-ministerial and multi-disciplinary approach had to be adopted to achieve significant results. Bringing the misguided youth back into the national mainstream is a delicate task and without appropriate inputs from various sources, programmes devised for this purpose may either lose focus or have little consequence.

The letter was also marked to Margaret Alva, minister of state for youth affairs and sports. Alva chaired a meeting between the central and the state governments on 23 March 1987 in which the state officials stressed the importance of national integration camps in Punjab to clear misconceptions about the government's intentions among the youth. An officer from Punjab also pointed out that positive media coverage could be an important aspect of the effort.

Alva mentioned during the meeting that it was not only necessary to take youth from Punjab to other parts of the country, but it was equally necessary to take youth from other parts of the country to Punjab so that they could have a balanced view of the development of the country.

Prime Minister Gandhi chaired a meeting on 11 November 1987 at Room No. 9, Parliament House, where Punjab's governor Siddhartha Shankar Ray was also present. Gandhi indicated that the state government should come forward with concrete proposals within two weeks, which could then be considered in the central government ministries concerned. Ray had submitted a note to the prime minister on behalf of the state government and it categorically said that the youth in Punjab was being buffeted by a separatist ideology based on fundamentalism and obscurantism. The need of the hour was, therefore, to inculcate and foster a nationalistic ideology based on secularism, democracy and rule of law and to disseminate this ideology throughout the social spectrum. The Punjab government believed that it needed to establish an intimate and direct relationship between the youth and the community, by involving them in need based programmes for rural reconstruction during or soon after their graduation. Such activities, the state government argued, had successfully been implemented by countries like Yugoslavia and China where they formed youth brigades. A note said:

> There would be little point in investment of resources for motivating the youth in schools and colleges towards the

> society and the nation if frustration is to be their fate right after they leave schools and colleges. The issue of providing avenues of employment to the educated youth, therefore, is more important than it may appear to be when viewed as an isolated objective of giving them employment. Socially destructive activities are sometime sought to be rationalized on the ground that the society has done nothing for the individuals. While it is not possible for the society and the nation to eliminate this problem in the short term, any improvement in this area would definitely be very rewarding to the society.

Battle of Wits

While Rajiv Gandhi's PMO was working on political tools to capture the hearts and minds of the younger generation in Punjab, Mohan Krishna, a R&AW field agent in Toronto, was facing a tough task. The covers of two R&AW officers who had successfully penetrated the inner sanctum of the World Sikh Organisation, the International Sikh Youth Federation and the Babbar Khalsa, had accidentally been blown. An officer codenamed SKS was taken out by a hardcore Babbar Khalsa supporter and his true identity was revealed to the Sikh community through their internal publicity arm which included a newsletter. A potential recruit, the editor of a Punjabi newspaper in Toronto, compromised another R&AW officer codenamed Colonel. Colonel's informal meeting with his would be source was splashed in this newspaper the next day, blowing open not only the R&AW operation inside the Sikh community, but also leaving hundreds of informers in the cold. Even to this day, almost three decades later, it is still being argued that a rivalry between the IB and the R&AW had compromised the operation and soured India's relationship with the Canadian Security Intelligence Service (CSIS). The two officers were declared Persona Non Grata and put on flights back to New Delhi in 1987.

Krishna, who was sent to Canada undercover in late 1987, said it was a battle of wits. At least two R&AW stations had been closed in Toronto after the fiasco. In Delhi, he had been briefed that the ISI had been behind the damage to the Indian spy agency's operation, but later he learnt that a turf war between the IB and R&AW, which the ISI had taken full advantage of, was the real reason the operation failed.

Trouble in Canada had started around September 1971, when Jagjit Singh Chohan began to give media interviews. At that time, his movement was portrayed as communist, owing to an affiliation with the Hindustan Gadar Party that operated from mailbox 144, Victoria, BC. On 21 September 1971, during a function at a gurudwara organised by the Khalsa Diwan Society of Victoria, a few young men attempted to distribute cyclostyled copies of a leaflet in Punjabi. This, however, was not allowed by the Sikh worshippers.

R&AW agents managed to get a copy of the leaflet and reported it was somehow linked with the Naxalbari movement back home. The propaganda material said:

> Is India independent? No! Absolutely not. Handfuls of looter do not stop utilizing the fruit of hard labour, done by farmers and labours for their personal benefit. Today India owes more than tri-billion dollars. Foreign pressure increasing day by day. The major portion of the industry of the country is directly or indirectly under the control of foreign capitalists. Is this independence? Or it is socialism of India and her henchmen. The struggle by the armed Kisan of India is continuing under the leadership of comrade Charu Majumdar of communist party. This struggle started in May 1967 from Naxalbari and had since spread all over India. Therefore Indian government is afraid of such elements. In spite of all the efforts including use of force these parties are marching ahead. In view of the traditional volunteers question arises what is the contribution

> of Indians residing in Canada to help those struggling Kisans and what should be the attitude of the masses. We invite the attention of the Gadar party which is looking after the interest of Indian Kisan in Canada to join their hands with the Gadar party of India to succeed in this mission.

That there were threats from multiple sources was quite clear and it was precisely for that reason that the IB was allowed to operate in Canada, even though foreign operations were not in their jurisdiction. The spies believe the decision to allow the IB to operate in Canada had been taken sometime in 1981 when a large number of Sikh immigrants began arriving in the country. India's deputy high commissioner in Ottawa, J. Jacob, had highlighted the issue in his report of June 1981:

> A matter which has been of growing concern has been the increase in number of cases of people from India arriving in Canada and continuing their stay here by declaring themselves as refugees. Though Canadian government has not notified acceptance in any such case, the law has loopholes which permits a refugee to stay for extended periods in Canada with facilities to work.

The then Canadian prime minister, Pierre Elliot Trudeau, was fighting many battles on several political and economic fronts. His government was pushing for a charter of rights in Canada's constitution, policy experts were facing the heat over rising inflation, and the inflation provided enough ammunition to political parties like the Conservatives and the New Democrats to target Trudeau's government. Above all the Canadian government was unnerved by revelations that two former Canadian envoys had been working as moles for the Soviet Union. Trudeau strongly denied these charges, but the scandal did not die down.

Back in India, the government's conscious decision to deploy the IB, the domestic spy agency, for espionage operations abroad, was an extraordinary step that had rattled the R&AW which guards its territorial jurisdiction jealously. In Krishna's candid opinion, the IB proved to be far superior in the Canadian theatre than the R&AW. Under suitable diplomatic cover, they operated from 10, Springfield Road in Ottawa, and managed to cultivate and recruit sources close to Sikh separatist leaders including the Babbar Khalsa's Talvinder Singh Parmar, Surjan Singh Gill and Manjit Singh Kohli.

Talvinder had played a key role in the crash of Air India Boeing 747 'Kanishka' on 23 June 1985, in which three hundred and twenty-nine people were killed. After the crash, Indian authorities played the usual blame game, accusing each other either of lack of intelligence or failure to act on available forewarnings.

A US embassy report said that the possibility of an attack on Air India had been widely known in the weeks before the bombing. They were right. The terror modules that executed the attack had slipped into Montreal from the USA. Though the FBI had been keeping an eye on suspected Sikh militants in Queens, New York, since 1983, their surveillance was merely to ensure that the militants did not carry out terror activities on US soil. Two Sikh militants, Ammand Singh and Lal Singh, thus managed to secure false passports and fly out of New York to take down the Air India flight.

Many Khalistan supporters in Canada had called for a boycott of the airline and when Talvinder Singh Parmar made a fiery speech at a Sikh temple in South East Calgary in the summer of 1984, he said that Air India planes would fall from the sky. The report said:

> The local press has described a controversy that has developed between the Royal Canadian Mounted Police (RCMP) and Canadian Intelligence over the conduct of the investigation and whether or not the tragedy could have been prevented. According to press reports, months before the bombing the

> RCMP investigated a tip that an Air India plane out of Montreal would be bombed. The RCMP had asked Canadian intelligence for a threat assessment of its likelihood. Police critics suggest that Canadian intelligence ignored clues that could have prevented the bombing. There have also been allegations that there was a Canadian intelligence mole working with the alleged bombing conspirators.

The FBI on its part raided Sikh localities in Queens and interrogated suspects. The agency claimed to have arrested some Sikh militants including Gurpartap Birk, an alleged gang leader, but trails leading to many others were untouched.

The US Committee on Foreign Affairs asked the CIA director William Casey whether press reports indicating the involvement of foreign powers and the role of the American spy agency in dividing India had any truth. The CIA believed that if Rajiv Gandhi continued to follow the policy of his late mother, Indira, Sikh unrest might create a problem for USA–India relations. The CIA also denied any role by Pakistan, claiming there were no terror camps for Sikh militants in the neighbouring country:

> Despite the Indian charges, we do not believe the Pakistan government has provided training to Sikh militants—in part because Pakistan fears that New Delhi might retaliate militarily. Officials of the World Sikh Organisation (WSO) told US diplomats in Mumbai late last summer that even when representatives of their organisation asked Pakistan's President Zia-Ul-Haq for assurances of asylum, citizenship and property rights for Sikh refugees, he merely advised them to avoid antagonizing Hindus.

This report made it clear that the CIA's interest in the situation was much deeper than it appeared on the surface. Prime Minister Rajiv Gandhi tried not to blame the USA and Canada directly for sheltering hardcore militants, but other government functionaries on various occasions minced no words in indicting Washington for the trouble in Punjab. After Prime Minister Gandhi signed a peace accord with moderate leader Harchand Singh Longowal in July 1985, Minister of State for External Affairs Khurshid Alam Khan informed Parliament that Lal Singh, the most wanted militant, had been trained at a safe house in Alabama, USA. The CIA believed that allegations of a foreign hand in the Punjab trouble was merely a byproduct of the Soviet intelligence agency KGB's disinformation campaign. This denial was as chilling as some of the intelligence reports that CIA agents were filing. These reports admitted that Khalistan supporters in the UK, Canada, the US, West Germany, Malaysia and elsewhere had demonstrated publicly against New Delhi, in several instances attacking Indian government-owned facilities abroad, and India's determination to curtail foreign based support for Sikh extremism risked undercutting other foreign policy objectives without significantly reducing dissidence at home. Another CIA intelligence report acknowledged that Khalistan supporters in the USA were lobbying with state and federal officials for support and India objected through diplomatic channels, calling this interference in its internal affairs. In a chilling report, US intelligence officials said:

> New Delhi will welcome Washington's assurances that it is investigating the propriety of Sikh political activities but is likely to press for concrete results. The Indian government particularly hopes the US will curb the activities of pro-Khalistan groups in New York and Washington, if necessary by deporting resident aliens. We do not doubt that Pakistani intelligence officials have contacted visiting Sikhs or that local officials have aided them, probably with Islamabad's knowledge. Officials in Lahore, for example, apparently provided Sikh hijackers with a pistol last summer—a charge that Pakistan's President Zia no longer denies. Last June (1984) we had an isolated report from US diplomats in Toronto that a Sikh

> approached them with an offer to assassinate Indira Gandhi if they would provide him with travel papers. The Indians probably would cite recent reports—noted by US diplomats in New Delhi—that Sikh extremists have rearmed themselves for a new round of anti-government operations with weapons intended for the Afghan insurgents.

Although the USA was willing to cooperate with India, partly due to Rajiv's open-minded approach on the world stage, the CIA had made it clear that cooperation is a two-way street and Washington would expect New Delhi to provide assistance in return. This literally meant that New Delhi was required to be vocal on the issue of international terrorism. The CIA was perturbed by India's stand that that terrorism unrelated to India was none of its business. The Americans were particularly peeved that India had privately condemned Iran's 1979 seizure of the US embassy, making its staff hostages, but turned aside US pressure to be part of official statements condemning the act and also did nothing to help ease the crisis. They were also angry that New Delhi had reacted to the bombing of the US embassy in Beirut in April 1983 by suggesting that Washington's refusal to recognise Palestinian rights of self-determination was a key source of US troubles in the Middle East.

In September 1985, Prime Minister Rajiv Gandhi met his Canadian counterpart Brian Mulroney and expressed concerns over the free run of Sikh extremists in several cities of Canada. In the meantime, the ISI tried to sabotage the Indian espionage network by feeding information to the Canadian media about Indian spies penetrating Sikh militant outfits in Vancouver and how Indian agents were bankrolling moderate groups in the local Sikh community to counter the hardcore fringe groups.

Krishna told me that the Babbar Khalsa, founded in the late 1970s with the aim to establish an independent Sikh state, was the most powerful Khalistan organisation, with branches in Canada,

Pakistan, the US and European countries. It was known to the CSIS that the Babbar Khalsa had been behind the bombing of the Indian aircraft, but the warnings about the terrorists' intentions were ignored.

Krishna was given a mandate and a blank cheque to neutralise the pro-Khalistan groups in Canada. 'I was told to do whatever it takes to get access to every bit of information on the plans made by hardcore Sikh leaders in Canada,' he told me.

Within months of his arrival in Canada in 1987, Krishna was running an asset linked to a gurudwara in Vancouver. He successfully harvested and shipped actionable intelligence on the Babbar Khalsa's activities in Canada and their terror plans against India. Just days after the launch of Operation Black Thunder II in Amritsar by top cop K.P.S. Gill on 9 May 1988 to flush out militants from the Golden Temple, Krishna dismantled a Sikh youth wing operating out of North Mississauga. Although the R&AW felt vulnerable in Canada, using its fledgling network of Indian spies against the strong separatist movement, Krishna often bypassed conventional means to gather productive intelligence.

'There was internal criticism about R&AW effectiveness in Canada. I remember an Indian diplomat had remarked during a party at the embassy that the R&AW survives because its reports are not read by the political bosses and they are lucky because no comments are offered. It was a bit humiliating. From that day on I swore to keep a step ahead of our adversaries. That became my priority. I successfully recruited informers in Ottawa and Winnipeg. I developed two assets deep inside Punjabi print media houses in Toronto and charmed a venom-spewing priest in a Vancouver gurudwara. I thought he might be a trickster, but that is the risk of our trade. He proved to be a great asset. We paid huge sums to keep the operation against militant groups going and it slowly took on a pace of its own,' Krishna told me.

Sometime in October 1988, the priest arranged a meeting with a potential recruit at Argo Café on Ontario Street. Krishna was told that the man belonged to the International Sikh Youth Federation and had been working closely with the group's leadership. The meeting revealed that the recruit, Tarvinder Singh, came from an affluent family in Ludhiana and since his arrival in Vancouver in 1983 for studies, he had been deeply involved in the separatist movement. But ever since the bombings executed by the Babbar Khalsa at Gurdaspur, Patiala and Hoshiarpur in February 1988, in which more than a hundred innocents were killed, he had been feeling trapped.

'So now what do you want to do?' Krishna asked him with a straight face.

'I want this mindless killing to end. I can do anything,' Tarvinder replied.

Within a month Krishna had a dossier on each of the International Sikh Youth Federation leaders with their contact addresses and photographs. A file was also shared with Canadian intelligence.

'We had no problem tracking them down if they planned terror attacks. Tarvinder had shared at least three actionable pieces of intelligence on the group's activities and that led to the arrest of a financier working closely with the ISI,' Krishna recalled.

No one at the R&AW cared about the source as long as the information had actionable details, was persuasive and included more details about Sikh activities inside Canada. The reports from Krishna in October 1988 rang alarm bells among the security agencies and the top echelon of the bureaucracy. Krishna saved countless lives with volumes of intelligence gleaned from Tarvinder about terror plans in India and a free run to operate helped him expand his espionage network by recruiting many more agents in Vancouver and Ottawa. Krishna travelled to Sikh localities in Winnipeg and Edmonton disguised as a businessman from Delhi and pretended to be a conscience keeper of society by raising the issue of militants imported from India who could eventually disrupt the peaceful lives and businesses of Sikh families settled abroad. This was a daring method with every possibility of boomeranging, but the spymaster continued to play with fire. His rendezvous with moderate community leaders enabled him to create sharp differences among the pro-Khalistani groups. A majority of them were for peace and secretly dreamed of having a better life away from the trouble and violence in Punjab. Within months Krishna was able to persuade a sufficient number of people to inform him about militant groups. They provided details of Khalistan supporters and financiers in Winnipeg and Edmonton. These dossiers along with further information of links with men in India were secretly shipped to New Delhi. Krishna's network was now producing accurate intelligence and the complete plans and intentions of Sikh militants based in Canada, allowing India to launch some remarkable counterstrikes.

Christmas in Maryland

Sometime in November 1988, Dinesh Mathur left his Washington residence for Annapolis. Sartaj, who drove the car a little above the speed limit, had secured a meeting with a Khalistan module codenamed Chatar. In about in an hour, the Indian spy and his aide stopped at a large house on Fairfax Road, which had a distinct wooden dome probably inspired by the Baroque style popular in the UK and France. During the drive, Sartaj told Mathur that Chatar was supposed to have vast knowledge of the pro-Khalistan network in the USA and R&AW secret maneuvers could help recruit this valuable source. Mathur was a man of steely resolve. His only advice to the unprecedented number of agents he recruited in various continents was to look for small details while collecting information and try to filter deception and motive before passing on intelligence reports. This worked to a large extent and his informers had penetrated the top echelons of the government, social organisations and even the scientific community in their various countries. Mathur had encouraged covert action where it was needed and no one in the foreign intelligence community knew his real name.

'There is no standard template for spying,' Mathur used to say. 'You have to use and exploit every possible tool available because spying is a dirty job.'

Chatar was waiting at the door when Mathur's car stopped at the portico. Unlike Jagjit Singh Chohan, Chatar had no bodyguards and his house appeared like any other in the affluent Maryland neighbourhood. Mathur recalled: 'Chatar had prepared a detailed agenda for our encounter. After about ten minutes of informal chat about life in general and the US's freezing weather in particular, he ushered us into his large and dark basement. When he switched on the light, Sartaj and I were shocked. There was a large table in the middle, full of explosives and ultra modern arms.'

'Do you really want to scare me?' Mathur's eyes locked on Chatar.

'No. I want to scare India. Your guys are fighting with .303 rifles, and here we have the most sophisticated weapons available in the world,' Chatar told him mockingly.

'Why did you want to show me these weapons?'

'So you can tell your bosses in the R&AW that our attacks in India are not going to stop.'

Mathur understood the situation and tried to ease the tension in the stuffy basement. 'But I don't know anything about weapons. I cannot tell which weapon this is,' Mathur said, picking up a gun from the table.

'Aren't you from the police service?' It was Chatar's turn to be shocked.

'No. Who told you this lie? I am from a teaching background and worked as a professor in Karnataka. Now I am just an analyst and my job is research,' Mathur replied.

Chatar's voice was filled with anger.

'Whatever you are, we know that you work for the Indian spy agency. Now I am going to do you a huge favour. Go and tell your bosses that Khalistan forces will soon blow up Connaught Place,' Chatar said disdainfully.

'But you are not my agent. Why should I believe you,' Mathur replied in similar tone. 'Perhaps what you are telling me is a complete lie. Do you have the exact date and time?' At last Mathur smiled at Chatar.

Chatar stiffened. Perhaps he knew he had underestimated Mathur's spycraft and realised that peddling propaganda through him would not be easy. He immediately guided Mathur and Sartaj out of his house. The fresh air cleared Mathur's head and before opening the door of his car, he handed Chatar his direct telephone number in case he 'would like to meet again sometime'.

'I will think about it,' Chatar said rudely.

They shook hands. 'I look forward to seeing you again,' were Mathur's last words before Sartaj switched on the ignition.

Back in his office, Mathur drafted a memo about his meeting with Chatar and kept it under lock and key. He had no technical intelligence support; the spy operation deep inside the USA was purely dependent on informers.

'Chatar would have been a trophy if only I was able to command him as I wished,' recalled Mathur about the days he spent thinking about the unusual meeting. 'I had a gut feeling he was well positioned to provide information on militants crisscrossing western countries to foment trouble in Punjab. I told Sartaj that if we could learn his weaknesses, it would be easy to lure him into working for the R&AW.'

By early December, Sartaj had produced a dossier on Chatar, with details of his family and business interests in the USA. Although there was no mention of his private life, the dossier noted that he was reckless and highly radicalised. Mathur recognised that any effort to make a dent in Chatar's loyalty to pro-Khalistan outfits would require psychological pressure as well as dollar bills. Chatar had not called Mathur even once since that strange meeting. It was a clear message that Chatar would not be an easy catch. Mathur asked Sartaj to fix a meeting with him sometime in mid-December.

On that December morning in 1988 as he drove to meet Chatar, Mathur was reading a report on civilian killings in Punjab—in the last six months, about six hundred and eighty-eight civilians had been killed, an average of four innocents a day. Although the number of terror incidents and casualties was significantly lower than in the previous year, militants were still able to strike at will.

Once they had settled down in Chatar's drawing room, Mathur began talking about Chatar's family and business. Chatar now knew that the Indian spy knew everything about him.

'I am not frightened of your government and agency,' he said.

Mathur nodded. It was obvious. Chatar was safely sitting in a foreign country that was aloof to the war far away in an Indian state.

'What do you want from me?' Chatar asked, staring directly at Mathur.

'Give me the name of financiers and operatives bleeding India,' Mathur said.

Chatar laughed. 'You want me to betray my friends.'

'No. They are not your friends. Your loyalty is to your home country, your family and business. They are just using you and when you are doomed they will not hesitate to pick another Chatar. These guys are not just a threat to India, they also disrupt the peace of the world. Think about your family and watch your interests. We live by the rules and you have my word I will always trust you with my life,' Mathur said.

'We are fighting for a cause, for our own nation. What makes you believe that I will abandon my friends?' Chatar asked.

'You are abandoning enemies and gaining friends in return,' Mathur said.

It took another hour for Mathur to persuade Chatar that he would be doing a great favour to his family by defecting. Just before he finished the psy op, Mathur walked to Chatar's chair and pulled out an envelope from his jacket. It contained ten thousand freshly minted dollar bills. Chatar quietly placed it on the side table.

'Come and see me on Christmas,' Chatar said, avoiding eye contact with Mathur.

Back in the safe house, Mathur began poring over his Punjab files and the dossier of agents who were his eyes and ears. As a spy, Mathur had recruited many smugglers, murderers and gangsters after meticulously checking their psychological behaviour. These anti-social elements or 'pure criminals' as Mathur called them, were regarded as the best operatives in the field; Mathur always said that outlaws were best suited to covert operations. In the USA, he applied the same tactic with utmost secrecy to sanitise the insurgents' den back home. 'They are temperamental but genuine, they are full of impurities but with the potential of gold, they are misguided but questing. If you make the right connection and play them right, they could be the best informers and saboteurs you needed,' Mathur once said.

He thought Chatar was a mad elephant, yet capable of dismantling the enemy's network. On Christmas evening in 1988, Mathur and Sartaj were ready to bring Chatar in, despite predictions from senior R&AW operatives that this would be a disaster. When they arrived at Chatar's home, Mathur noticed an expression of peace on his recruit's face.

'What followed was like a question and answer session. As Chatar answered each question, he looked anxious but satisfied. He rose from his chair a couple of times during our conversation and strolled around the room, sometimes glancing towards the windows. Sartaj was writing notes in a black diary. An hour later, Chatar took a deep breath, looked at me and asked, is it enough? I nodded and told him we would meet again in the new year,' Mathur recalled.

Chatar had given him a goldmine. He had provided details of Khalistan cadres in Amritsar and Ferozpur, areas of Punjab that saw more terror activities than anywhere else in the state. Mathur's intelligence report with its precise locations of hideouts and identities of modules was exceptional and powerful enough to change the course of the anti-insurgency operation. The report troubled the security establishment in India. At a top-level meeting at the Ministry of Home Affairs (MHA) sometime in January, it was decided to carry out a massive security operation in the villages of these districts. It took another month to bring together special commandos of the Central Reserve Police Force, Border Security Force and Punjab police to mount the operation. In the meantime, Mathur and Sartaj pulled together streams of intelligence reports about hotspots in the two districts and inputs about the cadres receiving arms and explosives from across the border with the help of the ISI. The Special Forces offensive began sometime in March 1989 and more than five thousand villages were sanitised. Reports in intelligence files suggest that a huge cache of weapons was seized and hundreds of militants were arrested in the month-long operation that severely damaged the terror capability of outfits like the Babbar Khalsa, Bhindranwale Tiger Force and Khalistan Liberation Organisation. By June 1989, the militants were overwhelmed, all thanks to Mathur's spy operation from the USA.

The then junior home minister, P. Chidambaram, made a statement in the Lok Sabha implicating Pakistan for supporting the militancy in Punjab. Chidamabaram was responding to a debate on whether Afghanistan jihadis and Punjab militant groups had forged an alliance to carry out terror strikes in India.

He believed that their contact was through the ISI, and not direct. Perhaps quoting intelligence reports, the minister said that Punjab extremists in the UK and the USA had established contacts with Afghan jihadis in 1985–86 purely to procure arms and money. One such report had indicated that Sikh militants in 1987 had planned to buy Stinger missiles from the Afghan rebels. Chidambaram also disclosed that Jagjit Singh Chohan had held a meeting with Afghan terror leaders in London in early 1989.

In a report in July 1989, based on information provided by Chatar, Mathur warned his top bosses in Delhi about the financial support extended to a few Panthic Committees from the USA and Canada. The leaders of the committees were operating from Pakistan and safe havens in Nepal. His report specifically mentioned Dr Sohan Singh, a surgeon turned Khalistan leader. Mathur said Sohan Singh had been rattled by the reverses in the last few months and was desperately trying to recruit more militants to keep the secessionist movement alive. He described the USA and Canada based organisation's role as the fountainhead of Punjab's insurgency. 'My close friendship with Chatar was risky but I did not see any other way to execute covert operations to neutralise the senior echelons of the Khalistan movement,' Mathur told me.

His special access to Chatar landed him another blind date—Dr Gurmeet Singh Aulakh. A research scientist turned self-proclaimed Khalistani leader, he had become the face of the Khalistan movement and a prominent figure in the USA, lobbying hard with American lawmakers for a separate state for Sikhs in India. With considerable influence at the Capitol, Aulakh and his associates had declared an independent Khalistan in late 1987 and his efforts in subsequent years were focused on getting the status of a sovereign state for Punjab as a new Sikh nation. According to Mathur, unlike other Khalistan leaders in the USA who were involved in terror attacks, Aulakh's primary focus was propaganda against the Indian government. While militant outfits disintegrated in Punjab, Aulakh launched a massive war against the Indian government, accusing it of Sikh genocide. Indian diplomats and spies followed his activities in Washington DC with growing alarm and voluminous reports were sent to New Delhi. Mathur said he was the first R&AW spy to gain access to Aulakh and he confronted the Khalistan leader with documentary evidence of his involvement with US officials to create political instability back home.

'He was soft spoken but very gritty. I thought he would be apologetic after seeing the documents, but I was wrong. Aulakh had utter contempt for India and was deeply in love with the USA. He had no intention of stopping his organisation's activities. He was aggressive and we decided to keep a watch over his frequent visits to US officials and keep New Delhi informed on all aspects of lobbying in those crazy days,' said Mathur, still barely able to control his anger towards the USA and particularly the CIA.

One of Aulakh's contacts, John Taylor Doolittle, a politician from California, frequently accused India of human rights violations. He referred to Punjab as Khalistan and believed that the USA should support the rights of the minority people of Khalistan, Kashmir and Nagaland to a free and fair vote on independence from India.

Mathur's case officer in Delhi, N. Vishwanathan, was particularly worried by the propaganda unleashed by Sikh leaders abroad. In his own words, 'India was paying a huge price because some pathetic men sitting in air-conditioned rooms were exploiting flaws in youngsters.'

On a foggy morning in mid-December 1989, the top spies of the R&AW made their way to a glassed conference room that was regularly subjected to bug sweeping. Rajiv Gandhi had lost the election and V.P. Singh, riding on the popular anti-corruption sentiment, had captured the prime minister's seat at Raisina Hill. In Kashmir, the kidnapping of Rubaiya Sayeed, daughter of then Home Minister Mufti Mohammed Sayeed, jolted the security establishment. Meanwhile in Punjab, the over ground activities of pro-Khalistan supporters was gathering a pace that triggered another round of effective political lobbying abroad. In the meeting, Vishwanathan suggested a counteroffensive to eliminate the propagandists' network. He later recalled that the arguments were mostly focused on the US, but it was decided that something must be done before the virus spread and fanned international opinion against the Indian government. After all the options were carefully weighed, the R&AW spies decided that the task should be handed to the MEA.

The Shocker

As the intelligence agency continued to run spies in the USA, the MEA hired filmmakers to make propaganda videos targeting the Sikh community abroad. The objective was to present the reality of the Khalistan movement in India; it had been hijacked by criminal gangs who were accumulating large amounts of money via donations and smuggling. They had enough to buy properties abroad and there were widespread rumours that many had sent their families away from the area of conflict.

These films were shipped to the USA in the diplomatic pouch. For broadcasting purposes on paid media networks, the government had directed external affairs officials based in Washington to convert them to BETA, which yielded high-resolution visuals and quality sound. Around a hundred thousand dollars was sanctioned from secret funds to finish the task by March 1990. Mathur and other spies waited for almost two months, but there were no BETA tapes. Queries from the R&AW headquarters went unanswered. Sometime in July that year the government was informed by the bureaucrats that all the BETA tapes they had made in Washington had become obsolete.

'No one had seen a single tape. This was the greatest mystery during our spy operation against Khalistan elements in the USA. What happened to all the money? Well, it was secret funds and perhaps the booty was equally distributed among the officers handling the propaganda operation,' Mathur speculated.

Given this situation, it was decided that the R&AW, while pursuing espionage operations, should also be tasked with successfully executing psychological warfare. Intelligence operations are conducted by rules and operatives are free to apply and use all kinds of ammunition to defeat inimical forces.

There are tough lessons for the R&AW from both intelligence successes and setbacks in the Khalistan operation as Pakistan looks to revive the militancy on the basis of the global exposure expected during referendum 2020 agitations in foreign countries. There is a growing need for analysts in the digital battlespace. A proposal has been moved by the government extending immunity to cyber decoys recruited to counter propaganda and criminal activities in the virtual world. For successful future operations on the ground, a decision has been taken to set up a joint counter operation centre involving the R&AW, the National Investigation Agency (NIA), the IB and the Punjab Police. The decision taken during a meeting of top security officials in early 2019 also finalised a blueprint to hire the services of retired officers and spies who had served in Punjab during the peak of the Khalistan movement. The aim is to ensure the Indian spies have superior resources to pre-empt any ISI move.

6

HUNTING THE R&AW TRAITOR

As hundreds of people braved the winter of 2003 to attend a special Christmas prayer at a cathedral in central Delhi, Rabinder Singh stepped into a waiting car at the Gole Market roundabout, took out his cell phone and called his wife, Parminder Kaur.

'I will reach in about an hour,' Singh said as his driver struggled to change gears in the traffic jam.

When he finally arrived in the upmarket neighbourhood of Defence Colony in south Delhi, Singh strode into his house without uttering a word to the driver. Minutes later, Parminder poured him a glass of scotch. 'I need to send an email to Suki,' he said. 'Did you speak to her about the exams?'

Parminder shook her head.

Rabinder took out a copy of the Bhagavad Gita, turned to chapter five and started typing Krishna's message to Arjuna from the fifth verse. The wisdom was meant for Suki, his daughter in the USA: 'That man perceives reality who regards the Way of Knowledge and the Way of Selfless Action as identical, because the liberation attained by knowledge is also achieved by selfless action.'

He went on to add that selfless action is the most important aspect of human life and the attainment of God is possible only with complete devotion to the almighty.

Then, he shut down the laptop and took out a sleek notebook from the cupboard along with a grey leather bag containing documents. He then took out a web camera and as he attached it to the laptop, Parminder walked in with another glass of whisky to replace the empty one. She walked out quietly as Singh started placing top-secret documents on the table to take pictures. These included a report on the insurgency in India's north east and an analysis on Sri Lanka by the National Security Council (NSC). He stored the images in the hard drive, then opened a secure file transfer protocol and signed in as 'Spring Flowers.' The transfer began and Rabinder let out a sigh of relief. The entire process took twenty minutes. Then, he switched on the shredder and thrust all the documents into it. He was pleased.

For years, R&AW joint secretary Rabinder Singh had been working as a double agent for the Central Intelligence Agency (CIA), consciously trading his country's secrets. R&AW sources who knew Rabinder Singh and even interacted with him socially, believe that he was recruited by the CIA while working as a counsellor in The Hague in the late 1990s. His desk at the Indian embassy was his cover as a R&AW officer serving abroad. Soft spoken and suave, Singh had served in the army before joining the spy agency in 1987. His handler was Annie, perhaps a codename for a CIA officer in Langley, Virginia.

Recruiting a spy to work as a double agent is the finest art in espionage. It requires a combination of tools ranging from persuasion to pressure. On that Christmas day in 2003, when Singh passed on valuable intelligence to Annie, he was not aware that he had been under the surveillance of the Counter Intelligence and Security unit of the R&AW since July. He never realised that the bearded, middle-aged fruit vendor selling fruit near his house was a R&AW spotter and his driver had been especially recruited to report on his activities. He often preached the wisdom of the Bhagavad Gita to his son and daughter, both settled in the USA. Was this a conscious attempt to cleanse himself of the sin of betraying his country? Or was he the perfect example of a person who defended and sold his country in same breath?

Even before the birth of the R&AW, India's only spy organisation, the Intelligence Bureau (IB) had been on the lookout for traitors and peddlers of valuable information, including government servants who handled sensitive files. There were rules for identifying and isolating such suspects. For instance, one kept an eye on anyone staying at the office during odd hours, anyone making extra copies of documents, being inquisitive about matters with which she or he was not directly connected, unauthorised absences from office, leave at regular intervals or on fixed days, bad habits, drunkenness and living beyond their means.

Intelligence organisations believe that weakness in character often prompts a person to barter official secrets for money or other considerations. The rulebook said: 'Musings with suspected persons or those who have certain political affiliations should be avoided to prevent leakages. The wide range of governmental activity and the increased complexities of administration have greatly added to the number of those who possess information, which must be safeguarded. Precautions are needed not only to prevent foreign powers from obtaining unauthorised information but also to avoid disclosure, which might bring improper financial or commercial advantage to people outside the government service.'

At diplomatic missions abroad, the threat of information leaks and defections was real. Sometime in mid-1950, the government issued instructions to keep information under lock and key. It also issued a top-secret note warning officers against slips in handling secret files. The note said:

> Instances have come to notice where top-secret documents have been lost or mislaid and also where certain documents have been destroyed by heads of missions without the knowledge of the government of India. This is irregular. In some cases, heads of missions or posts have taken away top secret or other classified documents on the grounds that the documents in question were addressed to them by name. It may be added, in this connection, that if an occasion arises when an officer feels that a document cannot be left with the person temporarily taking over from him, he should obtain government orders beforehand for the disposal of such documents. Under no circumstances can an officer take away secret or other classified documents with him.

It was considered the duty of every spy and individual government servant handling state secrets to ensure their safety, prevent them from falling into the hands of unauthorised people and ensure that their contents were not disclosed to anyone. Unless every person employed in clandestine work made the utmost effort to protect classified documents and information, it would be impossible to prevent leaks.

According to the R&AW spies, there are three possible reasons for a spy to become a double agent. The first motive for defection and betraying the country is monetary gain. Ideology, such as a certain political affiliation, is another reason. And third, careless talk and mishandled documents could lead to leakage of secrets.

A note objectively described the problems faced in the prevention of betrayal. It said:

> It is obvious that if there is a thief in the house, it is impossible to prevent thefts. It is, therefore, necessary that all the chances

> of an unreliable person finding position in a secret branch should be eliminated. It is by strictly following this precaution that the chances of leakages due to the first two causes may be minimized.

The increasing penetration of US intelligence in India had begun immediately after the Indian Independence but it intensified in 1954 when the CIA, with a larger focus on India and Pakistan, roped in various American organisations operating in India to prepare an assessment of a particular issue known as the National Intelligence Estimate (NIE). According to the Council on Foreign Relations, an NIE represents the US intelligence community's most authoritative and coordinated written assessment of a specific national security issue. Various government agencies participate in drafting the documents for the same. In India, the United States Information Agency (USIA) founded in 1953 and later, dissolved in 1999, played a crucial role in the collection of intelligence and drafted intelligence reports for Dwight Eisenhower's government. To do this, they did recruited Indian government officials to access key documents on New Delhi's future policies to forewarn Washington about India's activities. The US officials, working under the protective cover of an overt organisation, were told to focus on critical areas of influence in India. The targets were a few selected cities; the USIA was told to stay out of the villages. A memorandum of a meeting held on 26 May 1954 in Pennsylvania reveals the contours of the US espionage against India:

> There was considerable discussion of the possibility for intelligence reporting by public affairs officers and their staffs. Mr. Handley (William Handley, USIA, New Delhi) pointed out the dangers that might arise through the attempt to obtain information from local employees, who, after all, owe their alliance to their own government. He did recognize that the written reports currently submitted by mobile units

> every two months could be submitted to Washington. He doubted it could be wise to go any further. While additional information is secured through discussing the trips with the local employees, it must be remembered that preparing reports takes time away from operations and that there is always a shortage of clerical help.

The intelligence analysis focused on examining India's internal political and economic situation, its social problems, and the relative importance of India in the framework of US policy and strategic plans. The agents were also told to look into factors that tend to influence India to look favourably on the USA and the free world and monitor any factors that could lead India unfavourably towards the communist world. They also had to keep tabs on various US activities in India and assess the priorities of existing US government programmes and actions in India. The USIA conducted a survey in 1959 with the help of International Research Associates Inc., New York, and its Indian affiliates, to gather data on changes in attitude towards the USA and Soviet Union. The survey conducted in Delhi, Bombay, Madras and Calcutta also analysed issues pertaining to the East-West conflict and China. The intelligence report suggested that China had dropped sharply in general esteem primarily for its interference in Tibet and its border problems with India. However, Russia continued to be most frequently cited as India's 'real best friend,' with the USA and the UK tied for second place. Pakistan was identified as the chief 'danger to India,' but Russia and the USA were regarded as the greatest danger to world peace.

In the early 1960s, the focus of US intelligence shifted to India's nuclear programmes. Their primary aim was to assess India's nuclear capability. An intelligence report from October 1964 reveals the CIA's penetration and big brotherly attitude:

> The Indian government has all the elements necessary to produce a nuclear weapon and it has the capability to assemble

> a bomb quickly. India does not plan to commence work on the bomb as yet because the government of India is convinced that CHICOMS (Communist Chinese) will not have an offensive nuclear capability for at least five years. In the meantime, should the situation change, India is relying on President Lyndon Johnson's assurance to come to the aid of any nation menaced by China. When Parliament convenes early in November, the government expects pressure from some deputies for India to produce a bomb. However, the government plans to resist these pressures.

A year later, when the Lal Bahadur Shastri government came to power and an Indo-Pakistan war engulfed the region, the CIA worried that an Indian nuclear weapon programme was a certainty. William Raborn, the then CIA director, argued that proponents of a nuclear weapon programme were strengthened by the war, but the main trigger could be the political strengthening of Prime Minister Shastri's position. Raborn also agreed that India might continue to postpone a decision on nuclear weapons for the time being in return for continued high-level US economic aid, a renewal of military assistance and less US pressure on the Kashmir issue. The US spymaster, however, did not believe that such conditions would result in India holding on to its non-nuclear policy indefinitely. So, he warned the US government that within the next few years, New Delhi would probably detonate a nuclear device and proceed to produce nuclear weapons.

The formation of R&AW in 1968 and its subsequent role in creating Bangladesh pushed the US to intensify its activities in India. The US National Security Advisor, Henry A. Kissinger advised the US government to stop sending all military supplies to India and suspend critical military programmes including a communication system for a defensive radar directed at China and spares for about sixty-two C-119s that formed a large portion of India's transport fleet. In an analysis, US intelligence said that the

IB working under the home ministry was gathering incriminating information about Chinese activities and turning it over to the appropriate state or national agencies. It further stated that IB's fingerprint bureau and forensic science laboratory was superior to those maintained by other organisations. Another US report stated:

> The threat from China has spurred the central government into creating several small specialized security forces for duty in the sensitive areas along the Sino-India border. The Directorate General of Security (DGS), an office that is formally part of the Cabinet Secretariat but apparently has direct access to the Prime Minister, commands three loosely related forces and an air arm: the Special Frontier Force, the Indo-Tibetan Border Police and the Air Research Centre (a cover name for the air arm). The three men who have headed the DGS since the creation of the office in 1965 have all been drawn from the police, other elite civil services, and the three military services. The DGS has a good working relationship with other governmental security organizations as well as with the military.

On 24 May 1974, Paul V. Walsh, acting deputy director of intelligence, said that they had prepared a study that presented a stark picture of India's future. Walsh alleged that staffers, while analysing intelligence on India, clung to an extraordinarily optimistic view of India's future despite the weight of evidence to the contrary and had succeeded in mucking up earlier analyses of India's problems. Walsh argued that virtually all observers of the Indian subcontinent would agree that the problems confronting the Indian government would become extremely serious over the next few years. After the invasion of Afghanistan by Soviet forces and the collapse of the Shah in Iran, the strategic significance of the South Asian region for the US global interests had heightened. A secret Indian government report made it clear that India would not tolerate any foreign military presence under any pretext. In 1979, the Soviet Union, Poland and Czechoslovakia showed great interest in strengthening bilateral economic relations with India. To that end, these countries decided to restructure their import-export strategy towards India, taking into account the changed profile of India's industry and economy. The Janata Party government led by Morarji Desai was wary of spies and their methods, but bureaucrats in the Ministry of External Affairs (MEA) praised Desai's diplomatic niceties. A note prepared in June 1979 said:

> Contrary to what political analysts had predicted in 1977 both inside the country and outside, the Janata government has developed a healthy and mutually profitable relationship with countries of Eastern Europe without in any way sacrificing India's friendly relations with other countries. We do expect a new impetus to our economic relations with Eastern Europe.

At the same time, the Indian establishment was worried that the ultimate goal of the Soviets and the Americans was not the nuclear disarmament. Their priority, the bureaucrats felt, was arms limitation rather than disarmament measures. The primary concern of both the USA and the Soviets was the reduction of sophisticated, strategic arms while concentrating on greater firepower, accuracy and killing capacity.

In the early 1980s, for the USA and the CIA, the primary concern was to stop the Soviet expansion and create a balanced approach to tackle India and Pakistan purely for Western interests. The USA bolstered Pakistan's ability to resist the growing Soviet pressure while supporting the Afghan mujahideen that it called 'freedom fighters.' A note from Ronald Reagan's White House stated:

> Historic Indo-Pakistani animosity and the opportunity it affords the Soviet Union constitute the main obstacle to our

> objectives in South Asia. Pakistan's weapons supply relationship with the US and its continued nuclear explosives development program are viewed in New Delhi as threatening to India's vital interests. Pakistan suspects and fears Indo-Soviet collusion, believing that New Delhi and Moscow could maneuver in tandem to weaken or even destroy Pakistan. Since Moscow's invasion of Afghanistan, Pakistan and India have sought at various times and with varying success to construct a normalization dialogue.

The US objectives were very clear: 'Provide enough support to Pakistan to maintain an active Pakistani involvement in Afghan policy and ensure the stability of a key partner in South and Southwest Asia and thus weaken Soviet influence in the region.'

In those troubling times, the shadowy war unleashed by the CIA on Indian soil was intense. A story on the CIA's activities that appeared in the *Washington Post* in November 1979 triggered a political storm. The newspaper report, citing the biography of former spy chief Richard Helms, suggested that the CIA had planted an informer in Indira Gandhi's cabinet during the 1971 war to liberate Bangladesh. In August 1971, continued the report, this informer in Gandhi's cabinet told the CIA that the Soviet Union had signed a friendship treaty with India to forestall the Indian recognition of Bangladesh. The cabinet member—a CIA recruit—had told the American spy agency that the Indians planned to extend the war to West Pakistan. The news report, citing excerpts from the book, further said that the CIA was very upset by intelligence leaks about the mole at the heart of Indian government and their displeasure was made known to officials in the executive branch.

In 1983, a CIA spy working under the cover of a policy planning officer in New Delhi was found recruiting four Indians: three former military officers and a civilian. India didn't want to make a fuss so he was quietly asked to leave the country. To counter foreign agents, the IB was authorised by the government to conduct operations, including searches and arrests, with the help of law enforcement agencies. In September 1985, the IB and Delhi Police unravelled a CIA espionage ring involving a South Delhi businessman with links to politicians along with nine American agents working undercover at the US embassy. The US government was quick to deny any allegations of spying and recruitment of agents. An official statement was issued to claim that no US government official sought or received classified information. While denying the allegations, the Americans conveniently ignored the details of the matter that emerged in Indian courts.

R&AW officials who had helplessly watched the CIA's activities in the country believe that the lure of easy money had made the Indians vulnerable. Though the majority of the compromised people were civilians working in different ministries, the American intelligence agency had consistently tried to plant a double agent in the top echelon of the Indian spy agency.

The opportunity to invade the R&AW came in the mid-1990s when Indian decision makers approved increased liaisons with foreign intelligence organisations and exotic locations were chosen for rendezvous. A senior R&AW officer told me that such meetings hardly ever produced anything relevant to India's interests. He said: 'There is always a well-established mechanism within intelligence organisations across the world to share actionable inputs relevant to the countries concerned. But it is done within a *Lakshmana Rekha* (refers to a strict convention or rule, never to be broken). We went overboard and liaison meetings that yielded absolutely zero results were conducted without due diligence. Over a period of time, the exercise turned out to be counterproductive; it exposed our officers and some sensitive operations. The CIA was very keen to have R&AW harvests on Pakistan, China, Myanmar, Bangladesh, Afghanistan, Sri Lanka and Nepal. The Indian spy agency had developed a formidable network of informers in these countries and the steady flow of intelligence to R&AW headquarters was closely guarded.'

In the case of Rabinder Singh, there were apprehensions in various quarters during his visit to the CIA headquarters at Langley. This trip took place just before his posting at The Hague in mid-1999 and there were murmurs that his loyalty was up for sale. But the fervent pleas of several senior officers to mount surveillance against suspicious intelligence operatives fell on deaf ears. The USA was embarrassed by India's nuclear test in May 1998 and the CIA was blamed for not warning the US administration that the Atal Bihari Vajpayee government was about to change the security and strategic dynamics of the region.

For some US lawmakers it was the worst intelligence failure ever. And within the US intelligence community, even louder voices asked: what if we had a mole inside the system?

The Senate Intelligence Committee believed that the CIA had been surprised by India's nuclear test. The director of the CIA, George Tenet, asked retired Admiral David Jeremiah to chair a team of external experts to examine this failure on the part of the CIA and also examine the quality and quantity of intelligence reporting and analysis on the Indian nuclear tests. Jeremiah admitted that US spies failed to see India's nuclear test coming: whatever resources and assets the CIA had inside the Indian establishment had failed to analyse the true intentions of the BJP-led NDA government. In fact, Jeremiah believed that the Indian assets had fooled them. He said: 'There is a good deal of reporting, there is a good deal of activity inside the community on the nuclear issue but it was working against the criteria that you would expect for our systems, not necessarily the way they went about doing it. And it was ameliorated a little bit by the feedback coming back from the Indians. And nobody is required to tell us the truth. But it was ameliorated a little bit by their responses that laid out for instance this business about establishing the National Security Council and then subsequently I think we had some evidence that suggested that not all the leadership knew what was going on, and therefore, were not able to deal with it.'

The CIA had placed at least one intelligence analyst at Langley to specifically monitor India's nuclear programme and after the furor, Jeremiah proposed scrubbing the American intelligence community with a wire brush and polishing it up to make sure it worked right; that everyone understood their responsibilities, that somebody was in charge of certain areas and that they had a reporting mechanism and authority.

Jeremiah was also asked whether the US intelligence community lacked assets and understanding about India, Indian cultures and how Indians react to certain problems or behave in certain ways. More specifically, he was asked that if there were no people in the CIA who understood India, would he get people like that? Jeremiah replied that he had recommended acquiring sources that might be in a better place to predict the future.

A press reporter commented to Jeremiah that American's Human Intelligence (HUMINT) capability, as far as India was concerned, was limited. He said: 'There was comment after this episode that it underscored the idea that there simply were no solid sources inside India, and that pointed to a larger weakness in the human intelligence community.'

The admiral's responses were brutally honest, indicating that the USA needed to aggressively recruit human sources: 'I think that generally across the board without being specific to India ... I think we could say our human intelligence capacity is seriously limited. It is limited because of the tremendously expanded coverage that we are required to deal with in today's world. We are no longer looking at Russia and China as sort of the key places—we now have to be able to look at almost anywhere in the world for that kind of problem.'

Days after the nuclear test in Pokhran in May 1998, CIA analysts said it was a sign that the country's Hindu nationalist BJP-led NDA government believed it would be able to follow through with its long-range agenda to remake the country as a powerful Hindu state in accordance with party mythology about India's past, and if true, the party's widely popular security posture would help grow its political base and prepare the ground for more controversial domestic reforms down the road. American intelligence believed that the BJP was sending out mixed messages on its foreign policy priorities beyond the confines of South Asia, at least in part to keep foreign powers guessing about its intentions. Intelligence analysts argued that India had calculated that demonstrating its nuclear prowess made it a state that the international community could no longer ignore and provide it a permanent seat on the United Nations Security Council and a place at the table in various regional forums.

On the other hand, Admiral Jeremiah made certain recommendations, pointing out that few of them were India-specific. Although the classified report is still out of reach, a three-page sanitised version was released for public consumption. The panel headed by Jeremiah recommended that the US intelligence community must realign collection priorities. Besides tight surveillance on rogue states, the panel recommended that American intelligence should also monitor geo-political temperatures especially in India and Pakistan to ascertain whether they have the capabilities to develop WMD (Weapons of Mass Destruction) programmes.

Jeremiah's sanitised list of recommendations in four different areas—integration of intelligence community, manning and training, collection management and tasking and analytic assumptions—said:

> Empower an inter-agency group to offer specific recommendations on how to improve collection and analysis

> on the South Asia WMD problem, including both technical aspects and leadership decision-making. If such a group is established, the DCI (Director of Central Intelligence) should consider personally appointing a Chairperson who has the DCI's authority. Ensure that these types of collaborative, inter-agency groups are not hamstrung by compartmentation. To some degree, this means delegating and empowering senior levels within Intelligence Community organizations to speak for the organization but also to free up senior leaders to focus on the needs of the nation. In order to accomplish this, there must be more risk-taking on the part of the Intelligence Community's senior leadership in pursuing what needs to be done, whether specifically directed or otherwise.

Pakistan had responded to India's nuclear test with Chagai-I, the underground nuclear explosion in Balochistan province on 28 May 1998. This had escalated the tension between the two hostile countries and the US Defence Intelligence Agency (DIA) in November 1999 observed in a background paper that the nuclear weapons race may intensify in the future. DIA argued, 'Both nations are expected to try to improve their nuclear weapons, increase the explosive force, reliability and variety of types, as far as possible and scientists in both countries could learn better how to do this from further nuclear testing.'

Senior Indian intelligence officers confirmed that the USA had increased its HUMINT collection activities in India. For CIA officials though, Afghanistan and Pakistan were more troublesome and during various meetings in Delhi, the R&AW reminded them that the Taliban and its ally Al-Qaeda were being groomed by Pakistan's Inter Service Intelligence (ISI) and the USA must act now to prevent inevitable catastrophe. After the hijacking of Indian Airlines Flight 814 and the subsequent open support by the Mullah Omar regime in Afghanistan to Pakistani terrorists, Indian intelligence warned the US government that soon, with the help of the ISI, these terror outfits would become a potent force and may strike beyond Afghan boundaries.

'I think the Americans listened to us but didn't believe that terrorists in Afghanistan and certain pockets of Pakistan were a real threat. In our closed-door meetings, some of them raised apprehensions about our analysis and intelligence inputs, terming them too farfetched. Some US officials even observed that our assessment was a by-product of our animosity with Pakistan despite the fact that we gave them proof that the Taliban and Al-Qaeda were being nurtured by the ISI and the state machinery of the neighbouring country,' said Surendra Sinha, a R&AW officer.

His observation seems plausible. The Americans were watching the Taliban's growth and the unhindered Pakistani support to hardcore militants from the sidelines. A November 1994 cable from the US embassy in Islamabad said that the Taliban's origins and future remain an enigma, with even the most well-informed speculation confronted with paradoxes. The Americans were certainly not able to judge between what was considered the 'good' Taliban and the 'bad' Taliban. However, a US Department of State memorandum in December 1994 disclosed that the Taliban was directly supported by the ISI.

During his meeting with US Acting Secretary of State Strobe Talbott on 9 February 1996, Pakistani Foreign Minister Asif Ali denied any Pakistani involvement in the growth of the Taliban. A US Department of State cable said:

> Ali categorically denied that Pakistan provided military assistance to the Taliban and urged the US to work with Pakistan on the basic principles of a peace plan, which would become the United Nations plan.

Pakistan's ISI chief Naseem Rana, who also attended the meeting, assured Talbott that Pakistan gave 'not one bullet' to the Taliban movement. Several documents released by the US government under the Freedom of Information Act, heavily sanitised though they may be, revealed that the US government was eager to engage with the Mullah Omar-led Taliban government despite knowing its terror capability and its attempts to protect and sponsor Al-Qaeda elements including Osama bin Laden.

A US Department of State cable dated 26 September 1996 said:

> In our initial contacts with the new authorities in Kabul, we will seek information about the new government and its intentions, and reiterate our key concerns—the importance of a broad-based government and the need to address quickly the twin problems of narcotics and terrorism.

The cable further observed that US government would be interested in knowing the location of ex-Saudi financier and radical Islamist Osama bin Laden.

> We had heard previously that he was in the eastern provinces. His continued presence here would not, we believe, serve Afghanistan's interests.

Indian agents with deep penetration in various provinces of Afghanistan had better and more polished intelligence on the Al-Qaeda network and the Taliban than the Americans. When the Americans descended on Afghanistan after 11 September 2001 to pick up information on the unholy nexus between the ISI, Taliban and Al-Qaeda, they had to rely on local paid informers and ISI officers who hated the presence of American spies in Afghanistan.

Great Betrayal

Intelligence officers in Delhi and abroad confirmed to me that aside from accessing intelligence reports, the CIA's other important task was to gather a list of R&AW officers posted abroad. Rabinder Singh's great betrayal, which was discovered in

2003, revealed the extent of the network of moles the CIA had managed to set up in countries of interest to them.

Intelligence sources told me: 'After Rabinder Singh's escape from India to the US, the investigation revealed that he indeed gave a list of R&AW officers posted abroad to his handler, Annie. He had compromised the cover of our officers and no one was even remotely aware of this horrific fact. The internal investigation conducted by the Counter Intelligence unit of the R&AW divulged six hundred emails sent by Rabinder Singh to his handler. He used multiple email addresses to sell the country's secrets. This was an indication that Singh, who was technologically handicapped, had been well trained by the CIA.'

The traitor, however, used one email address undisclosed to the R&AW to communicate with Suki, his daughter. The conversations later recovered by R&AW investigators, which I have seen, frames a picture of a loving father who values hard work. In one such email Rabinder told Suki: 'There is no alternative to hard work and honesty. If you are honest and truthful, you will never suffer in your life.'

While he was under R&AW surveillance, Rabinder received an email from his daughter. She was complaining about a financial crunch and her tough life in the USA. He told her: 'You must trust in God and let him take care of everything. Just believe in God.'

It appears that if not God, then at least the CIA heard her plea. Two days later she wrote to Rabinder, informing him that a certain Jeffrey uncle had come and given her $1,200.

'Jeffrey uncle was very nice. Is he your good friend, Papa?' she had asked.

Rabinder wrote back that he was happy to hear that and yes, Jeffrey was a good friend. In another email, he again quoted the Bhagavad Gita and reminded Suki that life has to be perceived like a vast sky.

'Learn the value of Karma from our scriptures. It will teach you that you need to have dedication and devotion. Leave everything else to God,' he wrote.

These communications were frequent and during the course of the investigation, senior officers were intrigued to discover that Rabinder Singh always wore a mask.

'The evidence collected from his two personal laptops shows he lived a very conflicting and complicated life. We tried to find out more on Jeffrey from one of our assets in USA, but it was a cover name and we realised there was no such officer posted at Langley. However, Annie's details were procured and shipped to the Indian agency to corroborate the events leading to India's biggest spy scandal,' said Vijay Nambiar, a R&AW officer.

Were R&AW officials knowingly passing information to Rabinder Singh? According to an officer codenamed K.K. Sharma, in the course of surveillance on Rabinder Singh between January 2004 and April 2004, more than fifty-five officers of the agency were discovered to have inadvertently supplied intelligence and documents to the double agent. It was a trap laid by Rabinder, Sharma said, to innocent officials to feed him with intelligence and analysis on immediate neighbours such as the growing relationship between Myanmar and China, the Naxal penetration in Nepal, how the Taliban operated in Afghanistan, the activities of the Liberation Tigers of Tamil Eelam (LTTE) in Sri Lanka and their illegal procurement of weapons with the help of arms dealers in Eastern Europe.

I asked Sharma: 'How does it feel when you know there is a traitor working with you in the organisation, a person who is passing on intelligence that could compromise the lives of hundreds of agents working abroad?'

Sharma was baffled by this question. 'You want to sack that bastard,' he said. 'You also want to torture the traitor. That is the easiest thing to do. But what do you do thereafter? If you want to nail a traitor, you need to have solid evidence of betrayal. You need to have the details of his handlers so that the leaking line can be plugged for the future. When Rabinder was put under surveillance, there were reports that he was regularly having lunch meetings with an intelligence officer handling Pakistan operations and a desk officer handling some African countries. It could be assumed that they might have innocently given the traitor certain pieces of intelligence that he could sell for dollars. How one sanitises such activities was the biggest challenge.'

Sharma also revealed that many spies involved in the surveillance on Rabinder Singh were often agitated whenever he copied classified intelligence reports procured from colleagues, charming them with praise and treating them to meals at expensive restaurants.

'Since his room was bugged, they could hear every discussion he had with the officers manning different desks. These officers never suspected that while he shared a cup of coffee with them, he was stabbing them in the back. Welcome to the treacherous terrain of espionage. You never know who is spying against whom, which officer has been compromised and being run as a double agent by the foreign intelligence outfits. You feel as though you're living in a black hole. For me, it was like seeing an Aldrich Ames behind his innocent face,' said Sharma.

Aldrich Ames worked at the CIA from 1962 and got his first overseas assignment in Turkey in 1969. In 1985, while working in the CIA's Soviet division, he switched sides and walked into the waiting arms of the KGB, the Soviet intelligence organisation. The CIA admits that Ames may have compromised at least a hundred operations and may have endangered the lives of dozens of Soviets working for the American agency. In 1986 when CIA agents started disappearing, a hunt was launched to find the leak within the American intelligence apparatus. The CIA counterintelligence team led by well-known spy hunter Jeanne Vertefeuille discussed three possibilities for the failed and compromised operations: One, the KGB had infiltrated the agency's communications and read the traffic. Two, the KGB in Moscow had obtained access to CIA documents regarding the compromised cases or placed a bug or three, there was a mole within the agency.

As with the Rabinder Singh case, the CIA spy hunter team's biggest challenge was to establish that there was a mole within the agency and once they did this in 1989, as they brought Ames under the scanner, they were required to collect solid proof that his lavish lifestyle had been earned by selling secrets and betraying his comrades in arms. After years of patience and carefully analysing Ames's ill-gotten wealth, the CIA spy hunters came to believe that there was a link between his meetings with Soviet diplomats and the huge deposits in his bank accounts. He was arrested by the Federal Bureau of Investigation (FBI) just as he prepared for a trip to Moscow, a journey the investigators believed was one way. CIA officials said that during his career as a mole, Ames had received $2.5 million from the KGB and another $2.1 million had been earmarked for him at a bank in Moscow.

How much did Rabinder Singh receive from the CIA? There are only speculations, no concrete figures. How much damage did he cause to the country's national security by compromising ongoing operations? This too remains in the domain of speculation but the investigation revealed that he might have passed on over twenty thousand documents. Singh's modus operandi was simple. Bring a classified report home, photograph it with a sophisticated camera provided by the Americans, store the files in an external hard disc and later transfer them to his handler using secure internet protocol. He subsequently erased all the files from the external disc and the two laptops he frequently used to transfer the nation's secrets.

Only after his escape did the investigators from the Counter Intelligence unit start weaving together threads from his past.

Right on top were his frequent trips to Nepal. Although the counter-espionage unit operatives did not have elaborate details of the people Singh interacted with in the Himalayan country, they had reason to believe that his trips there were primarily to meet the Americans, especially the CIA station chief at Kathmandu who was working under the cover of Counselor, Economic Affairs. Later, the R&AW agents learned that days before he flew to Washington, Rabinder Singh and his wife Parminder had been booked into a hotel in Nepalganj, close to the Indian border and the CIA station chief had paid the bill. The two were then shifted to a CIA safe house in Kathmandu and two American passports were issued in the names of Rajpal Sharma and Deepa Kumar Sharma. On 7 May 2004, an American escorted them on board the Austrian Airlines Flight 5032 headed to Washington.

Spying is the product of betrayal. Someone in the business needs to betray a country, organisation or source to acquire protected intelligence. Rabinder was a seasoned spy and a double agent. He was trained in the craft of surveillance detection but only got suspicious about surveillance at his residence about two weeks before his escape. A R&AW surveillance team was deployed at his residence 24/7. His car and house were bugged. The R&AW officer handling the team believes that Rabinder had asked an officer in the security unit to sweep his office. This, he thinks, was proof of Rabinder's suspicion that he was being monitored. The R&AW officer requested the then National Security Advisor Brajesh Mishra to sign the order for Rabinder's arrest. But Mishra kept delaying the matter. It appears he wanted to get rid of Rabinder anyhow or perhaps waited for him to disappear because the existence of a CIA mole deep inside the R&AW was nothing less than a coup. He asked for more evidence and details of Rabinder's handlers in the US. This was a huge mistake. The capture and subsequent interrogation of Rabinder Singh could have unravelled the CIA network in India and Nepal as well as other moles or facilitators if there were any.

The night Rabinder Singh fled to Nepal, the surveillance team posted at his residence had spotted his wife leaving the house. She then came back with a family friend. Rabinder was in the house. The friend left after dinner. The team never saw Rabinder and his wife leaving the house. They only learned of the couple's escape the next day when there was no activity in the house and the spotters panicked. When an officer barged into the house on the pretext of delivering office circulars, the family servant disclosed that Sahib and Memsahib have gone to Punjab for a wedding. This was the last lie Rabinder Singh uttered before he vanished.

According to R&AW officers, neither Rabinder's wife nor his children were aware that Rabinder was a double agent. For them, he was a senior officer in the Cabinet Secretariat.

Sharma said that Rabinder's betrayal haunted the R&AW for months. In the aftermath of his defection to the USA, the government initiated proceedings to remove his services under article 311 (2) (C) of the Constitution.

'Sometime in mid-May, the CIA station chief was summoned to find out whether the US government had been in the loop about Singh's recruitment and defection. We all knew that the CIA had done the job, but this was a procedural formality. As expected, the Americans feigned ignorance about Rabinder Singh and his wife and denied that any R&AW officer had been in touch with the US intelligence agency. The CIA personnel who had helped Rabinder and his wife, retired from the agency in 2012 after serving for almost twenty-six years and nowadays, he occupies a top position in an Arizona-based defence group,' Sharma told me.

After switching loyalties, Rabinder Singh settled in Florida. Since the R&AW and the CIA had a long-standing relationship and had collaborated on some major security events in the past, Rabinder Singh's defection was given a quiet burial for some time. But he wasn't forgiven. An encrypted message that was shipped through the diplomatic pouch from Washington in late 2016 confirmed that the double agent was dead. Further information revealed that Singh had died in a road accident in Maryland. It also came to light that after switching loyalties, Rabinder Singh lived as a refugee in the USA when the CIA dumped him months after the dramatic extraction to the USA via Kathmandu in May 2004. He had been beset with financial problems since the CIA had stopped sending him pay cheques and his attempts to get a job at a think tank run by a former CIA deputy director were stonewalled, pushing him into a deep depression. A remorseful Singh, burdened with the sin of betraying his country, spent almost twelve years as a recluse in New York, Maryland and neighbouring Virginia, where his extended family lives. A senior officer codenamed Delta neither confirmed nor denied any role the R&AW might have played to eliminate the traitor. He did, however, say that Singh couldn't bear the guilt of betraying his country after his US dream collapsed, thanks to the CIA's use and throw policy.

'Singh was left in the cold. He had told his children and US-based relatives that there was a threat to his life in India. Despite so much material about his treachery available in the public domain, his relatives revered him as a loving and kind-hearted person. His death is seen as the closure of the case that was vigorously pursued till 2007. The betrayal of Rabinder Singh is one that R&AW would rather like to forget,' said Delta.

7

R&AW IN SHACKLES

Sometime in early 1990, the Indian government negotiated a defence deal for fighter aircraft from a developed country. Since the Indian embassy had to act as a coordinator, the ambassador asked a R&AW officer to help him finalise the deal. The officer readily agreed to activate a long-term asset who could swing the deal in favour of the Indian government. In the meantime, the bureaucrats in Delhi were about to clinch the contract through an Indian dealer for Rs 110 crore.

In April 1990, the R&AW officer returned to the ambassador, informing him the deal could be a little sweeter at Rs 65 crore, thanks to his shadowy asset. The ambassador duly informed New Delhi of this massive discount.

'No one knows what discussion took place behind closed doors at Raisina Hill but I was told that the government had already decided to go ahead with the dealer's offer of Rs 110 crore. Our asset was disappointed and completely withdrew. And we couldn't say a word since we are not supposed to fix commercial deals on behalf of the government. But given a chance, we can do a better job than most of the agencies tasked with such activities. On this front, R&AW remains highly underutilised,' a R&AW spy codenamed P. Narasimhan told me.

India had been doing a lot of defence shopping in the UK and the Soviet Union since Independence. The bureaucrats at Raisina Hill were the deciding factor, aside from the top brass of the defence forces. The Indian government bought Canberra jet bombers, trainers and reconnaissance aircraft from the British in the late 1950s. It had been a conscious decision not to become dependent on Soviet resources, although the USSR remained India's major supplier. The US and the UK imposed an arms embargo on India during the 1965 war with Pakistan, forcing the Indian government to look to Moscow for fighters, helicopters, air defence missile systems, tanks, armoured vehicles, artillery, tactical air defence systems, destroyers and submarines. Unlike the Western countries, the Soviets were ready to sell modern weaponry systems on easy credit terms and in some cases, they did not demand hard currency, but allowed the Indian government to pay with commodities.

After Prime Minister Indira Gandhi's government came to power, bureaucrats were sent to Paris to buy the Mirage 2000 as a counter to the F-16s provided to Pakistan by the USA. The CIA suggested that India's purchases in the Western arms markets were primarily aimed to supply its armed forces with the latest available weapon systems and military technology and to build a more modern and powerful defence establishment. The CIA officers believed India's first move to shop outside the USSR in the 1980s also served to reduce criticism at home and abroad of India being a Soviet proxy by reducing the Soviet share of overall Indian military imports.

In 1983, a CIA intelligence note said:

> Achieving a better balance of Western and Soviet arms, however, will be a slow, long-term process, and Western arms sales to India over the next five years are likely to be a comparatively small, albeit important, part of the overall modernization process. The Indian armed forces probably

> will seek selected weapons from the United States, and, in so doing, are likely to request progressively more sophisticated military technology. Prime Minister Gandhi, however, is likely to proceed slowly in concluding new major arms contracts with the United States because of suspicions of US intentions in the region and dislike for US foreign military restrictions.

And then in 1986, the Indian government signed a $285 million contract with the Swedish arms company Bofors for four hundred and ten Howitzer field guns. A year later, the deal turned out to be a massive scam, triggering a political storm in New Delhi. The opposition hammered Rajiv Gandhi's government as the alleged middleman in the deal, Ottavio Quattrochi, was closely linked to his family. It was during this period that R&AW officers posted abroad began verifying the credentials of arms sellers. Information picked up from assets and paid informers hired for limited operations was passed on to the government. Although the spy agency's role was limited and it was never directly involved in deals, it provided intelligence on suppliers and arms dealers operating in the global market.

Narasimhan's view that the R&AW is underutilised in this area is echoed by several other R&AW spies. The intelligence officials argue that R&AW officers are better trained to understand the shadowy world of arms dealing than a civilian bureaucrat posted abroad. And they could utilise their assets within the establishment of the target country to secure better deals. But they are shackled by the bureaucracy in many ways, including a turf war with the Indian Foreign Service (IFS). With a staff strength of about six thousand people, the spy agency finds it tough to maintain the cover of its agents abroad, particularly because of internal rivalries and a war with officers from diplomatic services.

An officer codenamed Alok Singh told me: 'In various instances, the diplomatic community exposed the identity of a R&AW officer within days of her or his arrival in the target country. In some cases, officers from other agencies inadvertently or deliberately identified the spy. Despite this pressure, the extraordinary men and women of the Indian intelligence community have done remarkable jobs. But the shackles need to be broken before R&AW can realise its full potential.'

For example, the arrival of a R&AW spy codenamed R.K. Singh in Dhaka sometime in the first week of June 1990 was disclosed to the Bangladeshi regime. Singh, whose primary task was to check Pakistan's sphere of influence in Bangladesh, learned from a junior officer at the embassy that his cover had been blown the moment he landed at Dhaka airport. From his first day at the embassy, he had been constrained in his tasks to neutralise Pakistan's proxies and shape a Bangladeshi government for India's advantage.

Once he knew his cover had been blown, Singh decided to follow a routine to counter the 24/7 surveillance on him. Every evening when he left the embassy, he would go to a video cassette shop close to his residence, borrow a Hindi movie and go home. Every Friday, he shopped for vegetables and groceries. A week later, the Bangladeshi counterintelligence officials opened a vegetable stall in front of his house to intensify their surveillance, because it appeared to them that Singh was doing nothing to justify their eye on him. Unperturbed, Singh continued his routine. In September 1990, an informer within the Bangladeshi establishment told him that his file had been closed because the counterintelligence officials had found nothing suspicious about him.

'The Bangladeshi counterintelligence thought R.K. Singh was not a R&AW officer. He goes to same video shop every day, comes back home and goes nowhere else to meet contacts or possible assets. What operation could he run? So they turned their surveillance on a brigadier who was working as the defence attaché at the embassy. R.K. Singh's four month long exercise in patience paid off, and now he was able to carry out spectacular operations in Bangladesh, crafting new alignments and informal networks to neutralise our adversaries,' chuckled Alok.

Indian spies also faced obstacles in Europe in the 1980s when Pakistan-linked forces became even more radical. In early 1981, it was learned that some Pakistani sympathisers based in London were raising funds for a Kashmir jihad. The R&AW used Prague as a launch pad to mount an operation against this campaign. Prague, the capital city of Czechoslovakia was receiving a host of visitors from the Soviet Union, Cuba and India to explore business opportunities in various sectors during this time. The strengthening of business ties provided a way to gain a foothold in the country and establish safe houses. The Indians quoted a market survey that showed a demand for a wide range of textiles, ready-made garments, hosiery, goods made of natural leather, sports goods, jewellery and cosmetics. Many Indian firms signed contracts with state agencies for regular supplies of spices, tea and other foodstuff. The president of Czechoslovakia, Gustav Husak, who became the long-term secretary general of the Communist Party of Czechoslovakia, was a bitter critic of imperialism and his close ties with Moscow were an added advantage for the Indian intelligence organisation.

But India was not the only country running spies from Prague. France, just a thousand kilometres away, was equally interested in expanding espionage operations through its attachés. In mid-February 1981, two French defence attachés were caught spying, which led to the expulsion of diplomats from both sides. It was a nerve-racking time for the Indian spies who were launching operations in Europe and Africa. But they survived despite little assistance from the officials of the diplomatic service.

R&AW and its operatives have successfully conducted several operations without inviting much attention, but certain areas in the ever-changing dynamics of security remain vulnerable.

According to Narasimhan, the R&AW, like the CIA, wants a hand in everything. Even with a friendly government, the R&AW needs to play both sides—the ruling party and the opposition—to ensure it remains unaffected by electoral outcomes in the future. Narasimhan also argued that any changes introduced in the workings of Indian intelligence agencies had been cosmetic, made without consideration for long-term strategy. He also tossed me a question: 'Why has the Chinese growth been exemplary?'

Fortunately, he answered the question himself. 'There is only one answer—economic espionage. Chinese intelligence has been stealing technology right from the start. They did it in automobiles, defence, space and various other sectors of manufacturing. We all know that some of the world's best spy organisations carry out commercial espionage. But though Indian agents are seeking a mandate for it, it has not been granted. If we can make commercial espionage a part of the R&AW's obligations, agents working undercover abroad could produce wonders. As of today, the scientific and economic advisors posted abroad just read and write reports on the basis of publicly-accessible literature, while the R&AW is confined to political and security espionage. Meanwhile, the Chinese Ministry of State Security mostly uses its agents to clone the best available technology. The R&AW has the experience and capability even for scientific espionage, but some of the best operatives in the trade remain underutilised,' Narasimhan said.

For many retired R&AW personnel, the half-century-long career of the spy agency was both good and bad. What they most wanted, they said, was clear priorities from the governments they served. On a daily basis, spying can be a routine job: gather information, analyse it and corroborate it. If the information has been procured from other sources, it needs to be verified again and again before the finished product is sent to the government of the day. Many veterans in the field agreed that the relationship between policymakers and the R&AW had been at its best during the R.N. Kao and Indira Gandhi's period, and its worst period was when the Janata Party government led by Morarji Desai was in power. There was almost a complete breakdown of the relationship in the years Desai served as the prime minister, thanks to a mutual sense of distrust. Direct communication between the R&AW and the prime minister was just 2–3 per cent of what it ought to have been—and it would have been even less if not for the institutional set up. According to a seasoned spy codenamed Rita Wadhawa, bureaucrats don't understand the need for intelligence, so they can't appreciate the products of spycraft.

'The major problem is that they treat the R&AW like any other government department,' she said. 'You ask for a post and the bureaucrats will point to other organisations to demonstrate the existence of a sanctioned strength. If we asked for fifteen positions for Mazar-i-Sharif, the bureaucrats told us to justify the number. We argued with the cabinet secretary and officials in the Prime Minister's Office that certain requirements cannot be put on file in black and white because we are not an ordinary institution. Even financial advisors posted with R&AW can be major obstacles in certain projects. They don't have the expertise of espionage and their primary responsibility is to create roadblocks.'

'The same jagged relationship exists between R&AW operatives abroad and the staff at diplomatic missions. The civilian officers posted abroad suspect that the intelligence agency spies on them, which is absolutely baseless,' Rita said. The R&AW plays no role in vigilance, but the hostility persists.

'Suppose the cover of the counsellor of information is given to an officer from the Ministry of External Affairs (MEA). In that scenario, the officer will never involve R&AW officers, which makes the life of bright spies very difficult. Even during visits of VVIPs from the country, the foreign officers make sure that the R&AW officers are kept at an arm's length during preparations. In recent years, we have seen that agency officers are not allowed to participate in trade delegations. This is quite worrisome,' said Rita.

Ashok Sethi, a spy earlier posted in a European country, said that the relationship between R&AW officers posted abroad with foreign office officials is on many occasions limited to 15 August and 26 January celebrations, and sometimes, a house party. Even Intelligence Bureau (IB) agents who are posted abroad as security officers often blow the covers of R&AW operatives. It's like a cold war within the set-up, he said.

'There cannot be any better example for this than the frozen relationship between MEA officers and R&AW agents in Bangladesh when Narasimha Rao was the prime minister,' said Sethi. 'Whenever we want to raise the strength of our teams in the neighbouring countries, the first opposition is always from the foreign office. They don't know anything about the functioning of the R&AW and the intelligence we pick up abroad for the security of the country, but they are authorised to write reports about our operatives and their functions. The biggest damage to a R&AW agent abroad came from one of its own agency chiefs, who exposed all the cover posts with the justification that "everyone knows you are R&AW, so why do you need the cover?" Sometimes foreign service officers are more than willing to show that the agency is dysfunctional without realising they are causing irreparable damage to not only ongoing operations but also to the lives of the agents and paid informers.'

Tactical Decision-making

Most older R&AW agents felt that only three customers—Indira Gandhi, Rajiv Gandhi and Narasimha Rao—genuinely appreciated espionage tradecraft. Rao in particular, a senior officer mentioned, was very shrewd in his dealings with the agency. He would listen to important reports narrated by the chief and other officers without uttering a word. At the end of the presentation, his only response was, 'Okay.' This perplexed a newly appointed chief who thought Rao did not like what they were doing or were planning to do because he never interrupted, did not question, and never said that he agreed. 'I told the chief not to worry because the PM agrees with what we are doing. If he had any objection, he would convey it immediately,' said a spy codenamed Madhav Anand. 'Once, when we informed Rao about an impending exchange of nuclear-installation lists with Pakistan to ensure that the Indian government is not attacked from any side, he said, "Okay." On another occasion, the government needed some help from a Middle East country and the PM spoke about it. But this was rare. He just listened to us attentively and meetings ended in half an hour. He never openly expressed his feelings, though we knew he admired our courage. We achieved a great degree of success in the Middle East during Rajiv Gandhi's tenure. The backroom manoeuvring by the R&AW reflected in open diplomacy. We created assets in Egypt, Algeria, Morocco, Tunisia and Iran, and tried to strike a balance between Israel and Palestine. In April 1985, Yasser Arafat was invited to attend a meeting with Rajiv Gandhi despite the reservations of Israel's intelligence agency, Mossad.'

In many ways, the R&AW spies have been lucky too. For instance, they have never had to face interference in tactical decision-making about covert operations. 'This is because we don't acknowledge our failures and never highlight our achievements,' said Madhav Anand. 'But we have been troubled for quite some time because our meticulous reports, prepared on the basis of spectacular intelligence, rarely get a response from the decision makers. We don't know why, but one thing is certain: there is tremendous institutional bias against the R&AW and on several occasions, it has been the victim of misinformation. For example, R&AW never operates inside the country and never interferes with domestic issues, but politicians are always scared of the agency. I would like to make it clear that gossip about rivalry over internal intelligence is not correct. We could disagree with the IB or the Defence Intelligence Agency (DIA) on some issues but that is like friendly banter.'

According to Sethi, the only time R&AW officers are genuinely perturbed by the bureaucracy is when there are unnecessary obstructions by civilian officers at times of great urgency. For instance, Sethi added, suppose a certain situation in Nepal was hot and the agency needed to urgently move a unit from Myanmar to Nepal. In such a situation, bureaucratic obstructions and questions about expenditure are major roadblocks. Mobile units simply don't have freedom to move from one place to another, said Sethi.

The bureaucrats don't understand the perils and dangers of covert operations, said Rita. Spies have no legal backing and yet they must operate in hostile territory. 'You are on your own if you are caught. This is not an easy life. You not only need to cultivate assets but also a network of informers. There is always a risk of failure while running an intelligence operation and vulnerability due to possible double agents. It requires great skill and courage to vacuum up the secrets of your enemy and survive to fight another day. A single miscalculation can cost hundreds of lives. And this is much more difficult for agents working overseas on long-term assignments because they do not have any cover. They live and work under bogus identities created for a particular operation,' Rita said.

In 2002, the Indian media echoed with whispers that a R&AW spy named Ravindra Kaushik had died in a Pakistani prison. The undercover agent who had managed to infiltrate the Pakistan army before his cover was blown in 1983 had been incarcerated for eighteen years and succumbed to pulmonary tuberculosis in November 2001. A fictional account of his life was published sometime after his death and Bollywood produced a film to highlight the larger than life figure of a superspy. There are various versions of his life floating on public platforms, each claiming to be authentic. Since there is no file on Kaushik in the R&AW and the MEA has petitions filed by his family in Rajasthan, it would be inappropriate to comment on the authenticity of those papers. But it is a known fact that agents were recruited for low-level operations abroad and Kaushik was perhaps not the only one. According to the R&AW insiders, hundreds of operatives were recruited for tactical operations in the 1980s.

'We have no information of such a person (Kaushik) in our operational record,' said an agency insider. 'I don't think we did this task because the stories seem like fantasy. I would say that any story about Kaushik is completely bogus. The idea behind any low-level operation is to get a continuous flow of information through different routes. It was said that Kaushik was initially paid some money, but after the controversy broke in the media, an internal investigation did not reveal anything about him or the person who might have been his handler.'

Intelligence agencies are now facing increasing pressure from various social groups who demand accountability for their functions. In 2012, the Centre for Public Interest Litigation filed a writ petition in the Supreme Court seeking a proper mechanism, following the models of other democratic countries, to ensure the accountability of the government's three intelligence agencies, namely IB, R&AW and the National Technical Research Organisation (NTRO). The petition argued that the intelligence agencies are public authorities that have operated since their inception under executive orders issued by the government without accountability to the Indian Parliament or any other democratic institution. The petition also noted that India has the dubious distinction of being the only democracy in the world whose intelligence agencies have no legitimacy in the eyes of the law and are not accountable to the people or the Parliament. Further arguments highlighted that in the

USA, two Congressional committees were set up in 1976 and 1977 to document the systematic abuse of power by the US intelligence agencies within the country and abroad. This led to the establishment of oversight mechanisms in the USA. Other countries, such as the UK, Australia, Canada and South Africa followed suit. In the UK, the Security Service (SS) known as MI5, responsible for domestic espionage, and the Security Intelligence Service (SIS), called MI6, responsible for external intelligence, are governed by the Security Services Act 1989 and the Intelligence Services Act 1994, respectively. The Canadian intelligence, known as Canadian Security Intelligence Service (CSIS), is governed by the Canadian Security Intelligence Service Act 1984, while the Intelligence Services Act 2001 (ISA) governs the Australian intelligence organisation. In Germany, the Federal Intelligence Service, called Bundesnachrichtendienst (BND) was established after the enactment of the Federal Intelligence Service Law in 1990. With these examples, the petitioner in India's Supreme Court demanded oversight mechanisms such as accountability to a Parliamentary Committee to ensure that the intelligence agencies function in accordance with the law and the democratic ideals of the nation.

The apex court rejected the petition in 2016, observing that any attempt to get into the domain of intelligence may create a dent in national security. Between the filing of the petition and the judgment, the intelligence community in India seethed with counter arguments that the Indian political condition was not suitable for a Parliamentary oversight. According to a senior intelligence officer codenamed Vijay Giri, the country's intelligence organs cannot afford to have political oversight for one simple reason—politicians cannot keep a secret.

'Suppose you wanted $30 million for an operation. Can you expect the political leaders to keep it a secret? It is not fair to compare Indian intelligence agencies with their counterparts in the developed countries. The political atmosphere is very different here and our operations would not survive for even a day. Even in the current scenario, we have unrealistic expectations from the R&AW despite the fact that the decision makers are not letting us work. We are not able to exploit the R&AW's full potential,' said Giri.

In the half a century since its inception in 1968, the R&AW has developed the capability to harvest excellent intelligence with the help of hundreds of analysts, strategists and committed field agents. Indian spies have graduated from sniffing out secrets to carrying out spectacular and effective covert operations. They are not motivated by the limelight or by money. The only thing that drives them in the treacherous world of espionage is loyalty for their country. They have set a new standard in the world of espionage by shunning publicity. Unlike the CIA, the MI6 and Mossad, little is known about the feats and sacrifices of Indian spies.

'We have seen glorious days and some unfortunate failures, but dealt with all the situations fearlessly,' said Giri. 'With changing global dynamics, we need to make certain changes ourselves and break the shackles of bureaucracy to allow ourselves more freedom to carry out spy missions. Spying is like walking on water; it can produce miracles.'

8

THE GLOBAL FOOTPRINTS OF R&AW

Since its inception in 1968, the R&AW spies and analysts have been trained to decode not just complex global issues, but also domestic matters with international ramifications. From secret encounters against inimical forces to long-term undercover operations, the R&AW spies gather information which the agency's analysts ensure is polished, put in context, compared with existing information, tested for reliability and then finally disseminated to the customers—India's decision makers, with the prime minister on top of the list.

As per the agency's training manual, there are four stages before a final report is dispatched for action—intelligence collection by field agents, collation at the desk concerned, evaluation and analysis by the analyst and country expert and finally circulation to the customer. While field agents require agility and a light footprint in the target country, analysts must have brains that could beat high-speed computers. The two need to work together to ensure that the intelligence gained is delivered with speed and accuracy.

Five professionally processed reports in this chapter give an insight into the world of intelligence analysts who are rarely mentioned by the media or portrayed in films. Two sections show how espionage operations can sometimes be more dramatic than fiction, and one section describes how the R&AW and the government of the day discuss issues and make decisions. Finally, this chapter also explains the strict rules of espionage tradecraft followed by every person involved in the generation of intelligence.

For instance, spies and officers posted abroad are forbidden to discuss any sensitive matter over the phone. No form of telephonic communication, either on a direct line or between two extensions from the same switchboard, is secure from casual interception through cross-connections and the possibility of telephone operators and engineers overhearing conversations while performing their duties. The spies are clearly instructed to keep in mind: The telephone is not secure.

A note on secure communications adds that the scramblers used by government departments offer no security against any expert with facilities for 'descrambling.' The government note says:

> It must be assumed that all line telephone conversations with our missions or by our missions and representatives abroad and all telephone conversations in foreign countries to and from official premises are intercepted. The danger of interception is not limited to the country in which the mission is situated but extends also to those countries through which the telephone lines pass. As the principle on which the scrambler works is well known, its use on foreign controlled lines confers no security. Telephone instrument is 'NEVER SECURE'. Telephone should never be used as a means of communication of any message of a secret nature. Nor should telegrams be dictated or gist given over the phone even in an Indian language, in view of the risk of a compromise.

To protect coded messages, guidelines have been prepared for personnel handling cypher units abroad. Authorised users are prohibited from divulging the methods of enciphering to any unauthorised person and it is made clear that those working on cypher jobs will never be released from their charter of secrecy even when they are no longer employed on cypher duties, don't have access to the cyphers or aren't with the service any longer. During their training, those coding messages are forbidden to discuss cypher matters even amongst themselves in any place where they are likely to be overheard by potential eavesdroppers. The identity of personnel handling cyphers is kept top secret and only a handful of top officers posted abroad know about their activities.

During the fledgling years of the R&AW, certain rules were formulated to keep the coding of information safe and secure. For instance, cypher officers have separate accommodation, which have to meet certain conditions:

(i) It does not in any way form a passage to another room or office, which is not used for cyphers.
(ii) Windows, skylights, etc. should be of translucent material, barred and protected by wire mesh to prevent papers from blowing away.
(iii) Doors should be strong and fitted with a secure locking arrangement.
(iv) Walls and ceiling should not be made of canvas or light boards.
(v) Persons walking or standing outside should not be able to hear or see what is being said or done inside.
(vi) All cypher material will be kept in a locked, heavy combination safe or in a security box permanently cemented to the floor, exclusively used for the storage of cypher material. Even when the cypher material is locked up, the building, office or room in which it is normally kept must be under surveillance twenty-four hours a day.
(vii) Access to cypher offices is confined strictly to cypher personnel and especially authorised personnel by the head

of the mission concerned, which should be kept to the absolute minimum necessity.

(viii) There must be only one entrance door to a cypher office, so that persons seeking admittance may be identified without allowing them access to the room or to a view of the room's interiors.

Rules were framed even for the disposal of paper from wastebaskets to ensure that any papers linked to the operatives and officers working abroad are not disclosed. To destroy cypher documents, the rules say that the books need to be unbound and then each page is to be rolled up as a whole and not torn into pieces before burning, and in the case of cryptograms the pages should be crumpled, because rolled and crumpled up paper burns quicker than small pieces. The officers are also told that cypher documents should be burnt in an incinerator used exclusively by the cypher office and while the papers are burning, they must be stirred with a rod to ensure that only ashes are left at the bottom.

Cypher personnel supervising the burning of such papers are directed not to leave their position near the incinerator till only ashes are left. Any carbon paper used while making copies of secret telegrams has to be burnt immediately after use.

For physical security and to guard secrecy, some more dos and don'ts are circulated among officers:

(a) All persons connected with the operation of cyphers on arrival into and departure from the cypher office will check to confirm that no cypher documents and papers have been left behind in an insecure manner.

(b) When there are two sets of keys for safes containing cypher documents, one set should remain with the cypher operator and the other should invariably be deposited with the head of the mission or controlling officer in a sealed cover. They should be checked periodically. Cypher keys should, under no circumstances, be deposited in a foreign bank.

(c) All packages containing cypher documents will be thoroughly examined on receipt and seals will be checked to ascertain that the packages have not been tampered with in transit. A thorough check of documents will be made with the accompanying issue note, and suitable entries made in the ledger, which should be kept up to date.

(d) Their official designation should never be disclosed.

(e) They should avoid informal contacts with foreigners, but at the same time, they should be discreet enough to not rouse suspicion of the nature of their work by exhibiting too much seclusion.

(f) In missions abroad when cypher personnel have to do general duties in addition to cypher work, and come into contact with foreigners in discharging their general official duties, they should carefully see to it that such acquaintances are strictly confined to the performances of their official duties only.

(g) Persons deployed in the operation of cyphers should be extremely careful of the dangerous influence of alcoholic drinks, that so often lowers moral standards. They should strictly avoid all social contacts with persons who are anxious to entertain them in any surreptitious manner.

As time passed, the job of the spies became even more gruelling. Many spies believe that certain documents related to crucial operations should be distributed among fresh recruits to help them learn the craft of the trade and lessons from triumphs and failures. In the early 1980s, the R&AW was a rising star in the global intelligence community and hundreds of Indian spies worked across the world in often hostile environments to harvest information with the potential to change the course of the future.

Back in the Delhi headquarters, analysts were busy with 'for your eyes only' reports for the customers. Here are some nuggets gleaned from the R&AW.

Iran–Iraq Conflict

On 22 September 1980, a year after the Islamic revolution in Iran, Iraq, governed by Saddam Hussein, invaded the fragile Iran led by the religious leader, Ayatollah Khomeini. The Islamic Republican Party (IRP) of Iran that was born amidst the revolution in 1979 was averse to the ceasefire proposal hurriedly drafted by the Islamic Summit, a coalition of several Islamic countries. R&AW spies picked up intelligence from field agents on the conflict that destabilised the region and slowly but surely, turned Khomeini into Iran's godfather. Three months after the war, the Ministry of External Affairs (MEA) created an Islamic Cell: a separate administrative division to carry out regular and intensive studies of Islamic affairs and their implications for India in all aspects.

India's growing interest in the region was primarily for two reasons: oil and the increasing penetration of Pakistan. In 1980, Pakistan had the second-largest armed forces in the Muslim world and all the Muslim countries turned to Pakistan for study material for their training institutions, officers and men to train combat units, engineers for construction work and retired officers to induct into paramilitary organisations. By the time of the beginning of the hostility between Iran and Iraq, Pakistan was providing personnel from its three services to both countries aside from support to the UAE, Jordan, Qatar, Kuwait, Libya and Saudi Arabia. Before the outbreak of war, Indian intelligence agents had picked up chatter on possible Pakistan-Iraq cooperation in the nuclear sphere.

India also had deep economic interests in Iraq and the topmost priority of Indira Gandhi's government was to defuse the situation and ensure peace. But Iran had taken a tough stand and all attempts for peace drew a blank. In an intelligence report dated 19 March 1981, the R&AW said that because of Khomeini's stand, the IRP had suggested that the first task of any peace mission should be to identify the aggressor and to punish him, directly naming Saddam Hussein. After the ceasefire proposal was handed to both countries, Iran was prepared to concede at most to a simultaneous ceasefire and Iraqi withdrawal in contrast to the recommendation by the Islamic Countries' Coalition for a week's gap between the two and a phased withdrawal of the Iraqis over a period of four weeks.

India too played an active role in peace-making efforts while expanding its economic relationship with Baghdad. Special peace envoys were sent to both Iran and Iraq a month after the invasion. The then foreign secretary, R.D. Sathe, made a secret trip to Tehran and Romesh Bhandari, the then secretary in the MEA, was sent to Baghdad to broker peace between the two neighbours as India had close and longstanding ties with both countries. The Iranians, however, were in no mood to reconcile. On 14 March 1981, the Iranian Prime Minister Mohammad-Ali Rajai said that the victory of the Iranian revolution depended upon the victory of Iran in war and defeat to Iraq meant the defeat of the revolution. R&AW spies reported that even while the peace committee's efforts to resolve the conflict continued, Iranian planes bombarded Nasiriyah and Kirkuk in Iraq. Apart from damage to the power station in Nasiriyah, four people, including a Russian national, were killed and several others were injured.

Rajai's rejection of the peace settlement led to a hardening of the Iraqi attitude. Saddam Hussein reaffirmed that Iraq would not withdraw its troops unless its sovereignty over the Shatt-al-Arab (the area surrounding the Tigris and the Euphrates rivers) was recognised along with the furnishing of legal and practical guarantees. The R&AW reported that Ahvaz, a city in southwest

Iran, was subjected to a heavy artillery attack on 10 March 1981 and people were reportedly leaving the town. Saddam Hussein had declared that Iraq would soon take over Ahvaz and other cities and the R&AW anticipated that this power struggle might assume considerable significance.

The spies' forecast was prophetic. The conflict continued for another eight years, ending only in 1988. Informers pointed out that the power tussle was not limited to battlefields but had also triggered a shadowy war in Tehran between Prime Minister Mohammad-Ali Rajai and President Seyyed Abolhassan Banisadr. R&AW analysts said:

> The IRP and President Banisadr continued their effort to outmanoeuvre each other. In order to circumvent the President's prerogative of refusing to approve the candidates proposed by the Prime Minister for the three vacant ministries, the IRP controlled Majlis (Parliament) made a move to appoint supervisors for these ministries. In a letter addressed to the President, 120 MPs asserted the constitutional validity of their stand in this regard. President Banisadr was apparently driven to a situation in which he had to approve the appointment of Ardebelli as Minister of Finance and Hassan Nizami as Minister of Commerce on 12 March 1981. The next day, speaker Akbar Hashemi Rafsanjani managed to get a bill approved by the Majlis authorising the Prime Minister to head the vacant ministries. In the meantime, a great controversy arose over the identity of the persons responsible for creating disturbances in the President's public meeting in the Tehran University and the manner in which the troublemakers were dispersed. President Banisadr charged that some of the 200 persons, who had been arrested on this occasion, were not only armed but also connected with the special armed forces of the Prime Minister's office. While the Prime Minister denied the existence of such a force, the IRP blamed the President for creating disorder alleging that it had been stage-managed

> to challenge the Rajai government. Banisadr maintained that since police personnel were beaten up, he had to ask people to overpower the culprits. The IRP questioned the legal status of the President's bodyguards and the budget from which they were financed. It also alleged that those who intervened on behalf of the President were members of the leftists' armed bodies as well as elements purged from the Iranian Army. Prime Minister Rajai charged that anti-revolutionary elements had gathered under the banner of the President. Prosecutor General asserted that even the President could be called for questioning and investigation carried out as to what actually transpired after the President issued orders to deal with the troublemakers and the role played by the President's guards. Sadegh Khalkhali, a Shia Cleric called upon the Chief Justice and the Supreme Judicial Council to pronounce that Banisadr was politically incompetent to hold the office of the President.

This internal fight for supremacy amid the Iran-Iraq war continued and the complaint against Banisadr reached Khomeini. R&AW spies watched as four thousand clergymen gathered in the town of Qom in March 1981, demanding action against the president. In response to the call of the clergy, the bazaars were partially closed in Tehran, and pro-clergy as well as pro-Banisadr processions were taken out.

After keeping silence on this issue for several days to avoid taking a firm position between the warring groups, Khomeini finally summoned sixteen top leaders from among Banisadr's and Rajai's supporters to his residence. Each leader, apart from stating his position on the matter, submitted a written statement for Khomeini's perusal. His office subsequently issued a ten-point communiqué to control the domestic chaos. It was made clear that since President Banisadr had been appointed the supreme commander of the armed forces by Khomeini, the president's authority must be acknowledged and all armed forces commanders should obey him. The president and the prime minister were told to not make public speeches until the end of the war and the clergy leading the Friday prayers were restrained from saying anything that would create differences among the people.

The R&AW spies observed:

> In view of the wide divergence of views between the two antagonistic factions, it is extremely doubtful whether the deep-rooted differences among them could be ironed out easily and some semblance of cooperation forged for tackling the burning problems affecting the nation, including the conduct of the war. More probably the task of Khomeini, who has so far been performing a balancing feat, is likely to be rendered more difficult.

In the meantime, the R&AW agents noted the mass exodus of Indian workers from Iraq and Iran since that was a telltale sign that the war would be prolonged one. A special department of the MEA was created to ensure the safe return of Indian workers and arrangements were made to issue transit visas and travel documents on the spot. Around eleven thousand Indians were evacuated from Iran and Iraq, while seventeen people were killed and thirty injured. Under the shadow of war, the Indo-Iraqi joint commission meeting was held in New Delhi in April 1981 to strengthen economic cooperation. Back in Iraq, the R&AW watched Saddam Hussein's growing strength and the crackdown against the moles in his Ba'ath Party. The Indian agents reported: 'Several Shia members of the Ba'ath Party were reported to have been taken into custody on suspicion of their links to opposition groups. The process of screening of the Shia officers in the army was also continuing. According to a report, some army officers including three Brigadiers were executed in Baghdad at the end of last month on charges of disloyalty or incompetence.'

Away from the world of espionage, the Indira Gandhi government tried to normalise India's economic relationship with Iraq and by 1982, around ninety-seven Indian companies were settled in the region to execute infrastructure and other projects worth over five thousand crore rupees. The foreign minister of Iraq, Sa'dun Hammadi, made a trip to New Delhi in July 1982 as the personal envoy of Saddam Hussein to discuss vexing issues in the Middle East due to the continuing war. The R&AW's intelligence processed by analysts ensured that India could formulate a well-carved diplomatic strategy to deal with the countries hostile to each other. The raw political information and the roles of key players were double-checked to protect India's interest and to decide the scale of any interference made by India in such a crisis.

Russian Roulette

Another R&AW analysis provides a peek into the internal tussle for leadership in the friendly country of the USSR. Leonid Brezhnev was seriously ill in early 1982 and speculation was rife about his successor. The Russian president had enjoyed a very close relationship with two Congress party prime ministers of India—Lal Bahadur Shastri and Indira Gandhi. Ever since he assumed power in 1964, Brezhnev had made sure there were opportunities for both countries to expand and deepen their mutually advantageous cooperation in all fields without interference by either side in each other's internal matters. During a meeting with Indira Gandhi in New Delhi in 1980, against the backdrop of the Soviet intervention in Afghanistan, Brezhnev had promised a substantial increase in the supply of crude oil to India and also technological support to set up industries. Now that he lay ill, the R&AW needed to figure out the backgrounds, strengths, points of weakness and intentions of other prominent leaders, one of whom would replace Brezhnev after his demise. This report helped the government shape its diplomatic approach towards the Soviet Union until Brezhnev's death in November 1982.

The R&AW report on the political situation in the Soviet Union decoded Brezhnev's achievements as well as his ruthlessness in eliminating potential competitors in the power game. The Indian agency estimated that Brezhnev had eliminated almost all the possible leaders from the next generation, such as Voronov, Shalepin, Mazurov, Shelest and Polyanski, all of whom he perceived as threats to his authoritarianism. Despite this, the Indian agency said, the old guard were no longer in complete control of Soviet policy. Brezhnev had at least introduced some new blood into the executive positions to decide the future of the Soviet Union. The report said:

> Brezhnev's great achievement has been the transformation of top leadership without drama from a coalition of interests in 1964 to a fairly loyal group of junior men willing to accept his supremacy. This was accompanied by no interruption of the new rule of law in non-political matters, which obtains primacy in the country. Today, there are only three people born after Lenin's death in the top thirty-odd individuals who rule USSR. Most of the members of the cabinet were born during the second decade of this century and have been in power for an average of twenty-five years. The last ten years has seen a new willingness to discuss gaps in the Soviet practices in the sectors of technology, management and devolution of authority. The young men who will take over by 1985 would be those who grew up after 1945. Detailed speculation about their beliefs would be futile, except to say negatively that all ruling groups would be proud of the Soviet Union's status as a superpower and would defend it. If they are able to do this efficiently, the people of Soviet Union will forgive them many mistakes.

It appears that the Indian agency missed Alexei Kosygin who died in 1980. As chairman of the Council of Ministers of the

Soviet Union, Kosygin was instrumental in promoting friendly ties between the Indians and the Soviets. His statement, 'Let friendship between the Soviet Union and India grow and strengthen' in the presence of Prime Minister Indira Gandhi in January 1968 in Delhi was seen as a message to Pakistan and China. When there were murmurs in the corridors of power that the Soviets were ready to supply arms and ammunition to Pakistan and the issue was taken up by the opposition leaders in the Indian Parliament, both Indira Gandhi and Kosygin denied that the friendly nation had made any such move. A R&AW report highlighted that Kosygin's death in October 1980 provided 'lonely eminence' to Brezhnev, but added that Brezhnev had no future.

The intelligence analysis also deciphered the thinking behind the various factions that were contenders for Brezhnev's position. The West was apprehensive of an army takeover after Brezhnev's demise, with the Defence Minister Dmitry Ustinov as the ruler. However, the R&AW analyst cited precedents of politicians prevailing over generals and refuted this claim. The analysts were certain that the army would not rule the Soviet Union. The report said:

> The present ruling group very roughly consists of (a) the large Ukraine group (Dnipropetrovsk Mafia) each one of whom owes loyalty to Brezhnev, (b) A small Leningrad group, of which Kosygin earlier and today Romonov are the representatives. Leningrad has always been the outcast in the power struggles since the last days of Stalin. Only Kosygin made it to the second place. (c) The Moscow group, of which Grishen and Andropov, the KGB chief, are the most important. (d) Senior members from the other parts of the union will play a role only in a fairly equal power struggle. Speculations about the army taking over power are unjustified, unless something of truly catastrophic proportions happens to the economy. Parallels from China and Yugoslavia are irrelevant in a country

> which was originally founded by political parties and not by the army. The recent Polish parallel has a little more significance. Bonapartism is, however, a dirty word in the Soviet Union.

The USA on the other hand was concerned about growing Soviet influence in India, which it believed undermined its own interests. The CIA argued that the India–Soviet relationship had strengthened over the years for primarily four reasons. First reason was the Soviet support for India during the 1965 war with Pakistan, the creation of Bangladesh, and its total support to Indira Gandhi during the Emergency. Second, the USSR was a reliable partner to India, providing sophisticated weapons at concessional rates even during wartime. Third, the Soviet Union was not only India's largest trading partner but also responded quickly to any aid requests. And finally, the Soviet Union gave unconditional support to India in international bodies like the United Nations and agreed with India's independent foreign policy. A CIA report said:

> Indian receptivity to Soviet initiatives has been reinforced by Indo-US discord over Washington's support for Pakistan in the 1965 and 1971 wars, its provision of a large amount of weapons to Pakistan, and its presumed failure to restrain Pakistan's nuclear weapons programme.

However, the R&AW was untroubled by the CIA accusation that the Soviet Union was providing substantial funding to the Congress party through its embassy. The agency was keeping a close watch on Soviet embassy officials in Delhi and those found to be involved in suspicious activities were quietly deported by the Indian authorities to Moscow.

In this analysis, the R&AW predicted the strengthening of Indo-Soviet military ties if the KGB chief Yuri Andropov got the top position after Brezhnev, partly because Andripov had a very good relationship with N.F. Suntook and Girish Chandra

Saxena, the two senior most officers of the Indian spy agency. The R&AW report said:

> The KGB Chief, Andropov, could be the likely successor. Most people outside the Soviet Union do not know that the KGB is not merely an intelligence service under the Home Ministry, but a separate Ministry by itself, with a persona. Andropov is in no way comparable to the secret service chiefs in the western countries.

The Indian agency also warned the decision makers that comparing Andropov with Lavrentiy Beria, the secret police chief during the Stalin era, would be a mistake. In an article published on 27 May 1982, *The Washington Post* observed that Andropov was an extremely interesting figure who spent much of his time in the KGB's foreign policy realms.

The R&AW believed that Andropov enjoyed much more power and public respect than Beria had as the chief of the secret police and later, as minister of internal affairs in 1953. The report said:

> Beria is a misleading precedent; he was a part of Stalin's state apparatus, during twenty years of collectivisation, war and final paranoia. Andropov has no such image. The Chinese parallel is important; the Chinese have adopted the Soviet model and their Minister for Public Security corresponds to the Soviet KGB chief. Hua Kuo Feng became Supreme leader after being the security chief. No one batted an eyelid either in China or in the democratic West.

The R&AW analysis of India's position was proved correct during Indira Gandhi's visit to Moscow to attend Brezhnev's funeral. She met Andropov, now the leader of the Soviet Union, and the two reaffirmed their mutual desire to further strengthen friendship and cooperation between their countries.

Though the analysis of the repercussions of the power struggle in the Soviet Union seems quite simple and straightforward, it was and remains the most delicate task undertaken by the intelligence agency, given that the intelligence was related to a friendly power rather than an enemy state.

A Third Alternative in the UK

Intelligence analysis also looks into new security or political coalitions shaping up in countries of interests. The analysts use their bird's eye view to keep track of the competitive market economy, internal political struggles, changing social dynamics and strength and weaknesses of foreign countries to be able to coherently warn the executive of possible issues. In the 1980s, R&AW officers and analysts watching developments in the UK were pleasantly surprised when a new political outfit called the Social Democratic Party (SDP) was formed after four powerful members of the Labour Party decided to provide an alternative against Prime Minister Margaret Thatcher's Conservative Party. The R&AW believed that the split in the Labour Party was mainly due to the influence of hardcore Marxist leaders and the breakaway faction was ideologically suited to India.

But the December 2019 victory of British Prime Minister Boris Johnson, leader of the Conservative Party, was celebrated by right-wing supporters in India and the Hindu diaspora in the UK. The right-wingers, supposedly followers of the BJP's Hindutva politics, had criticised what they called the anti-India, anti-Hindu stand of the Labour Party's Jeremy Corbyn, who had questioned the Indian government's move to strike down Article 370 as well as the clampdown in the state of Jammu & Kashmir.

Criticism of the UK's Labour Party party is not new. After Margaret Thatcher became the prime minister in May 1979, the leaders of the Labour Party had demanded a more liberal and accommodative political front to counter the Conservatives. When the SDP was formed in January 1981 and its two of its leaders won the by-election the same year, defeating opponents from the Conservative Party, it was of paramount importance for the R&AW to acknowledge the change and inform the government to prepare its priorities. In its report, the R&AW said that the emergence of the SDP in the UK was a positive development. The analysis said:

> The party has some able and sincere leaders from the right wing of the Labour Party; they have at least one charismatic figure in Shirley Williams, who has not taken kindly to Mrs Thatcher. The social democrat liberal alliance has respectable British antecedents going back to the Lib-Lab coalition in the first decade of the country. The ideological basis of the party is a non-Marxist, even non-Fabian welfare state of the Scandinavian type. It differs from continental socialism in its total innocence of any Marxist links. The social democrats on the continent are all theoretically loyal to the pre-Leninist second international type of Marxism. Shirley Williams, David Owen and Roy Jenkins are all friendly to India and have a strong commitment to Europe. Their assumption of office would be, from our point of view, a positive development.

Although the Indian government headed by Prime Minister Indira Gandhi enjoyed an excellent personal equation with Margaret Thatcher, the agency's job was to warn the leader to not put all the country's eggs in one basket, but placate influential figures across the spectrum. Indira acted on the advice. She developed good relationships with both Shirley Williams and Roy Jenkins, the founding members of the SDP. According to a R&AW analyst, the change in British politics indicated a massive shift in the political dynamics of Europe which created modern mainstream parties and junked class as the basis for politics. The R&AW analysis observed:

> The Labour Party, in its new left-wing policies, would not stray away from the mainstream, even though it will make maximum

> tactical use of differences at home. The victory of President Mitterand and continuing viability of the S.P.D. in Germany have to be seen against the comparative success of the minor Italian Socialist party in influencing national politics. We have to also take into account the de-facto convergence between continental socialism and the communist parties of Italy and Spain. Then, there is the crucial role played by the socialists in Spain and Portugal. If the results of the next general election in Britain are ambiguous, there is theoretical possibility of the social democrats widening the support from the right-wing in the Labour ranks and the welfare state advocates among the conservatives. This could lead to a genuine centrist party.

Unfortunately, despite a heady start in 1981, SDP electoral dividends plunged two years later. After a poor show in the 1983 general election in which party president Shirley Williams lost her seat, a debate started on its political future. The leaders, though, remained close to India. Finally the SDP was merged with the Liberal Party in 1988 and became part of a coalition government in 2010.

The Nuclear Arms Battle

Besides predicting political futures, R&AW has also been involved in passing on information to India's military strategists. This is particularly important because the poor relationship with Pakistan means that India is vulnerable to having developed countries play good cop-bad cop. It was common in the 1970s and 1980s for American and Soviet agencies to provide tip-offs against one another as part of their respective disinformation campaigns. After India's nuclear test in 1974, the Americans sold F-16 fighter jets to Pakistan but sent feelers to Delhi about signing up for nuclear disarmament. India was in favour of total nuclear disarmament but asked for other countries in possession of weapons of mass destruction to do the same. The Americans,

Soviets and other developed countries were unwilling. Thus, the R&AW, coordinating with the MEA, helped the Indian government formulate its strategy and ensure that the country was not pressured to sign the discriminatory piece of international legislation.

When Pakistan joined the nuclear arms race as a deterrent to India's capability, the R&AW had pointed out that though nuclear weapon states made public statements about non-proliferation, they conveniently turned into active collaborators for countries where they had high stakes. During the various United Nations meetings on nuclear non-proliferation, India made it clear that it had no intention to engage in any arms race but would never sign a discriminatory agreement that would allow some powers to keep their nuclear programmes but impose sanctions on some countries for working on nuclear capability.

In September 1981, India tabled a working paper at the UN Committee on Disarmament, suggesting that a universally acceptable system of controls and non-discriminatory criteria should be made applicable to all countries without exception. The MEA said:

> India believes that total nuclear disarmament has become a most urgent task in view of the perils facing mankind from an escalating nuclear arms race. Lasting peace cannot be built on the fear of nuclear weapons but must rest on the foundations of a general and complete disarmament under effective international control. To be meaningful, non-proliferation of nuclear weapons must cover both horizontal and vertical proliferation. Any discriminatory approach to this question is not only unjust but also unworkable. The principal task of our foreign policy, as before, will be to promote our ideals and preserve our interests in a rapidly changing international environment.

At around the same time, R&AW officers were keeping an eye on the political and public mood in Europe on the disarmament issue.

The agency's analysis prompted India to press for a resolution in the United Nations General Assembly in 1981 that any use of nuclear weapons would be a violation of the charter of the United Nations and a crime against humanity.

The analysis had observed that the unilateral disarmament campaign started in Europe in 1980 had turned into a public movement, with the left-leaning political section willing to even criticise Moscow for nuclear proliferation. It said:

> Today there is a feeling that it (disarmament movement) is pan-European and that it strikes strong responsive chords in Eastern Europe also. More important, a majority of people feel that there are already the beginnings of a powerful campaign on similar lines in the United States.

The intelligence agency further informed the government that the disarmament campaign in Europe was being pushed by the anti-nuclear and environment lobbies to protect the freedom of the individual against the overwhelming power of the modern state. 'The campaign itself is, however, much more broad-based and Ronald Reagan's idea of finishing them off by calling them Soviet stooges has not taken him anywhere,' the analysis continued. 'One part of this new disarmament campaign owes its origin to Martin Luther King Jr. and earlier, Gandhiji's technique of non-violent disobedience against unacceptable legislation by the authority in power. The absence of a grassroots movement like this in India is primarily due to the remoteness of the nuclear armament problem in our country. The European movement was the inevitable result of the new missile strategy of the two superpowers in Europe in 1979.'

It was obvious to the R&AW operatives and analysts that the Americans and Soviets were deceptive in their approach to nuclear disarmament. The proliferation of technology only added to more speculation. After Indira Gandhi's assassination, the Rajiv Gandhi government continued to call for an equal and non-discriminatory agreement between nuclear and non-nuclear weapon countries. According to the R&AW reports, India wanted the destruction of all nuclear arsenals across the globe before complete disarmament agreements were signed. It took the lead in the United Nations in January 1987 by suggesting that all countries must suspend nuclear testing with immediate effect. The Indian view was simple: disarmament is necessary not just for the maintenance of global peace but for the very survival of mankind. India was elected President of the United Nations Disarmament Committee meeting in August 1987. However, the USA did not attend the meeting and this absence deepened R&AW's suspicions about America's true intent.

While India refused to sign the non-proliferation agreement because of the discriminatory nature of its provisions, it continued to play the leading role at multilateral disarmament forums, calling for the complete destruction of nuclear arsenal and a universal ban on nuclear testing. After the cold war ended, there was a perceptible shift in the stand of countries with nuclear weapons. Due to India's tough stand and leading role on the issue, the United Nations General Assembly in December 1993 adopted a resolution for the early conclusion of the Comprehensive Nuclear Test Ban Treaty (CTBT). Though India did not sign the treaty due to its discriminatory nature, it maintains even today that it is in favour of a world free of nuclear weapons, though in the presence of nuclear weapons elsewhere in the world, it needs to protect the country's interests first.

The R&AW is credited with significant accomplishments on the disarmament issue. Its role was not limited to generating intelligence and analysis; it also engaged with friendly counterparts to convey India's concerns and reservations on nuclear non-proliferation treaty.

Today, thanks to the enormous amounts of data available in the public domain, India's intelligence analysts can quickly review breaking issues around the world and provide the government with candid assessments of various situations.

A False Link between Hindus and Corruption

Wars are not always conducted on battlefields. Disinformation campaigns can also produce destructive results. When the Janata Party led by Morarji Desai came to power, the R&AW's activities were curtailed because of Desai's deep suspicion of intelligence agencies. Within a year, the socialist government was in disarray and the international press was flooded with reports of intense feuding within the political establishment. British spies stationed in Delhi drafted a report linking Hinduism with corruption and sin and this was leaked to the international press in the early 1980s.

R&AW analysts were surprised by the excitement in the global media over the leaked report and the poor interpretation of Hinduism that the agency believed was part of the UK's imperial hangover. According to the leaked report, corrupt behaviour in Indian society was linked to Hindu beliefs, which emphasises individual rather than collective redemption. A more damaging allegation in the report was that, 'In Hinduism, there is no good or evil as in the case of Christianity, Judaism and Islam.'

This was followed by the inference that 'a natural concomitant of the absence of sin is the lack of ideas about truth. To a Hindu, the truth is usually that which most suits his convenience at any given moment. There is little place in Hindu ethos for truthfulness, unselfishness, social service or moral courage.'

According to a R&AW analyst codenamed Krishan Bhandari, this was psychological warfare, hitting at the faith of India's majority community. There are a number of ways to make a country and especially its intelligence agencies irritated, said Bhandari. The British had used the detonator of religion to explode propaganda and the American press had used it to undermine India, a country it perceived to be close to the communist Soviet Union.

An analysis produced by the R&AW in 1982 said:

> It will be noticed that the level of the discussion is fairly low. It is Eurocentric, in other terms, it is a highly parochial view of a person whose experience has been limited to the western European–Judaism–Christian–Islamic body of beliefs, the related faiths of people who believe in the Kitab. The answer to this, of course, is that dilemmas about truths both at normal times and during crises are universal phenomena. The famous question of Pontius Pilate to himself when asked to judge the accusation against Jesus is central to Christian history. 'What is truth?' asked the jesting Pilate and paused for an answer. It should not be difficult after research to locate similar problems in the Confucian–Taoist–Buddhist ethic of East Asia. The British reaction is not new. It was always there during the imperial period. In a notorious episode in 1936, Baden Powell, the founder of the Boy Scout movement, made a similar charge about Indians and truth. Mahatma Gandhi and Jawaharlal Nehru answered the wild allegation in appropriate terms. Khushwant Singh has now done the same effectively in the newspapers. The preoccupation, indeed, an obsession with truth in the original Hindu scriptures cannot escape any reader. This attitude towards the Indian civilisation is connected with the retrospective vindication of British rule. This is also linked with the fairly common left-handed compliment paid to Jawaharlal Nehru as 'India's last governor general'. The idea is that the momentum of British ethos survived during the leadership of this most British of Indian politicians.

According to the intelligence analysts, these allegations and wild thoughts about a religion would have had very little immediate significance if it were not for the fact that there was a lobby in the USA which had similar ideas. Although, not much was revealed in the public domain about the CIA's penetration in the Middle East, it was a fact that the Americans had a big stake in the region.

A secret note from the MEA in 1979 had informed the Indian government that the USA was training the Saudi intelligence service and that the CIA kept an eye on internal developments in Saudi Arabia. In 1948, after Independence, the Indian government had opened a consulate at Jeddah which was raised to the status of consulate general in 1954. In 1961, India established its embassy in the city with an emphasis on a policy of peace. But after King Faisal came to power in 1964, his inclination towards Pan-Islamism opened avenues for Pakistan's anti-India propaganda, resulting in a tilt in Saudi policy in favour of Pakistan. This increased India's anxiety and the country strengthened its monitoring of anti-India propaganda. When the attack on Hinduism exploded, intelligence operatives perceived it as a move to weaken India's global influence. The analysts said:

> British eccentricities of opinion can be dismissed as of minor importance. American perceptions controlling global policy are another matter. The attitude of the new Ronald Reagan Republicans to our part of the world is based, in part, on the revival of a fashionable cliché of the 50s. Professor Northrop, a leading American Indologist, put forward a thesis that the edge of western civilisation is on the frontier between India and West Pakistan. In spite of all their differences, the Muslims of all sects, Christians of all types and the Jews share a common loyalty to one God and one law. To the east of the Indus was a riot of many gods and many laws. This peculiar idea had a certain geo-political rationalisation in the writings of Sir Olaf Caroe. From this point of view, the beginnings of the orient are in India and also, to some extent, in the eastern parts of Russia, Stalin being a typical oriental. Today, the attempt is being revived to find a deeper, more satisfactory linkage between Pakistan, the oil-rich Muslim world and the west European civilisation. Ideas like that discovered by the British official in the High Commission would be grist to this propaganda mill.

Intelligence operatives like Bhandari believed that a propaganda and disinformation campaign like this had several motives. One such motive was to add more power to the growing influence of the Vatican. The R&AW analysis of this psychological operation claimed that there was some exaggerated interest in India about Pope John Paul II's attempts to have a dialogue with Islam and the several discussions with Libya. The Pope had visited Ankara in 1979 but the dialogue failed to take off because Christians are in a minority in Turkey. Another attempt was made in Nigeria where the northern parts are Muslim majority areas, but it failed despite strenuous efforts on the part of the Vatican. The R&AW report said:

> The background of the Catholic Church's interest in reconciliation, first with other Christendom, then with Islam and Judaism and then with all other living faiths lies in the new nervousness in the Church about a general skepticism cutting across all religious barriers. It is under this inspiration that the Church in India has made an attempt to Indianise itself. There is an institute in Rome which is devoted to the study of the Hindu religion and more particularly, the Vedas and Upanishadas. It can thus be seen that the Vatican's attempts at a dialogue with Islam are not necessarily malevolent towards us, but there is the danger they might be seen in many places as a part of an implausible attempt to isolate Hinduism.

The Indian counter-attack focused on corruption around the world. The intelligence operatives suggested that revelations in China after the Cultural Revolution indicated a high degree of corruption at every level. They also pointed out that even in the countries in the developed world, there was much greater awareness of actual corruption. There was the notorious example of the Lockheed scandal, which had touched senior politicians in Japan, Italy and the Netherlands, for instance. And corruption at all levels had also been noticed in Islamic countries of all types, ranging from Iran to Egypt. Therefore, the R&AW showed, there is no exclusive tendency towards corruption in the Hindu ethos.

For the spy agency, this was a bizarre task. But with its global contacts, it managed to dismantle the disinformation campaign. While agents in battlefields around the world steal secrets and recruit assets with critical information to ensure India's national security, an analyst job's is to provide clear pictures of both the sides of a coin—threat and opportunity—to the government.

Patience and Pillow Talk

The Indian spies were the first to spot the tall, silver-haired political figure when Soviet leader Mikhail Gorbachev landed at Palam Airport in Delhi in November 1988 with an entourage of diplomats and intelligence operatives. His visit was seen as a reaffirmation of the rock-solid relationship between India and the USSR as well as Gorbachev's determination to bring new thinking to Soviet foreign policy. In fact this new thinking, which eventually put an end to the decades-long cold war, was engineered by a man in President Gorbachev's core team. Gorbachev and the awe-inspiring political figure codenamed Nicholas Darchidze had decided to move away from confrontation and create a peaceful atmosphere across the world. Known for his anti-corruption campaign in the communist nation, Nicholas knew when to switch sides in political battles and had swiftly moved from Leonid Brezhnev's team to Konstantin Chernenko's camp before being picked by Gorbachev in 1985 for his cabinet.

At the banquet that evening, an intelligence officer codenamed Ashok Khurana met the man. Soon after, Nicholas's younger brother Aleksandre Darchidze interrupted the polite conversation between the two. Khurana was introduced to Aleksandre and the handshake that followed made the Russian a welcome guest on the list of the R&AW's 'prized possessions.' Aleksandre was in love with India. Khurana, considered to be the agency's best spy recruiter, took him the next day on a daylong trip to the Taj Mahal in Agra. In the shadow of the monument of love, Khurana cajoled and wooed the powerful Georgian who later became the most important asset the R&AW spies had ever recruited.

The espionage recruitment process has an immense coolness about it. When they were driving back to Delhi, Khurana told Aleksandre that no one knows the ultimate value of freedom better than spies because they risk everything. 'I may not have a doctrine for life but you will find me always there for you through the chaotic moments the world will witness soon,' Khurana said.

Aleksandre, well aware of the working style of intelligence organisations, smiled at Khurana. A spy remains a mystery till his last breath. But Aleksandre and Khurana had a sentiment in common against Hamid Gul, chief of Pakistan's Inter-Service Intelligence (ISI), for breeding terrorism in the subcontinent. Aleksandre was part of the Soviet group that had supervised the KGB's training of the Afghan intelligence services to fight Gul's spies.

'Just remember, I don't want to be crucified like Jesus and never try to be a shepherd,' was Aleksandre's parting advice.

Khurana told me that he had devised a unique mechanism to interact with Aleksandre. They always met in foreign locations and exchanged books and periodicals containing loose sheets that were gibberish to others but a goldmine for Khurana. They never discussed politics in public places. The intense battles between spies and traitors due to the cold war had created new power blocs and India was quite interested in gleaning the secrets of both sides.

In July 1989, Prime Minister Rajiv Gandhi was in Moscow to hold talks with Gorbachev. While the two leaders discussed issues related to bilateral cooperation aside from developments in Afghanistan and Europe, Aleksandre introduced Khurana to Anastasia Korkia, a twenty-seven-year-old public relations executive. Born in Rustavi in southeastern Georgia, Anastasia had moved to Moscow about two months after the Chernobyl disaster and begun working for a lobbying firm that was liaising with the government and the International Atomic Energy Agency (IAEA). A tall, green-eyed beauty, she was fluent in English and a walking encyclopedia on global political affairs. Aleksandre told Khurana that he had been knocked off his feet when the two first met sometime in November 1986. Anastasia moved in with him and, bitten by the love bug, Aleksandre provided her with easy access to the top echelons of the Soviet government. During their brief interaction, Khurana was introduced as a 'special friend'.

Khurana remained in Moscow even after the prime minister returned to India and spent several evenings at the Aragvi café, a favourite joint of the Soviet elite and spies. The relationship between a spy and a potential recruit is exhausting because it requires patience. 'You have to see if there is a lock on the face,' Khurana explained. 'If there is none, the door of opportunity is open. No wait lasts forever, but we must leave the process in the shadows.'

Khurana waited patiently for Aleksandre's and Anastasia's reluctance to work for the R&AW to dissipate. Recruiting an agent can be a nerve-wracking task. The agent must use everything in her or his power to be persuasive, build the bond of friendship and prevail over the potential recruit's fear of betrayal. A recruiter cannot rush to buy a mole. So he waited for his moment. Before the fall of the Berlin Wall, the two agreed to be R&AW assets. And from November 1989, Khurana started receiving reams of intelligence on Soviet policies towards the USA, Europe and Asia. This was called Operation Azalea.

No intelligence is a waste. It helps the country calibrate its approach to the world and be ready for future incidents. Khurana's early harvests were Soviet communications linked to Europe and the USA and soon, he also started receiving inputs on the Soviet policy on Pakistan. Months before the demolition of the Berlin

Wall began in June 1990, Khurana was provided with roadmaps prepared by the Soviets and the USA for a united Germany. Although the Indian government had no major stake in either West or East Germany besides enhanced economic and trade ties since 1982, the intelligence dossier helped the government redraft its current policies and prepare for upcoming events, such as the way the reunified country would deal with issues like their political apparatus, commercial infrastructure, monetary and other social issues. When Aleksandre's brother Nicholas planned to visit Washington to hold talks with the Americans, the Indian intelligence was well informed in advance about the agenda on nuclear testing, counterterrorism and reconstruction of trade ties between the two superpowers. The two best-placed assets inside the Soviet regime then informed Khurana that the two sides discussed the withdrawal of their troops from Europe to bring stability in the region. The Indian spy continued to run the two significant assets even after the disintegration of the USSR.

Khurana was a professional. He wasn't interested in the personal lives of Aleksandre and Anastasia but he was aware that differences had begun to appear between them after the former's brother was made premier of the newly carved independent state of Georgia. Sexual entrapment is not new in the world of espionage and Aleksandre, Khurana learnt, had used Anastasia as a potent weapon to extract vital intelligence, knowing fully well the risks involved. Khurana said nothing. He continued to receive his harvest. Anastasia had found a lover in a keeper of Russian secrets at KGB headquarters in Dzerzhinskaya Square. The man had played a crucial role during the cold war and according to Aleksandre, was going to shape the new power structure in the next few years. Several intelligence reports about Pakistan's nuclear programme that Khurana dispatched to R&AW headquarters were the product of pillow talk. When the first BJP-led government came to power for a brief period of time, Khurana was moved to another operation, but he maintained ties with his assets. Khurana said that the intelligence picked up by Anastasia was so good that he had requested a transfer back to the Russian theatre within a year. In 1999, Anastasia's lover, codenamed Alexei, was at the helm of affairs in Russia. Now Khurana knew virtually everything happening and being planned at the Kremlin. Alexei was a close ally of India though Indian interest in him was limited to needing prior knowledge of his moves towards Pakistan and China. Sometime in late 2000, Alexei was promoted. Khurana met Aleksandre in Tbilisi. His brother Nicholas was facing political turmoil, yet the two discussed and planned the future of Operation Azalea. Nicholas had returned to power in the April 2000 election, but there was brewing discontent among his cabinet colleagues that was fanned by the opposition. He was worried that disgruntled elements inside Georgia were supported by social sector organisations operating from the USA.

Aleksandre, however, quietly dropped a bombshell. Anastasia could provide intelligence on other countries that Alexei's regime was gleaning from a variety of sources including double agents, but this would come at a heavy price. Khurana knew the agent was pushing the boundaries but he remained non-committal. In such a scenario, he said, the decision has to be taken by the top bosses. Khurana recalled that the offer was deliberated for some time at the highest levels of the R&AW. Questions were raised as to whether Anastasia's move was 'politically motivated' to spread disinformation. And above all, what was the utility of buying such intelligence at a high price?

'Any slack end may inflict enormous damage to a cordial relationship,' Khurana was warned.

Fearing a backlash, the government headed by Atal Bihari Vajpayee was not interested in continuing the operation. Since spies cannot operate in a political vacuum, Khurana had to accept the government's priorities. When he conveyed the decision to

Aleksandre in April 2001, the Georgian said nothing. He just smiled before leaving the Moscow café where they had met.

'I ran into Aleksandre in Berlin sometime in 2004. I was sitting in a café and having a chat with an old friend when he came over and patted my back. I was happy as well as embarrassed to see him,' Khurana told me. 'He whispered in my ear, "We could have prevented December 2001" and left. He meant that if I had continued running them, we could have prevented the December 2001 attack on the Indian Parliament. Tragedy can often be traced to mistakes we have made in the past. His words haunt me every time we pay homage to our brave security personnel on 13 December. No matter how good the deal was, for me personally, Operation Azalea ended in both massive triumph and failure,' Khurana said.

Illusions of a Relationship

In the early 1970s, the R&AW corridors were abuzz with whispers that the CIA had helped the Indian intelligence agency tackle an external influence fanning the Naxalite movement in West Bengal. A shadowy US operative at the US consulate in Calcutta had 'unofficially' helped the Indian agency in stopping the arms and money from flowing into Indian territory from abroad.

It is true that the R&AW and the CIA have collaborated on several occasions when the issue was of mutual concern. Many serving and retired R&AW officials have said so. The CIA and the US government, in fact, had provided the R&AW with sophisticated surveillance equipment to fight left-wing extremism because they hated communists the most. When the R&AW, sometime in 1972, reported that arms could be coming from Chinese territory, the USA helped the spy agency deploy a surveillance and state of the art communication network along India's border with China. The relationship bloomed when the Intelligence Bureau (IB) was the sole Indian spy agency and in the aftermath of the Indo-Chinese war, the CIA came a little closer to India. But there has always been the suspicion that the Americans are watching their own interests and a partnership with India is decided on the basis of the pound of flesh the CIA could extract. One such incident was the installation of a nuclear-powered monitoring station at the Nanda Devi peaks in the Himalayas to spy on China's atomic tests and missile programme.

One sunny morning in April 1978, Prime Minister Morarji Desai woke up to a report on the American broadcasting channel NBC that made a startling disclosure about a CIA operation in the Indian Himalayas to carry out espionage activities on China codenamed Operation HAT. The text of the news report was sent to the Prime Minister's Office (PMO). The report said: 'Somewhere high in the Himalayan mountain range that separates India and China, a nuclear power pack filled with plutonium 238 is buried in the snow and rocks. The story on the American television channel raised the question—how did the nuclear device get there in the first place?'

In a telegram to the prime minister, the Indian embassy in Washington claimed that the US media had picked up the story and it was bound to create a storm back home. It did. Joint Secretary A.G. Asrani, who looked after America and Canada in the MEA, wrote to the R&AW and IB chiefs on 14 April that the issue had triggered a political storm in Parliament. Asrani's note said:

> Reports have appeared in the Press regarding the planting of a nuclear monitoring device in the Himalayas by an American mountaineering team in 1965. As would have been seen in this morning's newspapers, our grave concern has been conveyed by the foreign secretary to the Ambassador of USA. The latter has told us that the US government is looking into the matter and that he would let us know as soon as he gets some information from Washington.

Later, *Outside* magazine released a comprehensive story stating that the spy station was set up in coordination with Indian spy agencies, though they wrongly named the CBI (Central Bureau of Investigation) instead of the Intelligence Bureau. The article clarified that the nuclear power pack filled with plutonium-238 would remain in the Himalayas until it deteriorated, becoming a radioactive menace that could leak into the Himalayan snow and infiltrate the Indian river system through the headwaters of the Ganges.

An Indian intelligence report said that the CIA had started up Nanda Devi after the autumn of 1965, but razor-sharp winds and unseasonal storms delayed them and then winter's approach forced them to retreat short of the top. Intending to return in spring to finish the mission, they found a sheltered cranny on the southern lee of the mountain and stashed the special pack. In all, fourteen American climbers signed on with the CIA though ultimately only nine were sent to India. They were joined by four of India's best mountaineers from the 1962 Indian Everest expedition. In addition, the CIA had the unofficial cooperation of its Indian counterpart. An American undercover agent on the Indian intelligence payroll co-opted Indian intelligence, setting up the arrangement on an informal basis to preserve the CIA's absolute authority over the project. The CIA had demanded that Indian intelligence, which relied heavily on the US spy expertise, keep the affair secret from Prime Minister Indira Gandhi and other top-ranking officials of the government that then ruled India. The CIA was concerned that the Gandhi government might veto the project as needlessly provocative, since India's relations with China were then at a flash point. The CIA did give the then US president, Lyndon Johnson, a general outline of the project, but the agency also asked him not to notify the Gandhi government, a circumstance that became another reason for the US cover up.

An MEA telex message further claimed that the author of the article, Howard Kohn, held a press conference in New York and accused the CIA of being arrogant and irresponsible for abandoning the two nuclear-powered devices without bothering to inform the government of India. Mr Kohn also alleged that Indian intelligence, which he again wrongly named as the CBI, as well as the Government of India, had been tricked by the CIA. He added that the Indian agency had supplied porters, transport facilities, etc., to the CIA team but alleged that the Indian officials (CBI officials as he called them) were double agents.

Who were these double agents? Perhaps no one knows because at that time, the R&AW was not in existence and the IB was India's primary intelligence organisation. Howard Kohn claimed that from the beginning the CIA took a very arrogant position towards India, did not inform the Gandhi government and tricked the Indian intelligence agency into going along with the project using double agents: CIA agents who were on the Indian payroll.

In the same breath, Kohn claimed that some IB officers were working as double agents for CIA and also that some CIA officers were on the payroll of the IB. If the claim was true then it was clear that the IB had recruited some CIA officers and Operation HAT was the brainchild of the Indian intelligence agency. But the question remains: who was the real puppeteer? The IB or the CIA?

The MEA was livid at the explosive news report and even angrier when Calling Attention notices were served by Member of Parliament Dalpat Singh Paraste and four others on 17 April 1978. Foreign secretary J.S. Mehta called on the US Ambassador to India, Robert F. Goheen, and told him that the issue was going to cause very grave concerns in the Indian government, Parliament and elsewhere. He wanted to know the truth.

Goheen told Mehta that he had received a message from the state department, informing him that an article on the subject had appeared in a radical left magazine which was a successor or sister magazine to *Rolling Stone*. 'The state department are looking into the matter and will let the Ambassador know as soon as they have ascertained the truth,' Goheen replied sheepishly.

Mehta, however, emphasised that if the allegation happened to be true, it was imperative that Indians should know as soon as possible what the hazards were. 'If it is to be assumed that no leakage of radioactivity has yet taken place, we must know what the dangers are of future leakage and what can be done to provide safety against such a danger. Meanwhile, there is bound to be a great deal of alarm all over the country,' Mehta told Goheen.

After the meeting, Mehta wrote a letter to IB chief S.N. Mathur, asking him to provide details of the involvement of Indian agents. He sent copies to the R&AW chief, the PMO and the home secretary. He believed that the IB's vault might have documents dating back to 1966.

'In view of the extremely sensitive and indeed explosive nature of the allegations made in the article, I would be grateful if you could ascertain whatever details are possible, including the alleged involvement of our own Intelligence agencies in the affair,' Mehta wrote.

There was no reply from the IB. But the government believed the report and wanted to know from the Indian Mountaineering Foundation based in Friends Colony, Delhi, whether any India or foreign mountaineering expeditions to the area of Nanda Devi and Nanda Kot were sent or allowed during the period 1963 to 1968. Meanwhile, two US Congressmen, Richard Ottinger and John Dingell, wrote to US President Jimmy Carter asking him to investigate the matter and inform the US Congress about the CIA monitoring station that was buried by an avalanche. The letter was shared with the then Indian ambassador to the US, Nani A. Palkhivala. It is interesting to note that before writing the story, Howard Kohn had contacted the CIA and sought documents related to the operation but his request was denied. The CIA had told him it was a matter involving intelligence sources and methods.

While all were waiting for confirmation in writing, the government on 15 April 1978 wrote to the Ministry of Defence (MoD) that there was an immediate need to take samples in areas like Haridwar and the upper reaches of the Ganga to make sure there was no contamination of the waters or the silt in the riverbed. The then foreign minister Atal Bihari Vajpayee considered that sampling the water to ascertain any kind of contamination should be carried out immediately.

The Atomic Energy Commission (AEC) was also alerted about the explosive news. The prime minister's secretariat believed that with the help of the MoD, a couple of AEC scientists should be flown to the upper reaches of the Ganges on a reconnoitring trip to decide the spots from which it would be most appropriate to take the samples.

Prime Minister Desai's statement in the Lok Sabha more or less settled the matter that the CIA did try to set up a monitoring station and a plutonium device was buried somewhere under the snow and earth on the Nanda Devi slopes. But he categorically denied the accusation made by Howard Kohn in his article that Indira Gandhi was not kept in the loop and that the IB was tricked into setting up the monitoring station. Desai said:

> In the light of the international situation prevailing at that time and the scientific developments which were taking place both far and near, it was decided by the Government of India and the Government of the United States at the highest level that a remote sensing device with nuclear power pack should be installed near the highest point on Nanda Devi with the object of securing information about the missile developments. Accordingly, a mountaineering expedition manned only by Indian mountaineers went up the Nanda Devi followed by a

> joint Indo-American expedition scientifically equipped with the device with a view to installing it at a height of 25,000 feet. When the expedition was approaching the summit, it was overtaken by a blizzard, which made further ascent impossible, and facing fatal hazards to the party, they were obliged to retreat to the lower camp at a height of 23,000 feet. In precipitate descent under very trying and exacting conditions, they had to leave the power pack securely cached. With the onslaught of winter, no attempt to locate and retrieve the device was immediately possible and had to be postponed. Another expedition was mounted in May 1966 with the intention of retrieving and installing the device. However, the expedition party on arrival at the areas discovered that a major avalanche had occurred around the area and the device could not be located. In May 1967, a new device was taken to the same area and was duly installed on a neighbouring peak. This functioned normally for a while but was removed subsequently in 1968 and the equipment was returned to the US. These operations as I said were apparently carried out predominantly by Indian personnel but under the joint auspices and in the know of and with the approval at the highest political level of the Government of India at that time.

Desai also clarified that after Howard Kohn's report, the Indian government had assembled the relevant details and the background of these expeditions with reference to available records and in consultations with the US and Indian agencies that were involved in this project. On the issue of the possible leakage of the nuclear device, Desai made the startling claim that samples of water had been taken up to 1970 and had been under observation for some years but no trace of contamination was detected.

Around the same time, at least two American mountaineering expeditions had been planned for the Nanda Devi sanctuary and the IB was told to keep an eye on the climbers led by

M.D. Clark. Since the clearance had been given before the newsbreak, there were some deliberations about whether these expeditions should be stopped at the last minute. But Desai was not in favour of recalling any expedition due to the revelation.

The army pitched in to help and provided six restricted map sheets of Nanda Devi and the Banbasa area to assist the scientists. The maps were subsequently sent to the PMO. Two scientists, P. Abraham and Dr K.C. Pillai, were picked up from Bhabha Atomic Research Centre to carry out the sampling of Ganges waters. In May 1979, the government said the tests of samples of silt and water collected in April 1978 from the upper Ganga and from the Sharada also showed that there was no radioactive contamination in the water and soil.

Desai promised Parliament that a committee would be set up to examine the issue and subsequently, the Cabinet Secretariat appointed a panel headed by Atma Ram to examine the possibility of nuclear pollution of the Ganges by the spy device left atop Nanda Devi by the CIA. The Atma Ram Panel comprising Dr H.N. Sethna, Prof. M.G.K. Menon, Dr Raja Ramanna, Dr V. Ramalingaswami, Prof. A.K. Saha and Dr K.T. Thomas submitted its report in April 1979 and it was tabled in Parliament on 18 May 1979. The panel unanimously expressed the view that the hazards of radiation because of the release of plutonium from the device are 'negligibly small in magnitude and should not be a matter for alarm.'

What happened to the device at the Nanda peaks? The Atma Ram panel suggested that new techniques needed to be adopted to locate the device. 'The committee has also considered the possibility of the device being still intact but lying buried somewhere. It has pointed out that even in this case there is no hazard unless the device is disturbed or disintegrated.'

India and the USA also collaborated after an Indian airliner was hijacked and blown up at the Lahore airport by two Kashmiri militants on 2 February 1971. The aircraft was hijacked on 30 January 1971. Indian government officials held a meeting with the Americans on 4 February 1971 and they confirmed a representation had already been made to Pakistan. The hijackers were treated as heroes by the Pakistan government and this worried both India and the USA. The Indian agencies believed that the premeditated criminal act of hijacking and wanton destruction of the Indian Airlines aircraft within the protected area of Lahore International Airport was the direct result of the government of Pakistan having permitted their territory to be used for instigating, abetting and encouraging unlawful and subversive activities against India.

What was more shocking was that an Indian intelligence warning in September 1970 about the existence of a conspiracy in Pakistan to hijack Indian aircraft had not been heeded. India and the USA were also peeved over the fact that the hijackers were given asylum and the ISI had publicly expressed their solidarity with the hijackers.

'The two criminals were allowed to destroy the aircraft in full view of the troops, police and other airport personnel. Pakistan permitted the two hijackers to move and act freely in the airport area and terminal building, including making long-distance calls to their accomplices in Pakistan and meeting political leaders like Zulfikar Ali Bhutto and Mahmood Ali Kasuri and others freely,' India had charged. India banned Pakistani flights over Indian territory and this move caused a little unrest in the US establishment, which wanted India to resolve the issue as per International Civil Aviation Organization (ICAO) norms. What was more intriguing was the fact that Pakistan's commission of inquiry constituted by President Yahya Khan blamed Indian intelligence in April 1971. The Indian government countered:

> Casting the hijackers into the role of some Indian 007, however flattering to Indian intelligence, is so grotesque that we cannot

> take the inquiry seriously. Commission says that the hijackers were armed with only dummy weapons. This totally repudiates the Pakistan foreign secretary's version that the hijackers exhibited hand grenades to prevent the Pakistani authorities at Lahore from gaining control over the plane. Again if the hijackers only had dummy weapons, who supplied them the detonating devices to blow up the plane?

Indian and US officials agreed that Pakistan couldn't escape responsibility. The US told Pakistan to either return the hijackers or prosecute them. Meanwhile, Indian intelligence operatives were told by their US counterparts that the 'US government would not like to get involved between the two countries.'

The message was clear. The USA was not interested in helping India on this issue at the cost of antagonising Pakistan, which it thought was a force to counter Indian hegemony in the South Asia region. Till 1971, Indian agencies believed that the USA tended to build up Pakistan as a counter to India in an attempt to maintain a balance of power in the subcontinent. But R&AW deputy director M.C. Pant in a note dated 26 June 1973 said the US outlook was changing. He said, 'During a private conversation in London where Daniel Patrick Moynihan, the US ambassador to India, had gone in the second week of May 1973 to attend a function at the London School of Economics and Political Science, he is reported to have expressed optimism regarding Indo-American relations. According to him, the American administration had realised that it had made some mistakes in its policies concerning the sub-continent during 1971 and that it was prepared to normalise and improve its relations with India.'

But as in any bilateral relationship, suspicions always remained. On 13 June 1973, foreign secretary Kewal Singh warned the Indian ambassador to the US, T.N. Kaul, that the USA was trying to create a rift between India and its neighbours.

'This is part of a larger and more subtle American attempt to sow seeds of suspicion between us and our smaller neighbours. Moynihan referred to Nepal being apprehensive of India's dominant role in the region. My own assessment is that it is not our smaller neighbours conveying their so-called anxieties to the Americans, but rather the US government trying to create misunderstandings between us. The USA is misinterpreting our relations with the Soviet Union to our neighbours with a view to create distrust against us, while the US itself is taking various steps to strengthen understanding and cooperation with the Soviet Union.'

This was an interesting analysis by the then foreign secretary, who had decided not to buy everything the Americans were selling. R&AW officers who have spent considerable time in the USA and the Soviet Union said that the US propaganda machinery was strong and they used various agencies including social institutions to mislead targeted countries.

Preacher Spy of the CIA

In December 1975, the Indian government was alarmed by a startling claim made by US Senator Mark Hatfield. He had accused the CIA of using missionaries to spy on other nations. In a statement in the Senate, Hatfield had said:

> Mr. President, this summer, various news sources reported that the Central Intelligence Agency has made it a regular practice over the years to use missionaries, clergy and members of religious organizations for intelligence activities. It is my firm belief that this practice tarnishes the image of the United States in foreign countries, prostitutes the church and violates the first amendment's separation of Church and state.

The CIA chief, William Colby, admitted that the agency recruited clergy and told Hatfield that it would continue to do so in the future. With this statement, espionage agencies the world over began surveillance on all foreign clergy visiting their countries.

Already distraught over its failure to detect India's nuclear explosion in 1974, the CIA began to be investigated for its working style in 1976. The Indian government learned that the agency had been spending huge amounts of money to buy liquor and cigarettes as bait to recruit officials in their targeted countries, but were still drawing blanks in terms of actionable intelligence. A telex to Sharda Prasad in the PMO on 21 January 1976 from the Indian embassy in Washington said it all:

> *The New York Times* on 20 January published a report on the House Committee panel investigating the CIA. In the course of which he said that the panel found the CIA's intelligence-gathering activities had often fallen short of the mark. In the course of his dispatch he said the committee report contains evidence of additional failures of CIA in predicting the explosion by India of a nuclear device in 1974 and the Soviet-led invasion of Czechoslovokia in 1968. Documents provided to the Committee illustrate the uncertainty of the intelligence community over whether India possessed the ability to explode a nuclear device or its intention to do so. The assessment chastised the intelligence community for having failed to interpret available satellite photographs that were later found to clearly show India's nuclear-testing facilities. The report added balance sheets provided to the committee staff also showed that a medium sized CIA post overseas purchased $86,000 worth of liquor and cigarettes over a five-year period to be given by agents to friendly officials of the host country.

This was hilarious. Not because the CIA was luring foreign officials with liquor and cigarettes, but because the methods adopted by the spy organisation did not match its image created over the years as the best espionage network across the globe. However, Indian intelligence officers agreed that the CIA came to India's rescue in a limited way whenever a partnership was required. In the aftermath of the 2008 Mumbai attack, the US government and its agencies—the CIA and the FBI—maintained a close working relationship with the Indian government as well as the IB and the R&AW. While the CIA shared intelligence on Pakistan terror groups and the FBI on suspects detained in the USA, the American government gave access to official information received from the Pakistani government to the then National Security Advisor M.K. Narayanan. The intelligence harvested by the CIA from its Pakistani sources was regularly shipped to the R&AW as the Americans were certain that the terror attacks had been carried out by the Lashkar-e-Taiba (LeT) with the help of the ISI.

Why didn't they do this before the attack? Because for the Americans, the ISI, though tainted and disgraced for breaking laws and sponsoring terrorists, remains its closest ally in South Asia. Despite being faced with the devastating consequences of this friendship in the past, the CIA needs a close ally in the ISI to do its bidding in the subcontinent. An example of the rogue behaviour of the ISI and the subsequent CIA support to the Pakistani agency was exhibited after the 2008 Mumbai attack, in which six Americans were also killed. The CIA knew of the ISI role in the attack but continues to maintain strong ties with the Pakistani agency for long-term gains.

For Indian spymasters, countering China, which has forged a deep nexus with Pakistan, is a formidable task. It is obvious that countries must spy on each other to keep a step ahead. China has mastered that art. But in the last two decades, the R&AW has devoted considerable resources to tackle Chinese moves in the grey world. The agency believes China is terrified by India's growing clout in Asia and always willing to engineer clumsy provocations, like the one in the Maldives in 2012, when it covertly supported the ouster of President Mohamed Nasheed, widely known for his pro-India stand.

Chinese expansionist designs now ensure that India will be riddled with more spies. In January 2018, Prime Minister Narendra Modi, National Security Advisor Ajit Doval and some senior intelligence officials met to discuss efforts to counter Chinese and Pakistani intelligence in India. The prime minister was told that Pakistani spies were increasing infiltration to monitor India's activities in nuclear, space and missile technology and money was being pumped in through recruits to obtain classified documents. An intelligence officer talked about Pakistan-backed espionage modules which were mostly concentrated in the border districts of Punjab, Rajasthan, Gujarat and West Bengal. There were increasing cases of honey trapping and the ISI was also using many Indian agents on its payrolls to lure disgruntled elements of the establishment through the Pakistan mission in India. The intelligence officer asserted that the ISI was compromising government officials posted in Indian embassies around the world by exploiting their weaknesses.

A decision was taken to keep round-the-clock surveillance on Pakistani pilgrims, business delegations and their links in India and to launch an operation to trace Pakistani nationals who arrived in India on valid visas.

In the same meeting, a seasoned spy who handled Chinese affairs warned that India needs to brace for aggressive espionage operations from China, especially in the light of China's geo-political ambition to become the pre-eminent power in Asia and a global power by 2050 and its ambitious projects, such as the Belt and Road Initiative (BRI). There are several contentious issues between the two nations that the R&AW is particularly worried about and this reflected in their presentation to Prime Minister Narendra Modi. The unresolved issue of the delineation of the India-China boundary area, lack of progress in clarifying the Line of Actual Control (LAC), China's concern about the presence of the Dalai Lama in India and India's concerns regarding a post-Dalai Lama scenario all remain a headache for Indian decision makers.

The spies were also worried about Chinese support to certain northeast groups, increased Chinese interests in the Indian Ocean Region, the China-Pakistan Economic Corridor (CPEC, a part of BRI), which passes through Pakistan Occupied Kashmir, the encirclement of India through China's string of pearls project and growing Chinese influence in India's neighbourhood, especially in Nepal, Pakistan, Bangladesh, Sri Lanka and the Maldives.

It is an undeniable fact that China is the most active nation in the world with regard to cyber espionage, with formidable capabilities aimed at economic sabotage. Two other modus operandi adopted by China are to exploit business and cultural exchanges to harvest intelligence in India. In fact, the government's top decision makers were given a list of institutes that are suspected of being used by China to gather intelligence in India. A classified note was also given to top officials about a Chinese institute planning to open branches in Tamil Nadu and West Bengal. China also exploits the legitimate cover of business in sectors like telecom, engineering and manufacturing.

A seasoned spy said:

> China is replicating the espionage method of using soft power under the cover of legitimate activities which had earlier been patented by the US and Russia. The Chinese are using academics, scholars, businessmen, professionals and even journalists to mount operations in India. In recent years, it has been noticed by the counterintelligence team that Chinese firms have emerged as the lowest bidders in many infrastructural projects in India, with the active support of the Chinese government. Such Chinese footprints are increasingly being noticed in states like Maharashtra, Chhattisgarh and Haryana. They are also targeting strategic locations. For example, a Chinese business delegation went to Betul Island in Goa, near INS Khadamba. Espionage threats are also emanating from non-Chinese firms which employ Chinese

> persons as happened with the Dhamara Port Company in Odisha, which is strategically located near Dr Abdul Kalam Island, earlier known as 'Wheeler' Island.

Since that meeting, the government has begun examining business proposals from Chinese companies from the espionage angle. However, the threats have not disappeared. The then home minister, Rajnath Singh, during a closed-door meeting in 2018 where the R&AW chief was also present, asked a pertinent question: Why is there a large scale presence of Chinese companies in states like Chhattisgarh? A senior officer in the home ministry responded to Singh's query by explaining to the spy chief the various fault lines in the political, economic and social structure of China and the need to exploit these vulnerabilities to counter Chinese intelligence operations against India.

One warning which will be acted upon in the coming years is increasing surveillance on Chinatown in Kolkata. The local intelligence unit has warned that relatives of people of Chinese origin living in the city of joy have suddenly started mixing with the local population. Methods of espionage and means of penetration to steal secrets and engineer subversion will be more refined in the coming years and major superpowers will continue to spy on each other.

9

SPIES IN NEPAL

On 19 September 2008, Nizam Khan was glued to an Indian satellite TV news channel in his money exchange shop at Nabi Plaza in Birat Nagar, Nepal. On the screen, Operation Batla House played out live. Security forces swarmed the street in Jamia Nagar, New Delhi, and a shootout ensued at Batla House between Indian Mujahideen (IM) terrorists and the Delhi police. Two terrorists, Atif Ameen and Mohammed Sajid were killed and two others, Shahzad and Ariz Khan managed to escape.

There has never been such an operation before, Khan thought, and dialed his friend Ayub Sheikh. Their conversation was brief. They decided to meet at the madrassa on Karsiya Road in the evening.

Khan was part of IM's sleeper cell in Nepal and had helped the terror outfit with money, shelter and the passionate conviction that had been indoctrinated in him by Pakistan's Inter-Service Intelligence (ISI) from where he drew his resources as well. His meeting with Ayub primarily discussed the chances of betrayal, which Ayub shrugged off with a smile. Khan, however, decided to keep a low profile for the next couple of weeks. He knew that Operation Batla House had not been a coincidence. Since early

2007 when Indian counterterror agencies launched a massive crackdown against the IM's parent organisation, the Students Islamic Movement of India (SIMI), Khan had been apprehending a sweep. He himself had helped finance several terror-training camps in Kerala where new recruits were provided physical training, arms training, firing practice and lessons in the art of making crude bombs, all to carry out jihad in India.

Ayub had assured Khan that any 'fleeing birds' would contact him if they survived a month. In the first week of November, Khan received a visitor. It was Ariz alias Zunaid, who had crossed to Nepal from Jogbani in Araria district, Bihar. Nizam Khan gave him a new identity—Mohammed Salim from Ward No. 18, Birat Nagar, Nepal, and managed to get him accommodation at a madrassa.

Zunaid was not the first fugitive terrorist to be welcomed in Nepal. Since the mid 1990s, the ISI with the help of underworld don Dawood Ibrahim had successfully raised a solid network in the Himalayan country, charged with carrying out anti-India operations including smuggling. This had partly been made possible by India's big brother attitude to Nepal, which created a strong feeling of resentment in the Himalayan country.

For the R&AW, Nepal is the perfect example of both the triumph and the failure of traditional spying. The Himalayan nation was once an excellent theatre for Indian operatives, where top assets had been recruited to eliminate actual and potential threats. These assets close to the people in power provided quality intelligence, more useful and effective than any surveillance and sophisticated monitoring of second rung officers in a government.

But political failures on the part of various Indian governments led to a situation where India does not have the influence over Nepal it ought to have and did have in the 1950s, when the first ever treaty of peace and friendship between India and Nepal had been signed by C.P.N. Singh, the then India's ambassador to Nepal and Shamsher Jang Bahadur Rana, the maharaja, prime minister and supreme commander-in-chief of Nepal.

The treaty stated that India had agreed to provide arms, ammunition and support for the growth of commerce and industry in Nepal, that the aim of the two countries was to maintain everlasting peace and friendship, that both governments would mutually acknowledge and respect each other's complete sovereignty, territorial integrity and independence, that the two governments had consciously decided that no third country should cause any friction in their relationship and in case there was any breach or friction, they would not hesitate to inform each other, and finally, that Nepal should be free to import arms, ammunition or any other warlike material and equipment necessary for its security from India.

Turbulent Past

A democratic political system was introduced in Nepal in 1951, after almost three hundred years of monarchy. However, the constitution was only approved in 1959, whereupon the first general election was held for parliament. The Nepali Congress won an overwhelming victory and formed Nepal's first popular government. But the government was dismissed in December 1960, when King Mahendra Bir Bikram Shah Dev, whose reign began in 1955, found himself locked in perpetual conflict with the cabinet.

R&AW had not yet been born and the Intelligence Bureau (IB) was the sole Indian intelligence organisation keeping an eye on domestic and foreign developments affecting India. The dismissal of the Nepali Congress government meant that Nepal was in turmoil again and a report of the Ministry of External Affairs (MEA) drafted by Joint Secretary K.L. Mehta on

13 February 1962 revealed that internal strife in Nepal was turning into national uprising. Several Nepalese Congress leaders had taken shelter in India and King Mahendra believed that these leaders in exile, with the support of the Indian government, were fanning the discontent in Nepal.

The constitution that had come into effect in 1959 was abolished in 1962 and a new constitution was written which returned authority to the throne of Nepal. India had been drawn into the picture when King Mahendra visited eastern Nepal in January 1962 and a cracker was thrown at his Land Rover at Janakpur. Though only two people sustained minor injuries, the Nepalese foreign minister, Tulsi Giri, accused India of political trickery, double standards and subversion on the lines of the US action in Cuba, by permitting Nepalese rebels to use Indian bases to train and organise and conduct hit and run raids in Nepal. The Indian government protested against this 'immoderate statement,' arguing that there was no evidence that Indian territory was being used for hostile actions against Nepal. In February1962, two violent protests took place inside Nepal which again were laid at India's door. The government of Nepal lodged a protest with the Indian embassy, alleging that the raiders wore uniforms and helmets and belonged to an armed organisation which operated from Indian territory against the government of Nepal. The Indian government responded to the accusation by claiming that several enquiries were conducted but none had shown that the offenders had either entered Nepal from India or later fled to India. Amid the growing animosity between the two neighbours, King Mahendra made a trip to New Delhi on 18 April 1962. An MEA officer, M.J. Desai, noted that during this visit, the king and his officials were in a jittery mood. They wanted the government of India to take all sorts of extra-legal measures against the Nepalese Congress leaders in India on the grounds that these people were fomenting rebel activities in Nepal. Desai wrote:

> We told them (Nepal) that Government of India is taking effective measures to prevent the passage of armed persons or smuggling of arms from India into Nepal and that according to our information, the rebel activities in Nepal were based on local discontent. This was propagandistic effort made by the Nepal authorities to blame India for their inability to check the rebel activities and to maintain law and order inside Nepal.

Nepal, under King Mahendra's authority, was wooing China and an agreement had been reached for the construction of a Kathmandu-Lhasa road. When the Indian government pointed out the security risks involved and the concerns felt in India, Nepalese officials observed that they would take all necessary precautions to prevent any danger to Nepal—and therefore India—from China.

IB officials operating from Karachi informed the Indian government that Nepal had also entered into an air agreement with Pakistan for a direct service from Karachi via Kathmandu to Dhaka. Desai said in a note to senior members of the Indian government that when the MEA put this matter to Nepal, they gave no reply but reassured the Indian officials that they could not dream of doing anything that would affect the traditional friendship between India and Nepal. Desai's note said:

> We pointed out to them that friendship is a two-way traffic and while we can understand their desire to improve their communications, trade and international contacts, they on their side should keep in view the reactions of public opinion in India to any arrangements that they may reach with China or Pakistan which affect the common Indo-Nepal security interests.

Indian officials believed that King Mahendra was a lonely man, ill-advised and ill-served by his ministers and officials and easily sent off at tangents every few weeks. This was evident from the king's rather strong comment when he arrived at Palam Airport on 18 April 1962, as recorded in a government dispatch:

> We firmly believe that friendship is not a one-sided affair and friendly exchange of views is the best way to dispel imaginary or prospective misunderstanding between friends [...] that we keep ourselves ever ready for heart-to-heart talks with all friends for removing mutual misunderstanding.

While speaking at the banquet hosted in his honour on the same day, King Mahendra tried to pacify the Indian side, claiming that the Kingdom of Nepal was taking strides along the path of progress in response to the demand of the times.

But India was suspicious. Besides Nepal's relationship with China, India was also wary of the growing bonhomie between Pakistan and Nepal. IB operatives believed that Pakistan was trying to strengthen its base in this tiny, landlocked Himalayan country. Pakistan's president, Mohammad Ayub Khan, landed in Kathmandu on 9 May 1963 to cement ties between the two countries. Indian ambassador Harishwar Dayal in his note on 15 June 1963 said that Ayub Khan's visit appeared to have been intended not only as a return of the hospitality extended to King Mahendra in Pakistan earlier but as a reminder that Nepal had other friends besides India.

Pakistan's charge d'affaires office was opened in Kathmandu in August 1963 and it began an operation to cultivate and transport information from Nepal. While Pakistan was trying to gain a foothold in Nepal, China was fully in control in Kathmandu. The editors of at least two pro-Chinese newspapers, *Motherland* and *Naya Samaj,* visited China sometime in 1963. After the editors returned, the two publications launched a massive propaganda attack on India, alleging that an Indian embassy official (the military attaché) had distributed three lakh rupees to the

Kampas in northwestern Nepal to create trouble in the country. The Indian government quickly issued a denial and made high-level representations to the Nepal government about these reports. Indian intelligence officers posted in Nepal at that time reported the growing number of magazines funded by the Chinese to create anti-India sentiments in Nepal. They also reported the arrival of a large number of Chinese spies in Nepal. This was reiterated by Dayal who noted in July 1963: 'It seems too much to expect that the Nepalese authorities will take heed of the evident presence of Chinese agents all over Nepal including the capital.'

A report sent to the IB headquarters in New Delhi from Kathmandu in January 1964 described the hidden Chinese intention. China was not interested in the development of Nepal but needed a formidable presence there to counter India's influence in the region. The report cited an attack by a newspaper called *Nepali* against China which said: 'It was apparent that China on her own could not undertake any big projects in Nepal for development as long as her quarrels and differences with the Soviet Bloc continued. It had to be clearly understood that it would be futile to expect the Chinese to put up any big industries.'

After the birth of the R&AW, Indian policymakers slowly came around to the idea that Pakistan and China would do everything possible to turn Nepal against India. The government expected R&AW to create a well-conceived plan to neutralise the objectives of China and Pakistan and maintain a sense of good governance for the Nepalese populace for better diplomatic relations with the Himalayan country.

But the abrasions in the relationship became visible in the 1970s when the Nepalese monarchy rejected India's demand to restrict the growing presence of China and Pakistan on its soil. King Mahendra died in January 1972 and was succeeded by his son King Birendra Bir Bikram Shah Dev, who decided to continue the policy set by his father, leaving the R&AW team in Nepal disappointed. This team, led by Rajesh Garg, who played a significant role in Nepal's espionage theatre, neutralised an ISI plot in the Terai sometime in mid-1972. By this time, Nepal had become the field of a spy wars.

According to Garg, ISI chief Lt. General Ghulam Jilani Khan, who had taken charge of the intelligence agency in 1971, directly supervised the Pakistani mission in the Terai. Meanwhile, the R&AW had recruited an agent serving in Nepal's foreign ministry, known as K136 in Delhi. This man had been a 'walk-in'—he had volunteered to serve as an agent of the R&AW, demanding a high price for shared secrets. Garg said it took him some time to understand that the man did not want to work for the R&AW out of pure greed; he wanted the excitement of living on the edge. When Garg finally decided to trust the man and recruit him, he turned out to be the most important spy that the Indian agency ever had in Nepal.

K136 provided Garg with information on all the Pakistani nationals arriving in the country, allowing the Indians to peep into the files of Pakistani officials, tourists and businessmen moving in and out of Nepal. The spies worked via the age-old system of making drops at particular places, signalling the necessity for pick up with signs such as the '+' mark. In late 1972, Garg and the other operatives launched an operation in which Pakistani agents masquerading as businessmen were exposed and nabbed. They had been tailed for days by Garg's team and had revealed their true identities and details of a meeting they had held with rebel groups to launch an attack inside Nepal, aiming to put the blame on India. It was a risky operation, but Garg was determined to neutralise the plot.

Meanwhile, the Indian government faced some hard truths in the domain of its diplomatic relationship with Nepal. The R&AW's

role was limited to preventing anti-India activities in Nepal and ensuring the country's policies were in favour of New Delhi and not Beijing and Islamabad. However, a US embassy report on 19 December 1973 from New Delhi observed that the friction in the Indo-Nepalese relationship could get worse, as India increasingly worried about the friendliness between Nepal and China.

India had consistently maintained that Nepal was within its security frontiers; any establishment of the Chinese in the Himalayan country would mean that Beijing had easy access to India's heartland across the porous five-hundred-mile border with Nepal. Concerns were raised that the Chinese embassy in Kathmandu was assisting the Maoists in India.

But while US analysts in 1973 believed that though India was still suspicious of the Chinese-Nepalese relationship, it seemed to have arrived at the realistic conclusion that with its established ties to Nepal and increasing Nepalese national unity, the relatively small Chinese presence in Nepal would not harm India, given India's ability to apply pressure with more overt support for democratic forces like the Nepali Congress, as well as the possibility of economic warfare. However, Nepal's silent support to Pakistan was an area that even US officials believed could harm the Indo-Nepalese relationship. A former Nepalese minister informed US diplomats that a top level Indian official had warned him that if any Chinese military unit was ever invited to Nepal, the Indian army would occupy Nepal. This was the time when the vast majority of Nepalese Congress leaders, including B.P. Koirala, Nepal's first democratically elected prime minister, lived in exile in India and were planning a violent revolution to re-establish democratic rules. India had maintained that it would never force these leaders away from the country because of its strong belief in the parliamentary democracy.

Pakistan's presence in Nepal worried India. The memories of Partition were alive and haunting and the distrust between the two countries had been born the day the British decided to divide India. Though Pakistan fought and lost many wars against India on battlefields, they also used proxy means to hurt their neighbour, such as raising and sponsoring an army of terrorists. Pakistan's penetration in Nepal was further deepened by its president, Muhammad Zia-ul-Haq.

After Zia-ul-Haq's death in August 1988, ISI chief General Hamid Gul continued the ISI's secret meetings in the royal palace of King Birendra. The R&AW informed the Indian government that every other shop on the streets of Kathmandu was sponsored by the ISI and later, Kashmiris with close ties to militant leaders were settled there to support terror activities on the Indian soil. King Birendra was facing tremendous pressure from democratic groups in Nepal who demanded the abolition of the monarchy and the rule of democracy in the country. Birendra suspected that India had a role in this uprising and when the Indo-Nepal treaties of trade and transit lapsed in March 1989, he did not renew them though several proposals were mooted by the Indian government. Nepal alleged that India was pushing for an economic blockade of the country. However, the records of the MEA reveal that despite the fact that there was no Indo-Nepal transit treaty in force, the government had ensured the import of goods by Nepal through the checkpoints of Raxaul and Jogbani, along with separate transit routes from Bhutan and Bangladesh, and it continued to implement economic development projects in Nepal as a part of its aid package.

Sanjay Arora, a R&AW officer, said that the situation in Kathmandu had become frightening in terms of India's security and though they tried to reason with King Birendra, arguing that the presence of the ISI and Kashmiri militants in Nepal would make a serious dent to the relationship between India and Nepal and cause irreparable damage to India's internal security, the monarch chose to ignore India's plea.

Arora told me: 'We were left with no option but to support the people's movement. The agency's Nepal unit, operating out of Lucknow, made sure that democratic Nepalese leaders with calibre and spine got unflinching support because they would need to take the hard decision and uproot terror factories. We had informed the then prime minister, V.P. Singh, early on in February 1990 that our peaceful neighbour had turned into a safe haven for anti-India elements. Though Singh had a very frosty relationship with the R&AW, he instructed us to create a well-defined mechanism to carry out our plans. There has been a lot of misinformation about the role that the agency played. It was said that we were disrupters, but in reality, we were supporting pro-democratic elements.The IB and R&AW both believed that we needed more assets and eavesdroppers on both sides of the border to maintain a grip on the events unfolding in the wake of the people's uprising.'

The Lucknow-based operational headquarters of the R&AW's Nepal unit buzzed with activity in the early 1990s. Many top Nepalese leaders had offered their services in building a strong movement for constitutional democracy. Since such operations need to be managed politically, every decision taken by the R&AW officers handling Nepal was conveyed to the top brass in Delhi. Arora said that every important conversation was monitored at the listening posts. These were shared with field agents for appropriate action including covert operations. In his words, 'It was a neat operation that successfully hunted down ISI elements and neutralised the forces obstructing democracy. These twin objectives could have only been achieved through clandestine activities. I cannot divulge the operational details, but we ran a spectacular spy mission with highly placed assets inside Nepal.'

A spy codenamed Ravi S. Sinha cultivated assets in the Nepalese Congress and the Communist Party of Nepal in support of Operation Mechi that had galvanised support for the people's movement. He was the driving force behind the move to end the monarchy in Nepal, which was helping forces inimical to India to use its land. Sinha said that he had held several rounds of meetings with his sources in Nepal primarily to make them understand Pakistan's deception and that the monarchy was more interested in maintaining the status quo than in cleaning up the country. He also explained his relationship with the assets.

'It was more than a working relationship,' he said. 'Some were initially reluctant to participate and I told them to take time to evaluate the mess Nepal was turning into. I also warned them that Nepal would sink under such a regime and the support to militants may turn out to be counterproductive. They could see trouble brewing in Kathmandu and Pokhara, the two major cities of Nepal, and they helped us stay a step ahead of our enemies for years. Unfortunately, our strategists in the last few years have not utilised these assets judiciously.'

When the conflict ended in April 1990 after months of violence, an interim government headed by Krishna Prasad Bhattarai was installed in Kathmandu. In June that year, the prime minister, fondly called 'KP' by the Indian intelligence community, made a trip to Delhi and reiterated that he would make every effort to usher in peace, friendship and cooperation with India. He promised not to allow activities in Nepalese territory that could be prejudicial to the security of India and assured the Indian government of prior consultations on defence related matters. In November 1990, Chandra Shekhar became the prime minister and made a reciprocal visit to Nepal in February 1991, where he held meetings with a wide spectrum of Nepalese political leaders. During Chandra Shekhar's period in office, a decision was made to set up a high-level task force for comprehensive economic cooperation that would function under the guidance of an Indo-Nepal Joint Commission. Attempts were made from both sides to begin a new era of bilateral cooperation and India left no stone unturned to extend additional credit facilities to Nepal to ensure the timely completion of phased development programmes. In May 1991, G.P. Koirala took over as the prime minister of Nepal and a month later, P.V. Narasimha Rao became the ninth prime minister of India. MEA papers observed that G.P. Koirala called on Narasimha Rao in New Delhi in December, a trip that had been preceded by four months of active and extensive consultations between the two sides. For the first time, an Indo-Nepal High-Level Task Force was set up, chaired by the cabinet secretary and including the foreign secretary, the finance secretary and the commerce secretary, which prepared a comprehensive programme for bilateral cooperation with an emphasis on the expansion of economic and industrial cooperation. According to the MEA, this was the first time such an approach had been adopted by Nepal and India. The relationship between the two countries steadily improved during the first year of the Narasimha Rao government, although on the security front, the ISI and the network of Kashmiri militants were getting stronger.

Veterans in the spy game believe that King Birendra played a crucial role in helping Kashmiri and Khalistani militants, turning Nepal into a launch pad of terrorism against India. Bipin Govind, an Indian agent, carried out several operations in the small towns of the Terai region, picking up information about the various meetings held by Muslim leaders to chalk out a strategy to rehabilitate Kashmiri militants in various parts of Nepal including Kathmandu. His intelligence reports created turmoil within the security establishment. Govind also watched as propaganda material was distributed among the militants, encouraging them to return to India to wage jihad after spending some time in Nepal.

'There was a whole area we had nicknamed Kashmiri Bazar. Each Kashmiri here was part of a sleeper cell and they enjoyed the absolute support of the king's men,' Govind told me. 'There were chances of influencing the king against these people, but he was blinded by the propaganda orchestrated by the Muslim leaders from Terai. The smaller a nation, the bigger its ego. It was not easy to carry out open operations when the plotters enjoyed state support. Some of our operations aimed to dismantle the militants' plans before they were executed.'

As the R&AW moved closer to the Kashmiri militants in the Terai and Kathmandu, the Muslim leaders began floating non-governmental organisations as fronts to camouflage their terror activities. Into this high-pressure atmosphere, the R&AW deployed an undercover spy codenamed Sajid. Anantnag-born Sajid's task was to infiltrate Kashmiri-linked organisations and engineer differences among the outfits supporting the militants. When Sajid began his espionage operation in the early 1990s, he developed close ties with two powerful Kashmiri militants. This enabled him to pass on vital intelligence inputs even as he worked on subverting these groups. He stole the bank account details of pro-Kashmiri organisations and manipulated them to create envy and anger among rival groups. Simultaneously, he sent messages to the security agencies about the arrivals and departures of militants to assist the agencies in their covert operations. Several terrorists were neutralised on the basis of warnings dispatched by Sajid. Flying solo, Sajid harvested actionable intelligence of high value for the R&AW. Working inside enemy territory, he had to have had nerves of steel.

In Govind's words: 'He was a confident trickster and a gifted operative, courageous and reliable. Sajid operated for more than a year and I believe he was instrumental in preventing at least a hundred terror attacks in Kashmir. He successfully created rifts within several groups and the internal chaos weakened them substantially. We had more than than a hundred spies and informers in Nepal, but Sajid was the king of spies.'

The Arrival of the Underworld and Mujahideen

Just before the 1993 bomb blasts in Bombay, Dawood Ibrahim fled to Dubai. India had been strengthening its relationship with the UAE at this time. Just a few months after the serial explosions in Bombay that killed more than two hundred and fifty people, Indo-UAE Joint Commission meetings were held in Abu Dhabi. On the Nepal front, India was working with the government as well as the king and Birendra Bir Bikram Shah was invited to New Delhi. These two events are significant because Dawood's move to Dubai cemented the Kathmandu-Dubai underworld network and provided the ISI with huge leverage to strengthen its base in Nepal. Dawood had found a trusted friend in Mirza Dilshad Beg, a Nepalese parliamentarian who had deep ties with the Pakistani intelligence agencies and even helped them set up safe houses in Nepal. Originally from Gorakhpur, Mirza moved to Kapilvastu in Nepal and subsequently to the Nepalese Parliament, winning two back-to-back elections in 1991 and 1993. India was developing better ties with the G.P. Koirala government at the time, but the Indian agencies watching developments in the spy world were not able to contain the growing clout of Mirza and the ISI. The underworld operated with impunity in Kathmandu and Pokhara, though the R&AW did warn the government on several occasions of cells trying to create a network of smugglers, terrorists and human traffickers in Nepal to launch anti-India operations. A spy codenamed Diwakar Sharma said that during the visit of Nepal's foreign secretary, K.B. Shrestha, to Delhi in June 1996, the Indian side had raised the issue of the underworld and made it clear that anti-India activities from the neighbourhood would not be tolerated. However, the R&AW informed the government that the network was gaining strength in various nondescript Nepalese towns and could become a nightmare for India's internal security.

'The Nepalese internal security apparatus, including its intelligence wing, was still learning the ropes,' said Diwakar. 'They did not know the repercussions of allowing underworld terrorists to operate in their territory since India was the primary target, not Nepal. Though our action was large in scale, local support was missing and that created a huge problem for us. We paid the price in 1999.'

In September 1999, External Affairs Minister Jaswant Singh was in Kathmandu for an official visit. While the two countries reaffirmed their commitment to ensuring their territories were not used for activities prejudicial to the security of the other, Singh was keen on a clear demarcation of the porous boundary that was proving to be a major advantage for smugglers and terror outfits. India had freshly emerged from the Kargil War and the focus of the government under National Security Advisor Brajesh Mishra was to ensure that troubles in the neighbourhood were neutralised in a timely manner. Two months later, Indian Airlines flight IC 814 with one hundred and seventy-eight passengers and eleven crew members on board, took off from Kathmandu for New Delhi on 24 December 1999 and was hijacked by Pakistani terrorists. Although the hostages were released on 31 December in exchange for three jailed militants including Maulana Masood Azhar, questions were raised over the lack of forewarning. Two months later, it was learned that a R&AW operative in Kathmandu had informed his senior about the terror plot, but the memorandum was never sent to New Delhi.

'We learned that the R&AW officer was harassed when he filed the report warning the government about the terrorists' plan to hijack the aircraft. His immediate senior was very unhappy and kept the report in his drawer. It was never sent to headquarters for further action. So we were not sleeping. But there are times when you cannot do anything despite having an accurate input on future events. The IC 814 hijacking was one such example,' Diwakar said.

Nevertheless, due to the IC 814 hijack, the Indian government started looking at loopholes in the security apparatus of Nepal and found too many loose ends. After the intelligence fiasco that led to the Kargil war and the subsequent report submitted by the Kargil Review Committee, the then prime minister, Atal Bihari Vajpayee, set up a Group of Ministers (GoM) on 17 April 2000 to review the national security system. The GoM, headed by then Home Minister Lal Krishna Advani, with Defence Minister George Fernandes, External Affairs Minister Jaswant Singh and Finance Minister Yashwant Sinha, was mandated to formulate specific proposals for implementation. The GoM came to the conclusion that the ISI had been able to built new networks in Nepal. They also said that the dynamic nature of problems related to the management of borders was highlighted by the manner in which the India–Nepal border had changed over a period of time. The open boundary had once been peaceful and trouble-free, but with the increasing activities of the ISI in Nepal, the nature of the border had changed completely and the security concerns related to it needed to be addressed urgently.

After his release, Maulana Azhar formed a terror outfit named Jaish-e-Mohammed that aimed to unite Kashmir with Pakistan. The outfit, the R&AW suspected, had deep links in Nepal. The shadowy war was being fought on twin fronts—taking out terrorists and sleeper cells as well as helping Nepal tackle the growing menace of the Maoist movement that used hit squads to target infrastructure and was tying up with Indian insurgents.

The Maoists' overground leadership though, had developed an incredibly close connection with the Indian intelligence agency. An agent runner codenamed Nirmal Khatri said that they knew practically everyone in the cadre. Khatri and a handful of trusted men identified assets in the cadre for use in future operations. But sometime in 2000–2001, everything just collapsed. This was largely due to the one-way policy of the government, which believed that supporting just the Nepalese Congress was the wisest thing to do. And so it stopped cultivating Nepalese Marxists. In Khatri's words, 'It was the beginning of hostility towards India as we did not expand our network among the Marxists.'

Khatri said that while the R&AW argued strongly in support of the Maoist leadership, the NDA government headed by Atal Bihari Vajpayee had a different take on the issue. The then defence minister, George Fernandes, even went on record to say, 'The fight against Nepalese Maoists is also India's fight.' This perturbed many Nepalese Maoist leaders, who had been getting covert support from the R&AW.

The R&AW was also fighting a turf war in the neighbourhood with the CIA. Citing a Wikileaks cable of 2003, Khatri said that the US government was trying to occupy space that India had inadvertently conceded to other powers operating in the region. The secret cable drafted by the then US Ambassador to Nepal, Michael Malinowski, just months before the CIA successfully executed the defection of R&AW officer Rabinder Singh, reveals the US's frustration as well as India's inflexible policy towards Nepal. The cable said:

> On December 3 (2003) the US Ambassador raised with Indian Ambassador Shyam Saran reports that Intelligence agents assigned to the Indian Embassy in Kathmandu have been characterizing US government policy and motives in Nepal as malevolently aimed at undermining Nepal's sovereignty. The Ambassador told Saran that the reports had been passed to us by several Nepali political sources, who claimed to have had such conversations in the recent past with R&AW agents based at the Indian Embassy. He also briefed Saran about unsubstantiated reports suggesting that some Nepali Maoist women may have received training at a security facility in Dehradun in Northern India. Noting that Nepalese, both

> within the government and in the opposition, sometimes attempt to play off Indian and American interests, he stressed that the information passed on by these sources had not been verified. He noted that the reports predated the meeting between Nepali Maoists and Communist Party of Nepal United Marxist-Leninist General Secretary Madhav Nepal in Lucknow—an event that has set Nepali nationalists teeth on edge against India. The Ambassador emphasized that he was communicating these concerns to Saran as a friend and ally. In a separate meeting on November 30, Saran briefed the Ambassador on the just-concluded policy deliberations in New Delhi. He stressed that his interlocutors had expressed concern about possible spill-over of the insurgency onto Indian territory. Saran noted, however, that certain quarters within the Indian government had argued that India should maintain contact with the Maoists in order to influence them and to keep open communication channels in the event of a worst-case scenario in which the Maoists ultimately gain power. We cannot discount the possibility that our Nepali sources, many of whom resent India's influence in their country, may have their own motives in conveying to us reports of Indian double-dealing. We have always found Saran professional, collegial and cooperative, and believe that he does not sanction—and may probably not be aware of—all of R&AW activities in Nepal. His acknowledgement that some in the government of India 'go off on their own' and that some advocate maintaining contact and influence with the Maoists is his first admission to us that some elements within his Embassy may be working at cross-purposes to official Indian government policy.

While the cable is self-explanatory about the growing divisions among the decision makers, Khatri argued that there were strong undercurrents of resentment in Nepal in early 2000 because of the feeling that India had never allowed Nepal to grow. Such public perception was built largely due to the Indian government's unwillingness to have top leaders as Indian assets and its ambivalent approach in dealing with pro-India elements in Nepalese politics. It was also partly due to the aggressive propaganda against India by a certain section of Nepalese Maoists and Pakistani operatives.

This perception was wrong because India did enough. But the massive hype created by anti-India elements was more visible. The government's approach was also partly responsible for the Nepalese Maoists' attitude to India. According to Khatri, during the Atal Bihari Vajpayee govenment, the Indian intelligence agency was not in favour of completely banning the All India Nepali Unity Society, the political front of the Maoist movements in Nepal. The group was active in India and its political leadership was looking for support to enter mainstream politics. But to please King Gyanendra of Nepal, the Vajpayee government not only blacklisted the outfit but also arrested its leaders, Maheshwar Dahal and Partha Chhetri, who were in Delhi in July 2002. A R&AW officer privy to several discussions on Nepal in the government said that the Himalayan country was non-committal about the extradition of third country nationals despite the fact that Pakistani extremists, sheltered by a large delegation of ISI officers under diplomatic cover, were operating from its soil. He said that during a meeting over the mutual legal assistance agreement in February 2003, Nepal's discomfort was more than visible. The Nepalese officials were reluctant to deport Pakistani extremists and were also concerned about India's demand for the grant of access to Indian investigators on a reciprocal basis. On the political front, though India had started putting pressure on King Gyanendra to step back and allow democracy to flourish, it was a delayed response and various parties with leaders flirting with Pakistan and China had become active.

Meanwhile, India was dutifully executing a request from the Royal Nepalese Army and handing over Nepalese Maoist leaders hiding in India, including those who had come seeking medical treatment. India had to pay the price for this when King Gyanendra, after seizing power in February 2005, turned hostile towards India. The king had been playing both sides. He had secretly been in talks with Maoists back home, while asking India to capture the leaders of the movement. He was also angered by India's desire for democracy in Nepal and believed that India was hostile to him since it preferred democracy to monarchy. He was so anti-India that the then foreign secretary, Shyam Saran, went on record to say that the king was taking steps against India's interest.

While India had begun a crackdown against the Nepalese Maoist leadership, it accused King Gyanendra of strengthening the red forces back home. This warning about the growing cooperation between Nepalese and Indian Naxals received a snub from Gyanendra's palace, which R&AW officers believed was a major embarrassment for India. Saran was more emphatic when he said, 'There is no way in which we are able to engage with the government of Nepal in even making a proper assessment of what is happening.'

Khatri said, 'Over the years, a feeling was nurtured among the masses that India was the root cause of Nepalese problems. Our policy towards Nepal since the beginning has been myopic. The royalists, whom we used to call Nepalese oligarchs, and the Maoists were not cultivated and eventually, the ISI and China took advantage of a vast pool of assets ready to switch sides. Nepalese hostility towards us became global news when we started highlighting our aid to Nepal. Even one of our Nepalese assets posted abroad showed discomfort. This was the result of bad diplomacy. Several important individuals who were considered to be R&AW assets two decades ago now occupy executive positions in the present Nepalese dispensation. They have not forgotten that R&AW had refused to help them in need.'

King Gyanendra also played a crucial role in the confrontation with the Indian government when he sacked Prime Minister Sher Bahadur Deuba in early 2005 and became the absolute ruler of the kingdom. R&AW officers had strong reservations about the king's power in the democracy and even when the Manmohan Singh government tried to keep the veto power in Gyanendra's hands, the R&AW warned that the monarchy had to go if India wanted a stable and peaceful neighborhood. Gyanendra had started cultivating the Chinese and according to a R&AW intelligence report, favoured a large arms deal with Chinese, ignoring the Indian bid. The report added that Gyanendra's relatives were the alleged beneficiaries of several deals in other sectors, such as mobile technology.

But India failed to re-calibrate its approach to Nepal, leaving developments in the Himalayan kingdom out of its reach.

Nepal as a Safe House for Terrorists

The intelligence officers who relentlessly pursued the Indian Mujahideen's terrorists said that their spy missions in the neighbourhood confirmed the fear that little villages and towns in Nepal were turning into safe houses for terror modules fleeing India. By 2008, the R&AW had started to track and intercept the phone numbers of suspected sympathisers inside Nepal. An intelligence note that I accessed revealed the dual life of terror cells in Nepal. Immediately after the Batla House encounter in September 2008, Ariz Khan alias Zunaid managed to escape. The intelligence note said that he reached Aligarh and met Masood, briefing him about the police's crackdown and receiving some financial assistance. Subsequently, Zunaid, accompanied by Shahzad, shuttled between Mumbai, Jodhpur, Noida and Muzaffarnagar. The duo travelled to Azamgarh in UP, and Zunaid later went to Katiyar and Jogbani, where he crossed the India-Nepal border. A taxi awaited him there, arranged by Nizam Khan. When Zunaid got to Birat Nagar, Khan arranged for his stay at Karsiya road and helped him acquire a citizenship card and a passport in the name of Mohammed Salim, son of Noor Mohammed, Ward Number 18, Birat Nagar, Nepal. Now he was a Nepalese citizen.

In November and December 2008, Zunaid visited the madrassa often and in 2009, he stayed at Ghuski for two months, working as a teacher at Hilaal Public School. Intelligence sources revealed that the school was operated by Islami Sangh Nepal which claimed to have been formed in 1985 to establish Islam in its totality. The organisation was on the R&AW's radar, but not much was known about its ties with the ISI. R&AW spies believe that the Islami Sangh Nepal supported terrorists under the garb of charitable works. Nizam was closely linked to the organisation and carried out its activities on the ground. The year 2009 was spent by Zunaid in Kawasoti and Palpa in Nepal and in early 2010, he was introduced to the Indian Mujahideen veteran Abdul Subhan alias Tauqeer, who had fled India due to raids on SIMI and the IM after the Batla House encounter, and was also sheltered by Nizam Khan in Gorkha city. The intelligence report said:

> In January 2010, Zunaid talked to Abdul Subhan through Abdul Hakim's mobile phone. The meeting was fixed at Gorkha city and Zunaid shifted his base for next three to four months. Subsequently, he went to Ahle Village and started teaching at a Madarasa. Sometime in July 2010, Zunaid returned to Gorkha city and opened a restaurant. It was closed down within months after his partner and IM terrorist Tauqeer had an altercation with Tablighi Jamaat and the terrorists shifted their base to Kathmandu. Later, Zunaid moved to Pachera and joined Paradise Public Academy as a science teacher and stayed there till December 2014. During this period, he also got married to

a newly converted Sara, a widow. Towards the end of the year, Zunaid got a new passport with the help of Jalaaldin Miya, who was running a travel agency near Taj Bakery, Kathmandu. Both Zunaid and Tauqeer took a flight to Saudi Arabia on 10 January 2015. They got the visa through the Panda Supermarket Chain and continued to work for two years in Dammam. He worked at Panda (401) Ibne-Khaldoun Plaza, Dammam and stayed at Panda Employees Villa, Souq-Al-Ganam. In Saudi Arabia, Zunaid and Tauqeer went for scouting of young recruits but were unable to make contacts. Thereafter on 22 March 2017, Zunaid returned to Pachera and started teaching at Paradise Public School. He was nabbed by Indian intelligence officials while visiting his in-laws' house at Kathmandu in early 2018.

Tauqeer crossed Raxaul border for Nepal in a rickshaw and stayed at a hotel in Birganj. Later, he traveled to Bhutta, Birat Nagar and met a sympathizer Mannan at Dr. Gaffur's clinic. Islami Sangh Nepal helped him to set up a base. In December 2008, Tauqeer managed to arrange a Nepalese identity card in the name of Abdul Rehman Sheikh, resident of ward 18, Birat Nagar. Tauqeer also asked for a Nepalese Passport but his handler Nizam Khan denied it arguing that he doesn't know Nepali language and he must stay at Gorkha for sometime and learn the local language. Nizam also invited Tauqeer at his house in Kathmandu and arranged his stay at Dera village and started teaching at a government school. Three months later, he moved to Ahle village and stayed at a Madarasa but within few months, he shifted back to Dera and started teaching English at Tehfuzul-Quran Madarasa till December 2009. In the early 2010, Tauqeer moved to Gorkha city and opened a coaching centre in partnership with another IM sympathizer Abdul Karim. The centre was closed down in January 2011 and Tauqeer once again started pursuing his dream of leaving Nepal for Saudi Arabia. He was helped by another IM sleeper cell man Ayub, who runs a travel agency at

> Bagh Bazar, opposite Taj Lodge in Kathmandu. Ayub arranged a computer-teaching job for Tauqeer at Arjun Boarding School in Tamgaas, near Palpa Nepal. Subsequently, he taught at Rudra Ganga Boarding School. This job too was arranged by IM's cells deeply entrenched in the system. In the end of 2014, Tauqeer renewed his effort to get a Nepalese Passport and Nizam Khan provided some documents needed for it. Within 15 days, he was officially a Nepalese citizen. On Ayub's reference, he met one Hafiz, who arranged Saudi Arabian visa for him. On 12 April 2015, Tauqeer boarded Emirates flight for Riyadh. He worked at two supermarkets 'Exit 8' near the international airport and Imtiyaz al Uruba earning approximately 2600 Riyal per month. He returned to Nepal during Ramzan in 2016 and spoke to his family in Mumbai. The Indian spies intercepted the call. In January 2018, he was arrested from Nepal.

This intelligence report may not reflect the painstaking work done by the R&AW spies. It is a plain and simple internal memo drafted for the official file. However, according to insiders, the chase for the fugitives was exhausting. On many occasions, they hit roadblocks owing to the obscure network of sympathisers operating in Nepal and using circuitous routes to finance jihadi elements against India. There was also a gridlock in the Nepalese system that prevented them from acting on intelligence inputs received from secret sources.

For intelligence operatives like Khatri, the arrests were both a success and a failure. He was shocked by the fact that terrorists wanted in India easily spent ten years in Nepal. And as more and more Pakistan-sponsored madrassas are sprouting in the neighbourhood, the situation looks grim. He also rules out sealing the border as it may make the Nepalese even more hostile, allowing China and Pakistan to get the Himalayan nation firmly on their sides. According to the home ministry, the main challenge is to check infiltration by terrorists and criminals along the 1,715 km open border, and thirty-one battalions of the Sashtra Seema Bal (SSB) have been deployed to do so. Aside from institutional mechanisms at the home secretary and joint secretary levels, the two countries also have district coordination committees which discuss issues of mutual concern, such as containing cross-border crimes, smuggling and terrorist activities.

Can we close the border? That is not feasible or possible since the Chinese intelligence has now launched an offensive in Nepal. Mandarin teaching institutions have come up and a recent minor explosion in front of the Indian consulate was just a warning that the Chinese can get to us. An opportunity to mend ties came in January 2006 when officers of both the countries sat down for a meeting in New Delhi to discuss the Indo-Nepal transit treaty for the smooth movement of supplies to Nepal through fifteen transit points. More than 60 per cent of Nepal's total trade was with India and Nepal wanted to strengthen commercial ties for its development. The Indian government, however, worried by the nexus between the Indian and Nepalese Maoists and the unhindered access to the Chinese and the Pakistanis, asked Nepal to abide by certain preconditions, such as rationalisation of transit points, protection of third-country shipments through a guarantee system and access for the transport of goods from one point in India to another via Nepal. This discussion and India's strong views on certain conditions damaged the positive outcome of this meeting. There was at least three months' delay in the renewal of the treaty that had first been signed in 1950 and sent out a political signal that Nepal was totally dependent on India for its survival.

The Indian agency's view prevailed when the Maoists decided to abjure violence and enter electoral politics. Some Nepalese Maoists leaders were still among the R&AW's assets and this played a crucial role in the peace process and the safe arrival of the Maoist leadership in Kathmandu from their hiding places in the Terai region.

India had always enjoyed organic links with Nepal but changing global dynamics and the Chinese presence loosened India's grip on the Himalayan kingdom. The R&AW officer Diwakar recalled that even when the US government wanted something to be conveyed to Nepal, their diplomats requested India to pass the message on. But by 2009, Nepal had became so indifferent to India that an officer from the MEA was forced to turn down a proposal from the US embassy that wanted to convey that Nepal must look for political consensus and accommodate all the parties making efforts to strengthen democracy. This, he said, was a sign that the anti-India stand in the Nepalese political class was seen as pro-Nepal, though they remain politically and economically dependent on India.

Diwakar said, 'On the government level, we had decided to not give any direct message to the Nepalese government. The truth is that the intelligence agency was no longer in the position to persuade and influence the Nepalese. The R&AW also doubted the Nepalese intention since they were courting India's adversaries, China and Pakistan. Due to the unwillingness of the Indian government, the R&AW lost the opportunity to recruit and run top rung leaders who could have provided state secrets. There is no substitute for human intelligence collection and if the sources are drying up, the job of accurate prediction is nearly impossible. The government expressed doubts over the Maoists' intentions but we wanted our men everywhere. It can be dangerous to not have sniffers in the enemy camp. We continue to run our well-placed sources inside Nepal with proper control. Even when the use was limited—since it is always up to the government to decide how far we want to go—we recruited more informers to track every step the Nepalese decision makers were taking.

Handling agents is very difficult in such a hostile environment, but we cannot afford to be surprised. Our security concern was the Terai region and certain areas in Kathmandu since militants were setting up camps and safe houses close to the border and a renewed operation was launched to eliminate the radicals while the government continued to placate Nepalese politicians with aid for development and infrastructure projects.'

According to Khatri, political and diplomatic manoeuvring is for short-term benefits but espionage will give you long-term stability. 'Even today, the Nepalese government argues that India is a more vital and important neighbour than China, but you cannot blindly trust their words. The days of winning hearts are over. It is time to weaken anti-India elements. The priority is clear—we support an elected, stable and democratic government free from Chinese and Pakistani control.'

10

OPERATION HORNET

At the Café de Flore on Boulevard Saint-Germain, Paris, in November 1984, Sanjeev Jindal was lost in thought. In India, the funeral procession of Prime Minister Indira Gandhi was underway and her son Rajiv Gandhi was about to take charge of the Congress party. The French president, Laurent Fabius, had flown to New Delhi to attend the funeral. As the tourists and locals around him discussed Ernest Hemingway and Albert Camus, Jindal thought about his recent trip to London where he had met his recruit, Clarke Lee, a R&AW informer primarily concerned with picking up intelligence on anti-India elements, especially Pakistanis like Abdul Khan who sheltered extremists.

Reading Clarke's report on the night of 3 November, Jindal was filled with anguish and rage. Could he help take down anti-India networks operating in Europe despite the sharp division between politicians and intelligence officers regarding covert operations abroad? Since 1982, Khan had invited Pakistani intelligence officers, Indian fugitives and some local politicians to his Newham house in London. Among the reports sent by Clarke, there was a copy of a coded memo dated 9 December 1983, warning that Khan had had several rounds of meetings with an Indian recruited by the ISI which meant that they must be plotting something sinister against India. Jindal remembered forwarding a polished report to New Delhi in a diplomatic pouch, but thanks to the lax analysts back home, he had never received a response. This was a classic example of the uneasy relationship between desk analysts and field operatives. While field agents put their lives on the line, analysts filtered the information and corroborated it with different sources before sending it on to the top brass for further action.

Jindal, however, insisted that Clarke's loyalties were beyond doubt. So he called New Delhi in early December 1984, after the new government had settled in, and reminded his boss Anuj Bhardwaj about Clarke's warning against Khan and his cronies, including an Indian named B.N. Sandhu. Bhardwaj, known as the pop star of spies, had woke up late with a headache that cold winter morning and was feeling breathless. He listened to Jindal's coded complaint against the analysts and curtly told him to come to Delhi the next week for a one-on-one meeting.

At Bhardwaj's office, the two discussed high-grade intelligence sent to the agency before Indira Gandhi's assassination.

'Give me a quick rundown on your reports sent last year,' Bhardwaj demanded.

'I don't want to sound repetitive but you know our asset in London had warned that the ISI and Khan were plotting against India. It may have had nothing to do with the assassination of the prime minister, but I am worried about the increasing activities of these elements and if you check the reports, there is merit to his warnings,' Jindal said.

'It does make sense that Khan is working in collusion with Sandhu and the ISI and I am not ruling out their capability to subvert local politicians as well, but give me a solution and don't count your laurels,' said Bhardwaj harshly.

'Sir, we need to launch an operation. If we can bring down Khan and Sandhu together, it will have an adverse effect on all those standing in the queue to bleed us,' Jindal responded.

'Do you want me to launch an operation without knowing fully how to handle and operate it? I am also worried about the access of your agent, whether or not he has the keys to the inner circle of Khan and his chums. I won't allow it without proper control.' Bhardwaj's reaction was sharp.

'Give me a couple of days and I will respond to your queries in detail. We must do something urgently and I promise not to disappoint you,' Jindal assured him.

Bhardwaj had been told by a friend in the Ministry of External Affairs (MEA) that they were working out Prime Minister Rajiv Gandhi's future visits abroad and France could be one of the destinations in 1985. Thinking about Jindal's confidence in the intelligence he had received, Bhardwaj made up his mind that if any operation was going to be launched, London had to be the theatre and Paris could be used as an intelligence sub-station to plan the operation and hold meetings.

According to an intelligence analysis, India's relations with France had been rather formal for many years after Independence as it was the only European country to have a colonial pocket remaining in India after the Portuguese left Goa. Both countries had been too preoccupied with their respective problems to pay much attention to each other: France was deep in the task of post-war rehabilitation and reconstruction and India needed to build up a partitioned country. The world outlook of the two countries also differed substantially. India was non-aligned while France became a member of the North Atlantic Treaty Organisation in 1949. These differences were sharpened when France, along with Britain and Israel, invaded Egypt in November 1956. With Charles de Gaulle's advent to power in France in 1958, French foreign policy perceptions began to change. The new independent French foreign policy of rejecting bloc politics while seeking an East-West detente seemed to have elements in common with the policy of non-alignment followed by India.

By this time, India's problems with France over the French pockets had been amicably settled. The official visit of Prime Minister Georges Pompidou to India in February 1965, the first ever by a French prime minister, was an indication of the increasingly similar attitudes of the two countries on various international issues. Some differences resurfaced during the Soviet occupation of Afghanistan when France, following the US policy, believed that Pakistan needed to be strengthened to counter the Soviet might; nevertheless, Indira Gandhi visited France from 12–15 November 1981, which was considered an important landmark in Indo-French relations. Gandhi held discussions with President Francois Mitterrand and the two countries decided to strengthen their ties in various sectors. The relationship in the trade sector was strengthened by early 1982 with the decision of the Indian government to purchase the highly sophisticated Mirage 2000, for which the French government made credits available on short terms. This agreement, called 'intention to proceed,' was expected to secure India's air defence against Pakistan's acquisition of F-16 aircraft from the USA.

Later in December 1984, Bhardwaj began his day in office reading reports filed by Jindal from Paris as well as a few memos and observation reports from London. Sandhu, he realised, had vanished and then reappeared in the last couple of months. No one really knew where he had been but one of Jindal's reports, probably based on Clarke's input, had suggested Islamabad as a possible location. The report sent a quiver through Bhardwaj.

When Jindal showed up again, Bhardwaj said, 'I now see what you were hinting at. What is your plan?'

'Sir, we need to reach out to Sandhu. We should not let the ISI and Pakistan army seize this dangerous man and create a Bangladesh-like situation for us,' Jindal replied.

'Why are the British allowing him to go to Pakistan? Aren't they aware that Pakistan is creating a Frankenstein's monster?' Bhardwaj argued.

'For years, the British have been aware that the Pakistanis are supporting militants and armed rebels inside India. The conversation I had with some British officers makes it very clear that their thinking is that we are battling these militants, not they,' Jindal explained.

'Don't tell me the British are conscious collaborators in this?' Bhardwaj snapped.

'They are not collaborators but it is not on their priority list. They feel it is India's responsibility to wipe out the militancy and these guys have not harmed British territory, but have projected themselves as asylum seekers who have been persecuted by India,' Jindal replied.

'Are you suggesting the ISI is operating Sandhu?' Bhardwaj probed.

'My information suggests ISI chief Akhtar Abdur Rahman is directly supervising the operation. I have seen Clarke's harvest and that is why Khan and Sandhu's nexus is bothering me,' Jindal contended.

It was well past lunchtime when Bhardwaj asked Jindal for aggressive surveillance on Khan and Sandhu.

'What is in your mind about the operation?' Bhardwaj finally said.

'I need an officer posted undercover at the London embassy to coordinate with Clarke. He would just be a go-between. I will control the operation from Paris,' Jindal suggested.

'I hope your special operation pays off. Come back with an intelligence coup, not a disaster,' Bhardwaj said sceptically. No one could have guessed from his tone that Jindal was his favourite agent because of the younger man's methodical selection of targets and efficient handling of work.

This was the beginning of Operation Hornet.

Jindal had already identified the spy to be posted in London. The officer codenamed Mohan Narayanan had earlier worked in

Prague where, under the tutelage of Bhardwaj, he had carried out several operations. Narayanan was articulate, well-informed on militancy and the European landscape and above all, very charming. He could spin story after story without parting with even an iota of valuable intelligence. He could speak German and French besides a little Punjabi and could easily assimilate himself in an alien culture.

Operation Hornet was divided into two distinct areas. Intelligence collection and interpretation were the tasks for Narayanan and Clarke, while the covert operation was Jindal's responsibility. Sometime in late January 1985, Jindal was at Café Aida in Landstrasse, Vienna. He had waited for almost a week for this meeting with his old informer Sophie Klor. Jindal, known by a different name at the time, had dumped her two years earlier at the end of an operation he had run in Austria.

It is not unusual for an intelligence officer to dump her or his source or informer once the job is done. There are no permanent relationships in the world of espionage. Everyone has an expiry date. But Sophie was perhaps an exception. A history graduate, she worked with a non-governmental organisation based in Vienna. Jindal had met her at a human rights conference and was professionally drawn to her fierce condemnation of Pakistan's activities and American interference in South Asia, specifically Afghanistan. She came to admire Jindal's political and military knowledge of Europe and his strong views on the cold war. Their mutual respect helped Jindal earn her trust and he was able to recruit her as what the R&AW called a subconscious agent, meaning an agent activated not against her or his own country but a third country. Sophie assisted Jindal in his Austria operation. Like the R&AW's other subconscious agents in Europe in the 1980s and 1990s, she transferred money to moles, trained new assets in the target country and occasionally ran assets on behalf of the handler.

'So your socialist leader has got the Jawaharlal Nehru Award,' Jindal teased Sophie as soon as she pulled out a chair to sit down.

'You cannot discount Bruno's contribution to Austria. At least, he was firm and fought for equality like your great leader,' Sophie said curtly, referring to Dr Bruno Kreisky, who had been Austria's chancellor for almost thirteen years.

'I know he praised Nehru at the award ceremony and told the gathering that all his life he only followed the path shown by the Indian leader. He was beaming with joy recounting his encounter with Nehru,' Jindal replied in a lighter vein.

'You called me to discuss the friendship between Bruno and Nehru?' Sophie looked straight into his eyes before lighting a cigarette.

'You don't need to be sarcastic.' Jindal was defensive.

'What do you expect after showing up suddenly after two years? I don't know whether you are a friend or a foe,' Sophie snapped.

Jindal was silent. He was not an amateur. Abandoning the source was a part of his job. But renewing contact with a subconscious agent was something he had never done before.

'Just be honest with me. I am getting worried about your sudden reappearance,' said Sophie.

'Do you know where Harpreet Ahuja is?' Jindal asked.

'The Indian guy who worked with our organisation? He left about a year ago. Why are you looking for him?'

'I want you to dig him out for me,' Jindal said, placing an envelope containing $10,000 on the table.

Sophie looked at him quietly. She took the envelope and got up.

'Don't worry. Harpreet has always been nice to me.' Sophie winked at him and left the café. Jindal picked up the paper she had left on the table and put it in his pocket.

Two days later, Jindal was in Paris. He called Narayanan on a secure line at the embassy from a public telephone booth. The

London team—Narayanan and Clarke—had used cash to lure Abdul Khan's gardener, a Pakistani named Tariq Siddiqui, to betray his employer. Narayanan and Clarke's next move dealt a crippling blow to the Khan-Sandhu nexus. Tariq provided a huge amount of information, including the names and car numbers of visitors to Khan's house. The list included officials from the ISI, the Pakistani army and Pakistan's civil servants, as well as Sandhu and the two aides who were supposedly Sandhu's bodyguards and another Indian, who Tariq identified as Harbakhsh Singh. He also passed on classified information about Sandhu's and Harbakhsh's impending visit to Islamabad in February.

Jindal was delighted. 'You are doing a good job, Narayanan. Can you ask your guy to provide a photograph of the Indians with Abdul Khan? Also, push him to give us pictures of the ISI and Pakistan army officers meeting Khan in his house.'

'I am still not sure about his loyalty. Let me try,' Narayanan said.

Later that weekend, Narayanan informed Jindal that Tariq had refused to oblige, saying it was an impossible task. But after Narayanan paid him $5,000, Tariq promised to give him the letters arriving at Khan's residence. He had delivered about a dozen sealed envelopes in a plastic bag but most were invitations to public functions. One document about a money transfer from a bank was significant. It revealed that Khan was depositing small amounts of cash into two or three different accounts at a bank in London. Narayanan suspected that the accounts were linked to Sandhu and Harbakhsh as he knew they were living beyond their means.

'We do not know for certain what these guys are planning. Tariq needs to be handled carefully,' Jindal said when they spoke days later.

'I am getting optimistic about Tariq. But we must have a plan B. I will send it to you with my reports,' Narayanan replied.

A week later, Jindal forwarded a coded message to Bhardwaj. It brought a smile to his boss's tense face. Although Tariq's inputs were limited, the details about the key players arriving at Khan's house gave the R&AW top brass valuable insights into the ISI's plans and intentions.

Narayanan's plan B was to recruit a mole inside Sandhu's network. With Clarke's help, he started working on Harbakhsh's cousin, Amarjeet Singh, who had recently migrated to London and was seeking asylum. Clarke patiently waited for him to visit the immigration centre, where he deliberately bumped into him one fine March day in 1985 and asked whether Amarjeet needed any help. Amarjeet was surprised but not shocked and told Clarke his story. Clarke expressed sympathy and promised to facilitate his case, though he warned him not to discuss this with anyone, including the members of his family. Within two weeks, Clarke had won Amarjeet over and was able to move on from casual queries about Amarjeet's family and his life in India to more intimate questions regarding Harbakhsh's activities. He learnt that Amarjeet had never liked Harbakhsh, but was compelled to stay with him for a while.

'I want to settle down here and bring my family. I have two kids and my wish is to give them a good education,' Amarjeet confided in Clarke.

'I will help you. What does Harbakhsh do?' Clarke probed.

'He is a changed man, not the Harbakhsh I knew. Since he returned from Pakistan recently, I see a lot of Pakistani visitors in the house. I don't know what they are talking about as his drawing room doors are always closed but I don't get a good feeling about the visitors,' Amarjeet revealed.

Clarke now needed to test how far he could push Amarjeet.

'Why have you never confronted him about it? If he is meeting Pakistanis, that means he is up to something,' Clarke said.

'Look at my position. I am totally dependent on him. How

can I challenge him or ask him not to meet Pakistanis,' Amarjeet replied sadly.

'We will work on that. You tell me who is meeting Harbakhsh. Also, let me know if you overhear any conversation,' Clarke said. Before departing, he gave Amarjeet some money, knowing well that his betrayal could bring down Harbakhsh's empire.

Narayanan informed Jindal that they now had a better-placed mole and if operated ruthlessly, he could provide valuable intelligence on Khan's network. Jindal was happy but had developed concerns since it had been a while since he had last met Sophie. Vienna was one of the most critical and adventure-filled theatres of the cold war between the Soviets and the USA. CIA spies were on the hunt for intelligence on Soviet moves while Soviet spies were watching every move the Americans were making. With so much espionage activity in one place, Sophie could practically disappear.

But sometime in the first week of April, Sophie made contact.

'You have a right to your frustration but I have something for you. Can you come here over the weekend? I will be waiting for you,' she said softly.

'You know my heart. I forgive you,' Jindal said.

'Bring your head too,' Sophie said and put the phone down.

At their meeting at Café Aida, Sophie recounted her hunt for Harpreet Ahuja. It had taken her to Salzburg, Bregenz and finally to Innsbruck. She finally found him working as a manager at an Indian restaurant. At first, she was surprised that a man with a commitment to social causes was toiling away at an eating joint, but after some conversations with him, she learned that he had fallen on bad times and had grabbed this job although the pay wasn't great. She told Jindal about going out with Ahuja on a date.

'I broached the subject of resolving his financial problems and told him that an Indian businessman dealing in export-import could help him out. What are your intentions?' Sophie asked.

'My priorities are clear. I can't let this man slip out of our hands,' Jindal said.

They took the morning train to Innsbruck. Once they were seated, Jindal thought over what he knew about Ahuja. Before coming to Austria, Ahuja had worked in California for nearly a year with an Indian businessman named Avtaar Sethi who Jindal suspected was bankrolling Sandhu and his network. When Ahuja left for Austria in a huff, word spread in Sethi's circle and the R&AW spies marked Ahuja as a dissident who could be used in the future. Though there were no papers and documents to throw light on Ahuja's background, the Europe desk's reports on Sethi and Sandhu had described the man as intelligent, well-mannered and never afraid to speak his mind.

Sophie had arranged the meeting at Café Munding in the old town. Ahuja was polite but distant. Jindal was curious to know why he had left a comfortable life in California and ended up in Austria, struggling for money. Ahuja frankly told him that he had enjoyed his life in California but disliked the gatherings at Sethi's house, which he thought to be anti-national. 'Sethi has sold his soul. He is a traitor and working hand in glove with Sandhu to harm India. I couldn't bear the thought of betrayal,' he said.

Jindal was convinced that the intelligence reports about Ahuja and Sethi were correct. When they began a discussion about anti-India activities from the USA and Europe, Jindal told Ahuja that he worked for the R&AW and his business was merely a front.

'Our job is to secure the nation and insulate it from the influence of enemies,' Jindal stressed. Ahuja was surprised. He fumbled for words and looked at Sophie. She assured him he was in safe hands.

Jindal recruited Ahuja in Austria that April. Upon agreeing to work for the R&AW as a spy, Ahuja was given the codename Einsiedler. He agreed to revive contact with Sethi but asked Jindal for money to send back to his family in India. Jindal decided that

Sophie would be his handler to avoid any suspicion, but there would be minimum personal contact. Any intelligence Ahuja harvested would be transmitted through dead drops. In the espionage lexicon, a dead drop is a mechanism to receive and leave packets containing inputs and money at pre-decided secret locations to avoid one-on-one meetings with the source. Ahuja was taught spy tradecraft and techniques by Jindal and Sophie, including how to use dead drops by giving a signal of life before making the delivery.

A week later, Jindal was back in Paris. Narayanan and Clarke had dispatched a good harvest, proving that Tariq and Amarjeet were excellent assets. Amarjeet was able to access and deliver information on Harbakhsh's activities and the money he regularly received from an ISI officer posted in London under diplomatic cover. Jindal did not know what to do with this hot intelligence and sought Bhardwaj's help for the next step. A decision was taken to deliver the documents exposing Harbakhsh and the ISI officer's activities to British Home Secretary Leon Brittan sometime in June 1985 through a backdoor channel. Bhardwaj later informed Jindal that a copy had also been sent to the US, Canadian and British diplomats posted in New Delhi.

'They were embarrassed. Harbakhsh is soon going to be homeless. No one will welcome him except Pakistan,' Bhardwaj said.

But before the British could act, Harbakhsh disappeared from London overnight. Jindal and Bhardwaj suspected that he had been evacuated by the ISI before British security officials could interrogate him on his links with militants and Pakistan. The ISI officer identified by Amarjeet as Harbakhsh's handler had also vanished. A source based in Pakistan informed Bhardwaj about the arrival of Harbakhsh and his family in Rawalpindi, in the neighbourhood of Islamabad.

A month earlier in May, four civilians and a security person had been killed in Punjab. In July 1985, a Memorandum of

Settlement was signed between Prime Minister Rajiv Gandhi and Sant Harchand Singh Longowal of the Shiromani Akali Dal. The government agreed to make ex-gratia payments to the families of all the innocent people killed since 1982 and pay compensation for damaged property. The government had also agreed to withdraw the Armed Forces Special Powers Act from Punjab and put up a mechanism to expedite militancy related cases. But the accord failed to act as a deterrent to further violence and in the same month, seven civilians were killed.

Now Bharadwaj and Jindal chose a two-part strategy to target Abdul Khan, Sandhu and Sethi. Jindal had suggested that Sethi, being a businessman, could be lured by the agency if they could cultivate enough material to set his life ablaze. For Sandhu and Khan, Jindal suggested a covert operation.

'It all depends on Ahuja's sense of adventure. Has he been able to establish contact with Sethi? He has to stay one step ahead of these rascals,' Bhardwaj said.

Jindal informed him that Ahuja had spoken to Sethi a few days earlier and was planning a trip to California with Sophie, who volunteered to play the role of his girlfriend.

In October 1985, Sophie and Ahuja arrived in San Francisco. Sophie later told Jindal that the first meeting with Sethi took place in a cold atmosphere. 'He was very contemptuous but witty with a sharp intellect,' Sophie said of Sethi.

Despite his initial reluctance, Sethi made Ahuja an offer to stay and work with him in California, which he immediately accepted. Ahuja was also reunited with his old chum, Sethi's driver Puran Singh. Sophie was keenly interested in Sethi's business and social activities and Ahuja had a similar desire to bring down his friend's empire. He was mentally ready for betrayal.

By February 1986, the harvest was ready. Sophie and Ahuja left for Paris on the pretext of a vacation and an Indian embassy official was entrusted with the tough task of confronting Sethi with the evidence collected by the Indian assets. Jindal coordinated the plan from Paris. Narayanan, before flying to San Francisco, informed them that Sandhu was still in London and they swiftly moved to corner his friend in California.

The Indian official met Sethi in his swanky office. He explained to the Indian businessman that he had come as a friend and a well-wisher. Sethi knew something was wrong. In the next half an hour, the embassy official narrated all his dealings with Sandhu and the network that was working for the ISI. Sethi tried to counter this accusation by arguing that he had accidentally met Sandhu and had no dealings with the radical network. The embassy official took out a note with details of huge money transfers to Sandhu's account. Subsequently, he took out the copies of mails Sethi had received from his friend in London. At this point, Sethi dropped his cover story and admitted that he was closely working with Sandhu, who was employed by the ISI to launch attacks in India. Sethi was then taken to a safe house in San Francisco where Narayanan was waiting. He was interrogated for six hours. Narayanan later reported to Jindal that Sethi had finally decided to tell the truth. He informed Narayanan about Sandhu's activities, the names of the Pakistani officers he had met with his collaborator, and also the details of a meeting with Abdul Khan.

'He was cooperative and readily offered his services to the agency. He seems to be scared of being exposed and expelled from the USA in case we intimate the authorities. He has delivered some real nuggets,' Narayanan informed Jindal.

It was time for Jindal to meet the man. He wanted a fair assessment before forging an alliance with the defector so the agency was not misled into some sort of calamitous situation. He discussed the matter with Bhardwaj and they decided Paris would be the place to play out the deception.

In espionage, recruiting a defector is done by two primary methods—pressurise the person with overwhelming evidence so that he or she surrenders and is mentally ready for exploitation, and consistently feed the defector with misinformation so that in case of a double cross, the handler has the last laugh. In January and February that year, the ISI had substantially increased its terror operations in India and Pakistan's proxies were hell bent on damaging the social and economic structure of the country. Sethi took a circuitous route to Paris in order to avoid ISI surveillance on his movements. Bhardwaj, Jindal and Narayanan held two day-long meetings with the dangerous financier of terrorism in India. In Jindal's words, Sethi sang non-stop. He shared the smallest details of the Sandhu-Khan network, revealing the role of ISI officers posted under diplomatic covers in London. The ISI had a special detachment in London for the India operation and a team of six officers had been deployed to create and continue sponsoring terrorist networks to carry out activities inside India. At the time, an ISI officer named Mahmood was running Sandhu and Khan. Sethi said he was not aware if the ISI was handling any other anti-India module. He provided a list of the officers, profiles of people connected to Khan and Sandhu and above all, names of recruits in India who he believed were staunch supporters of the network. Jindal said there was one final hurdle that he had asked Sethi to resolve: what was the network's next move? Sethi promised to deliver the information. Bhardwaj handed him a miniature tape recorder and told him curtly that the proof needed to be solid. In the meantime, he forwarded the names of the Indian module to the R&AW headquarters. This subsequently landed on the desk of P.V. Narasimha Rao, who temporarily served as home minister from March to May 1986 before Buta Singh was handed the responsibility of internal security.

Jindal was informed sometime in April that eighteen people on the list had been neutralised in a covert operation and they had launched a manhunt for nine others. As promised, Sethi delivered a tape sometime in July 1986. The conversation among the network involving Khan, Sandhu and the ISI officers revealed a plan to expand the operation and the Pakistani intelligence officers assured substantial sums of money for the attacks. Bhardwaj decided that the R&AW should go head to head with the network. Through his contacts in MI5, he managed to convince the British about the covert activities of the ISI officers. As for Sandhu and Khan, Bhardwaj decided to escalate the matter to the top brass, seeking a go-ahead for further missions. In July and August, Bhardwaj was informed by his contacts in British counterintelligence agencies that the Pakistanis had been told to shut shop. He was, however, cautioned that the ISI might just shift the base of anti-India operations back to Islamabad. At that point, the MEA issued a statement for public consumption that Pakistan was unwilling to mend its ways and continued to support terror activities in India and was also making attempts to internationalise the Kashmir issue.

Sometime in September 1986, Narayanan received a call from someone who identified himself as Balwant Singh. Balwant disclosed that he had some information about the ISI-sponsored terror network in London but it was available for a price. During the conversation, he asked for a one-on-one meeting with someone of a higher rank in the agency's hierarchy. Narayanan informed Jindal about the strange volunteer. A background check at the agency's database revealed that Balwant was a wanted man and his name figured in the blacklist.

'If you decide to have a meeting with him, I need to be there,' Bhardwaj told Jindal.

Two days later, Balwant got in touch with Narayanan again. He agreed to a meeting in Paris. Narayanan later said that Balwant was desperate for the meeting. Clarke found out that Balwant was working for Sandhu, though his family remained in India. Bhardwaj, Jindal and Narayanan gathered for the meeting in Paris. What occurred was almost an interrogation that continued for three days. Bhardwaj's initial assessment was that Balwant was homesick and looking for a way out of the terror quagmire. The spy categorically told him that any visit to his homeland was only possible on one condition—if he provided details and evidence against his friends in the network. Balwant disclosed that Sandhu was making a huge sum of money for himself and using people like him to create mayhem in India.

'Sandhu is using the network for his own advantage. Abdul Khan is colluding with him to launch a recruitment drive next month. Details of other plans are not known to us, but three or four of us are desperate to return,' Balwant said.

In the coming days and weeks, with the help of information provided by Balwant and his friends in the inner circle, the Indian government escalated the matter with British Prime Minister Margaret Thatcher. Bhardwaj and Jindal provided superb intelligence that completely demolished Sandhu's defences. Sandhu and five of his close associates were picked up by British security agencies. Back in India, the government released a carefully-worded statement saying that British authorities were taking action against extremists operating from London and they would hopefully be convicted soon.

But this success came with a heavy price. The R&AW spies were worried about roping in other security agencies to remove Balwant and his chosen few from the blacklist.

'You cannot involve more than two or three agencies in any espionage operation and in this case, we needed to get the state government on board. I think Balwant is testing our willingness to go beyond the textbook for peace,' Bhardwaj told Jindal.

'We also need to avert the possibility of any of them joining the gang after resettling back home,' Jindal agreed.

'We cannot afford to let them loose. We want their visit to be limited to a week. They need to return to London after talking to their people and we must ask them to persuade their friends to give up their weapons. Resettlement can be dealt with later,' Bhardwaj said.

Later, only five people including Balwant were allowed to visit India. The defector was furious and insisted that all eleven people who had worked with him to demolish Sandhu's network had to visit their homeland. Jindal might have reacted more strongly to Balwant's demand, but he had some appreciation for the defector. Jindal told him: 'We need to be sure your guys are not going to betray us. Moreover, all five are dreaded and most wanted. We are arranging for new passports and identities for them.'

In December 1986, Balwant and his four friends were issued visas for all the routes they needed to take. The R&AW, in coordination with the immigration authorities and the state police, cleared their visit, which they were told was part of confidence-building measures. The domestic spy agency, the Intelligence Bureau, was informed that the men were on a peace mission to persuade others to abjure violence and build a new life. Two weeks later, Balwant returned to London, but one of his friends stayed on. Jindal and Bhardwaj were furious to discover a traitor among them. A secret operation was launched to locate the man, but he had disappeared. Bhardwaj later learned that he had been killed in an encounter. When the security agencies recovered documents from the dead man, the fabricated papers startled them. He was on the blacklist. How had he sneaked into India? They never received an answer to their question.

In January 1987, Bhardwaj sent Jindal to London. The aftermath of the operation against Sandhu and the slew of other arrests had weakened the ISI network but Abdul Khan was still trying to revive anti-India activities. While the ISI and Khan rushed to fill the vacuum, the R&AW took further steps to neutralise the recruitment drive. Simpson's Divan, a tavern in London, had become the meeting point for Jindal, Clarke and Narayanan. New plans were made every day to ambush Khan's remaining network but none worked out because Bhardwaj was against covert action in British territory. Finally, they zeroed in on Tariq, who had offered his services to R&AW to spy on his employer, Abdul Khan. He was summoned for a meeting sometime in late January at a safe house on the outskirts of London and for five hours the spies and the mole discussed and reviewed the plan to have Abdul Khan eliminated. Since the successful operation against the network, Tariq had become more helpful and confident. Jindal also enquired whether Abdul Khan was planning to travel to Pakistan. Tariq had no clue. He promised to inform them if there was any such plan. Jindal later flew to Delhi to discuss the idea of eliminating Khan while he was visiting Pakistan.

'This will put enormous responsibility on our assets in Pakistan. I also need to inform the chief and seek his sanction. Remember we need to play by the book,' Bhardwaj cautioned him.

Jindal meanwhile waited patiently for Tariq's information. In the first week of May 1987, Narayanan informed him that Abdul Khan was planning to visit his hometown, Lahore, sometime in June. His plan was to meet the newly appointed ISI chief, Lt. General Hamid Gul. Jindal and Bhardwaj decided that Abdul Khan had to be killed in Lahore. The terror financier was gunned down by two motorcycle-borne men as he entered his house that fateful day in June. He was shot nine times in the head and the neck. The Lahore police believed that the killing was the result of an old business rivalry but the ISI knew it was the R&AW that had chased and killed the fountainhead of terror. At his burial, a R&AW asset noticed that flowers had been sent from Hamid Gul.

11

A SPY AMONG THE DERVISH

Spying looks good on screen. In the films, a lone wolf armed with a gun wages a global war against a strong army, pausing every once in a while to court a beautiful woman as a part of his cover.

But the reality is quite different. Some of the greatest coups in the world have taken place without a gun in sight. How do you engineer dissent among the members of a strong adversary? How do you court a friend turned foe to the best advantage of your country? How do you spot and recruit double agents to help your organisation get a ringside view of events on the other side of the fence? How do you change political dynamics in a certain region by playing off one country against another? And how do you unleash a shadowy war to bring in a favourable regime when your country's economic interests are at stake?

Vipul Chandra was the complete opposite of James Bond. The young spy was known as 'Santji' (saint) by his close friends and within the intelligence community. He was a teetotaller, had never smoked and had had just one love affair during his training period with a Mumbai-born girl he later married. Vipul's entry into the R&AW coincided with fast moving events on the global map including the Shia revolution in Iran headed by religious leader Ayatollah Khomeini, Soviet aggression in Afghanistan and the arrival of the USA in South Asia to arm a group of Afghan mujahideen. His first posting was at Kabul; eight months later, he was dispatched to Syria. Upon his return a year later, Vipul was sent for an operation in Iraq. He was fluent in Arabic, Dari, Urdu, German and Russian. Languages and an ascetic smile were his weapons of choice. He loved Sanskrit and spent his free time reading about Sufi mystics. This colourful personality was just one side of the man. The other side was completely mysterious. As a professional spy, Vipul Chandra was cunning, possessed the ability to sniff out intelligence from miles away, a warrior loyal to his country and skilled enough in defence techniques to kill a man with his bare hands. His physique, friends teased, was made of steel.

While he was in Iraq sometime in mid-1984, Vipul received a call from Delhi, summoning him to an urgent meeting back home. India was facing both an internal and an external turmoil at the time and Vipul was needed in another theatre.

Since 1979, when the Khomeini-led movement had forced the Shah of Iran to step down and seek shelter elsewhere to survive, India's equation with Iran had turned hostile. Once a close friend, Iran viewed India as a power that had supported the Shah's rule and was now siding with the USA and other western powers.

Khomeini's apprehensions were true to a certain extent, Vipul's boss explained, but India had always followed the policy of non-alignment and talk about the India-US-Shah ties were part of a propaganda war launched by inimical forces to widen the rift between India and Iran.

Vipul was familiar with Khomeini's hard views on the USA. The cleric had once famously said: 'Any weapon whether it is a pen, a gun should not be employed against one another. Instead, they should be aimed directly at the enemies of humanity, on top of them the governments of United States.' Besides, the escalating war between Iraq and Iran further strained the relationship between India and Iran. India's overwhelming dependence on the Gulf region for oil had made it so desperate that sometime in 1981, the Ministry of External Affairs (MEA) had started examining the possibility of joining the same Organisation of Islamic Conference (OIC) that it had earlier found to be biased. Vipul was provided with top-secret analyses and classified documents on various issues. On the issue of India joining the OIC, he read carefully the analysis that said every Muslim state was eligible to join the conference on submitting an application expressing its desire and preparedness to adopt the charter, which defined the primary objective of the Conference to promote Islamic solidarity among member states. Considering the secular character of India's constitution, it was not possible for the country to adopt this charter and work for such aims. In addition, various resolutions adopted by the OIC since its inception in 1969 would be binding upon its members. For instance, a jihad fund had already been established by the member states at the Lahore summit held in 1974. The primary objective of this fund was to propagate Islamic culture worldwide and financially assist other Islamic countries in distress.

Some people argued that the membership of the OIC would help India meet Pakistani moves, but at the same time, constant confrontation with Pakistan in the Conference would expose the country to the charge of having a phobia against Pakistan. On important questions such as Kashmir and in the eventuality of an Indo-Pakistan war, there would certainly be pressure on India in the OIC for a compromise settlement and attempts at mediating the issue would be made by the OIC. A note said on Organisation of Islamic Conference prepared by the MEA:

> After our membership of the OIC, it is possible that a door may be opened for interference by the OIC in our internal affairs on a regular basis. Our past experience of participating

> in the Islamic conference at Rabat in 1969 was also not encouraging. In that conference India was treated shabbily, though the meeting was held at the government level. Our ambassador had even addressed the conference but no one raised an objection. It was on the behest of Pakistan that on 24 September objection was raised to our presence there. India's membership of this organization does not appear to be of any particular advantage for India. The development of bilateral relations by India with these countries is going on smoothly and may be further intensified. It seems to promise a brighter future for India's relations with Muslim states than the membership of OIC.

The India-Iran relationship was seriously compromised because of Khomeini's tough stand against the USA and its perceived allies. Diplomats struggled to find an important Shia leader who would stand up for India because without influence of that nature, any diplomatic effort would be futile. Vipul's boss, codenamed Anil Prasad, tossed him a difficult question: 'Can you win Khomeini's trust for India, mollify the agitating political leaders and neutralise the Pakistani influence in Iran? Are you capable and confident of launching a third-country operation without stepping into Iran?'

Vipul told me he felt as though his head had been struck by a hammer.

'But I have never said no to an operation,' he added. 'And here I was being handed a job that the entire diplomatic community had failed to deliver. It would be a lie to say that I was confident. I was damn nervous and it showed on my face. Nevertheless, I realised there was no choice. My boss was counting on this operation.'

To explore the major turning point in the relationship between India and Iran, Vipul sifted through several records that could shed light on how the USA played a key role in determining the relationship between the two countries that had always been perceived as non-aligned. He came across a conversation that took place on 3 October 1973 between the then foreign minister, Swaran Singh, and the then US secretary of state, Henry Kissinger at the state department office just hours before the two leaders sat down to lunch. Here is an excerpt:

> Henry Kissinger: Our only interest is to see success in your efforts. We do not support one side or the other. We have some concern only about Afghanistan. We have told Pakistan and Iran not to interfere in the internal affairs of Afghanistan unless Afghanistan tries to subvert their internal system.
>
> Swaran Singh: This matter came up when I went to Iran and spoke to the Shahenshah.
>
> Henry Kissinger: The Shah mentioned to me about your visit.
>
> Swaran Singh: I asked him plainly, is it your position that you will always side with Pakistan against India, whatever the merits of the question are? And he said that it was not a blanket commitment to Pakistan. He made two points–(1) if Pakistan was aggressed upon, he would support Pakistan, but he did not think it was India's policy to commit aggression against Pakistan (2) if there was a danger of disintegration of Pakistan, particularly in Balochistan, he would support Pakistan in resisting such a movement. I told him that my Prime Minister and I had made several statements that we had no interest in the internal affairs of Afghanistan and Balochistan.
>
> Henry Kissinger: The Shah was not accusing India but only mentioned various possibilities.
>
> Swaran Singh: He was mainly worried about Balochistan and indirectly about North West Frontier Province. I told him that we were not supporting any subversive movements there.
>
> Henry Kissinger: The Shah told me that you had asked him if he would consult you before he gave any arms to Pakistan and he said to you that he would.
>
> Swaran Singh: Yes, he said this to me.

This conversation reveals a very important point: the USA played the role of a mediator on certain vital issues and India's concerns were often transmitted to the Shah of Iran through the American government. Vipul said that a few other files clearly explained the hostility that began with Seyyed Abolhassan Banisadr, Iran's first president after the revolution. India's woes were compounded by Iraq's invasion of Iran in September 1980. The relationship turned worse after Ayatollah Khomeini appointed Ali Khamenei as president of Iran in 1981. The Americans believed that Khomeini's hatred towards nations considered to be supporters of the Shah had intensified after the US government gave refuge to the Shah, who had fled the country after revolutionary forces took over the capital city in 1979. Khomeini's protégé President Khamenei had similar views.

CIA analysts had observed that even after wresting power from the Shah in 1979, Khomeini's lust for vengeance was not satisfied. Their note said:

> The Shah's entrance into the US in October 1979, however, brought Khomeini's two hated enemies together. For Khomeini, commander in chief of the armed forces, the Shah's arrival in the US provided an external focus around which to rally the country. This was reflected in his rhetoric, which shifted from portraying the Shah as the prime opponent to the Shah as a puppet of the US.

On the other hand, Khamenei, who had studied under Khomeini, had been involved in activities against the Shah for a long time. Vipul said Khamenei was not only the president of Iran but also influenced society as Tehran's Friday prayers leader. India had very insignificant links with Khamenei's opposition led by Akbar Hashemi Rafsanjani, head of the assembly known as Majlis. He was busy with internal power tussles and several attempts to approach him had been futile. Rafsanjani had said that America continued to be Iran's enemy. In Khameini's view, Iran had no plan whatsoever to cooperate with or get near the United States. In contrast, Pakistan under Zia-ul-Haq had enhanced its ties with the Iranian government and Vipul informed me that by the end of 1984, military assistance from Pakistan to Tehran flowed unhindered. The ISI chief, Lt. General Akhtar Abdur Rahman, was a staunch supporter of close relations with Iran and other Arab states to keep a significant hold over Afghanistan.

Anil Prasad gave the go-ahead for the operation in 1984. Vipul was to work as a lone wolf. In January 1985, he landed in Damascus, capital city of the Syrian Arab Republic. He had an asset named Hayyan who worked in President Hafez al-Assad's Syrian Ba'ath Party regime. Vipul and Hayyan had earlier worked together in Lebanon. Hayyan had managed to enter the inner group of Ayatollah Mohammed Hussein Fadlallah, a Shia cleric and supposed supporter of the Hezbollah, a Lebanese militant organisation that arrived on the radar of the world's security agencies following the 1983 Beirut bombing in which hundreds of US and French soldiers had been killed. Vipul had been carrying out a limited operation in Beirut in 1983 when Hayyan introduced him to the religious preacher. Fadlallah told Vipul he could smell spies and if it was not for the painful experience of betrayal, he considered the profession the most important to protect a country.

'Even if it is not a pleasant work, it does make life pleasurable for the people of the country,' Vipul told Fadlallah. 'Spying is not just about betrayal and dualities, it is also about a love affair that gives colour to the superficial layer of security.'

Hezbollah was conceived during the successful Iranian revolution and spies believed it helped the radicalisation of Shias as well as militant activities in the neighbourhood with Khomeini as an idol. For Vipul, though, Fadlallah was a keyhole through which to peep into the affairs of the Middle East and carry out his operation quietly.

Now after almost two years since they had last met, the primary reason for Vipul to meet Hayyan against the backdrop of the Iran-Iraq war was simple—could he exploit Fadlallah's relationship with the Iranian leaders to get a foothold in the Iranian regime that was hostile towards India? For spies, it was no longer a secret that Hezbollah had been raised with Iranian support and both Fadallah and the outfit's leader Hussain Musavi were deeply entrenched in Khomeini's inner circle.

Hayyan sent a message through one of his contacts in Beirut to arrange Vipul's meeting with Fadlallah. They waited for almost two months for a response from the cleric when a newspaper report on 8 March 1985 triggered a shock. A car bomb had exploded in Bir el-Abed in south Beirut and initial reports suggested that Fadlallah was the target of the strike that had killed around eighty people. However, the preacher had narrowly escaped the attack.

In his first sermon after the attack, Fadallah blamed American intelligence for the bombing. Hayyan was later informed by a Hezbollah contact working as a sleeper cell in Syrian-controlled Bekaa Valley that the time was not ripe for a meeting with Fadallah. However, the contact added that Vipul and Hayyan should move to Kuwait and wait for a signal. The sleeper cell also warned Hayyan and Vipul that the Israeli intelligence agency Mossad and the CIA were keeping a close watch on Hezbollah contacts and a thoughtless move could spoil the espionage operation. The CIA believed that the Hezbollah posed a serious threat to American interests both as an aggressive terrorist network and as a rising fundamentalist political movement in Lebanon and its growing ability to strike the US personnel and installations would hamper the conduct of regular US diplomatic, military and commercial business in the Middle East and Western Europe.

In June 1985, Vipul and Hayyan, with the help of Fadallah, met Abdullah Shirazi in Kuwait. Shirazi headed a small Shia group known as the Jund al-Imam, but had a larger influence over Shia leaders in Iran. He promised to arrange a meeting with Abdul

Hakim, an Iraqi Shia leader considered to be a close friend of Rafsanjani, for a price that was immediately paid by the Indian spy agency in Baghdad. The meeting took place sometime in August 1985 at a R&AW safe house in Paris to avoid the CIA and Mossad's surveillance. Contact was established between Shirazi, Hakim and the Indian spy and it deepened.

Hakim was also running a Dervish group—followers of Sufism—in Paris. Vipul was invited to an evening of Sama meditation wearing a salwar and jameh with a wool skullcap. He later learnt that the group was primarily used by Hakim for intelligence collection in France and other European countries.

Between September and November 1985, Vipul and Hayyan made thirty-nine clandestine trips to Syria, Lebanon, Iraq and Afghanistan. On his three trips to Afghanistan to meet a powerful Shia leader, Vipul operated under the name of Khaled Faraj, a Kuwaiti businessman. The Afghan leader was flown to Beirut to meet Fadallah, carrying handsome gifts from the Indian agency. Vipul clarified that the Indian intelligence organisation never supported the activities of Hezbollah but they did not hesitate to take help from the leader widely considered to be a terrorist sympathiser.

'In espionage, there is no colour of your asset as long as it suits your interest and the asset continues to stay in the shadows,' Vipul once explained to me.

He also made five trips to Baghdad and Najaf where a group of Shia leaders supported the Iranian revolution and covertly worked against Saddam Hussein, a close ally of India. However, any visit to Tehran was deliberately avoided so this operation had to be conducted from a third country.

Finally in November 1985, a meeting was organised at the Hague in the Netherlands where Shirazi, Hakim, Hayyan and Vipul hosted Rafsanjani's man, Farhad. The meeting did not go well. Farhad asked to see the R&AW chief, G.C. Saxena. Vipul immediately sent a coded message to his boss, Anil Prasad.

'R&AW had always worked in the shadows and the demand from Rafsanjani was a bit unusual,' said Prasad. 'Nevertheless, Garry (G.C. Saxena) was informed and we advised him to meet Farhad at least once to satisfy whatever doubts Rafsanjani had in his mind. Garry went to meet Prime Minister Rajiv Gandhi, perhaps to brief him about the operation. A few days later, he asked me to arrange a meeting in Frankfurt.'

Prasad reached out to Vipul with little difficulty since he was staying in Najaf, a city in the south-central part of Iraq, with Hakim masquerading as Jamail, a Shia businessman from Kuwait. The Frankfurt meeting was held sometime in mid-December 1985, organised with the help of Hakim and Shirazi. The R&AW chief told Farhad that the Indian government was deeply committed to a bilateral relationship and whatever misconception had been spread about the India-Iran relationship was far from the truth. He also told Farhad that Vipul carried the word of the government of India and they should not suspect his authority. Farhad did not commit anything. But he assured them he would pass the message to Rafsanjani.

Farhad contacted Hakim sometime in January 1986 with a short message. His senior, Reza Bahram, would like to meet the R&AW spy Vipul. This time, a meeting was arranged in Madrid. Reza Bahram, a close aide of Rafsanjani, discussed the contours of the relationship between the two countries and they broadly agreed on several issues:

a) We continue to be friends, not overtly but covertly for the time being.
b) Iran should continue to meet India's energy requirements even in the worst times.
c) We will continue to hold meetings at the government level with Shia leaders in India and a delegation should visit Iran every six months.

d) An Iranian official delegation must visit India at the earliest to normalise the relationship.
e) An Indian diplomat would be deputed to meet Rafsanjani.

In March 1986, Rafsanjani, for the first time, gave a personal audience to an Indian diplomat owing to an outstanding operation carried out by the R&AW. The diplomat informed the MEA about the meeting and passed on an assurance that an Iranian ministerial-level delegation would soon visit India. It was a historic moment when the Iranian Foreign Minister Ali Akbar Velayati visited India in August 1986 for bilateral talks. Subsequently, informal discussions were held on the sidelines of a United Nations meeting.

Interestingly, the MEA took the entire credit for the Iran operation. In Prasad's words, basically the ministry became the face of a diplomatic coup engineered by a spy agency.

'You are listening to the whole orchestra but missing the conductor,' Prasad said. 'They claimed unhindered access to the Iranian government as well as the leader Khomeini, but the agent who made it possible quietly disappeared for another operation in another difficult terrain.'

Vipul, who had sort of turned into a recluse after the sixteen-month-long operation in a hostile territory, had an opportunity to meet Prime Minister Rajiv Gandhi along with G.C. Saxena.

'Gandhi asked Garry in a whisper whether he could give Vipul a Padma Bhushan award. The chief smiled and said, 'No sir. The reward for a spy is the success of the operation. He doesn't need any other decoration,' Anil Prasad told me later, when he recounted the various methods Vipul had used to turn a complete failure into a success. Those details, though, are classified as top secret and will remain buried in the R&AW vault for ages to come.

EPILOGUE

In an age when digital threats are as dangerous as non-state fanatics, intelligence officers often wonder: How far should spy operations go to eliminate threats to national security? They also ask this question: Is traditional spy tradecraft in which human intelligence (HUMINT) is tasked with recruiting and running spies in enemy countries still relevant in this age of electronic surveillance? Could data accessed via cyber espionage replace a good spy behind the enemy lines?

Today's debates on intelligence gaps and shortcomings at the National Security Council meetings in Delhi compare the harvests produced by men and machines, with more and more emphasis on eyes in the sky. But logically, such differentiation is treacherous. Threats faced by the country are multidimensional and not exactly black and white. Despite intercepting chatter about the Lashkar-e-Taiba's (LeT) plan to carry out terror attacks on Indian soil, the listening devices were not able to decode what was going on in Hafiz Saeed's mind. Where was he planning to attack? How was he going to execute it? Senior R&AW officials involved in counterterrorism sometimes wonder: If they'd had a mole inside the LeT, would 26 November 2008 have been just another day in Mumbai?

Chanakya's words on espionage clear up all doubts related to the need for human spies. He said: A king needs trusted spies not just to steal the secrets of his enemies but to also to sow seeds of dissension among the opposition. A fiery spy working undercover can change the destiny of a nation.

Chinese military strategist Sun Tzu said: 'If you know the enemy and know yourself, you need not fear the results of a hundred battles.'

These words are as true today as they were in the fifth century BC. That's why, though digital intelligence has revolutionised the working style of spy organisations across the globe, it has not been able to replace the ruthless efficiency of an agent on the ground.

Since 2008, India's intelligence gathering agency, like those of the rest of the world, began focusing on both digital and traditional espionage methods to keep pace with technological advances. The R&AW began to expand its HUMINT networks across the subcontinent and also formed a separate division for cyber espionage. A specialised group within the R&AW monitors secret codes, particularly in regional languages, that are used by foreign based anti-social elements to disseminate mischievous messages through social media platforms. Today, R&AW spy networks are used for more than stealing and defending state secrets. Spies monitor and neutralise drug and money laundering cartels, raise assets for sabotage in countries of interest, engage in psychological warfare and economic espionage, strengthen pro-India elements with the help of financial packages and also keep the Intelligence Bureau and other domestic security and law enforcement agencies informed about potential threats from terror groups and foreign organisations involved in subversive activities. Today, espionage collection by the R&AW is more efficient than it has ever been before.

On the other hand, a cyber security officer in Delhi or Bengaluru can shut down a power plant in Lahore at the press of a button or thwart a cyber attack launched by non-state actors operating in the dark web against vital installations in the country. In the new political landscape of India, digital intelligence, open-source intelligence and HUMINT must collaborate and act as a force multiplier for the government to create better informed policies. Since no single agency can tackle all the threats confronting policymakers today, the R&AW will also have to enhance its partnerships with friendly spy organisations in other countries. But above all, the government will always need a good spy to read the mind of an adversary.

In the late 1990s, the Indian spy agency had provided huge sums of cash to a Pakistani asset to start an Urdu newspaper. Civilian bureaucrats thought this was a complete waste of money. Today, the publication has grown into one of the most potent weapons in the R&AW's arsenal. But there have also been misjudgements. In 2002, the R&AW had spurned an outlaw from the neighbouring country when he sought the money to roll out certain business activities in Africa. The Indian operative handling the case thought that it was a brilliant offer, but his senior in Delhi did not respond. That outlaw is now an influential figure. If he had been recruited, he might have provided a number of critical intelligence inputs on terror groups, the ISI and the secrets of the Pakistani governments. There is simply no substitute for a ready-to-be-launched asset.

Despite certain failures, R&AW operations have helped safeguard the country's interests. As the first line of defence against overseas threats, the agency continues to provide intelligence to the prime minister and various security agencies, speaking truth to power. At the same time, the intelligence agency requires a clear political direction with zero interference if it is to maintain its neutrality, speed and efficiency.

NOTES

1. Bloodbath in Bangladesh

1. R&AW U.O. Note No. 6/BD/75(6)-VI. Bangladesh Assessment by Deputy Director A.K. Verma.
2. R&AW U.O. Note No. 6/BD/75 (12) Bangladesh scale of activity, N.F. Suntook.
3. Ministry of External Affairs, 26/TS/JS (PP)/75. Assistance to resistance groups and anti-government forces in Bangladesh.
4. High Commissioner to Bangladesh, Letter No. DAC/102/1/75. HC Foreign influence, political parties and political trends.
5. Ministry of External Affairs, Note (46) 3352-AS(SPP)/75. Assessment regarding Bangladesh after discussion with Joint Secretary (BD) Joint Secretary (Pak) Joint Secretary (E) Joint Secretary (Afr).
6. Ministry of External Affairs, 4/3388/JS(PP)75. Indian assessment after meeting with Bangladesh HC to India Shamsur Rahman.
7. D.O. No. BD.76/75, S. Chattopadhyay, Deputy Secretary to J.C. Ajmani (JS). Minutes of Meeting with Manoranjan Dhar, Minister of Law, Parliamentary Affairs, Bangladesh.
8. Note 95/75. R&AW assessment on Pakistan Mission in Bangladesh.
9. No. I/BD/103/1/76 MEA. Bangladesh Situation: Talking Points.
10. Government note: New policy orientation towards Bangladesh; a Summary.
11. Government note: Reasons leading to the coup.
12. D.O. 479/AS/82. R&AW assessment on coup in Bangladesh.
13. C-108-D-150111240-TELEGRAM-Big power rivalry.
14. Foreign Secretary Kewal Singh note-D/973-PP/75. FS and FM meeting with Abu Syed Chaudhury, Foreign Minister of Bangladesh at Lima.

15. MEA(BD) T/273/AS/(SPP)/75. J.N. Dixit Comment on military coup.
16. CCB No.12202. TELEGRAM Indian Embassy Warsaw to Ajmani, New Delhi.
17. CCB No. 12575, TELEGRAM HC Bangladesh to Ajmani, New Delhi.
18. CCB No. 12322, TELEGRAM from Indian Embassy Tripoli to Additional Secretary (WANA).
19. CCB No. 12326, TELEGRAM from Indian Embassy Baghdad to JS (BD), New Delhi.
20. China D650/PP/76, TELEGRAM on Chinese statements regarding Bangladesh.
21. MHA No. 9/18/75-G&Q. Letter of chief secretaries of West Bengal/ Assam/Tripura/Meghalaya/Mizoram on immigrants, insecurity among minorities, contingency plan, etc.
22. CIA RDP85T010, Bangladesh: Ershad's prospects.
23. CIA, Ershad's search for stability.
24. CIA, Ershad-the Man, visit to US.

2. Three Musketeers and a Bloody War in Fiji

1. Ministry of External Affairs, No. SUV/1/66, Suva (Fiji). Annual political report for the year 1966.
2. Letter to foreign secretary from Suva, No. SUV/101/1/70. Political report for March 1970.
3. CIA report P85T003. Fiji's Ratu Mara: Profile of a regional stateman.
4. Ministry of External Affairs, No. WEL/101/1/81, High Commission of India, Wellington. Annual political report of New Zealand for 1981.
5. No. Suv/101/1/70, Commission of India, Suva (Fiji). Economic report for May 1970.
6. Ministry of External Affairs, 1012/84/70. New constitution of Fiji.
7. No. CAN/101/1/81, High Commission of India Canberra. Annual political report for 1981.
8. Letter to Foreign Secretary from Commission of India, Suva. Political report for May 1970.
9. Consular report for 1981. High Commission of India, Wellington, New Zealand.
10. CIA report 05S0202, India-Fiji: Post-coup developments.

11. CIA report P85T003, Ratu Mara-Foreign policy.
12. CIA 85T008. Fiji: Economic prospects after independence.
13. CIA Intelligence Memorandum 70-137 on Fiji.
14. CIA report, Fiji-Consequences for leaving the Commonwealth.

3. A Warrior and the Warlords

1. Dispatch 458, Embassy of India, Kabul. Monthly records of events, December 1979.
2. Joint Intelligence Committee (JIC) report. Rebel groups based in Pakistan.
3. Joint Intelligence Committee (JIC) report, Pakistan-Soviet.
4. No. KAB/101/1/79, Embassy of India, Kabul. Monthly records of events, October 1979.
5. Intelligence note on presidium of revolutionary council of Afghanistan.
6. No. KAB/101/1/80, Embassy of Kabul. Monthly records of events, September 1980.
7. MOS/Pol/04/3/82. Record of discussion between A. Madhavan, Charge D' Affaires and Prof Kapitsa, Deputy Foreign Minister, Soviet Union at Moscow.
8. No. ISL/101/1/81, Embassy of India, Islamabad, Pakistan. Monthly record of events, April 1981.
9. No. ISL/ 101/1/81, Embassy of India, Islamabad. Monthly record of events, March 1981.
10. Joint Intelligence Committee (JIC) report. Review of developments in Afghanistan.
11. Joint Intelligence Committee (JIC) report. Country-wise aid received by Afghan rebels.
12. Joint Intelligence Committee (JIC) summary on Afghan situation, assessment on Pakistan, China, US and Soviet.
13. CCB No. 11196. TELEGRAM and Dy No. 10365/FS/81. Letters exchanged between foreign secretary and principal secretary to Prime Minister.
14. No. MOS/POL/104/1/81. Letter from L.L. Mehrotra, Deputy Chief of Mission to A.R.Deo, Joint Secretary (AMS), Ministry of External Affairs.
15. No. WII/12157/82. Letter from S. Jaishankar, Under Secretary

(AMS) to Siddharth Singh, Counsellor (Pol) Embassy of India, Washington.

16. No. WAS/POL/104/24/82. Letter from H.K Singh, First Secretary (Pol) Embassy of India, Washington to A.R.Deo, Additional Secretary (AMS) Ministry of External Affairs.
17. Dy.11166. Note from S. Jaishankar, Under Secretary (AMS) on US supply of F-16 aircraft to Pakistan.
18. Note 109/1/82. Analysis from S. Jaishankar, Under Secretary (AMS) on US arms supply to Pakistan, Prime Minister's proposed visit, etc.
19. No. WAS/POL/104/30/83. Letter from Siddharth Singh, Embassy of India, Washington to S. Jaishankar, Under Secretary (AMS) on US-Pak alliance.
20. Dy No.500. Consulate of India, Kandahar to Ambassador, Embassy of India, Kabul on record of events, December 1982 on Soviet troops, insurgency, Afghan Army.
21. No. KAB/101/1/82, Embassy of India, Kabul. Monthly record of events, November and December 1982.
22. No. JAL/101/1/78-5, Consulate of India, Jalalabad. Information on Soviet troops, insurgency, counter-insurgency, administration, law and order.
23. No. KAN/1/77. Consulate of India, Kandahar. Monthly record of events for November 1982.
24. JAL/101/1/78-7, Consulate of India, Jalalabad. Monthly record of events, November 1982.
25. CIA report, 82-10617. India and its neighbours: Cooperation or confrontation.
26. CIA report, PA79-10257. Afghanistan's relations with its neighbours.
27. CIA report, 83-10229. India-Pakistan: relations and security concerns.
28. CIA report, 10-C00522. Pakistan-China-US: Arms technology transfer.
29. CIA report, M87-20092C. India's actions and intentions in Afghanistan.
30. CIA report, M-85-10075. India's position in Afghanistan: prospects for change.
31. CIA report, P-06-0412. US support to Pakistan and implication for US policy, Soviet pressure on Pakistan.
32. CIA report, NIE31-83. India in the mid-1980s: Goals and Challenges.

33. Joint Intelligence Committee (JIC) report. Strength of Afghan Air Force, deployment of Soviet Air Force in Afghanistan.
34. No. WAS/POL/104/16/81. Letter from Siddharth Singh, Embassy of India, Washington to Dalip Mehta, Director (AMS) on Soviet military power.
35. No. CCB 12744, from Indian Embassy, Washington to Delhi. Record of discussion with US Assistant Secretary of State.
36. CIA report, 81-01036, Soviet exerted pressure on Afghanistan, prospects and implications of Soviet consolidation.
37. CIA report, 82-10366. Pakistan: tough choices on Afghanistan.
38. CIA report, 86-10044. India-USSR: Strains in relations.
39. CIA report, 85-10077CX. India: What Rajiv hopes for in Moscow and Washington.
40. No. WAS/POL/103/1/82. A.N.D. Haksar, Deputy Chief of Mission, Embassy of India, Washington. A report on visit to Pentagon and discussion with Francis J. West, Assistant Secretary for International Security Affairs, Department of Defence, US government.
41. No. WAS/POL/104/16/81. Letter and report from G.Parthasarathy, Counsellor (Political) on meeting and discussion with Assistant Secretary of State, Nicholas Veliotes.
42. No. KAB/101/1/80, Embassy of India, Kabul. Monthly record of events, October 1980. Political and constitutional developments, military situation, relation of Afghanistan with Pakistan, India and East European countries.
43. No. AS/AMS/154, TELEGRAM from Washington. US-Pakistan arms and discussion on avionics.
44. CCB No. 15037, TELEGRAM from Indian Embassy in Islamabad to Foreign, New Delhi on F-16 delivery to Pakistan.
45. No. WAS/POL/103/26/81. Letter and assessment report from A.N.D. Haksar, Deputy Chief of Mission, Embassy of India, Washington. Speech of Geoffrey Kemp, US National Security Council at India-US Business Council.
46. No. 4082-Secy East0/81. Note from E. Gonsalves, Ministry of External Affairs on India-US relations.
47. No.1-3/1/81, Ministry of External Affairs (Americas Division). Note on Afghanistan, US military assistance to Pakistan.

4. Sri Lankan Affairs

1. No. F(i) 234/10 (1)/80, Ministry of External Affairs. Brief note of stateless persons of Indian origin in Sri Lanka.
2. No. Col/HC/PS/380. Note from PE Kapadia, Deputy Secretary, Ministry of External Affairs to K.P. Fabian, Deputy High Commissioner, High Commission of India, Colombo on India's increased economic assistance targeting Tamil districts in Sri Lanka.
3. No. HC/PS/3/80. Government note on Sri Lanka-India's vital and permanent interest.
4. No. 11/124/NGO. Letter from C Dasgupta, Joint Secretary (BSM) to Thomas Abraham, Indian High Commission, Colombo on extending credit to Sri Lanka.
5. No. FIII/103/18/82. Indian Security-Current development in Sri Lanka.
6. CIA report, P85-T003. Sri Lanka: The challenge of communal violence, the Indian factor and possibility of Indian intervention.
7. CIA report, 86-10036. Sri Lanka: The growing insurgency, the insurgent groups, Sinhalese-Tamil conflict, insurgent leaders.
8. CIA report, 87-20116. Prospects for the Indo-Sri Lankan peace accord.
9. CIA report, P-88-T0009. Indian equities in Sri Lanka, increasing Indian military capabilities towards Sri Lanka.
10. No. COL/SCR/101/1/82. Cherry George, First Secretary, High Commission of India, Colombo. Lapse of state of emergency, Presidential election, amendments to the constitution, TULF, Tamil Congress, relation with India.
11. D.3799/JS/BSM. Letter and assessment report from Deb Mukherji, Joint Secretary (BSM), Ministry of External Affairs on Sri Lankan Presidential election, opposition disunity, Tamil factor, factors against Jayewardene, policies of new government and relations with India.
12. No. COL/ SCR/101/1/82, High Commission of India, Colombo. Assessment report from R.M. Abhyankar, Deputy High Commissioner of India.
13. No. COL/SCR/101/1/82. Arrest of Liberation Tigers, Tamil Eelam Liberation Front, relations with India.
14. No. COL/SCR/101/1/82. Liberation Tigers movement, TULF, US military aid.
15. No. COL/SCR/101/1/82. Trincomalee, Tamil United Liberation Front.

5. Shadowy War in Washington

1. PMO/295/PM/87. Note from Rahul Khullar on Punjab.
2. PMO note 1668/PM/V/87. Reference of letter from Ajit Jogi on Punjab militancy.
3. CIA report, M 84-10300. India: The Sikh Challenge, military crackdown, Rajiv's limited leeway for policy changes, Pakistan factor, implications for the United States.
4. CIA report, 0499/66. Sikhs threatens serious troubles in Indian Punjab.
5. US Congress Committee on Foreign Affairs, 84-3390. Letter to William Casey, Director, CIA. Sikh extremism and Pakistan support.
6. "Canada investigates charges of Indian covert operations." *The Washington Post,* 22 November 1985.
7. "Two Queens terrorists hunted in sky bombings." *New York Post,* 25 June 1985.
8. PMO note 2/PM/A/87. Rajiv Gandhi Approval on meeting over Punjab.
9. PMO note 10615/PM/V/86. Note from Rajya Sabha MP Ajit Jogi on Sikh militancy: Root of terrorism in Punjab lie in the alienation of the youth in Punjab.
10. PMO/2048. Brief for Prime Minister Rajiv Gandhi on Punjab militancy, government efforts.
11. DO No.F-4-1/86-D-III(SP)/629, Letter from R. Gopalaswamy to Sarita Grewal, Secretary Prime Minister's Office on Punjab issue.
12. No. 40/PMS. Letter from Sarla Grewal, Secretary, Prime Minister's office on Punjab situation.

6. Hunting the R&AW Traitor

1. Intelligence note No. F.52/NGO. Suspicious behaviour of intelligence officers and precautions.
2. Intelligence note No. F52/NGO. Handling of top-secret files, destruction of classified material, classification of top secret and secret files.
3. Intelligence manual 3/49. On disclosing information to unauthorised persons.
4. USIA memorandum of meeting at Pennsylvania. USIA intelligence survey, facilities and methods of meeting, types of intelligence for the USIS program for India.

5. CIA DB-315/01148-64, Intelligence information cable. Indian government policy on development of nuclear weapon.
6. White House, National Security Decision Directive 147. US policy towards India and Pakistan.
7. Doc ID-406297, Recommendations of Jeremiah report. Intelligence penetration in analyzing India target.
8. US National Security Council Memorandum No. 1026. Voluntary agencies in India.
9. "Who was the CIA informer in Indira Gandhi's cabinet?" *The Washington Post,* 22 November 1979.
10. CIA report-P86T00586. The Soviets in India: Moscow's major penetration in India, funding political parties and politicians.
11. CCB No. 4281-SAV, Ministry of External Affairs. Assessment reports on Prime Minister Morarji Desai's visit to Eastern Europe.
12. No. PRA/201/1/81-Com, Embassy of India. Political report from Czechoslovakia.
13. Note No. 253/FS(A)/76, KV Rajan, Embassy of India, Washington. Minutes of meeting with Dennis Kux.
14. Yatish Yadav. "Rabinder Singh, spy who defected to US, is no more: Double agent lived his last years as a remorseful recluse." *Firstpost,* July 2018.

7. R&AW in Shackles

1. Source based information.
2. CIA report-83-10063. India: Cautious Commitment to arms diversification.

8. The Global Footprints of R&AW

1. Intelligence note No. F.52/NGO. Cypher and handling communication, telephone, etc.
2. R&AW note-3372/50/82. Hinduism, truth and corruption.
3. R&AW FII/103/10/82. Unilateral disarmament campaign in Europe and northern protestant countries.
4. R&AW FIII/103/12/82. Liberal, socialist and democratic coalition in British politics.
5. R&AW U.O.No. 14/GU/81 (10). Iran-Iraq conflict, political development in Iran, situation in Iraq.

6. R&AW FIII/103/10/82. Soviet leadership, succession plan, Brezhnev achievements and opponents.
7. DO. No. 4302, Ministry of External Affairs (AMS) division, note prepared by A.G. Asrani, Joint Secretary for Nanda Devi expedition.
8. Ministry of Defence U.O. No. 2(32)/78/D (GS-I). Army aid for scientists of Atomic Research Institute, Bombay.
9. Rajya Sabha Secretariat No. RS/4/1/78-L. Bhupesh Gupta, Member, Rajya Sabha to mention to matter of urgent public importance: Latest reaction in US Congress circles regarding planting of nuclear device in Nanda Devi.
10. CCB No. 06792, TELEGRAM from Embassy of India, Washington to New Delhi.
11. DO.No. 2407, Ministry of External Affairs (AMS) division. American mountaineering expedition to Nanda Devi.
12. Ministry of Defence U.O. No. 1860-JS (AMS). US authorities placed nuclear-powered monitoring device in the area of Nanda Devi.
13. DO.NO. 5224, Ministry of External Affairs (AMS) division. Record of meeting with US Ambassador to India, Goheen on nuclear-powered monitoring device and controversy it had created in India.
14. Draft Note 20. J.S. Mehta, Foreign Secretary letter to Director R&AW and Director Intelligence Bureau on alleged attempt by the CIA to plant a nuclear-powered spy station in the Himalayas.
15. No.1877/GS/AMS, TELEGRAM from San Francisco regarding CIA spy mission India in 1965.
16. No. 1822/GS/AMS/78, TELEGRAM from Embassy of India, Washington. Officials involved in spy mission were double agents.
17. CCB No. 04469. Message from Principal Secretary to Prime Minister on monitoring device in the Himalayas to spy on Chinese nuclear tests.
18. MEA note No. 5640/T/78. "The Nanda Devi Caper: How the CIA used American mountaineers to plant a nuclear-powered spy station in the Himalayas." Howard Kohn, *Outside Magazine*, New York, May 1978.
19. Congressional Record-Senate S22053. CIA involvement with church/clergy and using preachers as spy in foreign countries. Statement of Hatfield and CIA director William Colby.
20. Telex 200 201600 from Washington to Sharada Prasad, PMO regarding US House Committee investigating CIA and how the intelligence gathering had often fallen short of the mark.

21. Minutes of the meeting, Prime Minister/NSA/Home Minister at DGPs conference from 6–8 January 2018 at Tanakpur, Gwalior.

9. Spies in Nepal

1. D2395/RHI/80, Ministry of External Affairs. Notes on Nepal, monarchy, economy, American assistance.
2. No. 12/1/63-C, Embassy of India, Nepal. Monthly political report No. 1 for 1963, calling off the rebel movement, China-India conflict, China-Nepal boundary protocol, Kathmandu-Lhasa road, Nepal trade agreement with China, Nepal relations with Pakistan.
3. No. 12/1/63-C, Embassy of India, Nepal. Monthly political report No. 2 for 1963. Nepal King statement, relations with China, Pakistan and the USA.
4. No. 27/286/NGO/Vol.III, Ministry of External Affairs. Nepal King visit to India from 18–23 April 1962 and discussion on various issues.
5. MEA file No. HI/1012. Speech by King Mahendra on arrival at Palam Airport in reply to the address of welcome by President Dr Rajendra Prasad.
6. MEA file No. HI/1012. Text of address of King Mahendra to Indian council of world affairs at New Delhi on 20 April 1962.
7. Ministry of External Affairs, External Publicity Division, 22 April 1962. Speech of King Mahendra at banquet given by the President Dr Rajendra Prasad.
8. MEA file No. HI/1012. Joint communiqué of India-Nepal on 23 April 1962.
9. No. 27/7/JS (PP)/82. Note on India-China relationship. Boundary issue, relations with neighbours.
10. Wikileaks US Cable: India foreign secretary Shyam Saran speaks from the heart on Nepal.
11. Wikileaks US Cable: Ambassador Michael Malinowski relays concerns about activities of Indian intelligence agents.
12. R&AW report on Nepal, Tauqeer, Shahzad. Escape after Batla house encounter, meeting with Riyaz Bhatkal, stay in Nepal and trip to Riyadh.

11. A Spy among the Dervish

1. The Organisation of Islamic Conference, MEA No. 2052/161/DD(PP)/81.
2. No. 1371/MIN/73, Record of discussions between Foreign Minister Swaran Singh and US's Secretary of State, Henry Kissinger.
3. CIA 180007, Khomeini and implications for Iranian policy.

ACKNOWLEDGEMENTS

While pouring four years of my life into this book, I've had opportunity to meet daring spies, agent-runners and spymasters who offered me a panoramic view of espionage missions. They don't seek credit and would like to remain in oblivion. I can't mention their names but I would like to express my deep gratitude for the trust they bestowed in me. I hope the book built on glimpses of clandestine operations and mysticism of this secret world is gripping to curious readers.

I have also benefitted from the generous help and suggestions of many former R&AW and Foreign Service officers who shared intricate facts on some of the complex events. I owe profound thanks to my closest friends, Dalip Singh, Ajmer Singh and Gyanant Singh. This book has had many inspirations. But two people stand out for encouraging me to go beyond 800 words: Ravi Shankar, a senior journalist and Karthika V.K., the publisher of Westland. Special thanks to my editor Kushal Gulab who worked on the structure and content of the manuscript with great skill and complete devotion. I also wish to express my gratitude to other outstanding members of Westland Publications for their immense contributions, especially Niyati Bhat and Vidhi Bhargava. My family deserves special mention for accepting my abrupt absence from their lives at regular intervals since writing this book has been consuming. My friends and colleagues at Network18, *The New Indian Express* too have been an endless source of strength. Finally, I feel deeply grateful to the elders in the profession, especially Ajay Singh and B.V. Rao for offering their wisdom.

I would like to conclude by expressing sincere gratitude to two people. I know I can't reveal your identity but this book is an ode to both of you.

INDEX

Abolhassan, Seyyed, 267, 358
Abraham, P., 297
Abraham, Thomas, 162
Achakzai, Abdus Samad, 108
Advani, Lal Krishna, 322
Afghan armed forces, demoralised and divided, 119
Afghan conflict, 137
Afghan Justice Project, 144
Afghan Mujahideen, 5, 124–25, 138, 231, 354
Afghanistan
- agreement with the Soviet Union, 116
- guerrillas, 23, 110, 130, 144
- India's concerns, 123
- India intensified cooperation, 114
- Indian intelligence, 112
- insurgency, 113
- invasion by Soviet forces, 230
- media propaganda against Indian intelligence, 124
- military coup in July 1973, 109
- seven-point political settlement programme, 122
- sharia rule in, 120, 139
- Soviet Afghan treaty of friendship, 118
- Soviet intervention, 106, 120, 133, 270
- Soviet occupation of, 121, 337
- Taliban and Al Qaeda's terror havens in, 149
- Taraki's secret execution, 117
- withdrawal of Soviet troops, 139

Afghan-Soviet friendship, 115
AGSA (Department for Safeguarding Interests of Afghanistan), 111, 117
Ahmad, Khondaker Mostaq, 11, 18, 21, 49
Ahmed, Kazi Zafar, 64
Ahmed, Moudud, 64
Ahuja, Harpreet, 340, 343
Air India Boeing 747, crash of, 207
Air India flight IC-814, hijacking of, 148, 237, 321
Akali Dal, 194, 196–97, 346
Al Qaeda, 145, 237–39
Ali, Asif, 238
All India Sikh Students Federation, 199
Alva, Margaret, 202–3
Al-Zulfikar, 123
Ames, Aldrich, 242
Amin, Hafizullah, 113, 117–18, 121
Amirthalingam, A., 164–65
Anand, Madhav, 255
Andropov, Yuri, 272–74
anti-Hindu propaganda, 28
anti-India feeling, 19, 28, 43

anti-India propaganda, 13, 32, 53, 283
anti-Mujib Bangladesh bureaucrats, 20
anti-Sikh riots in Delhi, 193
anti-Taraki army, 111
anti-Taraki elements, 111
Arafat, Yasser, 255
Arkhipov, Vasili, 112
Armed Forces Special Powers Act, 346
Arora, Pawan, 156, 174
Arora, Sanjay, 315
Asrani, A.G., 291
Association of South East Nations (ASEAN), 174
Asthana, Ved, 107, 135, 143–44, 146, 150–51
Atma Ram, 297
Atomic Energy Commission (AEC), 295
Aulakh, Gurmeet Singh, 219
Awami League, 24–27, 40, 42, 47–49, 54, 57–59, 62–63, 109
Azam, Shafiul, 15
Azhar, Maulana Masood, 321

Ba'ath Party, 269, 359
Babbar Khalsa, 204, 207, 210–12, 218
backroom manoeuvring, 255
Bahadur Rana, Shamsher Jang, 308
Bahini, Kader, 23–24
Bahram, Reza, 362
band of three, 85, 87, 93, 95, 96–98, 102
Bangladesh Chhatra League, 40
Bangladesh Nationalist Party (BNP), 46–49, 51, 57–59, 62–63
Bangladesh Times, 9
Bangladesh
  failure of Indian diplomacy in, 27
  illegal immigrants as well as illicit movement of arms from, 37
  Indo-Bangladeshi relationship, 26
  liberation of, 4, 23, 25, 55
  Soviet Union interests in Bangladesh, 16
Batla House encounter, 327
Bavadra, Adi Kuini, 98
Bavadra, Timoci, 5, 67, 77, 82, 91, 95, 97–98, 101
Beg, Mirza Dilshad, 320
Belt and Road Initiative (BRI), 303
Bengal Lancers, 14
Bhabha Atomic Research Centre, 297
Bhagavad Gita, 223, 225, 240
Bhandari, Krishan, 281
Bhandari, Romesh, 266
Bhattarai, Krishna Prasad, 317
Bhindranwale Tiger Force, 218
Bhindranwale, Jarnail Singh, 192, 201
Bhutto, Benazir, 60, 140–43
Bhutto, Murtaza, 124
Bhutto, Zulfikar Ali, 16, 18, 34, 124, 298
bilateral problems, 52, 54
Birendra Bir Bikram Shah Dev, King of Nepal, 308, 313, 320
Bofors, 97, 249. *See also* Gandhi, Rajiv
Bombay, bomb blasts (1993), 320
Border Security Force (BSF), 35, 37, 56, 218
Boy Scout movement, 282
Brezhnev, Leonid, 115, 270–74, 285
Brittan, Leon, 345

Calling Attention notices, 293
Canadian Security Intelligence Service Act 1984, 258
Canadian Security Intelligence Service (CSIS), 204, 210, 258
Canagaratnam, M., 162
Carter, James, 120
Carter, Jimmy, 294
Central Intelligence Agency (CIA)
  counterintelligence team, 242

informer in Indira Gandhi's cabinet, 232
intelligence operatives in Sri Lanka, 168
interest in Bangladesh, 51
involvement in murder of Sheikh Mujib, 12
network in India and Nepal, 244
neutralize Russian penetration, 54
operation in Indian Himalayas, 291–92
penetration and big brotherly attitude, 228
penetration in Middle East, 282
preacher spy of, 300–5
role in the military coup, 12
spy hunter team's challenge, 242
spy hunters, 243
supported Ershad government, 61
surprised by India's nuclear test, 234–35
use and throw policy, 246
Centre for Public Interest Litigation, 257
Ceylon Workers Congress, 166
Chakma movement, 24
Chandra, Vipul, 353–54
Chashi, Mahbub Alam, 15
Chattopadhyay, S., 12
Chaturvedi, Ashok, 181
Chaudhary, Mahendra, 80
Chaudhury, Abu Sayeed, 40
Chernenko, Konstantin, 285
Chernobyl disaster, 287
Chhatra Dal, 62
Chhetri, Partha, 325
Chidambaram, P., 218–19
China after the Cultural Revolution, 284
China-Pak operations, 30
China-Pakistan Economic Corridor (CPEC), 304
China-US relationship, intimacy of the, 173
Chohan, Jagjit Singh, 185–94, 196–99, 205, 214, 219
ciphers, handwritten, 59
Clark, M.D., 297
Colby, William, 300
Comprehensive Nuclear Test Ban Treaty (CTBT), 280
Confucian–Taoist–Buddhist ethic, 282
Corbyn, Jeremy, 275
Council Muslim League, 21
cryptograms, 263
'cultural conquest', 32
cypher, 261–64

Dahal, Maheshwar, 325
Dalai Lama, 303
Dalim, Major, 9–10
personal vendetta against Sheikh Mujib, 10
Darchidze, Aleksandre, 285
Darchidze, Nicholas, 285
Dastgir, Brigadier, 15
Dayal, Harishwar, 311–12
Defence Intelligence Agency (DIA), 142, 146, 237, 256
Desai, Morarji, 3, 45, 231, 253, 281, 291, 295–97, 309, 310
Deuba, Sher Bahadur, 327
Dhar, Manoranjan, 12
dictatorship, 58, 62
Dingell, John, 294
disarmament campaign, 279
Dixit, J.N., 12, 127
Dixit, Rakesh, 60–61, 63
Doolittle, John Taylor, 220

Dubey, Muchkund, 50
Dubs, Adolph, 110
Dutta, Subimal, 26

East Pakistan Communist Party, 42
economic collapse, 18
Eisenhower, Dwight, 227
Emergency, 3, 12, 45, 273. *See also* Gandhi, Indira
Ershad, Hussain Mohammed, 46–65
  agitations against corrupt and illegal rule, 63
  declaration of emergency, 63
  media censorship, 63
  pro-West policy, 60

Fadlallah, Ayatollah Mohammed Hussein, 359
Faridi, Javed, 158–59, 170, 172
Federal Bureau of Investigation (FBI), 198, 207–8, 243, 302
Fernandes, George, 322–23
Fiji Labour Party (FLP), 77, 102
Fiji
  background on, 69
  cultural survival for ethnic Fijians, 78
  demography of, 68
  economic sanctions against, 79
  independence from the British, 67
  India's efforts to strengthen ties, 77
  Indian techno-economic team in, 76
  Indians dominated business and the professional sphere, 71
  information war in, 96
  intention of the Australian and New Zealand investors, 76
  internal affairs, 81, 96–97
  operation big money, 96
  permanent representative to the United Nations, 103
  protests and pro-democracy demonstrations, 93
Financial Action Task Force, 6
Fonseka, Sarath, 153, 180
foreign relations strategy, 28
Freedom of Information Act, 239

Gandhi, Indira, 3, 12, 29, 32, 45–46, 52, 55, 66–67, 74–75, 77, 121–22, 125, 129, 155, 169, 193, 210, 232, 248, 252, 254, 265, 269–74, 276, 279, 292, 295, 334–35, 337
Gandhi, Mahatma, 98, 279, 282
Gandhi, Rajiv, 3–5, 56, 66, 74–75, 77, 78–79, 83–84, 97, 136–38, 156, 170, 175, 200–4, 208, 210, 220, 249, 254–55, 280, 286, 334, 336, 345, 362–63
Gandhi, Sanjay, family planning initiatives, 45
Ganga waters, sharing of, 60
Garg, Rajesh, 313
Geneva Accord, 139
Gilani, Syed Ahmed, 139
Gill, K.P.S., 211
Gill, Surjan Singh, 207
Giri, Tulsi, 309
Giri, Vijay, 258–59
Goheen, Robert F., 293–94
Gopalaswamy, R., 202
Gorbachev, Mikhail, 5, 136, 138, 285–86
Govind, Bipin, 318–19
Grewal, Sarla, 202
Griffin, George, 126
Gujaral, Inder Kumar, 60
Gul, General Hamid, 138–39, 141, 150, 192, 315, 352
Gulf War, 143
Gyanendra, King of Nepal, 325–27

Hamilton, Max, 86
Hammadi, Sa'dun, 270
Handley, William, 227
Harkat-e-Milli-e-Afghanistan, 139
Harkat-ul-Mujahideen, 149
Hasina, Sheikh, 9, 47–49, 57, 59
Hatfield, Mark, 300
Hawke, Bob, 90
hegemonistic tendencies, 31
Hekmatyar, Gulbuddin, 120, 130, 138–41, 144–45
Helms, Richard, 232
Heptulla, Najma, 97
Hezbollah, 359–61
Hinduism, 78
  attack on, 283
  Hindu-Muslim tension, 36
  Hindus and corruption, 280–85
  Hindutva politics, 275
  linking with corruption, 281
  poor interpretation of, 281
Hindustan Gadar Party, 205
Hizb-e-Inquilab-e-Islami, 139
Hizb-e-Islami, 130, 139, 144
Hizb-e-Wahdat, 143–45
holy warriors, 139–41
Homeland High Defence Council (HHDC), 113
Hossain, Kamal, 40–41, 47, 49
Huda, Mirza Nurul, 48–49
Human Intelligence (HUMINT), 157, 235, 237, 364–66
Husak, Gustav, 251
Hussein, Saddam, 265–67, 269–70, 361

Ibrahim, Dawood, 307, 320
illegal immigrants from Bangladesh, 37
illicit movement of arms from Bangladesh, 35–36, 56
India-Iran relationship, 356, 362
Indian diplomacy, 25, 28–29, 31
  efforts of, 31
  failure of, 27
  mutuality and equality, 29
  purposes and functioning of, 25
Indian Mountaineering Foundation, 294
Indian Mujahideen (IM), 306, 327–28
Indian Peace Keeping Forces (IPKF), 155–56
Indo-Chinese war, 291
Inter Service Intelligence (ISI), 5, 33, 60–62, 106–7, 119–21, 123, 136–39, 141, 145, 147–51, 192–93, 196, 205, 210, 212, 218–19, 222, 237–39, 286, 298, 302–3, 306–7, 313, 315–16, 318, 320, 322, 325–28, 334–35, 337–38, 341, 345, 347–49, 351–52, 359, 366
  agents in Afghanistan, 138
  Al Qaeda and, 238–39
  Khalistan movement and, 221–22
  partnership with mujahideen, 106–7
  presence in Nepal, 315, 320, 322
  support to Dawood Ibrahim, 307
  support to Taliban, 144, 238–39
  terror network in London, 349
International Atomic Energy Agency (IAEA), 287
International Civil Aviation Organization (ICAO), 298
International Sikh Youth Federation, 199, 204, 212
Iranian revolution, 266, 359, 361
Iran-Iraq Conflict, 265–70
Islami Sangh Nepal, 328–29
Islamic Countries' Coalition, 266
Islamic Republican Party (IRP) of Iran, 265

Islamic Summit, 265
'Islampasand' (Islam lovers), 21
Island (newspaper), 164
Ittehad, group of insurgents called, 131
Ittihad-e-Islami Barai Azadi Afghanistan, 139

Jabha-e-Najat-e-Milli Afghanistan, 139
Jacob, Ottawa, J., 206
Jagat Narain, Lala, 193
Jaishankar, S., 134
Jaish-e-Mohammed, 322
Jaleel, Abdul, 107, 143, 145, 147
Jalil, Major, 41
Jamaat-e-Islami, 36, 53, 58, 106, 130, 135, 139
Jana Sanghati Samiti, 24
Janata Party, 231, 253, 281
Jatiya Chhatra League, 9
Jatiya Samajtantrik Dal (JSD), 41–45
Jatiyatabadi Front, 46
Jatiyatabadi Gantantrik Dal, 45
Jatiyo Party, 56, 58. *See also* Ershad, Hussain Mohammed
Jayewardene, J.R., 160–63, 165–66, 168–70, 175
jihad fund, 355
Jindal, Sanjeev, 334–52
Jogi, Ajit, 201
Johnson, Boris, 275
Johnson, Lyndon, 229, 292
Junbish-e-Milli, 144
Jund al-Imam, 360

Kabul News Times, 120
Kabul Times, 120
Kader Bahini, 23–24
  strength of the, 23
Kallue, Shamsur Rahman, 60, 141
Kao, R.N., 1, 3, 10, 25, 32–33, 253
Kargari Astekhabarati Muassessa (KAM), 117
Kargil Review Committee, 322
Kargil war, 7, 321
Karmal, Babrak, 112, 118–19, 120–22, 127–28, 135
Karunanidhi, M., 176–77
Kashmir jihad, 251
Kashmiri militants, 315, 318–19
Kasuri, Mahmood Ali, 298
Kaul, T.N., 74, 299
Kaur, Parminder, 223–24
Kaushik, Ravindra, 256
Kemp, Geoffrey, 125
KGB, 136–37, 170, 209, 242–43, 272–74, 286, 288
KHAD, 120–21, 128
Khalis, Maulvi Yunus, 130
Khalistan Liberation Army, 197
Khalistan Liberation Organisation, 218
Khalistan movement, 185, 189–94, 196, 219, 221–22
  agitation and propaganda, 192
  Air India flight bombing, 193
  Jarnail Singh Bhindranwale, 192
  Khalistani elements on USA soil, 200
  long and complex history, 192
  reality of, 221
  targeted killings, 193
Khalistani militants, 318
Khalq Democratic Party, 110
Khalsa Diwan Society, 205
Khamenei, Ali, 358
Khan, Abdul Ghaffar Khan, (Seemant Gandhi), 108
Khan, Abdul Wali, 108
Khan, Ariz (Zunaid), 306, 327
Khan, Ashfaq, 104–5, 107, 117–18, 132, 136, 138, 140–41, 145–49, 151

Khan, Ayub, 108, 311
Khan, Ghulam Jilani, 33, 313
Khan, Ismail, 105, 142
Khan, Khurshid Alam, 209
Khan, Mohammad Akbar, 196
Khan, Mohammed Ayub, 108
Khan, Nizam, 306–7, 328–330
Khan, Yahya, 298
Khatri, Nirmal, 322–26, 330, 333
Khomeini, Ayatollah, 265–66, 268–69, 354, 356, 358–60, 363
King, Martin Luther, 279
Kissinger, Henry A., 229, 357
Klor, Sophie, 339
Kohli, Manjit Singh, 207
Kohn, Howard, 293–96
Koirala, B.P., 314
Koirala, G.P., 318, 320
Korkia, Anastasia, 286–89
Kosygin, Alexei, 271–72
Kreisky, Bruno, 340
Krishna, Baldev, 32–34
 operations from a safe house in Calcutta, 32
Krishna, S.M., 183
Kumar, Bob, 82

Laden, Osama bin, 146, 150, 239
Lahore summit, 355
Lashkar-e-Taiba (LeT), 302, 364
Laxman Prasad, 99
Liberation Tigers of Tamil Eelam (LTTE), 152–57, 168, 170–72, 174–76, 178–80, 183–84, 241
 espionage network, 178
 links with international arms market, 172
 operational command structure, 171
 politico-military structure of, 171
 Rajiv Gandhi's assassination, 175
 remnants in foreign countries, 183
liberation, euphoria of, 24
Line of Actual Control (LAC), 303
Longowal, Harchand Singh, 209, 346

Mahendra, King of Nepal, 308–12
Maheswaran, Uma, 164
Mahmud, Anisul Islam, 65
Malik, Anupam, 84
Malinowski, Michael, 323
Mara, Ratu, 70–72, 74–76, 77–78
martial law, 21, 43–45, 51–52, 57
Marwari businessmen, 27
Massoud, Ahmad Shah, 105–7, 130, 135–36, 138, 142–47, 149
Mathur, Dinesh, 185–92, 194, 201, 213–22
Mathur, S.N., 294
Mazar-e-Sharif, 104–5, 128
Mehta, J.S., 293
Mehta, K.L., 308
Menon, M.G. K., 297
Menon, Shivshankar, 180
MI5 [Security Service (SS) of UK], 258, 349
Mishra, Brajesh, 7, 244, 321
Mitterrand, Francois, 337
Modi, Narendra, 303
Mohammed, Yasin, 53
Mojadedi, Sibghatullah, 139
Moni, Sheikh, 9
Mostaq, President, 11–16, 18, 21, 49
Motherland, 311
mujahideen, 105–7, 114, 119, 123–25, 126, 129, 138–42, 144–45, 320
Mujahidi, Ibrahim, 111
Mujib Bahini, 22–23
Mujib, Sheikh, 9–10, 12–13, 18, 21–22, 24–25, 36, 40–42, 46, 50
 CIA's involvement in murder, 12
 friendly towards India, 10
 personality and charisma, 25

philosophy and aims of, 22
secularism, 19, 36
Mukti Bahini, 19
Mumbai attack (2008), 302
Muslim League, 21, 36, 44, 47, 49, 74
Mustapha, Ghulam, 10

Nair, K. Sankaran, 3
Najibullah, 127–28, 137, 139, 140–44, 146
Nambiar, Vijay, 241
Nankana Sahib, Pakistan, 192, 196–97
Narasimhan, P., 247, 252
Narayanan, K.R., 38–39
Narayanan, M.K., 180, 302
Nasheed, Mohamed, 302
National Awami Party, 108
National Federation Party of Fiji, 71, 73, 77
National Intelligence Estimate (NIE), 227
National Investigation Agency (NIA), 222
National Security Council, 48, 125, 224, 235, 364
National Technical Research Organisation (NTRO), 257
Nava Sama Samaja Party, 164
Naxalbari movement, 205
Naya Samaj, 311
Nehru, Jawaharlal, 4, 282, 340
Nepal, 2, 34, 134, 219, 234, 241, 244–45, 256, 300, 304, 306–32
Chinese presence in, 314
democratic political system, 308
diplomatic relationship with India, 313
Indo-Nepal transit treaty, 315, 331
Indo-Nepalese relationship, 314
internal security apparatus, 321
ISI and Kashmiri militants in, 315
launch pad of terrorism against India, 318
movement for constitutional democracy, 316
relationship with China, 311
as a safe house for terrorists, 327–33
spies and informers in, 319
undercurrents of resentment in early 2000, 324
Nepali (newspaper), 312
Neue Zurcher Zeitung, 126
New York Times, The, 194–95, 198, 301
non-alignment, policy of, 76, 336, 354
non-proliferation agreement, 280
North Atlantic Treaty Organisation, 336
North West Frontier Province (NWFP), 107–8, 357
Northern Alliance Forces (NAF), 146
nuclear arms battle, 277–81
nuclear disarmament, 231, 277–79
nuclear non-proliferation treaty, 280

Oakley, Robert B., 140
Omar, Mullah, 105, 145, 237, 239
Operation Azalea, 287, 289–90
Operation Batla House, 306
Operation Black Thunder II, 211
Operation Blue Star, 190, 193, 201
Operation Farewell, 61–65
Operation Fiji, 86, 95
Operation HAT, 291, 293
Operation Hornet, 334–52
Operation Mechi, 317
Operation Python, 23
Operation Satori, 177–78
Organisation of Islamic Conference (OIC), 355

Ottinger, Richard, 294
Outside (magazine), 292

Padma Bhushan award, 363
Pahlawan, Abdul Malik, 104–5
Pakhtoonistan, 107–10, 114, 135
Pakhtoonistan movement, 109–10
Pakistan
  Afghan refugees in, 118, 124
  anti-India propaganda, 283
  campaign against Awami League, 109
  Indo-Pakistan war, 229, 355
  interference in Afghanistan, 115–16
  ISI inside Afghanistan, 106
  Kargil war, 7
  madrassas, 330
  non-state actors' usage against India, 107
  penetration in Nepal, 314
  presence in Nepal, 314
  propaganda against Indira Gandhi, 125
  reconciled with Afghanistan, 108
  support to insurgents in Afghanistan, 147
  tactic support to Taliban, 105
  terror financing, 6
Pakistan People's Party, 108
Pandit, Vishal, 2
Pant, M.C., 299
Parmar, Talvinder Singh, 207
Patel, A.D., 73
Patwardhan, Krishna, 58–65
  coded message, 59
  vulnerabilities of operations in Dhaka, 58
People's Democratic Party of Afghanistan (PDPA), 111, 118, 128
people-to-people contact, 31
Pillai, K.C., 297
Pokhran nuclear test (1998), 236
Prabhakaran, Velupillai (LTTE chief), 153, 156, 164, 168, 171–72, 179–80, 183
Prasad, Anil, 356, 359, 361, 363
Prasad, Sharda, 301
Pro-Khalistan groups, 187, 209, 211
psychological warfare, 36, 96, 183, 222, 281, 365
Punjab Kesari, 193
Purba Banglar Samyabadi Dal, 42
Purba Sarbahara Party, 42

Qadir, General Abdul, 126
Quattrochi, Ottavio, 249

Rabbani, Burhanuddin, 105, 130, 135, 139, 144
Raborn, William, 229
Rabuka, Sitiveni, 5, 68, 76, 78–81, 82–84, 86–89, 90–102
Rahman, Akhtar Abdur, 136, 338, 359
Rahman, Farooq, 14
Rahman, Khalilur, 15
Rajai, Mohammad-Ali, 266–68
Rajapaksa, Gotabaya, 158, 179–80
Rajapaksa, Mahinda, 153, 158, 176–77, 179, 181, 184
Rajasingham, R., 163
Ramachandran, M.G., 165
Ramalingaswami, V., 297
Ramanna, Raja, 297
Rana, Naseem, 238
Rao, Nirupama, 181
Rao, P.V. Narasimha, 50, 52, 254, 318, 348
Rauf, Brigadier, 11
Ray, Siddhartha Shankar, 203

Reagan, Ronald, 124, 167, 173, 231, 279, 283
Reddy, K.S., 73
Reddy, S., 105, 107
Reddy, Sanjiva, 163
Rehman, Ziaur, 11, 15, 21–23, 41–44, 46–47
assassination of, 47
dominance of, 43
internal uprising against, 43
resistance force, 5, 22–25, 143
Ribeiro, Julio, 187, 201
Rolling Stone, 294
Royal Fiji Military, 78
Rustam, Mirza Murad, 104–5, 107, 110, 113, 125, 135, 143–45, 147–48

Saeed, Hafiz, 364
Saha, A.K., 297
Sahgal, Sanjiv, 86–87
Sahidul Islam, 9
Sandhu, B.N., 335, 337–38, 341–42, 344, 346–51
Saran, Shyam, 323, 326
Sarbadaliya Chhatra Oikya Parishad (All-party Students Council), 62
Sathe, R.D., 266
Sattar, Abdus, 45–49
Saudi Arabian recognition to Bangladesh, 11
Saxena, G.C., 170, 273–74, 361–63
Sayeed, Mufti Mohammed, 221
Sayeed, Rubaiya, kidnapping of, 221
Sayem, Abu Sadat Mohammad, 21, 45
Sayyaf, Abdul Rasul, 139
Second World War, 29
secularism, tenets of, 36
Serniabat, Abdur Rab, 9
Sethi, Ashok, 254
Sethna, H.N., 297
Shafifullah, Major General, 15
Shah, Ajeet, 183
Shah, Syed Siddiqui, 116
Shahi, Agha, 124
Shanti Bahini, 24
Sharma, Diwakar, 320–22
Sharma, Harish, 82
Sharma, K.K., 241
Shastri, Lal Bahadur, 229, 270
Shatt-al-Arab, 266
Sheikh, Ayub, 306
Sheikh's regime, economic degeneration during the, 25
Shekhar, Chandra, 4, 317
Shekhawat, Prem, 71, 74, 76–84, 86–90, 94–95, 100, 102
Shia revolution in Iran, 353
Shias, radicalisation of, 359
Shirazi, Abdullah, 360–62
Shrestha, K.B., 320
Siddique, Abdul Kader, 23
Sikh extremism, 198, 209
Singapore, 77, 170–71, 179, 183
Singh, Alok, 249
Singh, Amarjeet, 342
Singh, Ammand, 207
Singh, Balwant, 349
Singh, Buta, 348
Singh, C.P.N., 308
Singh, Chaudhary Charan, 3, 115
Singh, Dalpat, 293
Singh, Fateh, 200
Singh, Harbakhsh, 341
Singh, Jabir, 82
Singh, Jaswant, 321–22
Singh, K. Natwar, 74, 83
Singh, Kailash, 77, 80, 86, 87, 91, 94, 100
Singh, Kewal, 40, 299
Singh, Khushwant, 282
Singh, Lal, 207, 209
Singh, Manmohan, 181, 327

Singh, R.K., 250
Singh, Rabinder, 223–24, 234, 239–46, 323
Singh, Raja Man, 45–46
Singh, Rajnath, 305
Singh, S.K., 121
Singh, Sartaj, 185–86, 189–92, 213–18
Singh, Sohan, 219
Singh, Suchcha, 189–91, 194
Singh, Surendra, 67
Singh, Swaran, 357
Singh, Tarvinder, 212
Singh, V.P., 4, 60, 97, 157, 220, 316
Singh, Vijay R., 73
Singh, Vikram, 2
Singh, Zail, 57
Sinha, Avinash, 152–55, 157, 177, 179, 182
Sinha, Ravi S., 316
Sinha, Surendra, 238
Sinha, Yashwant, 322
Sivasithamparam, M., 165
Social Democratic Party (SDP), 275–77
Somiah, C.G., 36–37
South Asian Regional Co-operation (SARC), 56
Soviet Union
  friendship treaty with India, 232
  Geneva Accord, 139
  influence in Dhaka, 54
  interests in Bangladesh, 16
  relations with Afghanistan, 115–23
  repercussions of power struggle, 274
  unconditional support to India, 273
Spartacist, 141
Sreenivasan, T.P., 96–97
Sri Lanka, 4, 6, 66–67, 79, 137, 152–59, 161–66, 168–84, 224, 233, 241, 304
  aid from around the world, 161
  army's operation in Mullaitivu, 180
  Chinese covert interference, 173
  Chinese presence in, 181
  civil war in, 159
  civil war, 154
  foreign policy, 174
  guerrilla war of Prabhakaran, 153
  humanitarian situation in, 177
  Indian grant for humanitarian relief, 182
  indigenous population of, 159
  international intelligence agencies operations, 159
  labour migration from India to 159
  LTTE's string of suicide bombings, 154
  Nelliady attack, 164
  1987 peace accord with, 170
  Tiger Liberation Movement, 161–76
  victory against the LTTE, 154
  withdrawal of the IPKF, 157
State Trading Corporation of India (STCI), 27
sterilisation model, 45
Students Islamic Movement of India (SIMI), 307, 328
Subhan, Abdul (Tauqeer), 328
Sunday Leader, 157
Sunday Telegraph, 82
Suntook, N.F., 3, 21, 39, 40–41, 43–45, 110, 273
surveillance on Indian diplomatic staff, 50

Taher, Abu, 21
Taliban, 104–5, 107, 145–47, 149–50, 237–39, 241
  bad Taliban, 238

good Taliban, 238
growth of, 238
Pakistan's role, 145
takeover of Kabul, 145
Tamil Eelam Convention, 164
Tamil United Liberation Front (TULF), 161–66, 168
Taraki, Nur Muhammad, 110–21, 127
Taukei, Soqosoqoni Vakavulewani, 101
Taylor, Benjamin, 87, 93, 100
technical intelligence (TECHINT), 157
Tehzib, Nizamuddin, 111
Teja, J.S., 127
Tharakan, P.K.H., 154
Thatcher, Margaret, 275–76, 350
Thomas, K.T., 297
Thondaman, S., 160
Tiwari, N.D., 66–68, 74
Towab, A.V.M., 42–43
training manual, 260
Transnational Government of Tamil Eelam (TGTE), 184
Trudeau, Pierre Elliot, 206
two-nation theory, 34
Tzu, Sun, 91, 365

UK, third alternative in, 274–77
underworld, 307, 320–21
United Nations, 62, 81, 83, 103, 123, 144, 194–95, 236, 238, 273, 278–80, 363
United Nations General Assembly, 83, 279, 280
United Nations Security Council, 236
Ustinov, Dmitry, 272

Vajpayee, Atal Bihari, 7–8, 149, 234, 289, 295, 322–23, 325
Vakaturaga, Bose Levu, 98
Velayati, Ali Akbar, 363
Verma, A.K., 14, 16, 68, 73, 75, 100 138, 156
Verma, K.C., 181
Vibhas, 54–56
Vishwanathan, N., 220–21

Wadhawa, Rita, 253
Wadood, Major General, 128
Walsh, Paul V., 230
Washington Post, 232, 274
Wasiuddin, General, 11, 20
water-sharing problem, 54
Wickrematunge, Lasantha, 157
Wickremesinghe, Ranil, 159
Wikileaks, 171, 323
Williams, Shirley, 276–77
WMD programmes, 236
World Sikh Organisation (WSO), 199, 204, 208
World Trade Center, 150

Xiaoping, Deng, 4

Zia, Begum Khaleda, 48, 59, 65
Zia-ul-Haq, 123, 208, 315, 359
and the USA Nexus, 123
Ziyang, Zhao, 174